Adolescent Addiction: Epidemiology, Assessment and Treatment

Adolescent Addiction: Epidemiology, Assessment and Treatment

Edited by

Cecilia A. Essau

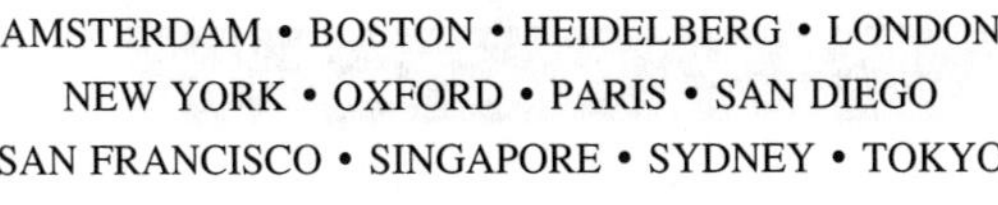

Academic Press is an imprint of Elsevier

Academic Press is an imprint of Elsevier
84 Theobald's Road, London WC1X 8RR, UK
30 Corporate Drive, Suite 400, Burlington, MA 01803, USA
525 B Street, Suite 1900, San Diego, California 92101-4495, USA

First edition 2008

British Library Cataloguing-in-Publication Data
A catalogue record for this book is available from the British Library

Library of Congress Cataloging-in-Publication Data
A catalog record for this title is available from the Library of Congress

ISBN: 978-0-12-373625-3

For information on all Academic Press publications
visit our web site at www.books.elsevier.com

Printed and bound in the United States of America
08 09 10 11 10 9 8 7 6 5 4 3 2 1

In loving memory of my parents

Essau Indit († 09.05.1992)
Runyan Megat († 26.05.1992)

Contents

List of Contributors

Gerald Adams, Department of Family Relations and Applied Nutrition, University of Guelph, Canada N1G 2W1

Bethany C. Bray, The Pennsylvania State University, Methodology Center, 204 E. Calder Way, Suite 400, Pennsylvania, PA 16801, USA

David W. Brook, Department of Psychiatry, New York University School of Medicine, 550 First Avenue, Millhauser Labs, Room HN323, New York, NY 10016-6481, USA

Judith S. Brook, Department of Psychiatry, New York University School of Medicine, 550 First Avenue, Millhauser Labs, Room HN323, New York, NY 10016-6481, USA

Janet D. Carter, Department of Psychology, University of Canterbury, Private Bag 4800, Christchurch, New Zealand

Linda B. Cottler, Washington University School of Medicine, Epidemiology and Prevention Research Group, Washington University School of Medicine, 40 N. Kingshighway, Suite 4, St Louis, MO 63108, USA

Louisa Degenhardt, National Drug and Alcohol Research Centre, University of New South Wales, Sydney 2052, Australia

Jeffrey L. Derevensky, International Centre for Youth Gambling Problems and High Risk Behaviors, McGill University, 3724 McTavish, Montreal, Quebec, Canada H3A 1Y2

Cecilia A. Essau, School of Human and Life Sciences, Roehampton University, Whitelands College, Holybourne Avenue, London SW15 4JD, UK

David H. Gleaves, Department of Psychology, University of Canterbury, Private Bag 4800, Christchurch, New Zealand

Mark Griffiths, International Gambling Research Unit, Nottingham Trent University, Psychology Division, Burton Street, Nottingham NG1 4BU, UK

Rina Gupta, International Centre for Youth Gambling Problems and High Risk Behaviors, McGill University, 3724 McTavish, Montreal, Quebec, Canada H3A 1Y2

Wayne Hall, School of Population Health, University of Queensland, Herston Road, Herston, Queensland 4006, Australia

Delyse Hutchinson, National Drug and Alcohol Research Centre (NDARC), University of New South Wales, Sydney, New South Wales 2052, Australia

Paul McArdle, School of Clinical Medical Sciences, 4th Floor William Leech Building, Medical School, Framlington Place, University of Newcastle upon Tyne, NE2 4HH, UK

Kerstin Pahl, Department of Psychiatry, New York University School of Medicine 550 First Avenue, Millhauser Labs, Room HN323, New York, NY 10016-6481, USA

George Patton, Centre for Adolescent Health, William Buckland House, 2 Gatehouse Street, Parkville, Victoria 3052, Australia

Michele Preyde, Department of Family Relations and Applied Nutrition, University of Guelph, Canada N1G 2W1

Ty A. Ridenour, University of Pittsburgh, Center for Education and Drug Abuse Research, Pittsburgh, PA 15260, USA

Heather S. Scott, Child, Adult & Family Psychological Center, State College, Pennsylvania, PA 16801, USA

Steve Sussman, Institute for Health Promotion & Disease Prevention Research, University of Southern California, 1000 S. Fremont Avenue, Unit 8, Building A-5, Suite 5228, Alhambra, CA 91803-4737, USA

PREFACE

Many books have been written on various aspects of adolescent addiction; however, almost all of them have focused on specific types of addiction, such as alcohol, drugs or gambling. The aim of this volume is to provide a comprehensive review of the state-of-the-art information regarding the major types of adolescent addiction which is scientifically (e.g., prevalence and comorbidity rates, risk factors of adolescent addiction) and clinically (e.g., prevention and treatment strategies) relevant.

Arranged in three parts, Part I deals with the general issues related to adolescent addiction, including an introduction to the topic, classification, and assessment strategies. Part II contains seven chapters, each of which addresses specific adolescent addictions: alcohol use, abuse and dependence; cannabis abuse and dependence; tobacco use and dependence; eating addiction; gambling practices; internet and video-game addiction; and teen sexual addiction. The topics covered in each chapter include definitions, epidemiology, risk factors, comorbidity, addiction course and outcome, prevention/intervention, and concluding remarks. Part III consists of two chapters, one on the assessment and treatment implications of comorbid addictive problems, and one that discusses some social and political implications of adolescent addictions.

The wealth of information regarding the definitions, prevalence, comorbidity, course, risk factors, prevention of and intervention into the various types of adolescent addiction will make this volume a valuable reference for both the novice and the expert, and for both clinicians and researchers interested in this field. It is hoped that this volume will not only serve to illustrate our current knowledge of adolescent addiction, but might also stimulate further research that may contribute to an improved understanding of the problem.

I am most grateful to the authors who have contributed to this volume, all of whom have made major contributions to the field of adolescent addiction.

I am especially honored by their contributions and dedication to this project, and, more importantly, their enhancement of our understanding of adolescent addiction. I would also like to acknowledge the support and patience of the staff at Elsevier Science Ltd.

Cecilia A. Essau

PART I

GENERAL ISSUES

1

Foundations of Addictive Problems: Developmental, Social and Neurobiological Factors

Michele Preyde and Gerald Adams

Adolescence is characterized in two opposing ways. The first is as a period of fun-filled excitement, growth and experimentation, a launch pad into a progressive and productive young adulthood. The second is as a period of inner conflict and familial perturbations that are necessary precursors to growth, but also possibly to dysfunction, apathy and alienation. Arguably, adolescence can be primarily one or the other, but there can be no doubt that it offers windows of both opportunity and vulnerability for each and every adolescent. This text focuses on one major window of vulnerability – addiction.

In this chapter we open the volume by concentrating our attention on a few tasks. Our efforts, if we are successful, will direct and guide your thinking as you read the remaining chapters. We will explore issues regarding the definitions of addiction, and indicate the challenges of conducting scientific inquiries into the subject – such as estimating its prevalence. Next, we shall explore some of the more interesting and promising theories of addiction. Finally, we will examine just a few of the many developmental, social and neurobiological factors contributing to adolescent addiction. This overview should help you bridge the many ideas and chapters in this book.

DEFINITIONS OF ADDICTION

Ideas about the concept of addiction abound. It is often conceived as being both a personal and a social problem – in the former case, addiction is viewed as a weakness residing within the adolescent who lacks control and motivation; in the latter, addiction is associated with impoverished environments and lack of opportunity. Definitional criteria regarding addiction are ambiguous.

There are at least two factors that contribute to a lack of clear understanding of the concept of addiction. The way addiction is conceptualized has changed over time, and there is no universally accepted (or utilized) definition – the definition of addiction has gradually evolved. In earlier times, addiction was equated with physiological dependence (West, 2006). Traditionally, addiction was considered to be a response to a substance taken by a person – as physiological adaptation to a drug, without which the person would experience withdrawal. That is, addiction was perceived as being a condition in which a person requires a substance (i.e., a drug) in order to function without physical and psychological reactions to its absence, and which often involves tolerance and dependence (Carpenter, 2001).

This idea that addiction results solely from substance use is believed even now. Some professionals (including addiction counsellors) still hold this view (Walters and Gilbert, 2000). Likewise, expert definitions can be found that restrict the object of addiction to drugs. For example, in *The Merck Manual*, a biomedical manual, addiction has been defined within the spectrum of substance use disorders (Berkow *et al.*, 1997: Sec. 15, Ch. 195), especially in comparing and contrasting ideas of physical and psychological dependence:

> **Addiction**, a concept without a consistent, universally accepted definition, is used here to refer to a lifestyle characterized by compulsive use and overwhelming involvement with a drug; it may occur without physical dependence. Addiction implies the risk of harm and the need to stop drug use, whether the addict understands and agrees or not.

Consistent with biomedical definitions, addiction has also been described as a biobehavioral disorder (Leshner, 2001) resulting from a series of changes in the brain, these neuroadaptations being caused by repeated exposure. It is hypothesized that damage to the frontal cortex of the brain impairs the decision-making abilities influencing behavioral inhibition toward, in this case, the drug. The concept of addiction portrayed from this perspective, although perhaps too narrowly focused on drugs, is helpful for understanding concepts shared with substance use disorders.

Even within the strict application of addition to a substance (i.e., a drug), there has been a loosening of the concomitant ideas of dependence. Current understanding of addiction appears to be moving even further toward a broader definition encompassing a syndrome with heterogeneous symptoms, including a problem of compulsive behavior (and perhaps compulsive cognitions) regarding an object of desire. There is an expanded application of the term "addiction" to a wide range of items of pleasure – that is, in other arenas it has been extended to include various objects of desire, such as gambling, the Internet, and sex addictions. Other key inclusions are ideas of compulsivity, risk of harm, and problems with motivation.

West (2006) provides a definition of addiction as a syndrome involving reward-seeking behavior which results in significant harm. In this view, addiction is defined as a problem in a person's motivational system. Addiction also involves impulses or cravings, perceived needs, and a person's sense of identity (West, 2006). It may involve dependence – physical or psychological – and intoxication. There does appear to be an effect on the choices people make, the emotional attachment they have to the object of desire; this has elements of habitual behavior, and largely involves behavior and feelings.

Common to these definitions is compulsive behavior, regarding an object of desire, which implies a risk of harm and problematic actions. How addiction is viewed influences how society and experts respond, and how research into addiction is conducted.

Walters and Gilbert (2000) have attempted to elucidate an operational definition of addiction. In previous work, Walters (1999) determined that there might be four key elements to an operational definition: a general progression element (comprising physical and psychological dependence), preoccupation, perceived loss of control, and persistence in the face of mounting negative consequences. Walters and Gilbert (2000) asked clients enrolled in a drug education class ($n = 31$), and Fellows ($n = 20$) of the American Psychological Association (Division on Addictions only), to define the concept of addiction. Not one subject provided a definition that contained all four elements. Furthermore, there was significant disagreement between the two groups. The modal response (50%) of experts was physical dependence, and collectively they defined addiction as a discrete set of behaviors. However, "older experts were significantly more likely to include physical dependence in their definition than younger experts" (Walters and Gilbert, 2000: 218). Younger experts were more likely to define addiction as compulsive-habitual behavior. This difference is perhaps an indication of the evolution of the concept. In contrast, the modal response (approximately 30%) of clients was diminished control, and collectively they defined addiction as a state of mind (a focus on loss of control, the perceived need to continue the behavior, and an overriding urge to reinitiate). Walters and Gilbert suggested that there might be formal definitions, but the person with the addiction may have a simple working definition. Thus, addiction criteria may vary as a function of age and expertise. Nonetheless, without an operational definition, it is difficult for the concept of addiction to have scientific credibility.

Addiction has also been described as a dynamic process (Shaffer and Albanese, 2005) which fluctuates in intensity – that is, people with addictions can experience episodes of abstinence, exacerbation, and control over the use of their object of addiction. Opinions regarding the concept of addiction also appear to differ somewhat *amongst* professionals and clients, but more so *between* professionals and clients (Walters and Gilbert, 2000). However, clients of psychological services for addiction tended to view addiction as needs, urges and diminished control. Experts (psychologists in addictions) revealed a tendency to view addiction as compulsive aspects of behavior, the presence of physical dependence, and diminished control.

Various definitions of addiction exist. An elusive meaning and a lack of consensus of clear definition promote problems in application in research and clinical practice, such as determination of prevalence rates and research on epidemiology, assessment and treatment. Nonetheless, a body of research evidence has accumulated on the nature of addictions and adolescence.

OVERVIEW OF THE THEORIES OF ADDICTION

Numerous theories have been offered to explain addiction, ranging from personal and interpersonal to contextual explanations. The seemingly opposing theories may suggest that the pathways to addiction vary for different people, and that addiction is manifested uniquely.

In the *stepping-stone hypothesis*, marijuana was believed to be the first step toward other drugs. Cohen (1972) suggested that people with drug addiction usually try several different drugs before becoming addicted. Kandel (1975) proposed a *multiple-stage progress theory*, suggesting that adolescents who used substances (drugs) usually progressed through four sequences or stages, starting with beer or wine or both, progressing to include cigarettes or hard liquor, then marijuana, and finally to prescribed psychoactive and other illicit drugs. Kandel asserted that legal drugs are necessary intermediates between non-use and marijuana. The stepping-stone and multiple-stage progress theories led to the development of the popular *gateway theory* (Demoss, 1992), in which it is postulated that individuals begin with a soft or less powerful drug and then progress to hard drugs. It is currently thought that there are no consistent or fixed patterns of drug use, such that:

> (1) a gateway drug may not necessarily be a licit or soft drug that leads to the use of an illicit or hard drug . . . (2) any drug can be a gateway drug of another drug or drugs as long as it is associated with increased risks for the use of the other drug(s) . . . (3) Two drugs each can be a gateway drug for the other.
>
> (Chen *et al.*, 2002: 802)

The understanding of gateway drugs has developed over 30 years. There seems to be no clear linear process from soft to hard drugs, but there does appear to be a likelihood of expanded drug use after the introduction of one or more drugs. How this theory may be applied to forms of addiction other than substances is not altogether clear.

The *peer-clustering theory* (Oetting and Beauvais, 1986) illustrates the relationship between adolescents' substance use and their peers' substance use. Associating with peers with substance use problems or addictions appears to normalize and reinforce the behavior. One of the important questions regarding the peer-cluster theory is, do adolescents choose or select peers who use substances, or do peers socialize adolescents to use substances? Simons-Morton and Chen (2006) have reported that there are in fact reciprocal influences; however, "socialization was a more consistent influence than selection" (Simons-Morton and Chen, 2006: 1211).

The *attribution theory* relates to how people explain the behaviors of others. The process of making an attribution is an attempt to explain people's behavior in an effort to make sense of the world. People's actions can be attributed to internal (e.g., dispositional) or external (e.g., situational) causes. One concern is that attributions are made with ease, and often with incomplete information. Another concern is that attribution errors are possible – in fact, fundamental attribution errors are common; that is, the behavior of people is frequently attributed to internal traits while external causes are often discounted. Negative attributions in adolescent addiction can be particularly harmful. Attribution theory has been utilized to illustrate how the use of addiction as a label can promote irresponsibility, learned helplessness and passivity (Davies, 1997). Similarly, there is concern regarding application of the label "addict", which may lead to a self-fulfilling prophecy fostering hopelessness, dependency and low self-efficacy (Walters, 1999). Attribution theory can help to explain adolescent addiction and how others view adolescents with addictions. It can be complemented by an examination of self-efficacy and social cognitive theory.

The *social cognition theory* (Bandura, 1977) has been used to explain behavior as being learned symbolically through the central processing of response information before it is performed – that is, an individual observes another person's behavior and then forms symbolic representations of that modeled or observed behavior. Individuals employ motivational processes when they select the behaviors they intend to model, or choose to model behaviors that they think are effective for their purposes. Reinforcement is a mechanical response that strengthens behavior by providing informational and motivational influences. People employ self-evaluative reactions and external outcomes to guide future actions. Self-evaluative reactions can lead to perceived self-efficacy. According to Bandura (2000: 212):

> self-efficacy is people's beliefs in their capabilities to perform in ways that give them control over events that affect their lives. Efficacy beliefs form the foundation of human agency. Unless people believe that they can produce results by their actions, they have little incentive to act.

Bandura (1999: 214) asserts that self-efficacy can promote desired changes through several processes, including affective, cognitive, choice and motivational processes. Self-efficacy beliefs can influence

> every phase of personal change – the initiation of efforts to overcome substance abuse, achievement of desired changes, recovery from relapses, and long-term maintenance of a drug-free life. A major explanatory challenge is resumption of a drug abuse by abstinent individuals after withdrawal symptoms are long gone to serve as motivation.

Areas of vulnerability may be identified when assessing an adolescent's perceptions of self-efficacy. In social cognitive theory, the family is generally the most influential shaper and regulator of an individual's behaviors and beliefs; however, many people can be involved in this process, including friends and support groups. For example, recent research suggests that smoking behavior in close friends appears to be highly influential among young male students, while older role models who smoke have considerable influence on young female students (Leatherdale *et al.*, 2006). Social cognitive theory has been useful for explaining some of the observations made regarding people with addictions, in particular the modeling of behaviors observed in families and peers, and the influence of an individual's self-efficacy on recovery.

West (2006) has conducted a comprehensive review of several theories to create a synthetic theory of motivation to explain addiction, and groups the large body of theories into three main typologies. The first group consists of those theories that suggest addiction has to do with the choices people make. These choices can be rational, irrational, stable or unstable preferences. The second group includes concepts of impulses, compulsion and self-control. Most notable is the disease model, in which addiction is described as overpowering impulses resulting from pathological changes in the brain. Within this grouping are other ideas, such as personality as a predisposing factor, self-efficacy, and self-regulation. In the third group, theories describing addiction as a habit or the result of instrumental learning are described. In particular, West describes classical, operant and social learning theories, among others. It might be argued, however, that in social learning theory, individuals actively seek out role models and choose to attend to and imitate certain behaviors – suggesting that this theory has been misclassified. Finally, West presents his synthetic theory of motivation, in which five top-level elements (plans, responses, impulses, motives and evaluations: PRIME) influence each other and are influenced by other systems, such as emotional state. In West's PRIME theory of addiction, addiction is described as (West, 1006: 147):

> a social construct, not an object that can be uniquely defined. According to the proposed theory, addiction can be usefully viewed as a chronic condition of the "motivational system" in which a reward-seeking behavior has become "out of control". It often forms part of a well-defined syndrome such as the "alcohol dependence syndrome involving cravings and withdrawal symptoms, but this need not be the case.

Addiction can vary in severity and be evident from different behavioral patterns, ranging from irregular bingeing to a chronic and sustained level of behavior. It is not always clear if the behavior constitutes an addiction. West (2006: 175) states that the three main types of abnormality that underlie the pathology of addiction are as follows:

1. Abnormalities in the motivational system of the individual that exist independent of the addictive behavior, such as a propensity to anxiety, depression or impulsiveness

2. Abnormalities in the motivational system that stem from the addictive behavior itself, such as acquisition of a strongly entrenched habit or an acquired drive
3. Abnormalities in the individual's social or physical environment, such as the presence of strong social or other pressures to engage in the activity.

This synthetic theory of addiction is appealing in that it spans neurobiology, psychology and social science. West attempts to address the multiple facets of addiction, including onset, quitting, chronic addiction, and relapse. In his PRIME theory of motivation, West illustrates the concept of addiction and fosters understanding of its numerous manifestations. This newly constructed theory may prove to be useful in understanding adolescent addiction.

DEVELOPMENTAL, SOCIAL AND NEUROBIOLOGICAL FACTORS ASSOCIATED WITH ADDICTIVE PROBLEMS

The etiology of addiction is not entirely clear, but what is known is that it is a complex process (Berkow *et al.*, 1997; West, 2006). Predisposing factors include physical characteristics such as genetic predisposition, personality, and socio-economic class. Psychological factors contributing to addiction include propensity toward anxiety, depression or impulsiveness, and, in particular, emotional distress where relief of symptoms is brought about by drugs. Cultural and social settings, such as peer or group pressure, social alienation, environmental stress and mass media, are also important factors to consider when developing an understanding of addictive problems in adolescents.

Although definitions vary, prevalence of substance use in adolescence has been thoroughly reported for several countries. In general, the vast majority (~80–90%) of adolescents in France and the United States have reported consumption of alcohol by the end of high school (Essau *et al.*, 2002). The prevalence rates of addictions, in general, are quite varied. For example, in Canada, the prevalence of adolescent gambling behavior was found to be widespread (Gupta and Derevensky, 1998). Over 80 percent of high-school students reported having gambled in the previous year, and 35.1 percent within the previous month; however, the rate of pathological gambling was determined to be 4.5 percent as measured with the DSM-IV. In the United States, alcohol is the most popular substance used by adolescents–25 percent of 13-year-old adolescents reported using alcohol in the previous 30 days (Grant and Dawson, 1997). It is important too that, in addition to definitional and methodological problems in the reporting of prevalence rates, it is unclear how many of these figures represent diverse groups of adolescents around the world.

Most risk factors have been organized according to classification/groupings. Beman (1995) has classified risk factors associated with addiction along demographic, social, behavioral and individual risk factors. Sullivan and Farrell (2002) have organized their classification in terms of early initiation to substance use, genetic-biological, psychological, peer-related, family-related, school- and community-related factors, traumatic and negative life events, and multiple risk factors. Others have developed classifications according to intrapersonal, interpersonal, and environmental or contextual factors. In this chapter, risk factors will be examined under the classification of developmental, social and neurobiological factors.

DEVELOPMENTAL FACTORS

• Psychosocial development can be compromised by addiction and mental health problems. The comorbidity of mental health disorders and addiction to substances is extremely high (Kessler and Walters, 2002). Research with adolescents who are community dwelling or institutionalized appears to confirm two models (Newcomb *et al.*, 1997): in one, adolescents' mental health problems can be seen to precede addictive behaviors; in the other, addictive behaviors have also been shown to exacerbate mental health problems. As the research literature on types of addictions develops, a similar pattern can be discerned in other areas, such as gambling addiction. Studies conducted in China illustrate the relationship between mental health and Internet or electronic addiction. College students with Internet addiction were shown to differ substantially from students without Internet addiction on a number of levels (Xiaoming, 2005). Students with Internet addiction reported more negative scores with regard to mental health problems, social support, life satisfaction, interaction anxiety, self-rating depression and self-esteem than did students without Internet addiction. Wang and He (2000: 316) have concluded that

> electronic game addiction causes personality problems (such as yearning for stimulation, emotionality, anxiety, and concealment) and mental health problems (such as somatization, sensitivity of interpersonal relationship, hostility and paranoia).

Of course, it is possible that a constellation of challenges, such as negative experiences in life, renders the adolescent vulnerable to developing an addiction.

The family is believed to have a fundamental influence on the developing child. A caregiver who is emotionally and physically available is essential for healthy child and adolescent development. Difficulties in the parent–child relationship can persist throughout childhood and adolescence. Formoso and colleagues (2000) have shown that dysfunctional caregiving, lack of positive parenting skills, and poor family management are strongly associated with substance use and delinquency in youth. Conversely, close monitoring and supervision by parents is associated with a decreased risk of starting drug use (Chilcoat *et al.*, 1995). Thus, positive parental interactions can protect youth, while dysfunctional parental interactions place youth at risk for substance use and for the development of an addiction.

Research is beginning to confirm the existence of correlates of addiction in adolescence with diverse ethnic groups. The association among substance use and adverse early experiences has been shown in relation to victimization among adolescents in South Africa (Morojele and Brook, 2006). The association between family conflict and other family difficulties and alcohol problems was reported in a remote indigenous Australian community (Kelly and Kowalyszyn, 2003). In Taiwan, there were slight differences between Han and aboriginal students in terms of their association with alcohol use and misuse (Yeh and Chiang, 2005). For the Hans adolescents, problem drinking was associated with males, paternal drinking, a single-parent household and peer drinking, while for aboriginal students, problem drinking was associated with males, paternal drinking and peer drinking – i.e., family structure only appeared to be associated with Han students' problem drinking. While similarities in the characteristics of adolescents with problems in addiction can be seen across various ethnicities, some ethnic groups experience unique constellations of personal, interpersonal, familial and socio-economic factors that influence the nature of the addiction. A prime example is provided by adolescents living on First Nations reserves in Canada.

SOCIAL FACTORS

Adolescents may be particularly vulnerable in their social interactions. They might have an awkward place in the family, be especially sensitive to peer pressure and experience angst in this time of enormous change. Furthermore, the decisions they make may have serious consequences, although the decisions are often made in an invincible frame of mind.

Attempts to explain patterns of addiction and substance use by adolescents have been proposed as psychosocial mechanisms that underlie health inequities. Health inequities are seen as particularly relevant in the key transitional period between childhood and adulthood. The relation between socioeconomic status and substance use has received some attention; however, the association appears to be complicated (Goodman and Huang, 2002). Evidence suggests an association between low socio-economic status and tobacco use in adolescents, but the relationship with other substances is variable. Similarly, those who are socially marginalized experience much higher rates of addiction.

In Canada, addiction in adolescents in Aboriginal communities has been linked to their history of displacement (e.g., relocation to reserves), loss of a way of life, mandatory residential schooling, and other governmental attempts at assimilation (Denov and Campbell, 2002). The impacts of this treatment of the aboriginal communities have been described as a significant loss of their traditional culture and identity, loss of control over living conditions, the destruction of the traditional economy, and considerable stress. These have led to disrupted patterns of behaviors "predisposing Aboriginal people to substance abuse, suicide, and other self-destructive behaviors" (Denov and Campbell, 2002: 25). The prevalence of cigarette smoking among Aboriginal Canadian youth has been reported as 50 percent for those aged 10–19 years, and 82 percent in those aged

15–19 years (Retnakaran *et al.*, 2005). These figures are considerably higher than age-specific national averages. In 1990 in Davis Inlet, 80–85 percent of residents who were at least 15 years old were alcoholic, with half reporting *daily* intoxication (Wadden, 1991). Gas-sniffing has been reported by many Aboriginal youngsters since the 1970s, when 62 percent of Cree and Inuit revealed that they sniffed gas (York, 1990), and is reportedly increasing. Persistent gas-sniffing is highly dangerous, harming the kidneys and liver, and permanently damaging the nervous system and brain. Social problems, namely antisocial and aggressive behavior, have also been associated with gas-sniffing. Over the past 15 years, many groups of children and youths have been found to sniff gas in unsafe conditions (for example, in freezing temperatures with burning candles) and even to attempt suicide by gas-sniffing (Denov and Campbell, 2002). The greatest prevalence of substance abuse appears to be among the geographically and socially marginalized. For Aboriginal youth, the high rates of alcohol abuse, gas-sniffing and suicide have been linked to the bleakness of their existence and confusion about their identity.

The course and outcome for substance use disorders in adolescents have been examined with respect to three main samples: community, treatment (mainly relapse), and untreated but recovered samples (Wagner and Tarolla, 2002). The results suggest that there is considerable heterogeneity in adolescent substance use problems, and that "there is wide variation in course and outcome" (Wagner and Tarolla, 2002: 132). Relapse within a year of treatment is common; in community samples, comorbid psychopathology is significant and has a negative impact on outcome. Many self-recovering adolescents reportedly relied upon their own efforts, positive social influence, and structured activities that did not include drugs (Wagner and Tarolla, 2002). Addictions in general may not be consistent with this research.

NEUROBIOLOGICAL FACTORS

Considerable research has been conducted in an effort to understand the effects of drugs as biological rewards. Drugs appear to have the ability to activate endogenous brain circuitry (Wise and Bozarth, 1985) and neural mechanisms – for example, blocking the dopamine reuptake mechanism (Wise, 1984). More recently, Koob and colleagues (2004) have conducted many studies and reviews to determine the neurobiological mechanisms involved in developing an addiction to drugs. Koob *et al.* (2004: 739) have defined drug addiction as "a chronic relapsing disorder characterized by compulsive drug intake, loss of control over intake, and impairment in social and occupational function". Koob outlined an heuristic framework of neuroadaptive changes in brain neurocircuitry which appear to account for different stages of the addiction cycle (Koob, 2000, 2003, 2006; Weiss and Koob, 2001). In this framework, it is suggested that major neurobiological changes in substance use disorders include a compromised reward system, over-activated brain stress systems, and compromised cortex function.

Koob arrived at this model through a review of several types of studies. From animal studies, it was found that dysregulation of specific neurochemical mechanisms in the brain reward system and recruitment of brain stress systems facilitated vulnerability to relapse. Vulnerability to addiction was revealed through an examination of genetic studies involving gene encoding and neurochemical elements in the brain reward and stress systems. From human imaging studies, it was shown that neurocircuits were involved in acute intoxication, chronic drug dependence, and vulnerability to relapse. Thus, great strides have been made in developing an understanding of the neurobiological mechanisms involved in drug addiction. While this understanding is still incomplete (Koob, for example, suggests that future research directions should examine specific neuropharmacological changes), other directions have involved attempts at understanding the neurocognitive factors associated with non-substance related addiction.

The notion that the concept of addiction is no longer restricted to drugs has gained popularity in many fields. Researchers have been attempting to demonstrate that the addiction can be broadened and reclassified to include non-pharmacological addictions. Some research to date has focused on comparing gambling with traditional concepts of addiction. In recent reviews, Potenza (2006) and Petry (2006) have established that the current state of knowledge on this matter would suggest that substantial similarities are apparent between pathological gambling and substance use disorders. Indeed, the similarity in neurocognitive functioning has also been demonstrated in a prospective study using samples recruited from addiction and general mental health treatment centers. Goudriaan and colleagues (2006) found that the group of pathological gamblers and the group with alcohol dependence were both characterized by diminished executive functioning (likely dysfunction of frontal lobe circuitry). Thus, there appears to be a common neurocognitive etiology for people with gambling or alcohol addiction.

The development of drug addiction and addictive behavior is complex, involving many pharmacological, genetic and environmental determinants. While considerable research has shown the effect of drug addictions on neural circuitry, not as much is known about the neurobiological factors associated with other objects of desire.

SUMMARY

A successful first chapter should capture your interest and introduce some of the mysteries to be found in chapters to come. Scientific writing may, at first glance, not appear to be filled with mystery, but rather the contrary. All we do as scientists-practitioners is explore the mysteries of the mind, body, setting, and even soul. Addiction still remains to some degree a mystery that we are beginning to unravel. In this chapter we reveal that the challenges of defining addiction are real and puzzling, and assessment and research may be limited by the lack of a universally accepted definition of addiction. Several theories can be used to examine the mechanism of action of addiction. Although different definitions and theories are used, we know that adolescents with addictions often face many developmental, social and neurobiological challenges.

REFERENCES

Bandura, A. (1977). *Social Learning Theory*. Englewoods Cliff, NJ: Prentice-Hall.

Bandura, A. (1999). Sociocognitive analysis of substance abuse: an agenetic perspective. *Psychological Science*, 10, 214–217.

Bandura, A. (2000). Self-efficacy. In: A.E. Kazdin (ed.), *Encyclopedia of Psychology*, Vol. 7. New York, NY: Oxford University Press, pp. 212–213.

Beman D.S. (1995). Risk factors leading to adolescent substance abuse. *Adolescence*, 30, 201–208.

Berkow, R., Beers, M., Bogin, R.M. and Fletcher, A.J. (eds) (1997). *The Merck Manual of Medical Information*. New York, NY: Pocket Books (available at http://www.merck.com/mrkshared/CVMHighLight?file=/mrkshared/mmanual/section15/chapter195/195a, accessed 20 October 2006).

Carpenter, S. (2001). Cognition is central to drug addiction. *Monitor on Psychology*, 32(5), 1–5. Available at www.apa.org/monitor/jun01/cogcentral.html (accessed 2 August 2006).

Chen, X., Unger, J.B., Palmer, P. *et al.* (2002). Prior cigarette smoking initiation predicting current alcohol use: evidence for a gateway drug effect among California adolescents from eleven ethnic groups. *Addictive Behaviors*, 27, 799–817.

Chilcoat, H.D., Dishion, T.J. and Anthony, J.C. (1995). Parent monitoring and the incidence of drug sampling in urban elementary school children. *American Journal of Epidemiology*, 141(1), 25–31.

Cohen, H. (1972). Multiple drug use considered in the light of the stepping-stone hypothesis. *International Journal of Addictions*, 7, 27–55.

Davies, J.B. (1997). *The Myth of Addiction*. London: Harwood Academic.

Demoss, B.C. (1992). Gateway drugs (letter). *American Family Physician*, 46, 666–668.

Denov, M. and Campbell, K. (2002). Casualties of Aboriginal displacement in Canada: children at risk among the Innu of Labrador. *Refuge: Canada's Periodical on Refugees*, 20, 21–33.

Essau, C.A. Stigler, H. and Scheipl, J. (2002). Epidemiology and comorbidity. In: C.A. Essau (ed.), *Substance Abuse and Dependence in Adolescence: Epidemiology, Risk Factors and Treatment*. Hove, East Sussex: Brunner-Routledge, pp. 63–85.

Formoso, D., Gonzales, N.A. and Aiken, L.S. (2000). Family conflict and children's internalizing and externalizing behavior: protective factors. *American Journal of Community Psychology*, 28, 175–199.

Goodman, E. and Huang, B. (2002). Socioeconomic status, depressive symptoms and adolescent substance abuse. *Archives in Pediatric and Adolescent Medicine*, 156, 448–453.

Goudriaan, A.E., Oosterlaan, J., de Beurs, E. and van den Brink, W. (2006). Neurocognitive functions in pathological gambling: a comparison with alcohol dependence, Tourette syndrome and normal controls. *Addiction*, 101, 534–547.

Grant, B.F. and Dawson, D.A. (1997). Age at onset of alcohol use and its association with DSM-IV alcohol abuse and dependence: results from the National Longitudinal Alcohol Epidemiologic Survey. *Journal of Substance Abuse*, 9, 103–110.

Gupta, R. and Derevensky, J.L. (1998). Adolescent gambling behavior: a prevalence study and examination of the correlates associated with problem gambling. *Journal of Gambling Studies*, 14, 319–345.

Kandel, D. (1975). Stages in adolescent involvement in drug use. *Science*, 190, 912–914.

Kelly, A.B. and Kowalyszyn, M. (2003). The association of alcohol and family problems in a remote indigenous Australian community. *Addictive Behaviors*, 28, 761–767.

Kessler, R.C. and Walters, E. (2002). The national comorbidity survey. In: M.T. Tsuang and M. Tohen (eds), *Textbook in Psychiatric Epidemiology*, 2nd edn. New York, NY: John Wiley & Sons, pp. 343–632.

Koob, G.F. (2000). Neurobiology of addiction. Toward the development of new therapies. *Annals of the New York Academy of Science*, 909, 170–185.

Koob, G.F. (2003). Neuroadaptive mechanisms of addiction: studies on the extended amygdala. *European Neuropsychopharmacology*, 13, 442–452.

Koob, G.F. (2006). The neurobiology of addiction: a neuroadaptiational view relevant for diagnosis. *Addiction*, 101, 23–30.

Koob, G.F., Ahmed, S.H., Boutrel, B. *et al.* (2004). Neurobiological mechanisms in the transition from drug use to drug dependence. *Neuroscience and Biobehavior Review*, 27, 739–749.

Leatherdale, S.T., Manske, S. and Kroeker, C. (2006). Sex differences in how older students influence younger students smoking behavior. *Addictive Behaviors*, 31, 1308–1318.

Leschner, A.I. (2001). What does it mean that addiction is a brain disease? *Monitor on Psychology*, 32(5), 1–3. Available at www.apa.org/monitor/jun01/sp.html (accessed 2 August 2006).

Morojele, N.K. and Brook, J.S. (2006). Substance use and multiple victimisation among adolescents in South Africa. *Addictive Behaviors*, 31, 1163–1176.

Newcomb, M., Scheier, L. and Benter, P. (1997). Effects of adolescent drug use on adult mental health: a prospective study of a community sample. In: A.G. Marlatt and G.R. VandenBos (eds), *Addictive Behaviors: Readings on Etiology, Prevention, and Treatment*. Sashington, DC: American Psychological Association, pp. 169–211.

Oetting, E.R. and Beauvais, F. (1986). Peer cluster theory: drugs and the adolescent. *Journal of Counselling and Development*, 65, 17–22.

Petry, N.M. (2006). Should the scope of addictive behaviors be broadened to include pathological gambling? *Addiction*, 101, 152–160.

Potenza, M.N. (2006). Should addictive disorders include non-substance-related conditions? *Addiction*, 101, 142–151.

Retnakaran, R., Hanley, A., Connelly P.W. *et al.* (2005). Cigarette smoking and cardiovascular risk factors among Aboriginal Canadian youths. *Canadian Medical Association Journal*, 173, 885–889.

Shaffer, H.J. and Albanese, M.J. (2005). Addiction's defining characteristics. In: R.H. Coombs (ed.), *Addiction Counselling Review: Preparing for Comprehensive, Certification and Licensing Examinations*. Mahwab, NJ: Lawrence Erlbaum Associates, pp. 3–31.

Simons-Morton, B. and Chen, R.S. (2006). Over time relationships between early adolescent and peer substance use. *Addictive Behaviors*, 31, 1211–1223.

Sullivan, T.N. and Farrell, A.D. (2002). Risk factors. In: C.A. Essau (ed.), *Substance Abuse and Dependence in Adolescence: Epidemiology, Risk Factors and Treatment*. Hove, East Sussex: Brunner-Routledge, pp. 86–117.

Wadden, M. (1991). *Niassinan: The Innu Struggle to Reclaim their Homeland*. Vancouver, BC: Douglas and McIntyre.

Wagner, E.F. and Tarolla, S.M. (2002). Course and outcome. In: C.A. Essau (ed.), *Substance Abuse and Dependence in Adolescence: Epidemiology, Risk Factors and Treatment*. Hove, East Sussex: Brunner-Routledge, pp. 119–142.

Walters, G.D. (1999). *The Addiction Concept: Working Hypothesis or Self-fulfilling Prophesy?* Boston, MA: Allyn and Bacon.

Walters, G.D. and Gilbert, A.A. (2000). Defining addiction: contrasting views of clients and experts. *Addiction Research*, 8, 220–221.

Wang, J., and He, M. (2000). Investigation of personality and mental health status of electronic game addicted adolescents and youth. *Chinese Mental Health Journal*, 14, 316.

Weiss, F. and Koob, G.F. (2001). Drug addiction: functional neurotoxicity of the brain reward systems. *Neurtox Research*, 3, 145–156.

West, R. (2006). *Theory of Addiction*. Oxford, Oxfordshire: Blackwell Publishing.

Wise, R.A. (1984). Neural mechanisms of the reinforcing action of cocaine. *NIDA Research Monograms*, 50, 15–33.

Wise, R.A. and Bozarth, M.A. (1985). Brain mechanisms of drug reward and euphoria. *Psychiatric Medicine*, 3, 445–460.

Xiaoming, Y. (2005). The mental health problems of Internet-addicted college students. *Psychological Science*, 286, 1476–1478.

Yeh, M. and Chiang, I. (2005). Comparison of the predictors of alcohol use and misuse among Han and aboriginal students in Taiwan. *Addictive Behaviors*, 30, 989–1000.

York, G. (1990). *The Dispossessed: Life and Death in Native Canada*. London: Vintage Books.

2

Classification and Assessment of Substance Use Disorders in Adolescents

Ty A. Ridenour, Bethany C. Bray,
Heather S. Scott and Linda B. Cottler

The existence of an adequate classification scheme for substance use disorders (SUD) enhances understanding of the etiology, treatment and prevention of such disorders (Cottler, 1992). Gauging the adequacy of an SUD nomenclature requires at least four standards (Cottler, 1992; Cottler and Compton, 1993; Crowley, 2006; Escobar and Vega, 2006; Saunders and Schuckit, 2006):

1. How well it distinguishes those who are addicted from those who are not
2. Its acceptability to addiction professionals
3. Its sensitivity to addiction severity
4. Its validity in diverse populations

Although the primary goal of accurate identification of persons with a SUD might appear simplistic, establishing an acceptable classification nomenclature has proven difficult (Cottler, 1992; Saunders and Schuckit, 2006). Criticisms of specific aspects of the most recent nomenclatures point to the need for continued development of SUD diagnostic systems (Morgenstern *et al.*, 1994; Hasin *et al.*, 1997a; Langenbucher *et al.*, 2000). Members of the DSM-V Substance Use Disorders Task Force recently specified additional aspects of SUD nomenclature in need of revision, including incorporation of dimensionality to SUD diagnoses, how diagnostic criteria could account for differences between cultures and ages and drugs, and accounting for persons who experience harmful substance use but do not meet DSM-IV diagnoses (Saunders and Schuckit, 2006).

Current SUD classification systems have been developed from theory and data pertaining to adults. The shortcomings of these nomenclatures relating to adults also apply to adolescents. Additional uncertainties exist regarding classification of adolescents' SUDs due to developmental differences between adolescents and adults (Lamminpaa, 1995; Weinberg *et al.*, 1998; Meyers *et al.*, 1999; Dawes *et al.*, 2000; Deas *et al.*, 2000; Spear, 2004; Caetano and Babor, 2006; Crowley, 2006). To illustrate, the duration and regularity of substance use (e.g., at least once per month over a 6-month period) are associated with the development of diagnostic criteria (Deas *et al.*, 2000; Mikulich *et al.*, 2001). On average, adolescents who consume alcohol and other drugs regularly have done so for shorter time periods compared with adults who consume the same substances. Likewise, adolescents with SUDs generally consumed the substance regularly over much shorter time periods than adults with the same substance use related diagnoses (Brown *et al.*, 1990, 1992; Deas *et al.*, 2000).

It might be hypothesized that psychotropic substances affect adolescents differently than adults, based on biological, social or cognitive reasons (Lamminpaa, 1994, 1995; Dunn and Goldman, 1998; Deas *et al.*, 2000; Spear, 2004). However, the specific mechanisms of these differences are complex and remain unclear (Barr *et al.*, 2004; Hill, 2004; O'Dell *et al.*, 2004; Turner *et al.*, 2004). Developmental differences have implications for SUD classification, etiology and intervention (Galanter *et al.*, 2005).

Revisions to one SUD classification system over the past two decades illustrate the challenges of classifying SUD pathology. A brief overview of the two widely used modern classification systems – DSM-IV and ICD-10 – will provide a grounding that will be referenced throughout the remainder of the book. Ways in which current classifications might not generalize to adolescents will be illustrated with examples from the growing research literature regarding SUD nomenclature for adolescents. Evaluation of current SUD nomenclature will focus on the instruments best equipped to assess the classification schemes, and briefly reviewing other, related, instruments.

RECENT EVOLUTION OF DSM PATHOLOGICAL SUBSTANCE USE CLASSIFICATION

The first diagnostic taxonomy of SUDs was presented in DSM-III (APA, 1980; Robins and Helzer, 1986). The taxonomy consisted of abuse and dependence in place of the single disorder in the Feighner Criteria and Research Diagnostic Criteria (Feighner *et al.*, 1972; Spitzer *et al.*, 1978). For dependence diagnosis, DSM-III required a physiological criterion (withdrawal or tolerance) and that social impairment due to substance use be experienced. The DSM-III SUD taxonomy was criticized on several bases, including the emphasis on physiological criteria and social impairment, lack of a specific theoretical underpinning, and inclusion of two disorders (Caetano, 1987; Rounsaville, 1987; Schuckit, 1993; Nathan, 1994). Within one year of the release of the DSM-III, a work group was designed to revise assessment of the nomenclature to test and prepare for these suggestions (Cottler *et al.*, 1995a). Although separate abuse and dependence disorders continued in the DSM-III-R, physiological, social consequences and occupational impairment criteria were not required for a dependence diagnosis, and the same nine criteria were used for all SUD (APA, 1987; Rounsaville, 1987).

The Edwards and Gross Alcohol Dependence Syndrome (Edwards and Gross, 1976; Edwards, 1986) served as the theoretical basis for SUDs in DSM-III-R, DSM-IV and ICD-10. Edwards and Gross characterized the alcohol dependence syndrome using the following criteria: narrowing of the drinking repertoire (alcohol consumption becomes invariable), continued alcohol consumption in spite of knowledge that alcohol is the source of problems, tolerance to alcohol's subjective effects, withdrawal symptoms, seeking relief or avoiding withdrawal symptoms by alcohol consumption, craving alcohol when not drinking, a compulsion to drink (a difficulty to stop drinking once alcohol consumption has ensued), and a return to alcohol consumption after a period of abstinence. In addition to these criteria, (Edwards and Gross, 1976; Edwards, 1986) acknowledged that the syndrome varies in severity, illustrating the difficulty in specifying a threshold that distinguishes the ill from the well. The narrowing of the drinking repertoire criterion was included in early ICD SUD nomenclature; however, it was not included in the DSM-III-R or subsequent classification systems of DSM and ICD because it was thought to be unreliable (Cottler *et al.*, 1995b).

Requiring three criteria for a dependence diagnosis maximized agreement between DSM-III and DSM-III-R in terms of who qualifies for a SUD (Rounsaville *et al.*, 1987). Substance abuse became a residual category in DSM-III-R for persons who did not meet dependence criteria but nevertheless had problematic substance use (Rounsaville and Kranzler, 1989).

DSM-III-R met the aforementioned standards of nomenclature adequacy (Cottler *et al.*, 1995a). An empirically driven approach to DSM-III-R revision included collecting information from over 50 experts, a literature review on research addressing specific questions regarding DSM-III-R classification, reanalysis of existing datasets, and collection of novel data to address issues that had not been sufficiently studied (Cottler *et al.*, 1995a). Moreover, an attempt was made to reduce discrepancies between DSM nomenclature and ICD-10 nomenclature to facilitate the comparability of international studies and communication (Pincus *et al.*, 1992). Specifically, dropping the narrowing of repertoire criterion from ICD-10 reduced discrepancies between the DSM-III-R and ICD-10 (Rounsaville *et al.*, 1993).

Thus, DSM-IV differed from the DSM-III-R in several ways (APA, 1994; Cottler *et al.*, 1995a). The abuse diagnosis was designed to be distinct from the dependence diagnosis rather than serving as a residual category for persons who do not meet dependence criteria. Abuse criteria were expanded from two to four. The "clustering" criterion was made more specific (at least three dependence criteria had to occur during a 12-month period). Dependence diagnoses were further specified as either physiological (with tolerance or withdrawal) or non-physiological.

CURRENT SUBSTANCE USE RELATED CLASSIFICATION SYSTEMS

Two co-existing classification systems are widely used to diagnose substance related disorders. The American Psychiatric Association's *Diagnostic and Statistical Manual of Mental Disorders – IV* (DSM-IV; APA, 1994) remains the current dominant taxonomy in the United States for mental health diagnoses. The International Classification of Diseases – 10 for research (ICD-10; WHO, 1993a), developed by the World Health Organization, is used to guide mental health diagnoses predominantly outside of the United States. The DSM-IV and ICD-10 systems serve to guide clinical practice, research and education. The functional utility of the two systems is most often associated with reimbursement for treatment services. DSM-IV also is used for research purposes. Two versions of SUD nomenclature are available for ICD criteria. The ICD-10 research criteria will be referred to throughout this chapter because they have been used in the literature.

The theoretical basis for substance use diagnoses of the two systems is the original alcohol dependence syndrome (Edwards and Gross, 1976). Each classification includes (a) a primary dependence diagnosis, (b) a secondary diagnosis abuse (in DSM-IV) or harmful use (in ICD-10), (c) similar substance-specific withdrawal criteria, and (d) similar substance-specific intoxication diagnoses. Additional diagnoses can be made, based on the patterns of symptoms and course of the disorder. For example, dependence diagnoses can be specified as including physiological criteria.

This chapter focuses primarily on the dependence and abuse/harmful use diagnoses because they are the most widely used diagnoses for identification of persons with addiction. Corresponding diagnoses from the DSM-IV and ICD-10 systems will be presented side by side to highlight their differences. Because DSM-IV provides a greater description of the disorders, characterizations of the diagnoses are quoted from the DSM-IV.

Substance Dependence: DSM-IV vs ICD-10

DSM-IV characterizes substance dependence as "a cluster of cognitive, behavioral, and physiological symptoms indicating that the individual continues use of the substance despite significant substance-related problems" (Edwards and Gross, 1976: 192). The dependence diagnosis applies to all psychoactive substance classes except caffeine. At least three criteria must occur within a 12-month period for an individual to qualify for either a DSM-IV or an

ICD-10 dependence diagnosis. Criteria that occur together over a 1-month period also qualify for ICD-10 dependence diagnosis.

The criteria used to define substance dependence diagnoses are physiological (tolerance or withdrawal) and non-physiological (the remaining behavioral or emotional criteria). If individuals have experienced either tolerance or withdrawal, their dependence diagnosis is further specified as physiological. Tolerance is defined as "the need for greatly increased amounts of the substance to achieve intoxication (or the desired effect) or a markedly diminished effect with continued use of the same amount of the substance" (Edwards and Gross, 1976: 192).

Substance withdrawal is defined in DSM-IV as "the development of a substance-specific maladaptive behavioral change, with physiological and cognitive concomitants, that is due to the cessation of, or reduction in, heavy or prolonged substance use" (APA, 2000: 201). For example, symptoms of cocaine withdrawal include "fatigue, vivid unpleasant dreams, insomnia or hypersomnia, increased appetite, and psychomotor retardation or agitation" (APA, 1994: 246), whereas opioid withdrawal can be experienced as "dysphoric mood, nausea or vomiting, muscle aches, lacrimation or rhinorrhea, pupillary dilation, piloerection, sweating, diarrhea, yawning, fever, and insomnia" (APA, 1994: 273). DSM-IV does not acknowledge cannabis withdrawal, a subject of intense debate at this time (Budney, 2006). For the withdrawal diagnosis, the DSM-IV nomenclature additionally requires distress or impairment related to social, occupational, or other important activities (criterion B).

Subtle differences between the ICD-10 and DSM-IV dependence criteria can lead to disagreements about which individuals qualify for diagnosis. Three differences are noted:

1. Inclusion of a craving symptom in the ICD-10
2. DSM-IV criteria (3) and (4) are combined into one criterion in ICD-10 (number (2))
3. DSM-IV criteria (5) and (6) are combined into a single criterion in ICD-10 (number (5)).

Craving is described as "a strong desire or sense of compulsion to take the substance" (symptom (1), WHO, 1993a: 57). Hence, individuals experiencing a strong desire to consume a substance in addition to having two other criteria would qualify for ICD-10 dependence but not DSM-IV dependence. Studies regarding the rates of disagreement between DSM-IV and ICD-10 diagnoses are described below.

DSM-IV Substance Abuse Versus ICD-10 Harmful Use

The abuse and harmful use diagnoses have been described by some researchers as similar because they are both residual categories to dependence. Individuals qualify for abuse or harmful use diagnoses only if the dependence criteria are not fulfilled. However, differences exist between the abuse and harmful use criteria.

DSM-IV substance abuse is characterized as "a maladaptive pattern of substance use manifested by recurrent and significant adverse consequences related to the repeated use of substances" (APA, 2000: 198). DSM-IV requires "impairment or distress" as defined by the repeated experience of one of four specific criteria in a 12-month period. The ICD-10 requirement of actual harm (criterion A) from substance use is vague compared with the substance abuse criteria. Another difference is noted in that the ICD-10 nomenclature specifies that harmful use must persist for at least 1 month or occur repeatedly within a 12-month period.

Substance Intoxication

Intoxication is characterized in the DSM-IV as "a reversible substance-specific syndrome due to the recent ingestion of (or exposure to) a substance" (APA, 2000: 199). Intoxication is defined primarily in physiologic terms, and varies across substances. For example, DSM-IV (2000: 239) diagnostic criteria for cannabis intoxication include two or more of the following signs that appear within 2 hours of cannabis use: "(1) conjunctival injection, (2) increased appetite, (3) dry mouth, and (4) tachycardia". Signs of hallucinogen intoxication include two or more signs that develop during or shortly after the use of the hallucinogenic substance: "(1) pupillary dilation, (2) tachycardia, (3) sweating, (4) palpitations, (5) blurred vision, (6) tremors, and (7) incoordination" (APA, 2000: 253).

Diagnostic Agreement Between DSM-IV and ICD-10

The most comprehensive study of (dis)agreement between DSM-IV and ICD-10 SUD across the world was conducted by the World Health Organization (WHO), the US National Institute on Drug Abuse (NIDA), and the US National Institute on Alcoholism and Alcohol Abuse (NIAAA) (Cottler *et al.*, 1997; Hasin *et al.*, 1997b; Pull *et al.*, 1997; Ustun *et al.*, 1997). The primary aims of this project were to develop internationally acceptable instruments for diagnosing SUD, and to investigate the reliability and validity of the instruments. The instruments that were tested were the Composite International Diagnostic Interview (CIDI, World Health Organization, 1993b), Schedules for Clinical Assessment in Neuropsychiatry (SCAN, World Health Organization, 1993c), and Alcohol Use Disorder and Associated Disabilities Interview Schedule – Alcohol/Drug Revised (AUDADIS-ADR, World Health Organization, 1993d).

Diagnostic agreement between the DSM-IV and ICD-10 was estimated using data collected from 1811 participants in psychiatric treatment, other medical and community settings at 12 international sites, including Amsterdam (The Netherlands), Ankara (Turkey), Athens (Greece), Bangalore (India), Farmington (Connecticut, US), Ibadan (Nigeria), Jebel (Romania), Luxembourg (Luxembourg), St Louis (Missouri, US), San Juan (Puerto Rico), and two sites in Sydney (Australia) (Hasin *et al.*, 1997b; Ustun *et al.*, 1997). Data were collected using the native languages of the locations. The level of agreement for diagnoses was estimated using the kappa statistic, which ranges from –1.0 (complete disagreement) through 0.0 (chance agreement) to 1.0 (complete agreement). Kappa estimates of 0.75–1.00 are considered excellent, of 0.60–0.75 are good, of 0.40–0.60 are fair, and of less than 0.40 are poor (Bishop *et al.*, 1975).

Estimates of diagnostic agreement were calculated for each instrument, providing a range of kappa values of the agreement between DSM-IV and ICD-10 for each diagnosis. Kappas were calculated using two-by-two contingency tables categorizing users of the substance who had a diagnosis versus users who did not have the diagnosis. Agreements for alcohol dependence in the past year were 0.90–0.92, and over the lifetime were 0.87–0.92 (Hasin *et al.*, 1997b). Corresponding kappas for dependence diagnoses were 0.84–0.88 and 0.89–0.90 for cannabis, 0.86–1.0 and 0.92–0.95 for amphetamines, 0.89–0.98 and 0.46–0.93 for sedatives, 0.96–0.98 and 0.98 (for each instrument) for opiates, and 0.96–0.98 and 0.96–1.0 for cocaine. With one exception (0.46 for sedative dependence measured with the CIDI), agreement estimates between DSM-IV and ICD-10 dependence diagnoses were excellent and consistent across instruments.

Agreements between abuse and harmful use diagnoses were poor to fair and less consistent between instruments (Hasin *et al.*, 1997b). One confound to estimating agreement between abuse and harmful use is that participants might meet criteria for dependence in only one diagnostic system, and consequently be eligible for only abuse or harmful use – which lowers agreement between them. Poor agreement between abuse and harmful use diagnoses has been reported for different age-groups, ethnicities and genders, as well as for community and treatment samples (Hasin *et al.*, 1996; Langenbucher *et al.*, 1994).

The poorer agreement and greater variation in instrument kappa values between abuse and harmful use could be due to poor conceptualization of abuse or harmful use, to poor operationalization of abuse or harmful use, or to both. Other studies suggest weaknesses in harmful-use nomenclature or assessment because of the poor reliability reported for harmful-use diagnoses in this sample (see, for example, Ustun *et al.*, 1997) and other samples (see, for example, Regier *et al.*, 1994). Importantly, the reliabilities of abuse criteria and of abuse diagnosis when the requirement of not meeting dependence diagnosis is ignored were fair to excellent (Horton *et al.*, 2000; Hasin *et al.*, 1997c).

Physiological Dependence Debate

The DSM-III requirement of a physiological criterion being present for a dependence diagnosis was controversial, but the debate continues. Perhaps the physiological criteria have been emphasized because they resemble a biological marker for the disease (Cottler and Compton, 1993). Among substance users, tolerance and withdrawal appear rare, whereas 86–99 percent of persons with dependence on alcohol, amphetamines, cannabis, cocaine, opiates, sedatives or nicotine report tolerance, withdrawal, or both (Cottler *et al.*, 1995a). In fact, it has been reported that the withdrawal criterion fails to distinguish persons with harmful substance use from other persons, particularly among adolescents (Langenbucher *et al.*, 2000). Less than one-third of adolescents in SUD treatment experience withdrawal (Stewart and Brown, 1995; Winters and Stinchfield, 1995; Langenbucher *et al.*, 2000; Mikulich *et al.*, 2001).

The emphasis and role of withdrawal has been more controversial than tolerance due to several factors. Tolerance is hypothesized to occur earlier ontologically than withdrawal – for example, Edwards and Gross (1976) argued that withdrawal cannot occur without tolerance. Withdrawal symptoms are more salient than tolerance symptoms. When physiological dependence is limited to withdrawal, such dependence is more strongly associated with substance use related problems and relapse in both adults and adolescents (Langenbucher *et al.*, 1997, 2000). Hasin and colleagues (2000) reported that persons recruited from the community with DSM-IV alcohol dependence who had experienced withdrawal were at nearly three times the risk for having alcohol dependence a year later, compared with persons who had not experienced alcohol withdrawal. Additional studies suggest that withdrawal is associated with more severe dependence (Schuckit *et al.*, 1998, 1999; Woody *et al.*, 1993; Langenbucher *et al.*, 1995; Bucholz *et al.*, 1996). However, data are inconsistent regarding withdrawal as a marker of severe SUD. In studies of drinkers recruited from the community, alcohol withdrawal was not as highly associated with a diagnosis of alcohol dependence as were other alcohol criteria (Hasin *et al.*, 1994; Muthen *et al.*, 1993).

Substance Use Disorder Severity and Continuum Debates

DSM-IV and ICD-10 nomenclature suggests that persons experiencing addiction should first experience abuse, and some of them will then progress to a more severe state of addiction – dependence. Some data suggest that adults and adolescents meeting criteria for DSM-IV abuse have less severe substance-related pathology than persons who meet dependence criteria (Pollock and Martin, 1999; Langenbucher *et al.*, 2000; Sarr *et al.*, 2000). However, other studies clearly demonstrate that abuse and dependence diagnoses fail to distinguish severities of substance-related pathology (Hasin *et al.*, 1997a; Schuckit *et al.*, 2001; Ridenour *et al.*, 2003; Hasin and Grant, 2004).

Additional studies have attempted to elucidate the levels of addiction severity that are associated with different DSM criteria. Langenbucher and colleagues (2004) found that in a sample of addiction treatment patients, the levels of severity associated with specific criteria differed between alcohol, cannabis and cocaine. Moreover, many of the dependence criteria were associated with less addiction severity than abuse criteria, but the addiction severities differed between drugs for most criteria. In all three substances, the criterion associated with the lowest severity of addiction was dependence criterion number (7) – not an abuse criterion. These results are highly consistent with DSM-IV criteria reflecting a continuum of addiction severity, but one that differs from DSM-IV nomenclature.

Martin and colleagues (2006) replicated the study with adolescents to find similar support for a severity continuum gauged by alcohol and cannabis use criteria rather than the distinct disorders of DSM-IV nomenclature. However, Martin and colleagues' (2006) results also differed from Langenbucher and colleagues' (2004) results with adults. Nevertheless, the evidence is so strongly in favor of a continuum of severity of SUDs that one revision being considered for DSM-V is to assimilate severity into the nomenclature (Helzer *et al.*, 2006; Muthen, 2006).

A recent test of the reliabilities of nomenclature for four types of inhalants illustrates complications that can arise when using adult-based criteria with adolescents (Ridenour *et al.*, 2006a). Inhalant use largely (though not exclusively) occurs during late childhood and early adolescence (Johnston *et al.*, 2006). Hence, the Substance Abuse Module inhalants module was tested in adolescent and young adult inhalant users who were recruited from the community. Briefly, reliabilities of abuse criteria and diagnosis were good to excellent whereas reliabilities of dependence criteria and diagnoses were poor to good across types of inhalants – which is the opposite pattern to that observed in adults (Ridenour *et al.*, 2007). Much improved reliabilities were found when inhalant SUD criteria were configured on continua, consistent with others' recommendations for continuous SUD nomenclature for adolescents regarding different substances (Harrison *et al.*, 1998; Fulkerson *et al.*, 1999; Pollock and Martin, 1999).

Diagnostic Orphans

Assimilating a severity continuum into SUD diagnoses is particularly compelling for adolescents because of the greater rate of "diagnostic orphans" among adolescents than adults. Diagnostic orphans meet one or two dependence criteria (but not diagnosis) and no abuse criteria (Hasin and Paykin, 1998, 1999; Pollock and Martin, 1999; Sarr *et al.*, 2000). Compared with persons who report no criteria, diagnostic orphans experience more severe substance use related problems (e.g., extent of use, number of psychiatric disorders, early age of substance use onset, proportion with dependence at 1-year follow-up). However, they experience less severe substance-related problems compared with persons who meet dependence criteria (Hasin and Paykin, 1998, 1999; Pollock and Martin, 1999; Sarr *et al.*, 2000). In fact, adult diagnostic orphans closely resemble persons meeting criteria for abuse in terms of the severity of their substance use pathology (Pollock and Martin, 1999; Sarr *et al.*, 2000).

Pollock and Martin (1999) found that adolescent diagnostic orphans resembled adult diagnostic orphans in some aspects. One difference they found was that in adolescent regular drinkers, nearly one-third fit the diagnostic orphan description, whereas diagnostic orphans composed only one-fifth percent of comparable samples of adults (Hasin and Paykin, 1999; Sarr *et al.*, 2000). At the least, persons fitting the diagnostic orphan description should be researched separately from other substance users (Pollock and Martin, 1999; Sarr *et al.*, 2000).

PRIORITIES OF DSM-V SUBSTANCE USE DISORDERS WORKGROUP

A special issue of *Addiction* outlined research topics to be addressed by the DSM-V Substance Use Disorder Workgroup *en route* to refining DSM criteria (Saunders and Schuckit, 2006). Workgroup members presented cases for re-examination of many nosological aspects of the criteria, including: categorical vs continuous nomenclature, social and cultural generalizations of criteria and diagnoses, (in)consistencies between DSM and ICD nomenclature, and substance-specific criteria. Of most relevance to this chapter will be the Workgroup's re-examination of how well criteria apply to adolescents (Caetano and Babor, 2006; Crowley, 2006).

CLASSIFICATION CRITERIA FOR ADOLESCENTS

The basic question "How appropriate are substance use-related diagnostic nomenclature for adolescents?" has been addressed in few studies. Social problems due to substance use were moved from dependence criteria in DSM-III-R to the abuse criteria in DSM-IV. It appears that this change has resulted in fewer adolescents being identified for dependence diagnosis but more adolescents being identified for abuse diagnoses for alcohol, cannabis, cocaine and hallucinogens (Winters *et al.*, 1999; Mikulich *et al.*, 2001). In contrast, fewer adolescents qualify for both of the dependence and abuse diagnoses of amphetamines, opiates and inhalants using DSM-IV criteria, compared with the DSM-III-R criteria (Mikulich *et al.*, 2001). An illustration of why social problems are so critical to diagnosis in adolescents is provided by the following scenario. Substance use by adolescents can lead to poorer academic performance and strain an adolescents' relationships with parents when parents are notified of their drop in academic performance. Moreover, adolescents who receive substance use treatment might do so at a parents' insistence before physical or psychological problems develop.

The social problems criterion is not the only one that differentiates adolescents from adults. Because they are younger, adolescents have had shorter time periods on average to use substances compared with adults. Thus, it might be hypothesized that fewer adolescents have experienced physiological symptoms. However, relatively high proportions of adolescents in SUD treatment report having physiological criteria (Mikulich *et al.*, 2001). Caetano and Babor (2006) demonstrated that at least part of the increased prevalence of physiological criteria in adolescents (compared with adults) could be poor comprehension or naïveté about the symptomotologies of physiological criteria.

Agreement between DSM-III-R and DSM-IV dependence diagnoses have generally been good to excellent for adolescents (Winters *et al.*, 1999; Mikulich *et al.*, 2001). Initial results suggest that no difference occurs regarding which adolescents meet criteria for dependence when the clustering criterion (at least three criteria must occur within a 12-month period) is dropped (Mikulich *et al.*, 2001). This finding may not be specific to adolescents, however, because similar results have been reported for adults (Cottler *et al.*, 1995a).

Limited research has investigated agreement between DSM-IV and ICD-10 substance use related diagnoses in adolescents. Pollock and colleagues (2000) investigated agreement between DSM-IV and ICD-10 alcohol diagnoses in adolescent regular drinkers from clinical and community settings of Pittsburgh, Pennsylvania. Assessments of substance use diagnoses were conducted using the Structured Clinical Interview for the DSM. The ICD-10 harmful use diagnosis was assumed to correspond approximately to the DSM-IV abuse diagnosis. Diagnoses were handled as though they represented thresholds on a severity continuum (i.e., dependence diagnosis was worst, abuse or harmful use represented a lower level of severity and no diagnosis was healthy). Only fair agreement was reported, with the greatest discrepancies occurring between ICD-10 harmful use and DSM-IV abuse diagnosis.

Agreement between DSM-III-R and DSM-IV abuse diagnoses has been reported to be poor to fair for adolescents receiving treatment using the Substance Abuse Module (Mikulich *et al.*, 2001). In contrast to these findings of less than ideal reliability for diagnoses, the cannabis abuse diagnosis provided useful prognostic information over a 1.5-year period for German adolescents (Perkonigg *et al.*, 1999). Of adolescents who met criteria for cannabis abuse at baseline, 44 percent also met abuse criteria at the 1.5-year follow-up, 5 percent met cannabis dependence criteria, and only 18 percent of the cannabis abusers abstained from cannabis use. Overall, Perkonigg and colleagues (1999) found that adolescents who used cannabis at baseline generally continued or increased their level of use at the follow-up.

At least four studies have led researchers to suggest combining DSM-IV abuse and dependence criteria into a single category for adolescents, and differentiating abuse from dependence in terms of the number of criteria experienced (Harrison *et al.*, 1998; Fulkerson *et al.*, 1999; Pollock and Martin, 1999; Ridenour *et al.*, 2007a). The literature regarding classification of substance use diagnoses among adolescents is scant, and research is needed to understand better how well or how poorly the DSM-IV and ICD-10 substance use classification nomenclature generalize to adolescents. Harmful use and abuse diagnoses should be interpreted with particular caution in adolescents. Harrison and colleagues (1998) reported a greater prevalence of dependence items than abuse items, and, interestingly, failure to fulfill role obligations and legal issues co-occurred more often with severe dependence symptoms than with other abuse symptoms. These findings are consistent with other studies among adolescents (White, 1987; Martin *et al.*, 1995, 1996; Winters *et al.*, 1999).

REMAINING QUESTIONS

In spite of these efforts to personify a substance use classification, a number of important questions have not been adequately resolved. One question is: Should the same criteria be used to define disorders for each substance? It was found that only for certain substances did the two definitions of withdrawal (use of a drug to get relief from withdrawal symptoms and experiencing withdrawal symptoms) overlap (Cottler *et al.*, 1993, 1995a). Hence, for some substances, using the two definitions of withdrawal will result in a greater number of persons meeting dependence diagnosis, whereas for other substances the later definition of withdrawal might suffice as the criterion. Other important questions not adequately addressed at the time of the release of DSM-IV SUD criteria included: Do the same criteria for dependence generalize to all substances? In what ways does the Alcohol Dependence Syndrome not generalize to other substances? Is abuse distinct from, a residual category of, or a milder form of addiction than dependence?

Recent studies by Ridenour and colleagues (2003, 2005) attempted to clarify how abuse and dependence are aligned and at the same time test how different their alignment was for four different drugs: alcohol, cannabis, cocaine and opiates. Analyses tested the connotation of DSM-IV nomenclature that persons with SUDs should progress through abuse to then experience dependence. However, they found that sizable proportions of clinically-recruited addicts experienced dependence either before abuse or without ever experiencing dependence (Ridenour *et al.*, 2003). Abuse was experienced well before dependence for alcohol and cannabis in 76 percent and 61 percent of the respective participants with those disorders, whereas abuse occurred before dependence in only 26 percent and 33 percent of cocaine and opiate SUDs, respectively. The alignment between abuse and dependence clearly differed between alcohol and the other substances, especially cocaine and opiates. Additional studies suggest that abuse and dependence do not align in the manner expected by DSM-IV or ICD-10 nomenclature (Hasin *et al.*, 1997a; Schuckit *et al.*, 2001; Ridenour *et al.*, 2003; Hasin and Grant, 2004). They also suggested that addiction occurs on a continuum, which is manifested differently for different drugs.

Ridenour and colleagues (2005) also demonstrated that the length of time between onset of abuse and dependence was not associated with previous SUDs or ethnicity, but was slightly associated with gender (females had faster progressions) and early initiation of drug use. Perhaps most the interesting result was that the average length of time between onset of abuse and onset of dependence resembled findings from studies of the relative addictiveness of substances from animal studies: cocaine is the most addictive, followed by opiates, then alcohol and cannabis (Ridenour *et al.*, 2005). Similar patterns have been observed in the general population (Wagner and Anthony, 2002). Their findings largely were replicated in a prospective study of adolescents (Ridenour *et al.*, 2006b).

Crowley (2006) posed additional considerations for DSM-IV nomenclature with adolescents. Perhaps SUD nomenclature should be linked to age, based on findings that SUDs mostly onset before age 25, most persons with SUDs also qualify for conduct disorder, and SUDs that onset during early adolescence may represent a more severe form of addiction. Given that adolescents with SUDs often qualify for diagnoses related to multiple substances, perhaps nomenclature should include the number of diagnoses or criteria experienced. Novel drugs of addiction often are first used among adolescents. Perhaps additional nomenclature should be created for forthcoming drugs with unknown syndromes such as intoxication or withdrawal.

ASSESSMENT

An issue that is equally important to developing accurate SUD nomenclature is the availability of an instrument to assess the classification system, along with indicators of harmful substance use that might be useful to consider for refining nomenclature (Cottler and Compton, 1993; Cottler *et al.*, 1995b). In certain respects, nomenclature and corresponding assessment(s) co-evolve because each informs the development of the other (Robins, 1989; Cottler and Keating, 1990). Characteristics of substance use other than diagnostic nomenclature ought to be included in the assessment because they can provide insight into substance use classification. Treatment outcomes can be predicted with increased accuracy using knowledge about patients' patterns of substance use, and treatment planning is often shaped, at least in part, by the antecedents and consequences of substance use (Babor, 1993). Knowledge of patterns of use, antecedents and consequences also provides insight into the etiology of SUDs (Babor, 1993).

CHARACTERISTICS OF THE IDEAL DIAGNOSTIC INTERVIEW

Cottler and Keating (1990) and Cottler and Compton (1993) have outlined the characteristics of a good diagnostic interview (Table 2.1). Before an instrument is useful for assessing SUDs, it must be demonstrated to be reliable (i.e., SUDs and criteria are consistent in persons regardless of variations in interview features, such as the person administering the instrument) and valid (the instrument truly measures the substance use characteristics that it is purported to measure).

Characteristics in Table 2.1 numbered (3)–(6), (10), (12), (14)–(16) and 20 augment the reliability of an assessment instrument. Structured interviews (number (3)) are those designed to have questions asked and scored in an identical manner in every interview. Instrument reliability generally is estimated by administering the instrument to the same individual twice, with a 1-week interval between interviews, and two different interviewers (test–retest, inter-rater reliability). The level of reliability is gauged using the kappa estimate of agreement between the two interviews.

Characteristics numbered (1), (2), (4), (11), (13)–(17) and (20) augment the validity of an assessment. The validity of an instrument can be evaluated in numerous ways. Face validity refers to the concept that items appear to assess the trait that they are intended to assess. Concurrent validity is estimated by administering more than one SUD assessment to the same individual. Someone

TABLE 2.1 Characteristics of a Good Diagnostic Interview for Substance Use Related Disorders

1. The nosologies of multiple diagnostic systems must be accurately operationalized
2. Persons who are ill must be distinguished from those who are well
3. Interviews should be highly structured (every question asked the same way by every interviewer)
4. Criteria or symptoms of medical origin must be excluded from contributing to substance diagnoses
5. Language should be non-idiomatic
6. Language should not be culture-specific
7. Interviews should be completed in one sitting
8. Interviews should be acceptable to everyone
9. Interviews should be error-free
10. Questions should be close-ended
11. Questions should be as brief as possible without sacrificing clarity of meaning
12. Questions should be comprehensible to persons whatever their educational level
13. "Skipouts" should be used only when it is impossible that interviewees have experienced any of the criteria that are skipped, based on the response to a probe question
14. The diagnostic criterion that is operationalized by each question should be transparent
15. Information collected should not be subject to individual interpretation
16. Information collected should not require external sources
17. Impairments not resulting from the illness should not be classified as symptoms
18. Enhancements such as reference cards or pictures should be available when needed to enhance interviewees' comprehension of questions
19. Training materials and course should be available
20. Empirical evidence (e.g., sensitivity, specificity, reliability, validity) from multiple datasets collected by different researchers should be good to excellent
21. Instrument should be computerized to maximize interview simplicity and minimize errors that might occur in the interview or data entry

From: Robins (1989), Cottler and Keating (1990) and Cottler and Compton (1993).

with a SUD on one assessment should qualify for the same SUD on the other assessment. Ideally, all persons who truly have a SUD will be identified as having the disorder by the assessment (high sensitivity), and all of the persons who truly do not have the disorder will not be identified as having the disorder by the assessment (high specificity).

The generalizability of an instrument also ought to be tested in terms of its reliability and validity with samples from cultures other than the original sample. In the afore-described WHO/NIDA/NIAAA international study, the Composite International Diagnostic Interview, Schedules for Clinical Assessment in Neuropsychiatry, and Alcohol Use Disorder and Associated Disabilities Interview Schedule – Alcohol/Drug – Revised were independently translated from English into the native languages used at each of the international research centers (Ustun *et al.*, 1997). Each of the translated instruments was then "back-translated" into English to ferret out errors in the original translation and further refine the translated instruments (Room *et al.*, 1996; Ustun *et al.*, 1997). Each assessment was tested for its cross-cultural acceptability (Room *et al.*, 1996). An illustration of why cultural differences must be considered when developing assessments comes from the translation of the Composite International Diagnostic Interview. In some cultures, regular consumption of alcohol is normative. In other cultures, interviewees were confused when asked "Were there ever objections from your family about your drinking?" (abuse criterion (4)) because any alcohol use was objectionable in that culture (Cottler and Compton, 1993).

The instruments with the largest influences on SUD classification to date are reviewed here. The Substance Abuse Module (SAM) was designed to thoroughly assess substance use nomenclature, as well as substance use characteristics that might be useful for clarification or revision of the current nomenclatures (Cottler and Keating, 1990; Cottler and Compton, 1993). The SAM meets the 21 characteristics of the ideal assessment; hence it will continue to be used to illustrate specific aspects of the ideal characteristics of a diagnostic substance use instrument.

SUBSTANCE ABUSE MODULE (SAM)

The SAM represents a continuation of a tradition of important mental health classification assessments (Cottler and Keating, 1990). Robins and colleagues (1981) based the NIMH Diagnostic Interview Schedule (DIS) on the DSM-III, Research Diagnostic Criteria (Spitzer *et al.*, 1978) and Feighner criteria (Feighner *et al.*, 1972). The Robins team also developed the CIDI, which is an expanded version of the DIS with additional items from the Present State Examination (Wing *et al.*, 1974; Robins *et al.*, 1988, 1990). The CIDI was designed for cross-cultural use, is highly structured, and was originally written to assess DSM and ICD psychiatric disorders. Field-testing of the CIDI was conducted in the Australia, Brazil, East and West Germany, France, Greece, India, Italy, Luxembourg, Norway, the People's Republic of China, Portugal, Puerto Rico, Sweden, the United Kingdom, and the United States. The CIDI was deemed acceptable in the field trials, and was reported to generally be reliable and valid (Robins *et al.*, 1988; Wittchen *et al.*, 1991, 1998). However, SUD items were reported to be too long, and certain SUDs had less than ideal reliability (Cottler *et al.*, 1991, 1997; Hasin *et al.*, 1997b; Pull *et al.*, 1997; Andrews and Peters, 1998). During validity testing of the CIDI and other SUD instruments, inquiries into why participants provided different responses to different interviews indicated that nearly 75 percent of discrepant answers were due to differences between the instruments – a result that was consistent across cultures (Cottler *et al.*, 1997).

The SAM, a revised and expanded version of the SUD section of the CIDI (Cottler *et al.*, 1989; Cottler and Keating, 1990; Cottler and Compton, 1993), assesses SUD criteria from nomenclatures of the DSM-III-R, DSM-IV and ICD-10. It has been used in numerous nosological studies of substance use classification (see, for example, Woody *et al.*, 1993; Morgenstern *et al.*, 1994; Cottler *et al.*, 1995a, 1995b; Langenbucher *et al.*, 1997, 2000; Horton *et al.*, 2000). Interviewees lifetime or preceding 12-month SUDs can be assessed for alcohol, amphetamines, caffeine, cannabis, club drugs, cocaine, hallucinogens, inhalants, opiates, prescription psychoactive medications, PCP, stimulants, sedatives, tobacco, and other miscellaneous substances. Separate SAM modules are available with detailed questions regarding club drugs and inhalants (Ridenour *et al.*, 2007). The SAM includes items regarding ages of onset and most recent occurrence of each criterion, individual withdrawal symptoms, specific physical, social, and psychological consequences for each substance, and quantity and frequency of use to estimate the severity and course of each disorder. The SAM also can be used to assess substance use patterns as well as the age of onset, most recent occurrence, duration, and course of each symptom and criterion.

Reference cards are used to aid comprehension of questions. Use of "skip-outs" in the SAM are minimal, and occur only when the response to particular questions only can be "no" based on previous questions (e.g., interviewees who report never having used opiates would not be asked about criteria related to opiate use). Page 27 from the SAM, Version 4.1, is presented in Figure 2.1 to illustrate qualities of the SAM that fit certain characteristics of the ideal assessment instruments. The SAM is a highly structured interview with all questions being close-ended. Interviewers read SAM questions and follow instructions that are presented in capitol letters.

The SAM has been thoroughly pilot-tested (Cottler and Keating, 1990; Cottler and Compton, 1993). An extensive training course is required to administer the SAM, during which training materials are provided. The SAM is computerized, which maximizes the convenience of administration of the interview and minimizes possible errors during the entry of data into databases (Cottler and Compton, 1993). The SAM has excellent reliabilities for DSM-IV SUD criteria, good to excellent reliabilities for DSM-IV dependence, and fair to excellent reliabilities for ICD-10 dependence in samples of African-Americans, Caucasians, drug users in treatment, and community substance-using samples (Cottler *et al.*, 1989; Compton *et al.*, 1996a, 1996b; Horton *et al.*, 2000). The SAM can be used alone or in conjunction with the CIDI or DIS to obtain information about psychiatric disorders.

ALCOHOL USE DISORDER AND ASSOCIATED DISABILITIES INTERVIEW SCHEDULE – ALCOHOL/DRUG – REVISED (AUDADIS-ADR)

The AUDADIS-ADR is an international version of the AUDADIS (Grant and Hasin, 1992; Grant *et al.*, 1995; Chatterji *et al.*, 1997). The AUDADIS is a structured interview that assesses DSM-IV, DSM-III-R and ICD-10 SUDs. It includes sections to assess mood and anxiety disorders, antisocial personality, substance

	C.	Was it before you were 15 years old?	NO .... GO TO E .... 1 YES 5
	D.	IF A IS <15 OR C=YES, ASK: Did you get drunk more than once before you were 15?	NO .... 1 YES 5
DSMALCAA	E.	Have you ever kept drinking for a couple of days or more without sobering up?	NO....(GO TO F)....1 YES 5
DSMALCMR DSMALCAR	REC:	When was the last time?	__/__ MONTH __/__ AGE
DSMALCAO	ONS:	How old were you the first time?	__/__ AGE
	F.	IN C2, IF TOTAL NUMBER OF DRINKS=20 OR MORE ON AT LEAST 2 DAYS, CODE F AND G YES WITHOUT ASKING. CODE 00 IN REC MONTH AND GO TO ONS. Have you ever drunk as much as 20 drinks in one day — that would be about a fifth of liquor, or 3 bottles of wine, or as much as 3 six-packs of beer?	NO....GO TO C7....1 YES 5
DSMALCAA	G.	Have you done this more than once?	NO .... 1 YES 5
DSMALCMR DSMALCAR	REC:	When was the last time?	__/__ MONTH __/__ AGE
DSMALCAO	ONS:	How old were you the first time you drank 20 or more drinks in one day?	__/__ AGE

			NO	YES
	C7.	Did drinking ever cause you to have:		
DSMALCAB	1)	problems with your family?	1	5
DSMALCAB	2)	problems with your friends?	1	5
DSMALCAB	3)	problems with people at work or school?	1	5
DSMALCAB	4)	Did you ever get into physical fights while drinking?	1	5

AA4A4 AD3RA6 AA3RA1	A.	IF ALL CODED NO, GO TO C8A. IF ANY CODED YES, CONTINUE. Did you continue to drink after you realized drinking was causing you any of these problems?	NO....GO TO C8....1 YES 5
MONTH ALCA4MR ALC3RMR DSMALCMR AGE ALCA4AR ALC3RAR DSMALCAR	REC:	When was the last time you continued to drink after you realized drinking caused you to have (LIST ALL CODED YES IN 1-4)?	__/__ MONTH __/__ AGE
ALCA4AO ALC3RAO DSMALCAO	ONS:	How old were you the first time?	__/__ AGE

FIGURE 2.1 Page 27 of the Substance Abuse Module, Version 4.1.

use related medical conditions, and family history of SUDs. AUDADIS questions are largely close-ended, and the SUD questions are asked for individuals admitting to having consumed alcohol at least 12 times over the course of a year or to have used a drug at least 12 times over their lifetime. Substance use frequency and quantity questions are included. Reference cards are used to enhance comprehension of items. Modifications to the AUDADIS for the AUDADIS-ADR include better representation of ICD-10 disorders, question refinements, and format changes to facilitate cross-cultural diversity. SUDs assessed in the AUDADIS-ADR include alcohol, amphetamines, cocaine, cannabis, hallucinogens, inhalants/solvents, opioids, PCP, sedatives/tranquilizers, and tobacco.

In a sample of substance-treatment patients, the AUDADIS had good to excellent reliabilities for DSM-IV dependence diagnoses but poor reliabilities for abuse diagnoses (Hasin *et al.*, 1997c). The poor reliabilities for the abuse diagnoses were reported when requiring that dependence diagnoses are not met. When participants who met dependence criteria were not disqualified for the abuse diagnoses, reliabilities for abuse diagnoses were good to excellent with few exceptions (Hasin *et al.*, 1997c).

The reliability of the AUDADIS-ADR was investigated using data collected from an international community sample of drug users or persons in drug addiction treatment (Chatterji *et al.*, 1997). Good to excellent reliabilities were reported for ICD-10 dependence diagnoses and fair to excellent reliabilities were reported for DSM-IV dependence diagnoses over the preceding year and lifetime. Poor to good reliabilities were reported for abuse and harmful use diagnoses in the preceding year and lifetime.

The AUDADIS-ADR was used as part of the largest epidemiological study of adults' psychiatric disorders to date. From 2001 to 2002, the first phase of the National Epidemiologic Survey on Alcohol and Related Conditions was conducted by collecting substance use related nomenclature, related mental and physical health disorders, and services utilization from a nationally representative sample of 43,093 in the US. A number of important contributions have already developed from this study and the follow-up survey of the sample. Among those contributions are further psychometric developments of the AUDADIS (Grant *et al.*, 2007).

SCHEDULES FOR CLINICAL ASSESSMENT IN NEUROPSYCHIATRY (SCAN)

The SCAN is based on the Present State Exam (PSE), and was developed in response to a request from the WHO Task Force on Psychiatric Assessment Instruments (Wing *et al.*, 1990). The PSE is a semi-structured interview designed for experienced clinicians to diagnose psychiatric disorders and evaluate their severity. Interviewers can use PSE questions or their own wording, as well as alter the order of diagnoses that are assessed. A computer program (CATEGO) can be used with the PSE to determine how an individual's symptom profile fits ICD classification. The PSE has been translated into approximately 40 languages.

The SCAN was first published in 1983 and used as a research instrument in England. It originally provided a format to assess ICD-10 diagnoses (Wing *et al.*, 1990). By 1987, SCAN items had been revised to assess DSM-III-R criteria as well. Like the PSE, the SCAN is a semi-structured interview, and open-ended questions may be used at the discretion of the clinician-interviewer. Follow-up questions can be devised to clarify interviewee responses. Hence, only clinicians who have graduated from SCAN training can use the SCAN. Unlike the PSE, the SCAN includes alcohol and drug use sections for DSM-IV and ICD-10 diagnostic classifications. No early "skip-outs" are specified for SCAN questions.

The SCAN was modified for cross-cultural acceptability and the SUD sections were tested for reliability in two international samples (US and Turkey) (Easton *et al.*, 1997). Drug users from general community and medical settings were included in the sample, along with drug treatment patients. Reliabilities of DSM-IV and ICD-10 dependence diagnoses were good to excellent, and the reliability of harmful use of alcohol was good when tested in alcohol users. Ustun and colleagues (1997) reported the test–retest, inter-rater reliability of the SCAN using the international sample of the WHO/NIDA/NIAAA study. In substance users, kappa reliability estimates ranged from good to excellent for DSM-IV and ICD-10 dependence. Kappas ranged from very poor to good for abuse diagnoses, and were poor for harmful use diagnoses. Compton and colleagues (1996a, 1996b) reported good diagnostic agreement for DSM-IV and ICD-10 dependence diagnoses between SCAN and CIDI-SAM diagnoses among general population drug users and drug treatment patients.

AGREEMENT BETWEEN INTERVIEWS IN INTERNATIONAL SAMPLES

ICD-10 Diagnoses

Ustun and colleagues (1997) and Pull and colleagues (1997) reported kappas of agreements in ICD-10 diagnoses between the CIDI, AUDADIS-ADR and SCAN using an international sample of 600–730. Agreements between the instruments were consistent across the pairs of instruments, and ranged from good to excellent for alcohol, opioids, cannabis, sedatives, and cocaine. However, estimates of agreement for harmful use diagnoses were poor in this sample for each instrument, as well as in other studies (e.g., Regier *et al.*, 1994). Hence it appears that the ICD-10 harmful use diagnoses require revision to improve their reliability and validity.

Slight differences were reported in the prevalences of dependence in Pull and colleagues' (1997) sample for specific drugs. The CIDI consistently provided estimates of prevalence that were similar to at least one of the other two instruments, whereas for certain substances the prevalences estimated by either the SCAN or the AUDADIS-ADR deviated slightly from the other two instruments. The AUDADIS-ADR estimate of alcohol dependence prevalence was greater (76%) than that with the CIDI or SCAN (69% each), and the AUDADIS-ADR estimate of sedative dependence prevalence was lower (36%) than that with the other instruments (43% and 47%, respectively). The SCAN prevalence estimates of cannabis dependence (36%) and amphetamine dependence (41%) were greater than the CIDI and AUDADIS-ADR estimates of cannabis dependence (24% and 21%, respectively) and amphetamine dependence (25% and 18%, respectively). Prevalence estimates of dependence on cocaine and opioids were similar with the three instruments.

Compton and colleagues (1996a) reported ICD-10 kappas between the SAM and SCAN for drug abuse patients and community-recruited drug users from St Louis, Missouri (US). Their estimates were similar to those of Pull and colleagues (1997) for the CIDI: good agreement for dependence on alcohol, opioids, cocaine and cannabis.

DSM-IV Diagnoses

Using community and clinical samples from Athens, Luxembourg and St Louis, Missouri (US), Cottler and colleagues (1997) investigated the agreement for lifetime DSM-IV diagnoses and criteria between the CIDI, SCAN and AUDADIS-ADR. Agreement between the three instruments for DSM-IV diagnoses of dependence, using kappa, was good for alcohol and opiates and fair for cocaine, sedatives and amphetamines. Kappas for cannabis dependence were mixed (0.35–0.55). Kappas for criteria of abuse and dependence were generally consistent with those reported for diagnoses, but slightly worse. Kappas generally were consistent across substance, regardless of which pair of instruments was analyzed.

In a sample of drug abuse patients and community-recruited drug users from St Louis, Compton and colleagues (1996b) reported agreement between the SAM and SCAN for DSM-IV dependence for alcohol, opiates, cocaine and cannabis. Kappas ranged from fair to good (Compton *et al.*, 1996b). Consistent with results from Pull and colleagues' (1997) study of ICD-10 diagnoses, a lower agreement between the CIDI-SAM and SCAN was reported for cannabis dependence (0.50) than for alcohol dependence (0.69) and cocaine dependence (0.61).

Although the SAM, AUDADIS-ADR and SCAN meet almost all of the 21 characteristics of the ideal diagnostic interview, few data are available for these instruments from adolescents. Such data also would be useful for investigating substance use classification nomenclature for adolescents. Other instruments either have been designed specifically for use with adolescents, or preliminary data have been collected for their use with adolescents.

ADDITIONAL INSTRUMENTS FOR SUBSTANCE USE RELATED DIAGNOSES IN ADOLESCENTS

Some long-existing instruments have recently been used to collect data from adolescents regarding classification of SUDs. Some novel instruments show promise for assessment of adolescents' SUDs and impairments associated with substance use, but will be presented only briefly because of their preliminary stage in development. Each of these instruments assesses substance use patterns, diagnoses, antecedents and consequences.

Adolescent Diagnostic Interview (ADI)

The ADI is a structured interview designed for use by laypersons specifically for interviewing adolescents in research and clinical settings. ADI items query DSM-III-R and DSM-IV criteria for SUDs using two to four questions for each criterion (Winters and Henley, 1993; Winters *et al.*, 1999). The ADI includes screeners for certain psychiatric disorders, level of functioning and psychosocial stressors, as well as memory and orientation deficits. Training is available for the ADI. The advantage of the broad range of persons who could administer the ADI is offset somewhat by the limited availability of psychometric data.

ADI reliability and validity were estimated for alcohol and cannabis disorders among clinical patients aged 12–19 years who had reported any alcohol or cannabis use during the preceding 12 months (Winters *et al.*, 1993a). Inter-rater reliability was estimated for the same interview using data from 72 patients. Kappa estimates were fair to good for alcohol abuse, cannabis abuse, alcohol dependence and cannabis dependence. Inter-rater reliability for individual symptoms ranged from good to excellent for alcohol and cannabis criteria. One-week test–retest, inter-rater reliability estimates were estimated using data from 49 participants. Test–retest, inter-rater reliability estimates were not presented for the abuse diagnoses because of their low base rates. Kappas for the alcohol and cannabis abuse criteria were fair; they were excellent for dependence diagnoses, and fair to good for dependence criteria. Estimating ADI diagnosis reliability could be enhanced using test–retest data from community samples of substance users.

Structured Clinical Interview for the DSM (SCID)

The SCID originally was designed to assess DSM-III diagnoses for clinical and research purposes. It has been adapted for DSM-IV and ICD-10 alcohol and drug diagnoses for adolescents (Spitzer *et al.*, 1987, 1992; Martin *et al.*, 2000; Pollock *et al.*, 2000). The SCID is designed for clinicians using a semi-structured format (Spitzer *et al.*, 1992). Extensive training is available for experienced clinicians. The SCID has been translated into Dutch, English, French, German, Greek, Hebrew, Italian, Portugese, Russian, Spanish, Swedish and Turkish.

One-week, test–retest kappas of SCID DSM-III-R diagnoses in psychiatric patients from Germany and the United States were good to excellent for substance abuse or dependence (Williams *et al.*, 1992). Data from community participants in the same study generated similar kappas for lifetime SUDs. Martin and colleagues (2000) reported inter-rater reliabilities of SCID diagnoses related to use of alcohol, cannabis, sedatives, hallucinogens and inhalants for a sample of adolescents ($n = 79$) recruited from clinics and the general community of Pittsburgh, Pennsylvania (US). Kappas for substance-related diagnoses were excellent.

Diagnostic Interview for Children and Adolescents (DICA)

The DICA is a semi-structured diagnostic interview of ICD-10, DSM-III-R and DSM-IV pediatric psychiatric disorders designed for layperson use in large-scale epidemiological research (Herjanic and Reich, 1982; Reich, 2000). Extensive training is required to use the DICA. However, interviewers are not required to have extensive clinical experience. Current and lifetime diagnoses can be assessed using the DICA. The DICA also queries psychosocial risk factors and the parent interview queries developmental milestones. A Structured Assessment Record of Alcoholic Homes (SARAH) module was developed to inquire of youths and their parents about youths exposure to parental drinking. A self-administered, computerized version of the DICA is available. A 1-week test–retest study with adolescents from community and clinical settings provided kappas of DSM-IV SUDs that ranged from good to excellent ($n = 50$; W. Reich, personal communication, 2001). The DICA assessment of adolescent SUDs will benefit from further investigation of psychometrics using larger samples of substance users, a broader range of SUDs, and additional substance use characteristics.

Diagnostic Interview Survey for Children (DISC)

The DISC-1 was designed for large-scale epidemiological studies of children's psychiatric diagnoses (Costello *et al.*, 1984; Shaffer *et al.*, 2000). The DISC is a structured interview for laypersons. The DISC 2.1 was used in the Methods for the Epidemiology of Child and Adolescent Mental Disorders (MECA) study. However, reliabilities were not reported for SUDs.

The latest version of the DISC, the DISC-IV, was published in 1997 and was designed for the diagnosis of DSM-IV and ICD-10 childhood disorders (Shaffer *et al.*, 2000). In addition to psychiatric diagnoses, the level of impairment caused by psychiatric symptoms is assessed. SUDs that are assessed with the DISC-IV are for alcohol, nicotine and illicit substances. The DISC-IV has a child self-report version and a parent-report version. Administration time is reduced by the use of "stem" questions, employed to omit SUD items for children who are very unlikely to qualify for a diagnosis. A disadvantage of stem questions is that specific criteria that individuals might have experienced might be missed. The DISC-IV also assesses the degree of impairment from SUDs regarding distress, academic/occupational functioning and relationship with parents, caretakers, teachers and employers, as well as participation in family and peer activities. The DISC-IV is available in English, French and Spanish, and has been computerized.

Recent studies of the reliability of DISC disorders in community samples have not included SUDs (Schwab-Stone *et al.*, 1993; Jensen *et al.*, 1995; Ribera *et al.*, 1996; Shaffer *et al.*, 1996; Breton *et al.*, 1998). Roberts and colleagues (1996) reported kappa estimates of the 1-week test–retest reliability of 0.532 for alcohol abuse and 0.477 for drug abuse using the DISC 2.1. Their sample consisted of 12- to 17-year-old psychiatric patients from southeast Texas, US.

Children's Interview for Psychiatric Syndromes (ChIPS)

The ChIPS was developed to provide a structured interview assessment of children's psychiatric diagnoses (Fristad *et al.*, 1998a, 1998b; Teare *et al.*, 1998). Compared with more established structured interviews of child psychiatric disorders, the ChIPS was designed to require less administration time, include less awkward procedures than other diagnostic interviews, and use age-appropriate language (Teare *et al.*, 1998). The ChIPS utilizes a skip-out procedure for each diagnosis, based on interviewees responses to several questions. The child's experience of abuse and psychosocial stressors is also queried.

Psychometric evaluations of the ChIPS suggest the instrument identifies childhood diagnoses similarly to the DICA (Fristad *et al.*, 1998b; Teare *et al.*, 1998). In a community sample of 40 children aged 6–18 (half of whom were aged 13–18), fair to excellent kappas were observed for abuse criteria for alcohol, cigarettes and drugs. ChIPS diagnoses were compared with diagnoses made by clinicians using clinical interview and DICA information. Total agreement between ChIPS and DICA interviews was reported for alcohol abuse and drug abuse, with 97.5 percent agreement for cigarette abuse. These estimates are tentative until data can be reported for a larger sample.

Pictorial Instrument for Children and Adolescents (PICA-III-R)

The PICA-III-R was developed to assess DSM-III-R disorders in children and adolescents, using pictures to illustrate criteria (Ernst *et al.*, 2000). The PICA-III-R is a semi-structured interview for clinicians. Interviewees are asked how much the person in the illustration (who has the criterion) is like the interviewee. Ernst and colleagues (2000) reported that children's comments about illustrations can provide insight to the child's pathology. Preliminary data suggest the PICA-III-R could be useful for diagnosing childhood and adolescent disorders. However, psychometric data were unavailable for the PICA-III-R substance use related diagnoses, presumably because of the very low prevalence of substance use in the sample.

Assessment of Liability and EXposure to Substance Use and Antisocial Behavior (ALEXSA)

The ALEXSA (Ridenour, 2003; Ridenour and Feinberg, 2007c; Ridenour *et al.*, 2007b, 2007d) is a computerized assessment to obtain 8- to 13-year-olds' self reports of risk factors for harmful substance use. ALEXSA subscales were designed to gauge 39 of the best predictors as well as drug-specific risk indexer of harmful substance use and antisocial behavior reported in prospective studies. Measurement innovations were incorporated into the

ALEXSA to enhance the validity of children's self-reports. Professional cartoon illustrations and audio readings accompany each item and response option. Carefully choreographed presentation of text, illustrations and audio readings, and use of a computer mouse to respond, permits the ALEXSA to be completed by even illiterate youth. The ALEXSA is computerized for a number of reasons, including the finding that greater frequencies of substance use and other risky behaviors are found using computerized self-reports compared with non-computerized self-reports (Turner *et al.*, 1998).

The test–retest reliabilities of ALEXSA predictors recently were estimated in 9- to 12-year-olds recruited from regular classrooms and academic enhancement programs (Ridenour *et al.*, 2007b). Reliabilities were categorized as excellent, good, fair, and poor. Eight factors derived from exploratory factor analyses had high good or excellent test–retest reliabilities. In spite of a lack of validity criteria (because of the few similar measures available for children's self-reports), validities of ALEXSA factors and subscales were demonstrated. In a separate sample of 8- to 16-year-olds from a summer camp designed to build resilience to chronic stress, 24 of the 25 ALEXSA subscales that were tested provided 1-year validities for predicting conduct disorder criteria, number of lifetime substances used, depression and academic achievement (Ridenour *et al.*, 2006d).

A second-order factor that was derived from the ALEXSA scores (Ridenour *et al.*, 2007d) demonstrated one mechanism by which the pathologies that are described in this book are associated. The four ALEXSA factors personal characteristics that measure (Problem Solving, Behavioral Disinhibition, Sensation Seeking and Social Contagion Risk) loaded onto a second-order factor named Disinhibition Risks. In turn, Disinhibition Risks correlated 0.71 with conduct disorder criteria, 0.24 with having used alcohol, 0.43 with the Alcohol Risk Index, 0.31 with having used tobacco, and 0.44 with the Tobacco Risk Index. This result also validated the ALEXSA because it was consistent with other studies implicating disinhibition as a core etiological risk for SUDs, antisocial behavior and other psychopathologies.

ASSESSMENT OF ADOLESCENTS' PSYCHOPATHOLOGIES RELATED TO SUBSTANCE USE DISORDERS

The importance of disinhibition, or poor impulse control, in the ontology of SUDs has been demonstrated in the research of several etiological research teams (Iacono *et al.*, 1999; Krueger *et al.*, 2002; Nigg, 2003; Tarter 2003; Clark *et al.*, 2005; Kreek *et al.*, 2005). The impulse control and disinhibition literatures represent research attempting to understand the etiological mechanisms of psychiatric disorders which have their greatest risk of onset during adolescence. Two other disorders with their greatest risk for onset occurring during adolescence that also involve impulse control deficits are eating disorders and pathological gambling

(Dawe and Loxton, 2004; Kreek *et al.*, 2005). Experiencing a SUD, eating disorder or pathological gambling increases the risk that the other two types of disorders also will be experienced (Courbasson *et al.*, 2005; Bray and Ridenour, 2007; Burge *et al.*, 2006; Measelle *et al.*, 2006). Not surprisingly, poor impulse control has been demonstrated to underlie the comorbidity between SUDs and eating disorders or pathological gambling (Dawe and Loxton, 2004; Kreek *et al.*, 2005). Although not directly linked, similar obstacles to SUD assessment in adolescents also have impeded development of assessments of eating disorders and pathological gambling for adolescents.

EATING DISORDERS

Hall (1883) described adolescence as "a time of storm and stress". The years surrounding puberty are marked by profound physical (e.g., Petersen, 1988), cognitive (e.g., Piaget, 1958), social and self-perceptual (e.g., Erickson, 1963) and impulse control or dysregulation developments (APA, 1994). It is not surprising, then, that puberty and the years following puberty mark a period of heightened risk for the onset of several psychiatric disorders, including eating disorders.

Eating disorders are characterized by intermingled and potentially devastating physical, emotional, cognitive and self-regulatory symptoms. Key points to consider regarding assessment of eating disorders include challenges of assessment and diagnosis, the importance of involving multidisciplinary health professionals, and the value of using multiple assessment techniques.

DSM-IV Eating Disorders

Disordered eating patterns specified in DSM-IV nomenclature include anorexia nervosa, bulimia nervosa, and a set of sub-diagnostic pathological eating patterns described as "eating disorders – not otherwise specified". Eating disorders frequently are misperceived as falling into mutually exclusive categories of starvation versus binge–purging. However, there can be much overlap among the symptoms of anorexia nervosa and bulimia nervosa. In fact, a core diagnostic criterion that DSM-IV and ICD-10 ascribe to both anorexia and bulimia is the tendency to derive much of one's self-image and/or emotional experiences from perceptions of one's own physique.

Assessment of Adolescents' Eating Disorders

Four diagnostic criteria contribute to a DSM-IV diagnosis of anorexia nervosa. The first is: "refusal to maintain body weight at a minimally normal weight for age and height". DSM-IV acknowledges that "minimally normal" is subjective. It offers the following guidelines to identify minimally normal weight: "body weight less than 85 percent of that expected" or "failure to make expected weight gain during a period of growth, leading to body weight less than 85 percent of that expected" (DSM-IV-TR: 589). To highlight the subjectivity of these guidelines, it is notable that the Metropolitan Life Insurance Company periodically revises its tables of "ideal" height/weight ratios. Thus, even well-accepted national standards for judging weight relative to height sometimes change abruptly. The ICD-10 takes a slightly more liberal position on what constitutes minimally normal weight, defined as a Body Mass Index (BMI = weight in kilograms/(height in meters^2)) of less than or equal to 17.5 (according to the World Health Organization, the normal range of BMI is 19.1–25.8 for women and 20.7–26.4 for men; for reference, a woman who is 5'4" tall and weighs 102 lb has a BMI of 17.5).

Given the subjectivity of the weight criterion, it can be challenging to judge the seriousness of a patient's weight loss, even with an adult patient whom a practitioner has known for a long time. The challenge is greater when judging the "normalcy" of an adolescent who has not yet reached a stable adult weight and whose growth has slowed, stopped or been replaced by weight loss. For this reason, medical practitioners with experience and extensive knowledge in interpreting growth curves, height and weight charts, and natural variations in adolescent growth patterns are essential members of eating disorder assessment teams. Such medical practitioners may also discern physical deficits incurred from eating disorders.

For a DSM-IV diagnosis of anorexia nervosa, post-menarcheal females must have amenorrhea (the loss of three or more consecutive menstrual periods). Medical knowledge and experience are also required to make sound judgments about whether underweight girls of typical pubertal age who experience delayed onset of their periods should be considered to have amenorrhea.

Other DSM-IV criteria for eating disorders are more psychological. A criterion for anorexia nervosa is that there is a "disturbance in the way in which one's body weight or shape is experienced, undue influence of body shape or weight on self-evaluation, or denial of the seriousness of the current low body weight" (DSM-IV-TR: 589). Similarly, a DSM-IV criterion for bulimia nervosa is that "self-evaluation is unduly influenced by body shape and weight" (DSM-IV-TR: 94).

A complicating factor in assessment of eating disorders during adolescence is that self-evaluation is an abstract and highly nuanced psychological concept (Miller, 1986). Adolescence is normatively a time for developing a system of self-evaluation (see, for example, Erickson, 1963). Adolescent patterns of self-evaluation are notoriously mutable and prone to emphasizing personal qualities that are salient to the individual at a given point in time. Hence, an eating disorder assessment team should include a mental health professional who has had ample time as well as a variety of opportunities to learn about an individual's means of evaluating him- or herself. Some of these opportunities might include clinical interviews, obtaining information from an individual's friends or family, observing the individual's social interactions, and self-report inventories (e.g., Eating Disorders Inventory-2, Garner, 1991) or other expressive mediums (for example, a journal, weblog, or collection of personal artwork).

The need for a variety of assessment tools is highlighted by the semi-conscious and/or secretive nature of many disordered eating symptoms (Pipher, 1995). A DSM-IV criterion for bulimia nervosa is that a person must engage in both binge eating (eating enormous amounts of food at one time, and feeling powerless to stop) and inappropriate compensatory mechanisms (purging behaviors such as self-induced vomiting, and/or non-purging behaviors such as fasting or excessive exercise) an average of two or more times each week for a duration of at least 6 months. People sometimes feel dissociated from their thoughts and emotions during eating binges (Pipher, 1995), and may not recall the binge – particularly if asked about it days or weeks later. It is common for people to feel secretive and/or ashamed of purging behaviors (Pipher, 1995), making them reluctant to offer honest accounts about the existence or frequency of such behavior.

Strategic Advantages in Assessment of Eating Disorders

Three strategies can improve eating disorder assessment. First, a skilled clinician can usually build a substantial sense of rapport with a client, particularly if given sufficient time. This rapport tends to decrease defensiveness about acknowledging eating disorder symptoms. Such rapport also can increase motivation to consider alternatives to disordered eating behavior. Second, a variety of self-observation and self-report strategies can increase on individual's accuracy in reporting behaviors. For example, the accuracy of information about the frequency of binges and compensatory behaviors can be improved if a chart is used to record what has been eaten and when, and any purging behavior that occurs. Finally, in cases where the individual undergoing assessment is unwilling or unable to honestly report his or her behaviors, other informants become most critical.

Though it is challenging to assess disordered eating patterns, teams of medical and mental health providers, using a variety of assessment techniques, usually are able to help individuals to clarify their health needs, risks and options. Compared to adults, assessment of adolescent eating disorders is more challenging because physical conditions, emotional experiences and self-perceptual and self-regulatory skills may be in flux. Nevertheless, these challenges are matched or exceeded by the potential to help persons recognize and address an eating disorder before it becomes an established way of life.

PATHOLOGICAL GAMBLING

Compared with SUDs and eating disorders, pathological gambling is a recently recognized psychiatric disorder with its origins occurring during or before adolescence. Pathological gambling was first designated as a psychiatric disorder in DSM-III (APA, 1980). Pathological gambling nomenclature has since evolved;

further revisions are being considered for DSM-V (Petry, 2006). Comorbidity, shared physiological substrates, overlapping genetic underpinnings, as well as parallels in developmental trajectories, treatment outcomes and risk factors, have led the DSM-V Substance Use Disorders Workgroup to consider subsuming pathological gambling within a category of disorders, "addictive disorders", with substance use disorders (Petry, 2006).

As legalized gambling spreads, gambling-related disorders are an increasingly important public health concern. It is estimated that 85 percent of adolescents have gambled at some point in their lives, and about 73 percent of adolescents have gambled in the preceding year (Shaffer *et al.*, 1997, 1999). Estimates of the prevalence of adolescents having pathological and sub-clinical problems related to gambling are highly variable. The proportion of adolescent problem and pathological gamblers may be up to three times that of adults (National Research Council, 1999).

Classification Criteria for Pathological Gambling

The first psychiatric nomenclature for diagnosis of problems due to gambling appeared in the DSM-III for the diagnosis of compulsive gambling. Revisions to gambling-related nomenclature were made to the DSM-III-R and DSM-IV. In addition, the diagnosis was renamed "pathological gambling".

DSM-III criteria were based on the clinical experience of treatment professionals; no testing went into their development, and they were criticized for a variety of reasons. In the DSM-III-R, the compulsive gambling diagnosis nomenclature was based on substance use related criteria (National Research Council, 1999). Additional debate and research led to a compromise between the DSM-III and DSM-III-R criteria, resulting in the current diagnostic criteria for pathological gambling defined in the DSM-IV.

Consequently, there are many similarities between DSM-IV nomenclatures of SUDs and pathological gambling. Similar to SUD criteria, DSM-IV criteria for pathological gambling include preoccupation with gambling, tolerance, loss of control, withdrawal, escape, lying, illegal behavior, and risking a significant relationship. It is likely that at least some shortcomings of the SUD criteria for diagnosing adolescents also apply to pathological gambling.

The most poignant difference between DSM-IV SUDs and pathological gambling may be the lack of a timeframe in which gambling criteria must be experienced ("clustering" criterion). Two criteria are unique to pathological gambling. The first is "chasing" behavior, which refers to returning to gamble after losing money in order to win back the lost money ("chasing one's losses"). It is possible to "chase one's winnings", although it is unclear whether this criterion refers to chasing behavior in general or only the chasing of losses. The second criterion that is unlike SUD criteria addresses the financial nature of gambling problems. This criterion is referred to as "bailout", and occurs when an individual must be aided financially by someone else to pay a gambling debt.

In DSM-IV, pathological gambling diagnosis is met by experiencing five or more criteria. Currently, there are no guidelines to identify sub-diagnostic problem gambling. Researchers have used DSM-IV criteria to define sub-diagnostic problem gambling using fewer criteria than five (National Research Council, 1999; Petry, 2005). There has been difficulty reaching a consensus about (i) how to label the condition of having one to four DSM-IV pathological gambling criteria, and (ii) nomenclature to use in identifying sub-diagnostic, yet problematic, gambling (National Research Council, 1999; Petry, 2005).

The ICD-10 also provides a diagnosis for pathological gambling. Two criteria (C and D) resemble the DSM-IV preoccupation and loss of control criteria in DSM-IV. The second ICD-10 criterion (B) includes characteristics described by several DSM-IV criteria. The first criterion (A) is unique in terms of being an explicit number of times of having gambled. DSM-IV nomenclature and assessments have been used nearly exclusively for research on gambling among both adolescents and adults. Therefore, the ICD-10 is not discussed further here, despite its potential benefits.

Assessment of Gambling-related Diagnoses in Adolescents

The gambling disorder nomenclatures of DSM-IV and ICD-10 were designed for adults. To date, three instruments have been developed to screen for problem and pathological gambling in adolescents, based on DSM-III-R or DSM-IV criteria. They are the South Oaks Gambling Screen – Revised for Adolescents (SOGS-RA), the *Diagnostic and Statistical Manual of Mental Disorders IV* Adapted for Juveniles (DSM-IV-J), and the Massachusetts Adolescent Gambling Screen (MAGS). The SOGS-RA was developed in 1993, the DSM-IV-J in 1992, and the MAGS in 1994. All three have had their psychometric properties evaluated with community samples of adolescents (National Research Council, 1999).

The SOGS-RA (Winters *et al.*, 1993b) assesses past-year gambling and related problems using 16 items. Adequate internal consistency and construct and concurrent validity have been reported (Winters *et al.*, 1993b). However, the SOGS-RA has not been well-tested in adolescent girls (Petry, 2005). Some SOGS-RA items appear easily misinterpreted (Ladouceur *et al.*, 2000), and some items are rarely endorsed (Wiebe *et al.*, 2000). The primary difference between the SOGS-RA and SOGS is that the SOGS-RA contains fewer items about the sources individuals use to procure money for gambling (Petry, 2005).

The DSM-IV-J (Fisher, 1992) assesses gambling and related problems using 12 items based on DSM-IV criteria. In addition, the DSM-IV-J contains items about procurement of money for gambling and crime involvement (Petry, 2005). The internal consistency of Fisher's DSM-IV-J has been reported to be satisfactory (Fisher, 2000). The primary difference between the DSM-IV-J and versions of the measure for adults is that the items about money and crime are age-appropriate – for example, DSM-IV-J items ask about using school lunch money and shoplifting, whereas adult items ask about fraud and forgery (Petry, 2005).

A multiple-response option version of the DSM-IV-J has been developed for use with non-clinical populations.

The MAGS (Shaffer *et al.*, 1994) assesses gambling and related problems in adolescents using 26 items. MAGS items are organized into two subscales. The first subscale (DSM-IV subscale) contains 12 items that operationalize DSM-IV criteria, while the second subscale (MAGS subscale) contains 14 items about gambling behavior. The MAGS originally was developed for the general population (Petry, 2005). Reliabilities of the two subscales have been reported to be good (0.87 and 0.83, respectively) (Shaffer *et al.*, 1994). There is no version of the MAGS for adults.

Considerations in Assessment of Adolescent Gambling

Regardless of the instrument, it is important to recognize the financial nature of problems with gambling in assessments for adolescents. Questions about finances have widely different meanings for adolescents and adults – in fact, items about finances may measure different underlying constructs in adolescents versus adults (National Research Council, 1999). Similar to SUDs, it is important to remember that different thresholds (especially for financial questions) may be appropriate (National Research Council, 1999).

An additional consideration regarding the SOGS-RA and the DSM-IV-J is that they were originally developed for clinical use, and thus they should be used cautiously when assessing problem and pathological gambling in general population and community samples because they were designed to protect against false positives (National Research Council, 1999). Alternatively, caution using the MAGS in clinical settings is needed. Further psychometric development of all three assessments is required, and much work is necessary to understand how best to assess problems related to gambling, let alone understand how to adapt such assessment for adolescents. As differences between adolescent and adult gambling behavior are clarified, improved assessment also should emerge.

SUMMARY

Classification of adolescent SUDs and related disorders has greatly improved over the past 15 years. However, large gaps remain in our understanding of these disorders, including basic questions regarding the generalization of existing SUD classification nomenclature to adolescents. Existing data suggest that classification schemes developed for adults do not generalize to adolescents. For this reason, "skip out" formats ought to be avoided in the assessment of adolescent SUDs and related disorders because critical pieces of information might be lost.

Encouraging preliminary data have been reported for several instruments designed to assess SUDs, eating disorders and pathological gambling in adolescents. Currently, however, an instrument designed to assist in the clarification of nomenclature for adolescent disorders is badly needed. Until our understanding of adolescent SUDs and related disorders deepens, assessments with adolescents ought to be supplemented with measures of substance use frequency and duration, age of onset and antecedents because they could provide critical insight for research, nomenclature and treatment of the disorders.

As the criteria for adolescent SUDs and related disorders are clarified, the accompanying instruments can be altered to fit such criteria. To illustrate the need to clarify adolescent psychiatric disorders, three drugs that are widely used by adolescents are among the least well understood. A withdrawal syndrome is not specified for cannabis in either the DSM-IV or the ICD-10 nosology. No criteria are specified for ecstacy, which is a combination of amphetamine and hallucinogen. "Inhalants" encompasses a highly diverse range of substances, each of which is highly toxic (Ridenour, 2005).

Simpson (1993) pointed out that, in spite of significant advances in theory and assessment, basic demographic variables such as gender, age and socioeconomic status continue to be characteristics associated with trends in substance use. For illustration, being male is associated with an increased probability of having a substance use diagnosis, although the association between gender and substance use is not entirely understood in terms of psychological or biological mechanisms. Other domains that ought to be evaluated to obtain a comprehensive assessment of an individual's SUDs include medical history and current health status (Barker *et al.*, 1993), comorbid psychiatric disorders and family history of psychiatric disorders (Helzer, 1993), family functioning (Olson and Tiesel, 1993), and social functioning and support (Orvaschel, 1993). Instruments designed to evaluate these specific domains typically are added to an assessment of SUDs, or screeners of these areas are used (Horton, 1993). Perhaps the variety of substance use characteristics associated with understanding classification and etiology is the reason for the hundreds of substance use related questionnaires that are in existence (Davidson, 1987; Cottler and Keating, 1990).

Unfortunately, these instruments have been largely designed for assessment of adults, and therefore represent another realm of knowledge that is lacking for adolescents (Weinberg *et al.*, 1998; Meyers *et al.*, 1999; Winters, 1999). Initial data regarding instruments designed for assessment of these domains in adolescents suggest that they are likely to enhance our understanding of the etiology, consequences and subtypes of SUDs in adolescents (Weinberg *et al.*, 1998; Meyers *et al.*, 1999; Winters, 1999).

Another concern regarding the assessment of adolescent SUDs is the way in which adolescents and children understand and respond to questions about substance use differently from adults. Using the DISC, Breton and colleagues (1995) found that pre-adolescent comprehension of questions about their experience of psychiatric symptoms was best if the question contained fewer than 10 words. Although pre-adolescents understood questions about the duration of a symptom, they had limited comprehension regarding the frequency of symptom occurrence and time period during which symptoms were experienced. This finding might be confounded by the complexity of questions used to ask about the frequency and time period of symptoms. Pre-adolescent comprehension of these questions might be enhanced by using visual tools that they are familiar with, such as a calendar (Breton *et al.*, 1995). Question complexity and questions about duration, frequency and time period also were associated with attenuation (the tendency to deny having symptoms during a second interview that were reported to have occurred during a preceding interview) (Lucas *et al.*, 1999).

Clearly, a great deal of research remains to be conducted before a classification nomenclature and assessment of adolescent SUDs will be completed. Progress is ongoing, however, and, because of the increased effort focused on classification and assessment issues, tremendous advances in this area should occur. Better understanding of SUDs should also enhance treatment for the disorders as well as our understanding of the course, etiology and prevention of SUDs.

ACKNOWLEDGMENT

This work was support by the following grants from NIAAA, NIDA and NIMH: AA12111, DA00434, DA05585, DA07313, DA10075, DA11622, DA017629, DA12900, MH17104.

REFERENCES

American Psychiatric Association (1980). *Diagnostic and Statistical Manual of Mental Disorders*, 3rd edn (DSM-III). Washington, DC: APA.

American Psychiatric Association (1987). *Diagnostic and Statistical Manual of Mental Disorders*, 3rd edn, revised (DSM-III-R). Washington, DC: APA.

American Psychiatric Association (1994). *Diagnostic and Statistical Manual of Mental Disorders*, 4th edn. Washington, DC: APA.

American Psychiatric Association (2000). *Diagnostic and Statistical Manual of Mental Disorders*, 4th edn, text revision. Washington, DC: American Psychiatric Association.

Andrews, G. and Peters, L. (1998). The psychometric properties of the Composite International Diagnostic Interview. *Social Psychiatry and Psychiatric Epidemiology*, 33, 80–88.

Babor, T.F. (1993). Alcohol and drug use history, patterns, and problems. In: B.J. Rounsaville, F.M. Tims and A.M. Horton (eds.), *Diagnostic Source Book on Drug Abuse Research and Treatment* (NIDA Monograph, NIH No. 96-3508). Rockville, MD: US Department of Health and Human Services, pp. 19–34.

Barker, S.B., Kerns, L.L. and Schnoll, S.H. (1993). Assessment of medical history, health status, intoxication, and withdrawal. In: B.J. Rounsaville, F.M. Tims and A.M. Horton (eds.), *Diagnostic Source Book on Drug Abuse Research and Treatment* (NIDA Monograph, NIH No. 96-3508). Rockville, MD: US Department of Health and Human Services, pp. 35–48.

Barr, C.S., Schwandt, M.L., Newman, T.K. and Higley, J.D. (2004). The use of adolescent nonhuman primates to model human alcohol intake. *Annals of the New York Academy of Sciences*, 1021, 221–233.

Bishop, Y.M., Fienberg, S. and Holland, P. (1975). *Discrete Multivariate Analyses*. Cambridge, MA: MIT Press.

Bray, B.C. and Ridenour, T.A. (2007). *Examining Late Childhood Predictors of Gambling Participation and the Desire to Gamble in the Future*. (Submitted for publication.)

Breton, J.J., Bergeron, L., Valla, J.P. *et al.* (1995). Do children aged 9 through 11 years understand the DISC Version 2.25 questions? *Journal of the American Academy of Child and Adolescent Psychiatry*, 34, 946–954.

Breton, J.J., Bergeron, L., Valla, J.P. *et al.* (1998). Diagnostic Interview Schedule for Children (DISC-2.25) in Quebec: reliability findings in light of the MECA study. *Journal of the American Academy of Child and Adolescent Psychiatry*, 37, 1167–1174.

Brown, S.A., Mott, M.A. and Myers, M.G. (1990). Adolescent alcohol and drug treatment outcome. In: R.R. Watson (ed.), *Drug and Alcohol Abuse Prevention, Drug and Alcohol Abuse Review.* Clifton, NJ: Humana, pp. 373–403.

Brown, S.A., Mott, M.A. and Stewart, M.A. (1992). Adolescent alcohol and drug abuse. In: C.E. Walker and M.C. Roberts (eds), *Handbook of Clinical Child Psychology*, 2nd edn. Oxford, Oxfordshire: John Wiley & Sons, pp. 677–693.

Bucholz, K.K., Heath, A.C., Reich, T. *et al.* (1996). Can we subtype alcoholism? A latent class analysis of data from relatives of alcoholics in a multicenter family study of alcoholism. *Alcoholism: Clinical and Experimental Research*, 20, 1462–1471.

Budney, A.J. (2006). Are specific dependence criteria necessary for different substances: how can research on cannabis inform this issue? (Special issue) *Addiction*, 101(Suppl. 1), 125–133.

Burge, A.N., Pietrzak, R.H., Molina, C.A. and Petry, N.M. (2004). Age of gambling initiation and severity of gambling and health problems among older adult problem gamblers. *Psychiatric Services*, 55, 1437–1439.

Caetano, R. (1987). A commentary on the proposed changes in DSM-III concept of alcohol dependence. *Drug and Alcohol Dependence*, 19, 345–355.

Caetano, R. and Babor, T.F. (2006). Diagnosis of alcohol dependence in epidemiological surveys: an epidemic of youthful alcohol dependence or a case of measurement error? (Special issue) *Addiction*, 101(Suppl. 1), 111–114.

Chatterji, S., Saunders, J.B., Vrasti, R. *et al.* (1997). Reliability of the alcohol and drug modules of the Alcohol Use Disorder and Associated Disabilities Interview Schedule – Alcohol/Drug – Revised (AUDADIS-ADR): an international comparison. *Drug and Alcohol Dependence*, 47, 171–185.

Clark, D.B., Cornelius, J.R., Kirisci, L. and Tarter, R. E. (2005). Childhood risk categories for adolescent substance involvement: a general liability typology. *Drug and Alcohol Dependence*, 77, 13–21

Compton, W.M., Cottler, L.B., Dorsey, K.B. *et al.* (1996a). Structured and semi-structured assessment of ICD-10 substance dependence disorders: CIDI-SAM vs SCAN. *International Journal of Methods in Psychiatric Research*, 6, 285–293.

Compton, W.M., Cottler, L.B., Dorsey, K.B. *et al.* (1996b). Comparing assessments of DSM-IV substance dependence disorders using CIDI-SAM and SCAN. *Drug and Alcohol Dependence*, 41, 179–187.

Costello, A.J., Edelbrock, C.S., Dulcan, M.D. *et al.* (1984). Report of the NIMH Diagnostic Interview Schedule for Children (DISC). Washington, DC: National Instituted of Mental Health.

Cottler, L.B. (1992). Commentary. *Annual Review of Addictions Research and Treatment.* Oxford, Oxfordshire: Elsevier Science, pp. 53–55.

Cottler, L.B. (1993). Comparing DSM-III and ICD-10 substance use disorders. *Addiction*, 88, 689–696.

Cottler, L.B. and Compton, W.M. (1993). Advantages of the CIDI family of instruments in epidemiological research of substance use disorders. *International Journal of Methods in Psychiatric Research*, 3, 109–119.

Cottler, L.B. and Keating, S.K. (1990). Operationalization of alcohol and drug dependence criteria by means of a structured interview. In: M. Galanter (ed.), *Recent Developments in Alcoholism.* New York, NY: Plenum Press, p. 8.

Cottler, L.B., Robins, L.N. and Helzer, J.E. (1989). The reliability of the CIDI-SAM: A comprehensive substance abuse interview. *British Journal of Addictions*, 84, 801–814.

Cottler, L.B., Robins, L.N., Grant, B.F. *et al.* and participants in the WHO/ADAMHA Field Trial (1991). The CIDI-Core substance abuse and dependence questions: cross-cultural and nosological issues. *British Journal of Psychiatry*, 159, 653–658.

Cottler, L.B., Shillington, A.M., Compton, W.M. *et al.* (1993). Subjective reports of withdrawal among cocaine users: Recommendations for DSM-IV. *Drug and Alcohol Dependence*, 33, 97–104.

Cottler, L.B., Schuckit, M.A., Helzer, J.E. *et al.* (1995a). The DSM-IV field trial for substance use disorders: major results. *Drug and Alcohol Dependence*, 38, 59–69.

Cottler, L.B., Phelps, D.L. and Compton, W.M. (1995b). Narrowing of the drinking repertoire criterion: should it have been dropped from ICD-10? *Journal of Studies on Alcohol*, 56, 173–176.

Cottler, L.B., Grant, B.F., Blaine, J. *et al.* (1997). Concordance of DSM-IV alcohol and drug use disorder criteria and diagnoses as measured by AUDADIS-ADR, CIDI and SCAN. *Drug and Alcohol Dependence*, 47, 195–205.

Courbasson, C.M.A., Smith, P.D. and Cleland, P.A. (2005). Substance use disorders, anorexia, bulimia, and concurrent disorders. *Canadian Journal of Public Health*, 96, 102–106.

Crowley, T.J. (2006). Adolescents and substance-related disorders: research agenda to guide decisions on Diagnostic and Statistical Manual of Mental Disorders, fifth edition (DSM-V). *Addiction*, 101(Suppl. 1), 115–124.

Davidson, R. (1987). Assessment of the alcohol dependence syndrome: a review of self-report screening questionnaires. *British Journal of Clinical Psychology*, 26, 243–255.

Dawe, S. and Loxton, N.J. (2004). The role of impulsivity in the development of substance use and eating disorders. *Neuroscience and Biobehavioral Reviews*, 28, 343–351.

Dawes, M.A., Antelman, S.M., Vanyukov, M.M. *et al.* (2000). Developmental sources of variation in liability to adolescent substance use disorders. *Drug and Alcohol Dependence*, 61, 3–14.

Deas, D., Riggs, P., Langenbucher, J. *et al.* (2000). Adolescents are not adults: developmental considerations in alcohol users. *Alcoholism: Clinical and Experimental Research*, 24, 232–237.

Dunn, M.E. and Goldman, M.S. (1998). Age and drinking-related differences in the memory organization of alcohol expectancies in 3rd-, 6th-, 9th-, and 12th-grade children. *Journal of Consulting and Clinical Psychology*, 66, 579–585.

Easton, C., Meza, E., Mager, D. *et al.* (1997). Test-retest reliability of the alcohol and drug use disorder sections of the schedules for clinical assessment in neuropsychiatry (SCAN). *Drug and Alcohol Dependence*, 47, 187–194.

Edwards, G. (1986). The alcohol dependence syndrome: a concept as stimulus to enquiry. *British Journal of Addiction*, 81, 171–183.

Edwards, G. and Gross, G.G. (1976). Alcohol dependence: provisional description of a clinical syndrome. *British Medical Journal*, 1, 1058–1061.

Erickson, E.H. (1963). *Childhood and Society.* New York, NY: W.W. Norton and Company.

Ernst, M., Cookus, B.A. and Moravec, B.C. (2000). Pictorial Instrument for Children and Adolescents (PICA-III-R). *Journal of the American Academy of Child and Adolescent Psychiatry*, 39, 94–99.

Escobar, J.I. and Vega, W.A. (2006). Cultural issues and psychiatric diagnosis: providing a general background for considering substance use diagnoses. *Addiction*, 101(Suppl. 1), 40–47.

Feingold, A. and Rounsaville, B. (1995). Construct validity of the dependence syndrome as measured by DSM-IV for different psychoactive substances. *Addiction*, 90, 1661–1669.

Feighner, J.P., Robins, E., Guze, S.B. *et al.* (1972). Diagnostic criteria for use in psychiatric research. *Archives of General Psychiatry*, 26, 57–63.

Fisher, S. (1992). Measuring pathological gambling in children: the case of fruit machines in the UK. *Journal of Gambling Studies*, 8, 263–285.

Fisher, S. (2000). Developing the *DSM-IV* criteria to identify adolescent problem gambling in non-clinical populations. *Journal of Gambling Studies*, 16, 253–273.

Fristad, M.A., Cummins, J., Verducci, J.S. *et al.* (1998a). Study IV: Concurrent validity of the DSM-IV Revised Children's Interview for Psychiatric Syndromes (ChIPS). *Journal of Child and Adolescent Psychopharmacology*, 8, 227–236.

Fristad, M.A., Glickman, A.R., Verducci, J.S. *et al.* (1998b). Study V: Children's Interview for Psychiatric Syndromes (ChIPS): psychometrics in two community samples. *Journal of Child and Adolescent Psychopharmacology*, 8, 237–245.

Fulkerson, J.A., Harrison, P.A. and Beebee, T.J. (1999). DSM-IV substance abuse and dependence: are there really two dimensions of substance use disorders in adolescents? *Addiction*, 94, 495–506.

Galanter, M., Lowman, C., Boyd, G.M. *et al.* (eds) (2005). *Recent Developments in Alcoholism: Alcohol Problems in Adolescents and Young Adults*, Vol. 17. New York, NY: Kluwer Academic/ Plenum.

Garner, D.M. (1991). *Eating Disorders Inventory-2*. Odessa, FL: Psychological Assessment Resources.

Grant, B.F. and Hasin, E. (1992). *The Alcohol Use Disorder and Associated Disabilities Interview Schedule (AUDADIS)*. Rockville, MD: National Institute on Alcohol Abuse and Alcoholism.

Grant, B.F., Harford, T.C., Dawson, D.A. *et al.* (1995). The alcohol use disorder and associated disabilities interview schedule (AUDADIS): reliability of alcohol and drug modules in a general population sample. *Drug and Alcohol Dependence*, 39: 37–44.

Grant, B.F., Harford, T.C., Muthén, B.O. *et al.* (2007). DSM-IV alcohol dependence and abuse: further evidence of validity in the general population. *Drug and Alcohol Dependence*, 86, 154–166.

Hall, G.S. (1883). The contents of children's minds. *Princeton Review*, 11, 249–272.

Harrison, P.A., Fulkerson, J.A. and Beebe, T.J. (1998). DSM-IV substance use disorder criteria for adolescents: a critical examination based on a statewide school survey. *American Journal of Psychiatry*, 155, 486–492.

Hasin, D. and Grant, B.F., 2004. The co-occurrence of DSM-IV alcohol abuse in DSM-IV alcohol dependence. *Archives of General Psychiatry*, 61, 891–896.

Hasin, D. and Paykin, A. (1998). Dependence symptoms but no diagnosis: diagnostic "orphans" in a community sample. *Drug and Alcohol Dependence*, 50, 19–26.

Hasin, D. and Paykin, A. (1999). Dependence symptoms but no diagnosis: diagnostic "orphans" in a 1992 national sample. *Drug and Alcohol Dependence*, 53, 215–222.

Hasin, D., McCloud, S., Li, Q. and Endicott, J. (1996). Cross-system agreement among demographic subgroups: DSM-III, DSM-III-R, DSM-IV and ICD-10 diagnoses of alcohol use disorders. *Drug and Alcohol Dependence*, 41, 127–135.

Hasin, D., Van Rossem, R., McCloud, S. and Endicott, J. (1997a). Differentiating DSM-IV alcohol dependence and abuse by course: community heavy drinkers. *Journal of Substance Abuse*, 9, 127–135.

Hasin, D., Grant, B.F., Cottler, L. *et al.* (1997b). Nosological comparisons of alcohol and drug diagnoses: a multisite, multi-instrument international study. *Drug and Alcohol Dependence*, 47, 217–226.

Hasin, D., Carpenter, K.M., McCloud, S. *et al.* (1997c). The alcohol use disorder and associated disabilities interview schedule (AUDADIS): reliability of alcohol and drug modules in a clinical sample. *Drug and Alcohol Dependence*, 44, 133–141.

Hasin, D., Paykin, A., Meydan, J. and Grant, B. (2000). Withdrawal and tolerance: prognostic significance in DSM-IV alcohol dependence. *Journal of Studies on Alcohol*, 61, 431–438.

Helzer, J.E. (1993). Psychiatric diagnosis, family psychiatric history. In: B.J. Rounsaville, F.M. Tims and A.M. Horton (eds), *Diagnostic Source Book on Drug Abuse Research and Treatment* (NIDA) Monograph, NIH No. 96-3508. Rockville, MD: US Department of Health and Human Services, pp. 49–57.

Helzer, J.E., van den Brink, W. and Guth, S.E. (2006). Should there be both categorical and dimensional criteria for the substance use disorders in DSM-V? {Special issue.} *Addiction*, 101(Suppl. 1), 17–22.

Herjanic, B. and Reich, W. (1982). Development of a structured psychiatric interview for children: agreement between child and parent on individual symptoms. *Journal of Abnormal Child Psychology*, 10, 307–324.

Hill, S.Y. (2004). Trajectories of alcohol use and electrophysicological and morphological indices of brain development: distinguishing causes from consequences. *Annals of the New York Academy of Sciences*, 1021, 245–259.

Horton, A.M. (1993). Future directions in the development of addiction assessment instruments. In: B.J. Rounsaville, F.M. Tims and A.M. Horton (eds), *Diagnostic Source Book on Drug Abuse Research and Treatment* (NIDA Monograph, NIH No. 96-3508. Rockville, MD: US Department of Health and Human Services, pp. 87–92.

Horton, J., Compton, W. and Cottler, L.B. (2000). Reliability of substance use disorder diagnoses among African-Americans and Caucasians. *Drug and Alcohol Dependence*, 57, 203–209.

Iacono, W.G., Carlson, S.R., Taylor, J. *et al.* (1999). Behavioral disinhibition and the development of substance-use disorders: Findings from the Minnesota Twin Family Study. *Development and Psychopathology*, 11, 869–900.

Jensen, P., Margaret, R., Fisher, P. *et al.* (1995). Test–retest reliability of the Diagnostic Interview Schedule for Children (DISC 2.1). *Archives of General Psychiatry*, 52, 61–71.

Johnston, L.D., O'Malley, P.M., Bachman, J.G. and Schulenberg, J.E. (2006). *Monitoring the Future National Results on Adolescent Drug Use: Overview of Key Findings*. Bethesda, MD: NIH, National Institute on Drug Abuse.

Kreek, M.J., Nielsen, D.A., Butelman, E.R. and LaForge, K.S. (2005). Genetic influences on impulsivity, risk taking, stress responsivity and vulnerability to drug abuse and addiction. *Nature Neuroscience*, 8, 1450–1457.

Krueger, R.F., Hicks, B.M., Patrick, C.J. *et al.* (2002). Etiologic connections among substance dependence, antisocial behavior, and personality: modeling the externalizing spectrum. *Journal of Abnormal Psychology*, 111, 411–424.

Ladouceur, R., Bouchard, C., Rheaume, N. *et al.* (2000). Is the SOGS an accurate measure of pathological gambling among children, adolescents, and adults? *Journal of Gambling Studies*, 16, 1–24.

Lamminpaa, A. (1994). Acute alcohol intoxication among children and adolescents. *European Journal of Pediatrics*, 153, 868–872.

Lamminpaa, A. (1995). Alcohol intoxication in childhood and adolescence. *Alcohol and Alcoholism*, 30, 5–12.

Langenbucher, J., Morgenstern, J., Labouvie, E.W. and Nathan, P.E. (1994). Diagnostic concordance of substance use disorders in DSM-III, DSM-IV, and ICD-10. *Drug and Alcohol Dependence*, 36, 193–203.

Langenbucher, J., Morgenstern, J. and Miller, K.J. (1995). DSM-III, DSM-IV and ICD-10 as severity scales for drug dependence. *Drug and Alcohol Dependence*, 39, 139–150.

Langenbucher, J.W., Chung, T., Morgenstern, J. *et al.* (1997). Physiological alcohol dependence as a "specifier" of risk for medical problems and relapse liability in DSM-IV. *Journal of Studies on Alcohol*, 58, 341–350.

Langenbucher, J., Martin, C.S., Labouvie, E. *et al.* (2000). Toward the DSM-IV: the withdrawal-gate model versus the DSM-IV in the diagnosis of alcohol abuse and dependence. *Journal of Consulting and Clinical Psychology*, 68, 799–809.

Langenbucher, J., Labouvie, E., Martin, C.S. *et al.* (2004). An application of item response theory analysis to alcohol, cannabis, and cocaine criteria in DSM-IV. *Journal of Abnormal Psychology*, 113, 72–80.

Lucas, C.P. Fisher, P., Piancentini, J. *et al.* (1999). Features of interview questions associated with attenuation of symptom reports. *Journal of Abnormal Child Psychology*, 27, 429–437.

Martin, C.S., Kaczynski, N.A., Maisto, S.A. *et al.* (1995). Patterns of DSM-IV alcohol abuse and dependence symptoms in adolescent drinkers. *Journal of Studies on Alcohol*, 56, 672–680.

Martin, C.S., Langenbucher, J.W., Kaczynski, N. and Chung, T. (1996). Staging in the onset of DSM-IV alcohol symptoms in adolescents: survival/hazard analysis. *Journal of Studies on Alcohol*, 57, 549–558.

Martin, C.S., Pollock, N.K., Bukstein, O.G. and Lynch, K.G. (2000). Interrater reliability of the SCID alcohol and substance use disorders sections among adolescents. *Drug and Alcohol Dependence*, 59, 173–176.

Martin, C.S., Chung, T., Kirisci, L. and Langenbucher, J.W. (2006). An item response theory analysis of diagnostic criteria for alcohol and cannabis use disorders in adolescents: implications for DSM-V. *Journal of Abnormal Psychology*, 115, 807–814.

Measelle, J.R., Stice, E. and Hogansen, J.M. (2006). Developmental trajectories of co-occurring depressive, eating, antisocial, and substance abuse problems in female adolescents. *Journal of Abnormal Psychology*, 115, 524–538.

Meyers, K., Hagan, T.A., Zanis, D. *et al.* (1999). Critical issues in adolescent substance use assessment. *Drug and Alcohol Dependence*, 55, 235–246.

Mikulich, S.K., Hall, S.K., Whitmore, E.A. and Crowley, T.J. (2001). Concordance between DSM-III-R and DSM-IV diagnoses of substance use disorders in adolescents. *Drug and Alcohol Dependence*, 61, 237–248.

Miller, J.B. (1976). *Toward a New Psychology of Women*. Boston, MA: Beacon Press.

Morgenstern, J., Langenbucher, J.W. and Labouvie, E.W. (1994). The generalizability of the dependence syndrome across substance: an examination of some properties of the proposed dependence criteria. *Addiction*, 89, 1105–1113.

Muthen, B. (2006). Should substance use disorders be considered as categorical or dimensional? (Special issue) *Addiction*, 101(Suppl. 1), 6–16.

Muthen, B.O., Grant, B. and Hasin, D. (1993). The dimensionality of alcohol abuse and dependence: factor analysis of DSM-III-R and proposed DSM-IV criteria in the 1988 National Health Interview Survey. *Addiction*, 88, 1079–1090.

Nathan, P.E. (1994). Psychoactive substance dependence. In: T. Widiger, A. Frances, H., Pincus *et al.* (eds), *The DSM-IV Source Book*, Vol. 1. Washington, DC: American Psychiatric Association Press.

National Research Council (1999). *Pathological Gambling: A Critical Review*. Washington, DC: National Academy Press.

Nigg, J.T. (2000). On inhibition/disinhibition in developmental psychopathology: view from cognitive and personality psychology and a working inhibition taxonomy. *Psychological Bulletin*, 126, 220–246.

O'Dell, L.E., Bruijnzeel, A.W., Ghozland, S. *et al.* (2004). Nicotine withdrawal in adolescent and adult rats. *Annals of the New York Academy of Sciences*, 1021, 167–174.

Olson, D.H. and Tiesel, J.W. (1993). Assessment of family functioning. In: B.J. Rounsaville, F.M. Tims and A.M. Horton (eds), *Diagnostic Source Book on Drug Abuse Research and Treatment* (NIDA Monograph, NIH No. 96-3508. Rockville, MD: US Department of Health and Human Services, pp. 59–78.

Orvaschel, H. (1993). Social functioning and social supports: a review of measures suitable for use with substance abusers. In: B.J. Rounsaville, F.M. Tims and A.M. Horton (eds), *Diagnostic Source Book on Drug Abuse Research and Treatment* (NIDA Monograph, NIH No. 96-3508. Rockville, MD: US Department of Health and Human Services, pp. 79–86.

Perkonigg, A., Lieb, R., Hofler, M. *et al.* (1999). Patterns of cannabis use, abuse and dependence over time: incidence, progression and stability in a sample of 1,228 adolescents. *Addiction*, 94, 1663–1678.

Petersen, A.C. (1988). Adolescent development. *Annual Review of Psychology*, *39*, 583–607.

Petry, N.M. (2005). *Pathological Gambling: Etiology, Comorbidity, and Treatment*. Washington, DC: American Psychological Association.

Petry, N.M. (2006). Should the scope of addictive behaviors be broadened to include pathological gambling? (Special issue) *Addiction*, 101(Suppl. 1), 152–160.

Piaget, J. (1958). *Judgment and Reasoning in the Child*. London: Routledge and Kegan Paul Ltd.

Pincus, H.A., Frances, A., Davis, W.W. *et al.* (1992). DSM-IV and new diagnostic categories: Holding the line on proliferation. *American Journal of Psychiatry*, 149, 112–117.

Pipher, M. (1995). *Hunger Pains*. New York, NY: Ballantine Books.

Pollock, N.K. and Martin, C.S. (1999). Diagnostic orphans: adolescents with alcohol symptoms who do not qualify for DSM-IV abuse or dependence diagnoses. *American Journal of Psychiatry*, 156, 897–901.

Pollock, N.K., Martin, C.S. and Langenbucher, J.W. (2000). Diagnostic concordance of DSM-III, DSM-III-R, DSM-IV and ICD-10 alcohol diagnoses in adolescents. *Journal of Studies on Alcohol*, 61, 439–446.

Pull, C.B., Saunders, J.B., Mavreas, V. *et al.* (1997). Concordance between ICD-10 alcohol and drug use disorder criteria and diagnoses as measured by the AUDADIS-ADR, CIDI, and SCAN: Results of a cross-national study. *Drug and Alcohol Dependence*, 47, 207–216.

Regier, D.A., Kaelber, C.T., Roper, M.T. *et al.* (1994). The ICD-10 clinical field trial for mental and behavioral disorders: results in Canada and the United States. *American Journal of Psychiatry*, 151, 1340–1350.

Reich, W. (2000). Diagnostic Interview for Children and Adolescents (DICA). *Journal of the American Academy of Child and Adolescent Psychiatry*, 39, 59–66.

Reich, W., Cottler, L.B., McCallum, K. *et al.* (1995). Computerized interviews as a method of assessing psychopathology in children. *Comprehensive Psychiatry*, 36, 40–45.

Ribera, J.C., Canino, G., Rubio-Stipec, M. *et al.* (1996). The Diagnostic Interview Schedule for Children (DISC-2.1) in Spanish: reliability in a Hispanic population. *Journal of Child Psychology and Psychiatry and Allied Disciplines*, 37, 195–204.

Ridenour, T.A. (2003). *Assessment of Liability and EXposure to Substance use and Antisocial behavior© (ALEXSA©), CORE Measures*. Allison Park, PA: Assessments Illustrated.

Ridenour, T.A. (2005). Inhalants: not to be taken lightly anymore. *Current Opinions in Psychiatry*, 18, 243–247.

Ridenour, T.A. (2006). "Factor Analyses of Children's Substance Abuse Risk Domains: Disinhibition Pervades Intrapersonal Risk." Presented at the Center for Education and Drug Abuse Research Seminar, Pittsburgh, PA.

Ridenour, T.A., Cottler, L.B., Compton, W.M. *et al.* (2003). Is there a progression from abuse disorders to dependence disorders? *Addiction*, 98, 635–644.

Ridenour, T.A., Maldonado-Molina, M.M., Compton, W.M. *et al.* (2005). Factors associated with the transition from abuse to dependence among substance abusers: implications for a measure of addictive liability. *Drug and Alcohol Dependence*, 80, 1–14.

Ridenour, T.A., Bray, B.C. and Cottler, L.B. (2007a). Reliability of use, abuse, and dependence of four types of inhalants in adolescents and young adults. *Drug and Alcohol Dependence* 91, 40–49.

Ridenour, T.A., Lanza, S.T., Donny, E.C. and Clark, D.B. (2006b). Different lengths of times for progressions in adolescent substance involvement. *Addictive Behaviors*, 13, 962–983.

Ridenour, T.A., Clark, D.B. and Cottler, L.B. (2007b). Reliability and validity of the Assessment of Liability and EXposure to Substance use and Antisocial behavior© (ALEXSA©) in 9 to 12 year old students. *Journal of Psychopathology and Behavioral Assessment* (manuscript submitted for publication).

Ridenour, T.A. and Feinburg, M.E. (2007c). Using correlational analyses to improve prevention strategies based on survey data from youth. *Evaluation and Program Planning*, 30, 36–44.

Ridenour, T.A., Gottschall, A., Ferrer-Wreder, L. and Greenburg M.T. (2007d). Predictive Validity of the Assessment of Liability and EXposure to Substance use and Antisocial behavior© (ALEXSA©) in 8 to 16 Year Old Youth. *American Journal of Preventive Medicine* (submitted for publication).

Roberts, R.E., Solovitz, B.L., Chen, Y.W. and Casat, C. (1996). Retest stability of DSM-III-R diagnoses among adolescents using the Diagnostic Interview Schedule for Children (DISC-2.1C). *Journal of Abnormal Child Psychology*, 24, 349–362.

Robins, L.N. (1989). Diagnostic grammar and assessment. Translating criteria into questions. In: L. Robins and J. Barrett (eds), *The Validity of Diagnosis*. New York, NY: Raven Press.

Robins, L.N. and Helzer, J.E. (1986). Diagnosis and clinical assessment: the current state of psychiatric diagnosis. *Annual Review of Psychology*, 37, 409–432.

Robins, L.N. and Regier, D.A. (eds) (1991). *Psychiatric Disorders in America*. New York, NY: Free Press.

Robins, L.N., Helzer, J.E., Croughan, J. and Ratcliff, K. (1981). National Institute of Mental Health Diagnostic Interview Schedule: its history, characteristics and validity. *Archives of General Psychiatry*, 38, 393–398.

Robins, L.N., Helzer, J.E., Orvaschel, H. *et al.* (1985). The Diagnostic Interview Schedule. In: W.W. Eaton and L.G. Kessler (eds), *Epidemiologic Field Methods in Psychiatry: The NIMH Epidemiologic Catchment Area Program*. Orlando, FL: Academic Press, pp. 143–170.

Robins, L.N., Wing, J., Wittchen, H.U. *et al.* (1988). The Composite International Diagnostic Interview (CIDI): an epidemiologic instrument suitable for use in conjunction with different diagnostic systems and in different cultures. *Archives of General Psychiatry*, 45, 1069–1077.

Robins, L.N., Cottler, L.B. and Babor, T. (1990). *WHO/ADAMHA Composite International Diagnostic Interview – Substance Abuse Module (SAM)* (1983, revised 1987, 1988, 1988, 1989). St Louis, MO: WHO/ADAMHA.

Room, R., Jounce, A., Bennett, L.A. and Schmidt, L. (1996). WHO cross-cultural applicability research on diagnosis and assessment of substance use disorders: an overview of methods and selected results. *Addiction*, 91, 199–220.

Rounsaville, B.J. (1987). An evaluation of the DSM-III substance use disorders. In: G. Tischler (ed.), *Treatment and Classification in Psychiatry*. New York, NY: Cambridge University Press.

Rounsaville, B.J. and Kranzler, H.R. (1989). The DSM-III-R diagnosis of alcoholism. *Review of Psychiatry*, 8, 323–340.

Rounsaville, B.J., Kosten, T., Williams, J. and Spitzer, R.L. (1987). A field trial of DSM-III-R psychoactive substance dependence disorders. *American Journal of Psychiatry*, 144, 351–355.

Rounsaville, B.J., Bryant, K., Babor, T. *et al.* (1993). Cross system agreement for substance use disorders: DSM-III-R, DSM-IV and DSM-10. *Addiction*, 88, 337–348.

Sarr, M., Bucholz, K.K. and Phelps, D.L. (2000). Using cluster analysis of alcohol use disorders to investigate "diagnostic orphans": subjects with alcohol dependence symptoms but no diagnosis. *Drug and Alcohol Dependence*, 60, 295–302.

Saunders, J.B. and Schuckit, M.A. (eds) (2006). The development of a research agenda for substance use disorders diagnosis in the Diagnostic and Statistical Manual of Mental Disorders, fifth edition (DSM-V). (Special issue) *Addiction*, 101(Suppl. 1), 1–5.

Schuckit, M.A. (1993). Keeping current with the DSMs and substance use disorders. In: D. Dunner (ed.), *Current Psychiatric Therapy*. Philadelphia, PA: W.B. Saunders Co, pp. 89–91.

Schuckit, M.A., Smith, T.L., Daeppen, J.B. *et al.* (1998). Clinical relevance of the distinction between alcohol dependence with and without a physiological component. *American Journal of Psychiatry*, 155, 733–740.

Schuckit, M.A., Daeppen, J.B., Danko, G.P. *et al.* (1999). Clinical implications for four drugs of the DSM-IV: Distinction between substance dependence with and without a physiological component. *American Journal of Psychiatry*, 156, 41–49.

Schuckit, M.A., Smith, T.L., Danko, G.P. *et al.* (2001). Five-year clinical course associated with DSM-IV alcohol abuse or dependence in a large group of men and women. *American Journal of Psychiatry*, 158, 1084–1090.

Schwab-Stone, M., Fisher, P., Piacentini, J. *et al.* (1993). The Diagnostic Interview Schedule for Children– Revised Version (DISC-R): II. Test–retest reliability. *Journal of the American Academy of Child and Adolescent Psychiatry*, 32, 651–657.

Shaffer, H. J., LaBrie, R., Scanlan, K.M. and Cummings, T.N. (1994). Pathological gambling among adolescents: Massachusetts Gambling Screen (MAGS). *Journal of Gambling Studies*, 10, 339–362

Shaffer, D., Fisher, P., Dulcan, M.K. *et al.* (1996). The NIMH Diagnostic Interview Schedule for Children Version 2.3 (DISC-2.3): description, acceptability, prevalence rates, and performance in the MECA study. *Journal of the American Academy of Child and Adolescent Psychiatry*, 35(7), 865–877.

Shaffer, H. J., Hall, M.N. and Vander Bilt, J. (1997). *Estimating the Prevalence of Disordered Gambling Behavior in the United States and Canada: A Meta-analysis*. Boston, MA: Harvard Medical School, Division on Addictions.

Shaffer, H.J., Hall, M.N. and Vander Bilt, J. (1999). Estimating the prevalence of disordered gambling behavior in the United States and Canada: a research synthesis. *American Journal of Public Health*, 89, 1369–1376.

Shaffer, D., Fisher, P., Lucas, C. *et al.* (2000). NIMH Diagnostic Interview Schedule for Children Version IV (NIMH DISC-IV): description, differences from previous versions, and reliability of some common diagnoses. *Journal of the American Academy of Child and Adolescent Psychiatry*, 39, 28–38.

Simpson, D.D. (1993). Demographic, socioeconomic, and criminal background data. In: B.J. Rounsaville, F.M. Tims and A.M. Horton (eds), *Diagnostic Source Book on Drug Abuse Research and Treatment* (NIDA Monograph, NIH No. 96-3508). Rockville, MD: US Department of Health and Human Services, pp. 11–18.

Spear, L.P. (2004). Adolescence and the trajectory of alcohol use: introduction to Part VI. *Annals of the New York Academy of Sciences*, 1021, 202–205.

Spitzer, R.L., Endicott, J. and Robins, E. (1978). Research diagnostic criteria. *Archives of General Psychiatry*, 35, 773–782.

Spitzer, R.L., Williams, J.B.W. and Gibbon, M. (1987). *Instruction Manual for the Structured Clinical Interview for DSM-III-R*. New York, NY: Biometrics Research Department, New York State Psychiatric Institute.

Spitzer, R.L., Williams, J.B.W., Gibbon, M. and First, M.B. (1992). The Structured Clinical Interview for DSM-III-R (SCID). *Archives of General Psychiatry*, 49, 624–629.

Stewart, M.A. and Brown, S.A. (1995). Withdrawal and dependency symptoms among adolescent alcohol and drug abusers. *Addiction*, 90, 627–635.

Tarter, R.E., Kirisci, L., Mezzich, A. *et al.* (2003). Neurobehavioral disinhibition in childhood predicts early age at onset of substance use disorder. *American Journal of Psychiatry*, 160, 1078–1085.

Teare, M., Fristad, M.A., Weller, E.B. *et al.* (1998). Study I: Development and criterion validity of the Children's Interview for Psychiatric Syndromes (ChIPS). *Journal of Child and Adolescent Psychopharmacology*, 8, 205–211.

Turner, C.F., Ku, L., Rogers, S.M. *et al.* (1998). Adolescent sexual behavior, drug use, and violence: Increased reporting with computer survey technology. *Science*, 280, 867–873.

Turner, L., Mermelstein, R. and Flay, B. (2004). Individual and contextual influences on adolescent smoking. *Annals of the New York Academy of Sciences*, 1021, 175–197.

Ustun, B., Compton, W., Mager, D. *et al.* (1997). WHO study on the reliability and validity of the alcohol and drug use disorder instruments: overview of methods and results. *Drug and Alcohol Dependence*, 47, 161–169.

Wagner, F.A. and Anthony, J.C. (2002). From first drug use to drug dependence: developmental periods of risk for dependence upon marijuana, cocaine, and alcohol. *Neuropsychopharmacology*, 26, 479–488.

Weinberg, N.Z., Rahdert, E., Colliver, J.D. and Glantz, M.D. (1998). Adolescent substance abuse: a review of the past 10 years. *Journal of the American Academy of Child and Adolescent Psychiatry*, 37, 252–261.

White, H.R. (1987). Longitudinal stability of dimensional structure of problem drinking in adolescence. *Journal of Studies on Alcohol*, 48, 541–550.

Wiebe, J.M.D., Cox, B.J. and Mehmel, B.G. (2000). The South Oaks Gambling Screen revised for adolescents (SOGS-RA): further psychometric findings from a community sample. *Journal of Gambling Studies*, 16, 275–288.

Williams, J.B.W., Gibbon, M., First, M.B. *et al.* (1992). The Structured Clinical Interview for DSM-III-R (SCID). *Archives of General Psychiatry*, 49, 630–636.

Wing, J.K., Cooper, J.E. and Sartorius, N. (1974). *The Measurement and Classification of Psychiatric Symptoms*. London: Cambridge University Press.

Wing, J.K., Babor, T., Brugha, T. *et al.* (1990). SCAN: Schedules for Clinical Assessment in Neuropsychiatry. *Archives of General Psychiatry*, 47, 589–593.

Winters, K.C. (1999). (Revisions Consensus Panel Chair). *Screening and Assessing Adolescents for Substance Use Disorders*. Rockville, MD: US Department of Health and Human Services.

Winters, K.C. and Henley, G.A. (1993). *Adolescent Diagnostic Interview Schedule and Manual*. Los Angeles, CA: Western Psychological Services.

Winters, K.C. and Stinchfield, R.D. (1995). Current issues and future needs in the assessment of adolescent drug abuse. In: E. Rahdert and D. Czechowicz (eds), *Adolescent Drug Abuse: Clinical Assessment and Therapeutic Interventions* (NIDA Research Monograph 156). Rockville, MD: US Department of Health and Human Services, pp. 146–171.

Winters, K.C., Stinchfield, R.D., Fulkerson, J. and Henly, G.A. (1993a). Measuring alcohol and cannabis use disorders in an adolescent clinical sample. *Psychology of Addictive Behavior*, 7, 185–196.

Winters, K.C., Stinchfield, R.D. and Fulkerson, J. (1993b). Toward the development of an adolescent gambling problem severity scale. *Journal of Gambling Studies*, 9, 371–386.

Winters, K.C., Latimer, W. and Stinchfield, R.D. (1999). The DSM-IV criteria for adolescent alcohol and cannabis use disorders. *Journal of Studies on Alcohol*, 60, 337–344.

Wittchen, H.U., Robins, L.B., Cottler, L.B. *et al.* and participants in the multicentre WHO/ADAMHA Field Trials (1991). Cross-cultural feasibility, reliability and sources of variance of the Composite International Diagnostic Interview (CIDI). *British Journal of Psychiatry*, 159, 645–653.

Wittchen, H.U., Lachner, G., Wunderlich, U. and Pfister, H. (1998). Test–retest reliability of the computerized DSM-IV version of the Munich-Composite International Diagnostic Interview (M-CIDI). *Social Psychiatry and Psychiatric Epidemiology*, 33, 568–578.

Woody, G.E., Cottler, L.B. and Cacciola, J. (1993). Severity of dependence: data from the DSM-IV field trials. *Addiction*, 88, 1573–1579.

World Health Organization (1993a). *The ICD-10 Classification of Mental and Behavioural Disorders: Diagnostic Criteria for Research*. Geneva: World Health Organization.

World Health Organization (1993b). *Composite International Diagnostic Interview, Version 1.1*. Geneva: World Health Organization.

World Health Organization (1993c). *Schedules for Clinical Assessment in Neuropsychiatry*. Washington, DC: American Psychiatric Press.

World Health Organization (1993d). *Alcohol Use Disorder and Associated Disabilities Interview Schedule – Alcohol/Drug – Revised*. Geneva: World Health Organization.

PART

II

Specific Adolescent Addictions

3

ALCOHOL USE, ABUSE AND DEPENDENCE

CECILIA A. ESSAU AND DELYSE HUTCHINSON

Alcohol is one of the most commonly used substances in most Western societies, especially among adolescents. The use of alcohol is so common in this age group that it has become a "normal" phenomenon, and socially acceptable. Adolescence is also a developmental stage during which experimentation with alcohol reaches its peak (Bukstein, 2000). Although experimental or occasional use does not generally cause any impairment, it may act as a risk factor for the development of problem alcohol use (Grant and Dawson, 1997). Problem drinking occurs when adolescents consume alcohol to an extent that it causes them to have occasional difficulties such as a hangover, being arrested for drinking, missing school, and causing breakages and damages (Reboussin *et al.*, 2006).

A small proportion of the adolescents who consume alcohol develop alcohol abuse or dependency, which is characterized by a maladaptive pattern of alcohol use leading to significant impairment or distress. Alcohol abuse is defined as a recurrent use of alcohol resulting in a failure to fulfill major role obligations at work, school or home; frequent use of alcohol in physically hazardous situations; use related to legal problems; or use causing or exacerbating persistent social or interpersonal problems (DSM-IV; American Psychiatric Association, 1994). The abuse of alcohol by adolescents ("youth") poses major problems to the user and his or her family, as well as to society at large. Examples of problems associated with alcohol abuse include increased risk for motor vehicle accidents, decline in academic functioning, antisocial behavior and legal problems, failing to fulfill major role obligations, and recurrent social or interpersonal problems (see review by Adams *et al.*, 2002). If adolescents with alcohol abuse continue to drink, they may go on to develop alcohol dependence. Alcohol dependence is characterized by tolerance, and a withdrawal syndrome when alcohol is discontinued or its consumption is reduced. The use of alcohol leads to the reduction or cessation of important social, occupational and recreational activities. Individuals with alcohol dependence tend to spend a great deal of time in activities required to obtain alcohol, in using alcohol and in recovering from its effects.

EPIDEMIOLOGY, COMORBIDITY AND COURSE

A number of studies have been conducted regarding the prevalence of alcohol use, abuse and dependence in adolescents. However, methodological differences such as variations in the case definition, assessment instruments, timeframe (lifetime, 6 months, current), age groups, informants (parent, self-report) and settings make it difficult to directly compare findings across studies (Essau *et al.*, 2002). Furthermore, the introduction of alcopops (soft drinks mixed with alcohol) and bottled mixed drinks in the mid-1990s has changed the patterns of adolescent alcohol use, again making it difficult to compare trends in drinking. Alcopops and mixed drinks are not only among the most popular alcoholic drinks, they have also accounted for an increase in alcohol consumption in 13- to 16-year-olds (Roberts *et al.*, 1999; Ter Bogt *et al.*, 2002).

ALCOHOL USE

The Monitoring the Future Study (MTF) is an annual survey of a nationally representative sample of both private and public secondary schools drawn from mainland United States (Johnston *et al.*, 2002). The survey was first undertaken in 1975, and originally set out to collect data on lifetime, past year and past month drug use by students in the twelfth grade. Since 1991 the MTF survey has also included eighth and tenth-graders in its sample, and has reported prevalence rates for lifetime, past year and past month substance use for all three grade year-groups. The most recent report, on data collected in 2005, is based on more than 49 300 students from 402 secondary schools who completed self-report questionnaires during a regular class period. Alcohol use is extremely common, with 75 percent of the students reported consuming alcohol by the end of high school. Furthermore, 58 percent of the twelfth-graders and 20 percent of the eighth-graders reported having been drunk at least once in their life. Binge drinking (i.e., having five or more drinks on a single occasion at least once in the past 2 weeks) showed a modest increase in the early part of the 1990s, leveling off in 1995/1996. A decrease in drinking and drunkenness appeared in all grades in 2002 and this continued into 2005.

The National Survey on Drug Use and Health (NSDUH), directed by the Substance Abuse and Mental Health Services Administration (SAMHSA), provides annual estimates of prevalence, incidence and demographic distribution of use of illicit drugs, alcohol and tobacco among 12-year-olds and above living in the US. According to the 2005 survey (SAMHSA, 2007), 28.2 percent of 12- to 20-year-olds reported drinking alcohol in the past month. Of these, 18.8 percent were binge drinkers (i.e., consumed five or more drinks on the same occasion) and 6 percent were heavy drinkers (i.e., consumed five or more drinks on the same occasion on each of 5 or more days in the past 30 days). The highest rate of binge drinking was found in Whites (22.3%), followed by American Indians or Alaska Natives (18.1%). The lowest rate was found in Asians (7.4%).

The European Schools Project on Alcohol and other Drugs (ESPAD; Morgan *et al.*, 1999) was comparable with the US Monitoring the Future study (MFT). Its main aim was to examine the alcohol and drug habits of young people, aged 16 years, living in various European countries. The first data collection was conducted in 1995 in 26 countries, and the second survey was performed in 1999 in 30 countries. The third and most recent survey was carried out in 2003 in 35 countries, and more than 10 000 students took part. The results of the 2003 survey can be summarized as follows:

1. The vast majority of the students (more than 90%) reported having consumed alcohol at least once in their lifetime
2. The highest rate of regular alcohol use (i.e., at least 40 times in a lifetime) were found in Denmark, Austria, the Czech Republic, the Isle of Man, the Netherlands and the UK, with rates ranging from 43 percent to 50 percent
3. Students with the highest percentages of frequent drunkenness (at least 20 times) came from parts of western Europe, namely Denmark, Ireland, the Isle of Man, the UK, Estonia and Finland (range: 26–36%).
4. The lowest rates of frequent drunkenness were reported in Mediterranean countries (Cyprus, France, Greece, Portugal, Romania and Turkey).

The differences in the frequency of alcohol consumption across European countries underscore the importance of cultural factors. For example, in some countries alcohol is associated with socializing and the feasting habits of the population. Furthermore, some countries (such as Greece) do not have any age limit on the sale of alcohol (Kokkevi *et al.*, 2007). The Trading Standards North West provided data on the frequency, quantity and location of alcohol use among 15- and 16-year olds in the northwest of England (Bellis *et al.*, 2006). These adolescents ($n = 10\,271$) were recruited from 147 schools. A total of 87.9 percent of students reported having consumed alcoholic beverages at least once every 6 months. Most of these drinkers were females, older (i.e., 16-year-olds), White, attended a school located in the least deprived regional area, had more spending money and belonged to a youth club. Of those who consumed alcohol, 38 percent reported binge drinking (five or more drinks in one session), 24.4 percent reported being a frequent drinker (more than twice a week) and 49.8 percent reported drinking in public places. Although still of an age where it is illegal to purchase alcohol, 40 percent of the adolescent drinkers reported buying their own alcohol.

Adolescents who purchased their own alcohol compared with those who did not were six, three and two times more likely to drink in public places, to drink frequently, and to binge drink, respectively. Obtaining alcohol from parents seemed to reduce the risk of adolescents' binge and public drinking.

The Australian Secondary Students' Alcohol and Drug Suvey (ASSAD) is a secondary-school based survey conducted throughout Australia, and commenced in 1984 (White and Hayman, 2006). In the 2005 survey, a high percentage of the 12- to 17-year-olds reported having consumed alcohol, especially among the older age groups. Specifically, 86 percent of 14-year-olds and 96 percent of 17-year-olds had tried alcohol sometime in their life. Among current drinkers, 2 percent of 13-year-olds and 21 percent of 17-year-olds had consumed alcohol at a risky level, as defined by the Australian Alcohol Guidelines (i.e., seven or more drinks in a single day for males and five or more drinks in a single day for females), on at least one occasion in the past week. Among females, the most common type of alcohol consumed was premixed spirits; among males it was beer. Parents were the main source of alcohol, especially among younger (39%) compared with older (35%) students. In terms of the drinking trend, the findings showed a decline in the prevalence of current drinking during the 1980s followed by an increase in the 1990s, with no significant changes in 2005.

In addition to these large surveys, a number of epidemiological studies have provided us with information on the prevalence of alcohol use among adolescents in several countries. In the US, findings from the Oregon Youth Substance Use Project (OYSUP; Andrews *et al.*, 2003) indicated that 20 percent of boys and 4 percent of girls in first grade had used alcohol in their lifetime. By the fourth grade, about 20 percent of both girls and boys reported use in their lifetime; by eighth grade this had risen to 65 percent. In the Oregon Adolescent Depression Project (OADP), three-fourths of the participants had tried alcohol during adolescence and 94 percent of them had tried alcohol by young adulthood (Lewinsohn *et al.*, 1996). In a study by Young and colleagues (2002), alcohol was the most commonly used substance at all ages, peaking at ages 17 and 18 years with rates of 88.1 percent and 86.7 percent, respectively. However, when "repeated use" was examined, these rates dropped to less than 70 percent. Adolescents not only used alcohol on a frequent basis, they also consumed it in large quantities. Specifically, 9 percent of females and 23 percent of males reported consuming five or more drinks per drinking occasion (Lewinsohn *et al.*, 1996).

In the Netherlands, 60 percent of males and 50 percent of females aged 12–13 years had used alcohol at least once in their lifetime. This increased to 90 percent by the age of 18 years (De Zwart *et al.*, 2000). Of the 12- to 13-year-olds, 20 percent of males and 15 percent of females had been drunk at least once. Among the 16- to 17-year-olds, 70 percent of males and 60 percent of females had been drunk at least once. A recent study by Poelen and colleagues (2005) on the trends of alcohol use and misuse among adolescents in the Netherlands showed an increase in frequency and quantity of drinking among 12- to 15-year-olds in

2000 compared with 1990. This increase in alcohol use has been attributed to an increased popularity of alcopops among this age group. Time-trends analysis by Hajema and Knibbe (1998) similarly showed that adolescents and young adults drank more in 2000 than in 1993. The use of alcohol, frequency and quality of drinking, frequency of drunkenness and problem drinking increased with age until the age of 25 years; after this the prevalence of these behaviors decreased, especially among females. The authors regarded this as being caused by changes in social roles – such as acquisition of partner and parental roles.

In Germany, two epidemiology studies have provided details of the prevalence of alcohol use. In the Early Development Stages of Psychopathology (EDSP; Wittchen *et al.*, 1998), almost all (94.5%) the adolescents and young adults studied reported having consumed any alcoholic beverages in their life. The proportion of adolescents who consumed alcohol on a regular basis increased with age, ranging from 13.2 percent in the youngest group to 75.6 percent in the oldest. Alcohol users who first consumed alcohol at the age of 14 years or younger were at a higher risk for meeting a diagnosis of abuse and dependence compared with those who initiated alcohol use at 15 years of age or older (Holly *et al.*, 1997). In the Bremen Adolescent Study (Essau *et al.*, 1998), 77.2 percent of 12- to 17-year-olds had consumed any alcoholic beverages sometime in their life. The high rates of alcohol consumption in these two German studies have been explained in terms of German law and societal views regarding the use of alcohol in adolescence. Legal access to alcohol beverages in Germany begins at 16 years, and is accompanied by widespread acceptance of alcohol use in this age group. This is in contrast to many other countries where the age for legal access to alcohol is much older. For example, in the United States the legal age for buying alcohol beverages is 21 years.

ALCOHOL USE DISORDER

Recent epidemiological studies have estimated that between 3.5 percent (Fergusson *et al.*, 1993) and 32.4 percent of adolescents (Giaconia *et al.*, 1994) meet the criteria for a lifetime DSM-IV alcohol use disorder (AUD). The 1-year prevalence was 10.4 percent (Feehan *et al.*, 1994), and the 6-month prevalence was 26.1 percent (Reinherz *et al.*, 1993). Significant discrepancies have been found between mothers' and adolescents' self-reports: the lifetime prevalence of AUD based on mothers' reports was 1.9 percent; based on adolescents' self-reports it was 3.5 percent (Fergusson *et al.*, 1993).

In Young and colleagues' study (2002), 10 percent of the adolescents met the criteria for alcohol abuse. In the 17- and 18-year-old cohorts, the rate of abuse was one in six adolescents. The prevalence of alcohol dependence in adolescents under the age of 16 years was less than 1 percent; among 18-year-olds it was 6.5 percent. Over 80 percent of those meeting the criteria for alcohol dependence endorsed at least one symptom of alcohol abuse, and over one-third endorsed three or four symptoms of abuse. Endorsement of abuse symptoms, however, showed gender-specific trends. For example, in the study by Lewinsohn and colleagues (1996), males reported greater hazardous use and alcohol-related legal problems whereas females reported greater failure to fulfill role obligations. In Young and colleagues' study (2002), the most frequently endorsed symptoms of alcohol abuse were "continued substance use despite persistent or recurrent social or interpersonal problems" associated with alcohol use, and "use when physically hazardous". Among those who met the diagnosis of alcohol abuse/dependence, significantly more females than males endorsed a failure to fulfill role obligations than males; significantly, more males than females were likely to report "recurrent substance use in situations in which it is physically hazardous". The most frequently endorsed symptoms of alcohol dependence were "tolerance" and "using alcohol in larger amounts or for longer periods than intended".

COMORBIDITY

AUD co-occurs frequently with other psychiatric disorders such as anxiety, depression and disruptive behavior disorders (Fergusson *et al.*, 1993; Lewinsohn *et al.*, 1993). In the OADP, over 80 percent of the adolescents with AUD met the diagnostic criteria for other psychiatric disorders: about 20 percent of the cases were of an internalizing type, 35 percent were of the externalizing type, and the remaining 45 percent consisted of both internalizing and externalizing disorders (Rohde *et al.*, 1996). Studies of clinical samples have also observed a high rate of anxiety disorders among youth with AUD (Clark *et al.*, 1995). For example, in a study by Clark and Jacob (1992), 50 percent of adolescents with AUD had at least one lifetime anxiety disorder, with PTSD being the most common.

Comorbidity of AUD with various types of SUD is also quite common (see, for example, Wu *et al.*, 2005). In the Bremen Adolescent Study (Essau *et al.*, 1998), about one-third of those with one type of substance use disorder had at least other types of abuse/dependence, with AUD being the most common comorbid disorder. Weitzman and Chen (2005) found a high comorbidity rate between alcohol and tobacco use among a nationally representative sample of youth. Specifically, 98 percent of current smokers in college reported drinking alcohol (Weitzman and Chen, 2005). Problem drinkers or those who met the DSM-IV criteria for alcohol abuse were 3.31 and 3.02 times, respectively, more likely to report current smoking than were drinkers who did not meet these criteria. The association between smoking and drinking was stronger among females than males, in that females who had consumed 20 or more drinks in the past month were 5.01 times as likely as their female peers to be current smokers. Females who met the DSM-IV criteria for alcohol abuse, or those using alcohol to "self-medicate" for problems and who did not seek/receive help, were about 1.4–1.5 times more likely to smoke compared with male problem drinkers who did not seek or receive help for their drinking habits. In the OADP study, the level of problematic alcohol use was associated with both daily smoking and drug use disorders (Rohde *et al.*, 1996). Specifically, the rates of daily tobacco use were 3 percent in alcohol abstainers, 10 percent in experimenters, 22 percent in social drinkers, 39 percent in problem drinkers and 59 percent in adolescents with a diagnosis of AUD. Rates of drug use disorder were 42 percent among those with AUD, at a follow-up investigation, compared with 12 percent of those who had no symptoms of abuse or dependence. Furthermore, alcohol and drug use disorders in adolescence were predictive of nicotine dependence by the age of 24 (Rohde *et al.*, 2004). In a study by Wagner *et al.* (2005), early-onset use of alcohol/tobacco was associated with high risk of drug use, and the risk was higher for males than for females – about 16 percent of males and 4 percent of females who had used alcohol/tobacco before the age of 14 transitioned to use of other drugs. By age of 15, 20 percent males with early alcohol/tobacco use used drugs, compared with only 8 percent of males with no early alcohol/tobacco use. Among 15-year-old females, 8 percent of those with early alcohol/tobacco use used drugs, compared with 2 percent of females who did not use alcohol or tobacco before the age of 14.

A high proportion of individuals with comorbid AUD and other psychiatric disorders reported the occurrence of a psychiatric disorder before that of alcohol abuse or dependence (Kessler *et al.*, 1996). This is not surprising, because many psychiatric disorders have their onset in childhood or early adolescence. However, patterns are far from clear-cut. In the OADP, 58.1 percent of adolescents with AUD who had a history of major depression reported the occurrence of depression before that of alcohol (Rohde *et al.*, 1996). Similar findings have been reported by Hovens *et al.* (1994), in that 53 percent of the adolescents with dysthymia and AUD reported dysthymia preceding AUD. However, in some other studies (see, for example, Milberger *et al.*, 1997) alcoholism seemed to trigger depression, with an associated progressive use of hard drugs. Furthermore, weekly use of alcohol, daily cigarette smoking and lifetime use of illicit drugs all increased the prevalence of depression to nearly 19 percent (Kandel *et al.*, 1997; Armstrong and Costello, 2002). The OADP data also indicated that, of those with both alcohol and drug use disorders, 51.5 percent had a drug disorder before their alcohol disorder (Rohde *et al.*, 1996). The finding that almost half the alcohol cases had an alcohol disorder before a drug use disorder was interpreted as failing to support alcohol as a gateway to a more serious drug use in adolescence.

Of adolescents with anxiety disorders and AUD, 87.5 percent reported anxiety disorders to have preceded AUD (Rohde *et al.*, 1996). Within anxiety disorders, social phobia and agoraphobia usually preceded alcohol abuse, while panic disorder and generalized anxiety disorder tended to follow the onset of alcohol abuse (Kushner *et al.*, 2000). In a clinical sample of adolescents, Ilomäki *et al.* (2004) found that the presence of a phobic disorder increased the risk for subsequent alcohol dependence up to 4.5-fold compared with adolescents without a phobic disorder. The onset of the phobic disorder occurred about 3 years before the onset of substance dependence, and boys with a phobic disorder had significantly earlier onset age for substance dependence (13.7 years) than did girls (15.4 years).

Using data from the National Household Surveys on Drug Abuse, Wu *et al.* (2005) found that adolescents who reported using both inhalants and marijuana were most likely to receive a diagnosis of past-year AUD (35%). Increased odds of recent alcohol abuse or dependence were associated with the following factors: lifetime drug use, older age, female gender, high level of family income, residence in non-metropolitan areas, recent mental health service utilization, a history of incarceration, delinquent behavior, a history of multi-drug use, and onset of alcohol use before the age of 13.

The comorbidity of AUD and other psychiatric disorders represents an important public health challenge, because such comorbid psychiatric conditions are generally chronic and severe and associated with greater functional impairment, and those with such a disorder are more likely to have received treatment for their AUD (Rohde *et al.*, 2001) and less likely to benefit from available treatments (Lewinsohn *et al.*, 1995). The presence of conduct disorder together with AUD has also been associated with an earlier onset of AUD and faster progression of problematic levels of alcohol use (see, for example, Windle and Davies, 1999), and tended to double the probability of future AUD (Rohde *et al.*, 2001). The finding of high comorbidity between AUD and other antisocial behavior was interpreted as being consistent with problem-behavior theory (Jessor and Jessor, 1977), which suggests that this problem behavior is a single syndrome which is associated with the underlying construct of unconventionality.

COURSE

Longitudinal studies among adults have been very informative regarding the course and outcome of AUD. In most studies, problem drinking or AUD generally begins early in life. As reported in the Epidemiologic Catchment Area study, over 80 percent of the adults with a lifetime diagnosis of AUD developed their first symptoms of the disorder before the age of 30, and over 35 percent had developed at least one symptom of AUD between the ages of 15 and 19 (Helzer and Burnam, 1991). Adult studies have shown different patterns of course, with changes in alcohol diagnoses over time. As shown by Grant *et al.* (2001), 53 percent of the community samples of young adults who met the criteria of alcohol abuse at baseline and 48 percent of those who met the criteria for alcohol dependence no longer had this disorder at a 5-year follow-up investigation. On the other hand, these authors found prior diagnosis to be a strong predictor of subsequent dependence in that 8 percent of those with abuse and 26 percent of those with dependence at baseline were dependent on alcohol at follow-up. These results indicated significant discontinuity, and that abuse and dependence have different courses.

Studies on the course and outcome of AUD in adolescents are rare. In the OADP study (Lewinsohn *et al.*, 1996), 7 percent of adolescents met the criteria for a lifetime diagnosis of AUD by the age of 15–19 years; by 24 this had increased to 30 percent. Another publication of the OADP showed that adolescents with AUD, compared with those with other disorders, were significantly more likely to have adulthood AUD, other SUD, depressive disorders, antisocial personality disorder or borderline personality disorder (Rohde *et al.*, 2001).

CONSEQUENCES OF ADOLESCENT ALCOHOL USE

Alcohol use during adolescence is associated with an increased likelihood of death from motor-vehicle accidents and from unintentional injury such as drowning and fatal falls. According to a report by the American Academy of Pediatrics (1995), alcohol-related motor-vehicle injuries were the main cause of death among 15- to 24-year-olds in the US, with about 7000 such fatalities occurring each year. Adolescent drinkers are also at an increased risk for engaging in other health-risk behaviors such as violence (White *et al.*, 1999; Swahn *et al.*, 2004), unsafe sexual practices (Cooper, 2002), use of illicit drugs (Wagner and Anthony, 2002), and sexual victimization among adolescent females (Champion *et al.*, 2004).

Alcohol abuse/dependence in adolescents is often associated with impairment in various life areas, such as negative interpersonal relationships, increase in family conflict, decline in academic functioning, antisocial behaviors and legal problems, failing to fulfill major role obligations, and recurrent social or interpersonal problems (Myers *et al.*, 1998). In the Bremen Adolescent Study (Essau *et al.*, 1998), 77 percent of adolescents with alcohol problems repeatedly used alcohol in hazardous situations. Adolescents with AUD were psychologically more distressed compared with those without these disorders.

In addition to its proximal consequences, alcohol use early in life is associated with an increased risk of AUD and associated psychopathology in adulthood (Anthony and Petronis, 1995; Lewinsohn *et al.*, 1996). It has been estimated that each year's delay in the age of onset of alcohol use before the age 14 decreases the risk of alcohol abuse and dependence by 8 percent and 14 percent, respectively (Grant *et al.*, 2001). Furthermore, adolescent alcohol abuse and dependence tend to be quite stable over time (Wagner and Tarolla, 2002), exerting negative development effects extending into adulthood.

However, the diverse nature of adolescent alcohol use makes it difficult to ascertain the direction of causality. For example, for some adolescents alcohol consumption maybe a reaction to certain problems (such as stress), and an increased involvement with alcohol may precipitate deterioration in psychosocial functioning; for other adolescents, alcohol use may be embedded within the "problem behavior" syndrome (Jessor and Jessor, 1977).

RISK AND PROTECTIVE FACTORS

A large body of research has examined risks for alcohol problems in young people; however, given the space limitations of this chapter, this section is not all-inclusive. The factors that are considered to be most important and for which there has been considerable empirical support have been selected for review. It should be noted that one of the complexities in this field of research is that risk and protective factors frequently co-occur and interact in complex ways across time, serving to increase or decrease the relative risk for alcohol problems. For instance, young people who develop alcohol problems typically report multiple risk factors at different developmental stages, such as early parent–child relationship problems, deviant peer friendships in adolescence, and co-morbid mental health problems in young adulthood (see, for example, Jacob and Leonard, 1994). Where available, we have endeavored to include research on the influence of multiple risks and/or protective factors over time – particularly studies that have prospectively examined the relative contribution of such factors in the development of youth alcohol use problems.

FAMILY FACTORS

It is well-established that the family plays a primary role in the formation of a child's social, cognitive and emotional development. It is therefore not surprising that a considerable body of empirical work has been dedicated to understanding the role of family and parenting factors in the development of adolescent alcohol problems. In the following section we summarize literature on a range of postulated risks, including family functioning and socio-economic status, disruptions in parenting and the parent–adolescent relationship, as well as parental attitudes and behavior relating to alcohol use. A brief discussion of the possible genetic determinants of alcohol problems is included in the section on parental alcohol use disorders.

Family Functioning

Adolescents who develop alcohol-related problems commonly report problems in family functioning. A cross-sectional community study of 445 adolescents aged 15–17 years in the United States found that problem alcohol use among young people was strongly associated with family dysfunction, characterized by family conflict and low levels of family organization (Colder and Chassin, 1999). An English study by Foxcroft and Lowe (1997) examined the relationship between perceived family life and drinking behavior in 11- to 16-year-olds ($n = 4369$). Results revealed that low family support and low family control were significantly linked with higher levels of drinking. More recently, Bray *et al.* (2001) conducted a 3-year longitudinal study of 7540 adolescents in the United States. The study found that lower family stress and conflict were associated with decreases in adolescent drinking across time, whereas increasing across-time levels of alcohol use were linked with greater family stress and conflict. In another 2-year longitudinal study, Duncan *et al.* (1998) found that high levels of parent–child conflict were associated with a greater likelihood of adolescent alcohol and other drug use. Moreover, individuals who experienced increasing levels of conflict with parents over an 18-month period also reported faster increases in substance use across time.

Theoretically, poor family functioning has been posited to increase the risk for adolescent alcohol use through its negative impact on parenting and disruptions to child socialization and development (Lowe *et al.*, 1993; Jacob and Leonard, 1994). In support, an 18-month longitudinal study by Ary *et al.* (1999a) found that families with high levels of conflict were less likely to have high levels of parent–child involvement. Such family conditions resulted in less adequate parental monitoring of adolescent behavior, making associations with deviant peers more likely. Poor parental monitoring and associations with deviant peers were in turn strong predictors of engagement in substance use and other problem behaviors. Although association with deviant peers was the most proximal social influence on problem behavior, family factors (high conflict and low involvement) and parental monitoring were key parenting practices that influenced this developmental process. Other work by Ary and colleagues (1999b) also supports the role of poor family functioning in the development of youth substance use.

Family Structure

While the relationship between family structure and adolescent alcohol use has not been widely studied, there is some evidence that non-intact family status is associated with an increased risk for youth drinking. Bjarnason *et al.* (2003) conducted a large cross-sectional study of adolescents aged 15–16 years ($n = 34,001$) in 11 European countries. Results indicated that adolescents who lived with both biological parents had significantly reduced frequency of heavy drinking compared with adolescents from single-mother, single-father or blended families. Notably, the significant positive effect of being part of an intact family was stronger in societies where heavy drinking was viewed more positively in adolescent culture. In the New Zealand Christchurch cohort, early family breakdown was identified as an independent risk factor for the development of youth alcohol use. It was associated with heavier alcohol use at age 14, after adjusting for age 8 conduct problems and earlier age of alcohol initiation (Fergusson *et al.*, 1995).

Family Socio-economic Background

Despite the consistent association identified between family socio-economic status and adolescent antisocial behavior, socio-economic status or class does not appear to be a strong predictor of youth alcohol use (Williams *et al.*, 2000; Hayes *et al.*, 2004). A number of studies conducted in the United States and Europe have identified positive associations between parental occupation and affluence, and adolescent drinking (Hawkins *et al.*, 1992; Richter *et al.*, 2006). These studies suggest that alcohol use is greater among adolescents whose parents are of higher socio-economic status. In contrast, other studies have found no or higher risk of excessive drinking behavior in lower socio-economic groups (Lowry *et al.*, 1996; Richter *et al.*, 2006). Poulton and colleagues (2002) conducted a longitudinal study using data from the Dunedin birth cohort in New Zealand ($n = 1000$). The study found that low, but not high, socio-economic status in childhood was weakly associated with alcohol dependence at age 26. In regard to low socio-economic status, Hawkins *et al.* (1992) argued that alcohol use increases only when poverty is extreme; however, the authors also pointed out that under such conditions most adolescent risk factors and problem behaviors are also likely to increase.

DISRUPTIONS IN PARENTING

Conceptual models posit that parenting deficits often occur in the context of adolescent alcohol misuse, and that these factors are often directly or indirectly linked to other individual (e.g., biological and psychological factors) and broader environmental influences (such as cultural and socio-demographic factors) (Barnes, 1990; Jacob and Leonard, 1994; Hayes *et al.*, 2004). Parenting constructs that have been empirically linked to adolescent and young adult alcohol misuse include inadequate parental support, poor parental monitoring, harsh or inappropriate behavior management, poor parent–adolescent relationship quality, and parents' own attitudes and behavior in relation to alcohol.

Parental Support

Parental support is a key dimension of effective parenting, incorporating constructs such as nurturing, attachment, acceptance, cohesion and love (Jacob and Leonard, 1994). Parental support has been defined as "parental behaviors toward the child, such as praising, encouraging and giving physical affection, which indicate to the child that he or she is accepted and loved" (Barnes *et al.*, 2000: 176). In general, research has consistently found that greater parental support predicts better adolescent functioning and fewer adolescent problem behaviors in a range of domains, including alcohol misuse (see, for example, Barnes *et al.*, 1987, 1994, 2000; Barrera and Li, 1996). Longitudinal research on parent–child involvement also indicates that low levels of such involvement are indirectly associated with later adolescent alcohol and other drug use, through poor parental monitoring and involvement in deviant peer friendships (Ary *et al.*, 1999a, 1999b).

Parental Monitoring

Parental monitoring refers to parental awareness, watchfulness and supervision of adolescent activities in multiple domains (i.e., friends, school and behavior at home), and communication to the adolescent that the parent is concerned about, and aware of, those activities (Dishion and McMahon, 1998). Poor parental monitoring and supervision of child and adolescent activities has been demonstrated to predict adolescent alcohol use in numerous longitudinal studies (see, for example, Barnes and Farrell, 1992; Barnes *et al.*, 1992, 2000; Duncan *et al.*, 1998; Ary *et al.*, 1999a, 1999b; Thomas *et al.*, 2000; Guo *et al.*, 2001). For example, Guo *et al.* (2001) conducted a longitudinal study of 755 adolescents aged 10–21 years. Results indicated that high parental monitoring, in addition to clearly defined rules at the age of 10 years, predicted lower alcohol use and dependence at 21 years. In this study, higher monitoring was associated with lower rates of alcohol abuse after controlling for both externalizing and internalizing behavior at 10 years of age. In another study, Barnes *et al.* (2000) conducted a six-wave longitudinal analysis based on interviews with 506 adolescents in a general community sample in the United States. Results indicated that higher parental monitoring directly predicted lower initial drinking levels in adolescents, and lower levels of adolescent alcohol misuse across time. Monitoring was also found to mediate other family effects; low levels of parental support were indirectly related to increasing adolescent alcohol abuse through poor parental monitoring. The authors therefore suggested that children who are reared in a supportive, nurturing environment are likely to be more receptive to parental monitoring. In turn, these adolescents are less likely to engage in alcohol misuse during adolescence.

In other longitudinal work by Ary and colleagues (Ary *et al.*, 1999a, 1999b), parental monitoring was shown to have a direct effect on alcohol use and other problem behavior, and an indirect effect through deviant peer associations. In a study by Duncan *et al.* (1998), high levels of parent–child conflict and low levels of parental monitoring were associated with a greater likelihood of adolescent substance use and deviant peer friendships. In other studies, poor monitoring has been associated with family dysfunction, parent–adolescent relationship difficulties and social disadvantage (Dishion and McMahon, 1998). In sum, poor parental monitoring appears to be an important risk factor for the development of youth alcohol problems. Monitoring also appears to interplay with other family, peer and socio-demographic risks in the development of youth alcohol use problems.

Behavior Management

Behavior management refers to "parents' active efforts to shape the behavior of their adolescent" (Hayes *et al.*, 2004: 32). Behavior management has also been referred to in the literature as "parental control". Researchers have suggested that the relationship between parental control and adolescent alcohol use may be curvilinear. According to this notion, optimal functioning is related to a moderate degree of parental control, with too much control (rigidity) or too little control (laxness) leading to problem behaviors. In addition to the level of parental control, the type of control has been shown to be important. In a cross-sectional study by Barnes and Farrell (1992) which examined various aspects of parental control, coercion (i.e., hitting, yelling) had a positive linear relationship with substance use and deviance – that is, more coercive control was associated with adolescent problem behavior, including alcohol use. The authors noted that in 12 separate analyses relating various adolescent outcomes (including drinking) to parental inductive control (i.e., telling adolescents why they should not do something and offering explanations for behaviors), no significant relationships were detected. Thus, it appears that coercive but not inductive parental control may promote the likelihood for adolescent drinking. This is also consistent with the finding that coercive control showed a significant negative correlation with parental support (representing negative support), whereas inductive control was related positively with parental support.

A small body of research provides evidence that harsh parenting or discipline and high levels of parent–adolescent conflict are associated with youth alcohol use, but that the links are often indirect. A three-wave longitudinal study by Brody and Ge (2001) found that youth self-regulation at wave two mediated the paths from harsh-conflicted parenting at wave two to both adolescent alcohol use and poor psychological functioning at wave three. Ary and colleagues (Duncan *et al.*, 1998; Ary *et al.*, 1999a, 1999b) revealed both indirect and direct prospective relationships between parent–child conflict (along with poor parental monitoring) and elevated levels of adolescent substance use. Interestingly, a longitudinal study on data from the Mater University birth cohort in Australia found that "strict" parental control of a child at age 5 years was associated with a reduced risk for AUD in males at age 21 years (Alati *et al.*, 2005). However, "strict" control reflected components of high quality monitoring without differentiating harsh or coercive control.

Other cross-sectional research on parenting style compared adolescents who were parented using a more cohesive authoritative style (high on parental responsiveness and demands) with adolescents who were parented in either an authoritarian style (low on responsiveness and high on demands), a permissive style (high on responsiveness and low on demands), or an indifferent style (low on responsiveness and demands) (Jackson, 2002). The study found that adolescents who were parented in an authoritarian or indifferent style (but not a permissive style) were significantly more likely to deny parental authority, which was in turn associated with higher alcohol use. Taken together, there is some evidence that authoritarian or harsh parenting and a more distant or lax style of parenting may increase the risk for youth alcohol use and misuse. However, further longitudinal research is needed to test whether these behavior management styles actually predict the later development of youth AUD.

Parent–Adolescent Relationship Quality

Parent–adolescent relationship quality has been described as the product of ongoing interplay between parents and their adolescent which underpins all aspects of parenting (Hayes *et al.*, 2004). A healthy parent–adolescent relationship is thought to be important in that it fosters open communication between parents and child, providing a foundation for better parental monitoring and the setting of appropriate boundaries relating to alcohol use and other behavior (Jacob and Leonard, 1994; Dishion and McMahon, 1998). In support, a number of studies have identified consistent relationships between poor parent–child relationship quality and youth drinking.

Adolescent perceptions of parental care have been shown to be related to alcohol misuse. Using a cross-sectional design, Mak and Kinsella (1996) assessed 493 Australian secondary students with an average age of 16.2 years. The study found that adolescents who misused alcohol were significantly more likely to report lower levels of perceived parental care than adolescents who did not engage in alcohol misuse. In Neighbors and colleagues' study (2000), difficult temperament was a significant predictor of AUD symptoms for both males and female adolescents, and was negatively related to parent–adolescent relationship quality. Interestingly, some gender differences were identified. For males, the relationship between difficult temperament and AUD symptoms was mediated by poor parent–adolescent relationship quality. For females, however, difficult temperament and poor parent–adolescent relationship quality independently predicted adolescents' AUD symptoms.

Longitudinal studies also provide evidence that parent–adolescent relationship quality influences adolescent drinking. For example, a 3-year longitudinal study of 7540 adolescents in the US found that more positive parent–adolescent relationships were associated with decreasing drinking across time, in addition to greater emotional autonomy and lower levels of family stress and conflict (Bray *et al.*, 2001). Conversely, adolescents who reported increasing across-time levels of alcohol use more frequently experienced parent–adolescent relationship difficulties, including emotional difficulties, separation and detachment, and greater family stress and conflict. Several longitudinal studies suggest that poor parent–adolescent relationship quality indirectly increases the risk for adolescent alcohol use through its impact on parental monitoring and deviant peer associations (Ary *et al.*, 1999a, 1999b; Barnes *et al.*, 2000). Taken together, research suggests that parent–adolescent relationship quality has both direct and indirect effects on the development of alcohol use and misuse.

Parental Attitudes Toward Drinking

Parental attitudes toward drinking represent an indirect means of social modeling, and may be communicated either explicitly or covertly through the setting of limits or communication of values by parents regarding alcohol use (Williams and Hine, 2002). Parents who drink alcohol are more likely to exhibit permissiveness toward alcohol use in their adolescent children (Wood *et al.*, 2004). These authors found that the more permissive parents were in regard to adolescent alcohol use, the more likely their adolescents were to engage in heavy binge drinking. Parental permissiveness also appeared to influence peer associations, with a significant relationship between greater peer influence and alcohol use demonstrated when parents were permissive. Parent's permissiveness regarding alcohol use may therefore be influential in determining adolescent alcohol initiation and the later transition to heavier drinking.

Williams and Hine (2002) examined the role of parental attitudes towards adolescent alcohol use in mediating of more global parental permissiveness in the prediction of alcohol misuse among adolescents ($n = 320$). The study found that parental permissiveness and both mothers' and fathers' level of alcohol use were indirectly related to adolescent misuse, as they were mediated by parental and significant others' level of approval of the adolescent's alcohol use. The findings of this study suggest that parental permissiveness towards alcohol use has a more influential role in determining adolescent alcohol misuse than does more general parental permissiveness.

Parental Drinking

Studies have consistently demonstrated that parents' own use of alcohol increases the likelihood that their adolescent children will engage in alcohol use, with this relationship being strongest among families in which one or both parents engage in problem drinking (Chassin *et al.*, 1999). Analysis of cohort data from the Australian Temperament Project identified significant associations between paternal and maternal drinking patterns (reported by the mother) and the level of alcohol use reported by the adolescent. Adolescents who drank at very high levels were significantly more likely to have parents who reported that they drank on an occasional or frequent basis. Conversely, adolescents who reported that they did not drink were significantly more likely to have parents who reported that they were occasional or non-drinkers. There was also a positive association between parents who drank alcohol, and allowing adolescents to take alcohol to parties (cited in Hayes *et al.*, 2004). In another study by Bonomo *et al.* (2001), 16- to 17-year-old adolescents who reported that their parents drank daily were at a significantly greater risk of alcohol-related risk-taking. These adolescents were also more likely to initiate alcohol use earlier and to engage in problem drinking at a younger age than non-exposed children.

Alati and colleagues (2005) recently examined the role of maternal drinking in the prediction of alcohol problems at age 21 years using data from the Australian Mater University cohort. Results indicated that those born to mothers who reported drinking more than one glass of alcohol a day at the 14-year follow-up had a two-fold risk of AUD at the 21-year follow-up. Moreover, adolescent boys exposed to moderate maternal alcohol consumption (at least one alcoholic drink per week) also had an increased risk of alcohol problems compared with boys of abstinent mothers. This finding remained robust after controlling for other adolescent, maternal and familial factors measured at birth, childhood and early adolescence. The researchers noted that although fathers were not included in the study, Australian men drink more than women. They therefore suggested that mothers' drinking patterns may reflect exposure to similar or more excessive paternal drinking and, possibly, similar patterns of consumption in the child's broader social environment.

The risk for alcohol problems in young people is particularly high among children of parents suffering alcohol abuse or dependence. While not all such youngsters go on to develop alcohol-related problems, statistics indicate that these children are at approximately four times greater risk of using alcohol or developing alcohol-related problems than children of non-alcohol dependent parents (Weinberg, 1997; Chassin *et al.*, 1999; Jacob *et al.*, 1999). Evidence suggests that both biological and social and behavioral learning are likely to be important determinants (Hawkins *et al.*, 1992; Jacob and Leonard, 1994; Jacob *et al.*, 2003).

There is now considerable evidence that genetic effects play a critical role in the development of alcohol abuse and dependence. In a review of this literature, Hawkins *et al.* (1992) reported that genetic effects have been identified among children of parents suffering alcohol abuse and dependence. For example, adoption studies have identified elevated rates of alcohol dependence (between 18% and 27%) among male offspring of such individuals (Hawkins *et al.*, 1992). Twin studies also show that male children of parents dependent on alcohol have a greater likelihood of developing alcohol abuse (Hawkins *et al.*, 1992). For example, Jacobs *et al.* (2003) examined male monozygotic and dizygotic twins concordant or discordant for alcohol dependence (AD) from the Vietnam Era Twin Registry. Offspring of monozygotic and dizygotic twins with a history of AD were significantly more likely to exhibit alcohol abuse (AA) or AD than were offspring of non-alcohol-dependent fathers. Offspring of an alcohol-abusing monozygotic twin whose co-twin was AD were also more likely to exhibit AD than were offspring of non-alcoholic twins. In contrast, offspring of an unaffected (i.e., no history of abuse or dependence) monozygotic twin whose co-twin was AD were no more likely to exhibit AA or AD than were offspring of non-alcoholic twins. These results suggest that family environmental effects do contribute to offspring outcomes; in particular, that a low-risk environment (i.e., the absence of parental alcohol dependence) can moderate the impact of high genetic risk in offspring for the development of AUD (Jacob *et al.*, 2003). In their review, Hawkins *et al.* (1992) also pointed out that approximately half the adults hospitalized for alcohol dependence do not report a family history of alcohol abuse, suggesting that biological linkages do not account for a significant proportion of cases.

Other research has attempted to tease apart possible social and behavioral learning links in the transmission of alcohol problems. In general, evidence suggests that parental AUD has indirect rather than direct social and behavioral influences on the development of youth alcohol problems. For example, longitudinal research by Dishion and colleagues (1999) examined the relative influence of parental substance use and parenting skills in the prediction of adolescent substance use. Parental substance use did not show unique influence after controlling for parenting practices or peer influences. The authors therefore argued that parenting skills and behavior management (i.e., parental monitoring) have more direct influence on adolescent substance use. In other studies, parenting deficits have also been found to exert more direct effects on adolescent drinking than parental drinking (Barnes *et al.*, 2000). For example, a six-wave longitudinal analysis of 506 adolescents in the United States found no direct effects of parental alcohol abuse on adolescent alcohol misuse (Barnes *et al.*, 2000); rather, parental alcohol abuse indirectly predicted adolescent alcohol use across time through lack of parental support and poor parental monitoring. It could be inferred from these findings that frequent or abusive drinking patterns have detrimental impacts on parenting, which in turn contribute to the development of alcohol problems in young people.

Other longitudinal research suggests that parental alcohol use may influence youth drinking via the selection of substance-using peer friendships. Using longitudinal data from the Christchurch Health and Development Study, Fergusson and colleagues (1995) found that parental alcohol use at child age 11 years did not directly predict abusive or hazardous drinking at 16 years; rather, the effect of parental alcohol use on the risk of later abusive or hazardous drinking was mediated by adolescent peer affiliations at age 15 years. This finding suggests that children of parents who use alcohol are more likely to have affiliations with peers who also use alcohol or other substances. In turn, deviant peer affiliations increased the risk for alcohol abuse at age 16 years. Taken together, the results of these studies suggest that regular parental alcohol consumption and parental AUD are important factors in the development of youth alcohol problems, but that there are likely to be multiple pathways of influence.

Parental Supply of Alcohol

Children are often first introduced to alcohol in the family home. In a national survey on Australian school students' use of alcohol in 2005 (White and Hayman, 2006), parents were reported to be the most common source for obtaining alcohol by adolescents who were current (weekly) drinkers. Of 12- to 17-year-old students, 37 percent indicated that their parents gave them their last drink, 8 percent of respondents indicated that they obtained their last drink from siblings, and a small proportion (4%) of students took alcohol from their home. Interestingly, the proportion of students indicating parents as their source of alcohol was significantly greater among the younger (39%) than the older students (35%). This suggests that parents are the major source of alcohol supply for many young people, and that their influence during the early stages of adolescence may be especially important (White and Hayman, 2006).

Students aged 12 and 17 years were also asked to indicate where they consumed their last alcoholic drink. The three most common places for students to drink alcohol were at a party (33%), in the family home (30%) or at a friend's home (14%). The proportion of students drinking at home decreased with age among both males and females, from around 50 percent of 12-year-olds to around 23 percent of 17-year-olds (White and Hayman, 2006). Both younger and older students drank less alcohol per week if they obtained their alcohol from parents than if they obtained it by having someone else buy it for them. Likewise, weekly consumption of alcohol was significantly lower among 12- to 15-year-olds if they obtained it from parents as opposed to friends. Younger students also drank significantly fewer drinks per week if they drank at home than if they drank at a friend's house or at a party. A similar pattern was seen among older students. These data suggest that students are more likely to drink at moderate levels when they obtain alcohol from their parents and drink in the family home than when they drink with their friends. On the one hand, it may be the case that drinking in the family home environment, under close parental supervision, reduces the risk of heavy drinking commonly associated with unsupervised alcohol use in the peer context. Alternatively, adolescents may consume less when they drink at home because their parents are present, and this moderation does not translate to the peer drinking context. At this stage it remains unclear whether parental supply of alcohol is a risk or protective factor for alcohol use problems in young people, but it is likely that this relationship is strongly mediated by parental monitoring.

PRENATAL EXPOSURE TO ALCOHOL

Prenatal exposure to alcohol increases the risk for a range of physical, cognitive and mental heath problems in young people (O'Leary, 2004). The full range of possible outcomes resulting from maternal alcohol use during pregnancy are referred to as Fetal Alcohol Spectrum Disorders (FASD) (Barr and Streissguth, 2001). The most severe outcome is known as Fetal Alcohol Syndrome (FAS), and the less severe forms are commonly referred to as Partial FAS (Abel, 1998; Moore *et al.*, 2002). The expression of full FAS is found in children whose mothers have a history of chronic heavy alcohol use or frequent heavy intermittent alcohol use in pregnancy. The diagnosis of FAS is based on a set of criteria comprised of abnormalities in three main areas: characteristic physical abnormalities, growth retardation, and central nervous system abnormalities with intellectual impairment (Abel, 1998; Moore *et al.*, 2002).

FAS and FASD have been associated with high rates of alcohol and other drug use disorders in later life (Famy *et al.*, 1998; Clark *et al.*, 2004). Recent research also suggests that more moderate exposure to alcohol in pregnancy is associated with the development of alcohol problems in early adulthood. Baer *et al.* (2003) conducted a 21-year longitudinal analysis of the effects of prenatal alcohol exposure on young-adult drinking. Prenatal alcohol exposure (one alcoholic drink of more per day in pregnancy) was associated with alcohol problems at 21 years of age, independent of the effects of family history of alcohol problems, nicotine exposure, other prenatal exposures, and postnatal environmental factors – including parental use of other drugs.

FAS is also associated with a complex pattern of cognitive and behavioral dysfunction which can have detrimental effects on youth later in life (O'Leary, 2002). Symptoms can include poor impulse control and hyperactivity; deficits in attention, memory or judgment; poor problem-solving and arithmetic skills;

language problems; and deficits in abstract thinking, perception and motor development. These effects place children at greater risk of experiencing difficulties in schooling and problems in relating to others (Moore *et al.*, 2002; O'Leary, 2004). In adolescence, FAS has been associated with attention, memory and information-processing deficits (Clark *et al.*, 2004). Moreover, alcohol consumption in pregnancy has been associated with antisocial and delinquent behavioral problems in adolescence and young adulthood, including poor impulse control, poor social adaptation, trouble with the law, inappropriate sexual behavior, difficulties with employment, and substance use problems (Jacobson and Jacobson, 2002). These risks often cluster together with youth alcohol problems, suggesting that there are likely to be complex and multiple pathways (i.e., both biological and environmental) from prenatal exposure to the later development of AUD in young people.

INDIVIDUAL FACTORS

Behavioral and Emotional Problems

Behavioral and emotional problems during childhood and early adolescence have consistently been linked with the development of AUD in young people (Sher, 1994; Smart *et al.*, 2005). These problems roughly fall into two main categories: outwardly directed externalizing problems, including symptoms of oppositional defiant disorder, attention deficit hyperactivity disorder, conduct disorder and antisocial personality disorder, and inwardly directed internalizing problems, including symptoms of anxiety and depression. Externalizing problems are more commonly found in boys, and internalizing problems are more commonly found in girls.

Among the longitudinal papers published on early risk factors for alcohol abuse, findings from the Seattle Social Development Project suggest that both externalizing and internalizing behaviors at age 10 years are important predictors of alcohol abuse and dependence at age 21 (Guo *et al.*, 2001). Examination of data from the Mater University birth cohort study in Australia indicated that externalizing but not internalizing symptoms at age 14 years is significantly associated with AUD at age 21 years, after controlling for other factors across three sensitive periods: birth, childhood and early adolescence (Alati *et al.*, 2005). In the Pittsburgh Youth Study, early signs of psychopathology, including conduct disorder, attention deficit hyperactivity disorder and depression at age 13, were all strongly associated with alcohol abuse in late adolescence (White *et al.*, 2001). Likewise, a prospective population study by Locke and Newcomb (2003) found that dysphoria was strongly associated with later heavy drinking, with a bidirectional relationship evident among females in adolescence. Findings from the Dunedin birth cohort study also support the notion that personality traits are important predictors of heavy drinking in young adults (Caspi *et al.*, 1997). Specifically, the study found that youths characterized by high negative emotionality and low constraint at 18 years were predisposed to engage in alcohol abuse as well as a range of other health-risk behaviors at 21 years (violent crime, unsafe sex practices and dangerous driving habits).

Elevated levels of externalizing behavior may be reflective of a "deviance proneness pathway" to youth alcohol problems (Sher, 1997). According to this pathway, a "difficult" temperament in combination with ineffective parenting leads to unsocialized behavior, which in turn results in poor adjustment and school failure. School failure and related low self-esteem are posited to lead to association with deviant, substance-abusing peers, which further reinforces problem behaviors. By early adolescence, these individuals typically display impulsive and antisocial personality traits, including elevated levels of risk-taking, sensation-seeking, poor school performance, and aggressive and antisocial behaviors (Jessor and Jessor, 1977; Sher, 1997; Smart *et al.*, 2005). Conversely, the link between youth internalizing and alcohol problems is theorized to be reflective of a "negative affect pathway" to AUD. This pathway focuses on temperamental proneness to experiencing negative affective states, a high level of life stress, and ineffective coping resources. By early adolescence, this often manifests in anxiety and depressive disorders, difficulties in family relationships and generalized distress and maladjustment (Harter, 2000). Alcohol problems purportedly develop in this context as an ineffective means of coping with psychological distress. Both the deviance proneness and negative affect pathways are thought to be significantly enhanced by a family history of AUD (Sher, 1994).

Early Initiation to Alcohol

Empirical evidence indicates that the younger the age at which a child or adolescent commences drinking, the greater the risk of alcohol misuse in adolescence and adulthood. Longitudinal data from the Christchurch Health and Development Study suggest that initiation to alcohol in childhood and early adolescence increases the likelihood of regular and high-risk alcohol use in adolescence, independent of a range of other influences (Fergusson *et al.*, 1994, 1995). In another study on early exposure to alcohol, children who had been introduced to alcohol before the age of 6 years were shown to be 1.9–2.4 times more likely to report frequent, heavy or problem drinking at age 15 than children who did not drink alcohol before the age of 13 (Toumbourou *et al.*, 2004). Other studies suggest that the later adolescents delay their first alcoholic drink, the less likely they are to become regular or problem drinkers. For example, results from the Victorian Youth Alcohol and Drug Survey (Premier's Drug Prevention Council, 2003) in Australia show that adolescents who start drinking later are more likely to report that they are light or occasional drinkers, and they are less likely to binge drink.

There is also evidence that early initiation to drinking increases the risk for more severe alcohol problems. Data from the National Longitudinal Epidemiologic Survey of 27 616 young people in the United States show that the lifetime alcohol dependence rates of people who initiate alcohol use by age 14 are four times as high as those who start at age 20 years or older (Grant and Dawson, 1997). Notably, the odds of lifetime dependence decreased by 14 percent with each additional year of delayed initiation, and the odds of abuse decreased by 8 percent, after adjusting for potentially confounding variables.

While studies suggest that early initiation to drinking increases the risk for problematic patterns of alcohol use in later life, other factors may also play a role in this relationship. It may be the case, for example, that adolescents who commence drinking at a young age and who subsequently go on to misuse alcohol in late adolescence or adulthood have been exposed to other familial and social risks that, together with early exposure to drinking, increase the risk for adverse outcomes (Foxcroft and Lowe, 1991). In support of this notion, Fergusson *et al.* (1994) identified correlations between the age of reported first use of alcohol and measures indicative of positive parental attitudes to alcohol use and approval of alcohol use by young people. The authors suggested that early alcohol use was to some extent, an indicator measure of home environments in which alcohol was used frequently and viewed positively. This suggests that although the early onset of alcohol use places individuals at greater risk of alcohol-related problems, this risk is greatest among young people who live in home environments that adopt generally permissive and encouraging attitudes to alcohol use in their children. Further research is needed to determine whether early initiation is itself a key risk factor or whether the presence of other factors (e.g., parental permissiveness regarding alcohol use, peer environment), in combination with early exposure, increases the risk for negative outcomes.

PEER ENVIRONMENT

Conceptual models suggest that while parents and significant family members are a potent and primary source of influence in childhood, peers become increasingly important during adolescence (Jacob and Leonard, 1994). The high prevalence of alcohol use among peers of adolescent drinkers has been demonstrated in large-scale community surveys such as the Australian National Drug Strategy Household Survey (AIHW, 2005). Data from this survey show that three-quarters of Australian recent drinkers (78.3%) reported that all or most of their friends consume alcohol. Numerous other studies have identified peer similarities in patterns of alcohol use and misuse among members of youth friendship groups (see, for example, Curran *et al.*, 1997). One explanation for these similarities is that the peer environment may act to promote and maintain alcohol use via modeling and imitation of specific behaviors, increased availability of and access to alcohol, and value transmission and social reinforcement. In support, longitudinal studies provide evidence for a direct effect of peers on the development of problematic drinking patterns. In a study by Fergusson and colleagues (1995), affiliation with substance using peers at age 15 was shown to directly predict alcohol abuse at age 16, after controlling for a range of confounds.

Peer similarities in youth drinking may also be accounted for by friendship selection. According to selection, adolescents choose friends with whom they share similar attitudes and behaviors. A number of longitudinal studies have assessed the comparative role of peer socialization and selection, with the available evidence suggesting that these processes are both linked to youth drinking. For example, a longitudinal study by Curran *et al.* (1997) found that an adolescent's earlier levels of alcohol use predicted later changes in peer use and, conversely, that levels of peer alcohol use at baseline predicted changes in later adolescent use. Similarly, a recent three-wave longitudinal study by Reifman and colleagues (2006) found evidence for both social influence and selection in the development of college students' heavy drinking and that of their social networks. Specifically, the study found that greater presence of individuals considered "drinking buddies" in a network predicted an individual's own later drinking. Likewise, wave-to-wave changes in average network drinking appeared to result from network members with different drinking levels being added to and dropped from the network. These studies suggest that young people who share certain prior attributes tend to associate with one another and subsequently influence each other's drinking patterns as a result of continued association.

Some studies have examined the relative contribution of parental and peer influences to youth drinking. Reifman *et al.* (1998) compared the role of peers and parents in the prediction of drinking among adolescents aged 13–16 years. Friends' drinking was the most significant predictor of progression to heavy drinking, followed by low parental monitoring. Rai *et al.* (2003) also compared peer and parental influence, using data from six cross-sectional studies conducted over 10 years. Overall, the results were similar to those of Reifman and colleagues, identifying an increased risk for alcohol use in adolescents whose peers were involved in risk behaviors (odds ratio = 1.62; range 1.37–1.92). Similarly, low parental monitoring was also associated with greater risk for alcohol use (OR = 0.65; range 0.35–0.69). These data suggest that the effect of peers mediates the influence of parenting factors on adolescent alcohol use. In a recent review, Hayes and colleagues (2004) therefore suggested that peer effects become particularly important when parent–adolescent relationships are of poorer quality.

While involvement in peer drinking culture is a risk factor for later alcohol misuse, young people at high risk for the development of AUD are often part of more deviant or counter-conventional peer networks. These networks are typically characterized by involvement in both licit and illicit drug use, antisocial behavior and aggression, school truancy, risky sexual behavior and criminal involvement (Spooner *et al.*, 2001; Smart *et al.*, 2005). Longitudinal studies suggest that the formation of attachments to delinquent and substance-using peer groups is one of the strongest predictors of both antisocial behavioral patterns and substance use disorders in young people (Hawkins *et al.*, 1992; Fergusson *et al.*, 1995; Fergusson and Horwood, 1996). Evidence also suggests that there is a complex range of childhood risks associated with the formation of these peer affiliations, including family social stratification (i.e., low socio-economic status, growing up in a problem neighborhood), poor family functioning, parental substance use disorder, and individual behavioral predispositions – including early anxiety and withdrawal, aggression, conduct problems and drug experimentation (Jacob and Leonard, 1994; Fergusson and Horwood, 1999; Smart *et al.*, 2005).

BROADER CULTURAL FACTORS

Drinking Culture

Cultural norms regarding adolescent alcohol use are thought to exert a powerful influence on youth drinking behavior. In European countries where there are permissive attitudes toward youth alcohol use, societal patterns of heavy adolescent alcohol use have been shown to be higher than in countries where the cultural climate is less favorable toward youth alcohol use (Bjarnason *et al.*, 2003). A recent study by Beyers and colleagues (2004) also identified differences in norms concerning adolescent alcohol use and patterns of use in three large, representative student samples from Victoria, Australia, and the American states of Oregon and Maine. Although there were many similarities between the two countries, the factors which were more strongly associated with risk for substance use in Australian youth reflected more tolerant norms and attitudes, whereas the risk factors identified for youth in the United States cohorts were reflective of social alienation, measured by individual factors such as academic failure, rebelliousness and poor social skills. Findings were interpreted in the context of policy differences between the two countries, with American abstinence policies associated with punishment for use and Australian harm minimization policies associated with greater tolerance toward experimentation with drug use. However, it is likely that other factors, not accounted for in the research, also contributed to differences between the countries (for example, laws relating to youth alcohol use, socialization practices surrounding alcohol, etc.).

Laws Regarding Adolescent Alcohol Use

Laws regarding adolescent alcohol use can exert considerable influence on adolescent drinking behavior and broader cultural attitudes toward youth alcohol use. Laws can also directly influence the availability of alcohol, and when availability increases so too does the prevalence of adolescent drinking (Hawkins *et al.*, 1992). There is now strong evidence from studies conducted in the United States, Canada, New Zealand and some other countries to show that decreasing the minimum legal age for both the purchase and use of alcohol can increase youth alcohol use and alcohol-related harm (Shults *et al.*, 2001; Wagenaar and Toomey, 2002; Kypri *et al.*, 2006). These studies have monitored the prevalence and patterns of youth alcohol use and alcohol-related mortality and morbidity before and after policy changes to minimum drinking and purchase-age laws. For example, a New Zealand study by Kypri and colleagues (2006) found that lowering the minimum legal purchase age for alcohol from 20 to 18 years in 1999 was associated with significant increases in both alcohol-involved crashes and hospitalized injuries among 15- to 19-year-olds. Likewise, a review by Shults and colleagues (2001) found that lowering the minimum legal drinking age produced a median increase of 10 percent in youthful crash involvements. This evidence supports the view that laws regarding adolescent alcohol are important, and that increasing the legal age for alcohol purchase and use can reduce risky drinking practices among youth and related harms. As such, laws can increase risk, but can also have a protective effect on youth drinking.

Ethnic Minority Groups and Indigenous Peoples

A considerable body of research has been conducted on ethno-specific substance use patterns in the United States. At present, the most comprehensive data available on ethnic/indigenous minorities are available on minorities, including Native Americans, Hispanics and African-Americans. Interestingly, prevalence data show that Anglo-Americans are relatively likely to have been drunk by twelfth grade compared with Hispanics and African-Americans (67.9% versus 63.8% and 40.5%), and are relatively likely to report having been drunk in the last 30 days (37.7% versus 12.0% and 25.5%; Johnston *et al.*, 2002). While Anglo-Americans report greater prevalence of alcohol use, there are important differences in the patterns and consequences of alcohol use by ethnic minority status. With significant variation across tribes, Native Americans show the highest rate of AUD-related harm among any ethnic/indigenous group in the United States, including driving and other accidents, and FAS (see, for example, Beauvais, 1998). Hispanic minorities have also been demonstrated to suffer significant alcohol-related consequences (e.g., Sussman *et al.*, 2002a), with Mexican Americans reporting higher drinking rates than Puerto Rican or Cuban Americans (Caetano, 1998). Among substances of abuse, alcohol is the most abused among African-American adolescents, and its use may remain stable with increasing age instead of decreasing as it does among Anglo-Americans (Henderson *et al.*, 2002). Since young people are at higher risk for alcohol abuse and dependence than older individuals, these ethnic and indigenous minority groups are at elevated risk for the development of alcohol misuse and AUD. Differential family acculturation and role reversal or loss of parental control over adolescents by parents who are less acculturated than their children have been associated with youth alcohol use among ethnic/indigenous minorities in the United States (Spooner *et al.*, 2001). Relatively low SES, social disorganization, chronic stressors and older age have also been associated with continued heavy drinking is some minority groups (e.g., Henderson *et al.*, 2002).

There is a considerable body of research indicating that young indigenous peoples in Australia are also at elevated risk for the development of alcohol problems. Prevalence data show, for instance, that while fewer indigenous than non-indigenous Australians consume alcohol, when they do drink they tend to consume alcohol at riskier levels than non-indigenous Australians (Saggers and

Gray, 1998). A recently published community survey indicated that among young indigenous people aged 18–24 years, 34 percent of young people consumed alcohol at risky/high-risk levels compared with 29 percent for non-indigenous people, with high-risk drinking being most common among young Aboriginal males (Australian Bureau of Statistics, 2006). Research suggests that there are multiple factors which youth from Aboriginal and Torres Strait Islander communities are exposed to that are likely to contribute to higher rates of alcohol misuse, including impoverishment, poor health, overcrowded housing, unemployment, lack of educational qualifications, high crime rates, racism, cultural bereavement, and elevated rates of family violence and abuse (Spooner *et al.*, 2001; Stanley *et al.*, 2003).

Young People Living in Rural and Low Population Density Areas

There is evidence that youth living in rural or other low population density areas are at greater risk for alcohol problems and consequences. Australian data show that young people living in rural populations engage in more alcohol and tobacco use than people living in metropolitan communities (Bond *et al.*, 2000). In 2004–2005, 13 percent of people aged 18 years and over in major cities of Australia had risky/high-risk levels of alcohol consumption, compared with 15 percent in inner regional Australia and 16 percent in outer regional Australia/other areas (ABS, 2006). Similarly, national survey data from the United States indicated that in 2001, lifetime prevalence for alcohol use (53.5% versus 49.1%) and having ever been drunk (26.7% versus 49.1%) was higher among eighth-grade students in relatively low population-density areas compared with students in metropolitan areas (Johnston *et al.*, 2002). D'Onofrio (1997) identified common risk factors for alcohol use and abuse among youth living in urban and rural sites (e.g., peer and family influences, sensation seeking). However, additional factors associated with living in a rural area are thought to compound the risk for alcohol use; these problems include greater economic disadvantage, more limited access to social supports and services, and vulnerability to external factors such as sudden loss of employment – for example, due to extreme weather conditions prevent farming, or closure of large industries (D'Onofrio, 1997; Spooner *et al.*, 2001).

PROTECTIVE FACTORS

Protective factors refer to "psychosocial influences that either have a direct effect on limiting or reducing drug involvement or may buffer or moderate the association between risk factors and drug use and abuse" (Newcomb, 1994: 163). Compared with the large body of research on the risks for youth alcohol problems, relatively few studies have examined protective factors that mitigate against these risks.

Not all adolescents who are exposed to the risks overviewed in this chapter go on to suffer alcohol problems. There appear to be a number of factors that enable children to weather the problems of their childhood (see, for example, Chassin *et al.*, 2004). Children least at risk appear to be from families with high levels of family support, control and cohesion, where there is a supportive caregiver who can mitigate the effects of other risks. Social supports outside the family, such as support from school, friends and the community, are also associated with better outcomes for children (see, for example, Hill *et al.*, 1997).

The relationship between parents' positive behavior management strategies and youth alcohol use has been studied as part of the Seattle Social Development Project (Kosterman *et al.*, 2000; Guo *et al.*, 2001; Oxford *et al.*, 2001). Using a sample of 808 adolescents followed from birth to early adulthood, these studies highlight the importance of positive parental practices. Specifically, the research found that delayed adolescent alcohol initiation was predicted by family standards and rules, parental monitoring and adolescent attachment, after taking into account the influence of deviant peer relationships. With respect to problem drinking, parental rules, a strong value system, rewards for behavior and well developed negotiation skills when adolescents were aged 10–16 years predicted lower alcohol abuse and dependence at age 21.

In families where parental drinking problems are a major factor, drinking patterns are important in determining outcomes. For example, there is evidence that an unpredictable pattern of parental alcohol abuse may result in greater disruption to family life than a more predictable, regular drinking pattern. Similarly, out-of-home drinking patterns may to some extent insulate family and children from disruptions that occur when drinking takes place at home (Jacob and Leonard, 1988, 1994).

Many protective factors that promote resiliency reflect the opposite end on the continuum of a single factor or construct. In the case of parent–child relationship quality, for example, whereas problems in this domain predict adolescent alcohol misuse, adolescents who report having a good relationship with their parents have improved outcomes in many areas, including reduced substance use, higher self-esteem, better academic achievement, the capacity to seek social support, and lower rates of social and psychological problems (Armsden and Greenberg, 1987). Similarly, high-level parental monitoring (in contrast to poor monitoring) has been identified as an important influence on general adolescent behavior, with specific links to the prevention of adolescent alcohol use and abuse (Dishion and McMahon, 1998). Numerous other factors identified through the chapter, including delayed initiation to alcohol use, affiliation with non-deviant peer networks, and broader cultural factors (i.e., laws and cultural norms) can also ameliorate the risk for youth AUD. While greater understanding of the factors that buffer children from developing alcohol problems is needed, it appears that the presence of fewer risks, for shorter duration and at less critical developmental time points, reduces the overall risk for adolescent and young adult drinking problems.

PREVENTION AND INTERVENTION

The previous section highlighted that alcohol use in young people is influenced by a range factors. This suggests that a multi-component approach is required to change youth drinking behavior (Mitchell *et al.*, 2001; Galanter, 2006). Specifically, interventions that target changes in families, schools, peers, communities, social norms and laws are needed, as well as programs that target the continuum of drinking behaviors linked to later drinking problems (e.g., delaying initiation of experimentation and limiting the progression to regular use, misuse and disorder). Prevention and intervention programs also need systematically to target identified risk and protective factors at critical developmental points. For example, in early childhood, preventative interventions need to address childhood risk factors prior to drinking onset (i.e., externalizing behavior; parent management strategies); in adolescence, interventions need to address drinking onset and related drinking attitudes and behavior alongside other risk factors (e.g., involvement in counter-cultural peer friendships; parent–adolescent relationship problems), whereas in early adulthood, more established drinking patterns and problems may need to be targeted. At each of these key developmental stages, selected interventions are also important to prevent the development of AUD among special or high-risk groups in the community.

Considerable progress has been made over the last decade in the identification and evaluation of prevention and intervention strategies that aim to reduce alcohol use and misuse among young people (Tobler *et al.*, 2000; Mitchell *et al.*, 2001; Loxley *et al.*, 2004; Galanter, 2006). A summary of the large number of intervention programs that have been conducted and evaluated is beyond the scope of this chapter, so we have chosen to focus on interventions and strategies that have been subject to more rigorous empirical evaluation and appear to show some effects on youth drinking behavior and the consequences or factors linked to youth alcohol problems. Given that the focus of this chapter in on adolescence, we have chosen to concentrate first on programs that span the late elementary to high school years, and second on programs that focus on intervening in the college/university years. The final section provides an overview of literature on prevention work in special and high-risk groups.

SCHOOL-BASED PREVENTIVE INTERVENTIONS FOR ADOLESCENT DRINKING

Many risk factors for youth alcohol problems occur during childhood, prior to the onset of drinking. For this reason, school-based programs often aim to prevent the development of alcohol and other drug use and misuse by targeting known risk domains (i.e., individual, familial and peer factors) when children are in their late elementary and early high school years. Developmental perspectives are consistent with this approach, suggesting that early interventions may facilitate wellbeing further along the developmental pathway. Indeed, it has been suggested that if a person's developmental trajectory is directed along problematic pathways, the more energy is required to change the course and the more difficult it will be to redress damage to developmental potential (Mitchell *et al.*, 2001). This perspective provides a rationale for intervening early in problematic pathways to alcohol misuse and AUD.

The Strengthening Families Program

The Strengthening Families Program (SFP; Spoth *et al.*, 1998) is a well-researched family program developed in the United States which aims to prevent the initiation of alcohol use in adolescents. It is a universal program for widespread application with parents and children in the general community. The program comprises seven once-a-week sessions for 10- to 14-year-olds. The goals of the program are to enhance parental skills in nurturing, communication and limit-setting, in addition to youth pro-social and peer resistance skills. The program involves separate parent training and children's skills training, followed by joint family life skills training sessions in which parents and children practice the skills learnt in separate sessions.

Spoth and colleagues (1999) tested the effectiveness of the SFP among 446 American families randomly allocated to treatment and control groups. The children were in sixth grade at the time of the intervention. At the 1-year follow-up, significantly fewer children in the intervention group had initiated alcohol compared with children in the control group, with a medium effect size of 0.29. This treatment effect remained evident 2 years after treatment, with a large effect size of 0.39.

The SFP was also examined as part of a comprehensive review conducted by the Cochrane Consortium (Foxcroft *et al.*, 2003), which involved the evaluation of 56 international studies in which an educational or psychosocial prevention program specific to adolescent alcohol use was undertaken. The review included investigation of the longer-term effectiveness of interventions, and required follow-up to be maintained beyond 3 years (Spoth *et al.*, 2001). Over the longer term, the SFP showed the greatest promise of all intervention and prevention programs under review. Using a conservative strategy for analyzing data in which all participants were included in the intervention or control group to which they were assigned, whether or not they completed the intervention, the review found that for every nine individuals who received the SFP, 4 years after the intervention there would be one fewer person reporting that they have ever used alcohol, used alcohol without permission, or ever been drunk. The program was one of only two prevention interventions judged by the review to show promise as an effective preventive intervention.

Life Skills Training program

The Life Skills Training program (LST; Baker *et al.*, 1990; Botvin *et al.*, 1995a) is a widely used school-based prevention program which consists of a 3-year prevention curriculum for junior or middle high school students. The curriculum addresses drug information, drug-resistance skills, self-management skills and social skills, and consists of 15 sessions in the first year, 10 sessions in the second year and 5 sessions in the third year. A long-term randomized trial of the LST program found that it had long-term effects on tobacco, alcohol and marijuana use through twelfth grade (Botvin *et al.*, 1995a). Specifically, the study reported significantly less self-reported drunkenness in those teenagers who received the intervention compared with the control group. Despite the effectiveness of the LST program in this study, it appears to be less effective than some other available programs. A randomized control trial by Spoth *et al.* (2002) evaluated the effectiveness of LST combined with the SFP 10–14 intervention, the LST program alone, and a control condition among 36 randomly selected rural schools. Results indicated that the average Substance Use Index score was highest in the control group, next lowest in the LST condition, and lowest in the LST + SFP 10–14 condition. However, only the combined condition was significantly different from the control condition. These results suggest that the additional family component included in the SFP significantly enhances the positive results derived from LST alone. Consistent with this study, the Cochrane Review also concluded that the LST program was less convincing than the SFP as an effective intervention over the longer term for the prevention of alcohol misuse (Foxcroft *et al.*, 2003).

Project Northland

Project Northland is a multi-component, community-based program for the prevention of alcohol use among adolescents. This program aims to boost the effects typically achieved by a classroom curriculum alone with the addition of other strategies designed to intervene directly in the social environment of youth. The program was evaluated in 20 school districts in northeastern Minnesota that were randomly assigned to either a treatment or a control condition (Perry *et al.*, 1993). The students participated in three intervention stages from sixth grade through twelfth grade. The first intervention stage was conducted when students were in sixth grade through eighth grade, and involved social behavioral training, peer leadership and extracurricular social opportunities, parental involvement and education, and community-based task forces. The interim stage of the study was conducted when students were in the ninth and tenth grades (Williams and Perry, 1998). Intervention at this stage was comparatively minimal, comprising a five-session classroom program. The final stage of the intervention targeted students in the eleventh and twelfth grades through various activities, including classroom curriculum, parent postcards, media involvement, youth development activities, and community organizing and policy development (Perry *et al.*, 2000).

Results from the first stage indicated that, after 3 years of Project Northland activities, a smaller proportion of students in the intervention communities reported alcohol initiation or use compared with students in the control communities (Perry *et al.*, 1996). Specifically, monthly drinking was 20 percent lower among students in the intervention school districts compared with students in the control districts, and weekly drinking was 30 percent lower. Students in the intervention group who were never-drinkers at the beginning of sixth grade not only drank significantly less than students in the control group; they also smoked fewer cigarettes and used less marijuana at the end of the eighth grade. In addition to these behavioral effects, the intervention had positive effects on family management regarding alcohol issues, peer influence, social normative beliefs, evaluation of consequences, and self-efficacy to resist alcohol use among baseline non-drinkers. Despite these positive outcomes, during the interim phase of the intervention drinking rates between the treatment and control groups began to converge, and by the end of tenth grade no significant differences were identified between the two groups (Williams and Perry, 1998). Following the more intensive final intervention in eleventh and twelfth grades, alcohol use patterns among the two groups were again shown to diverge (Williams *et al.*, 1999). By the end of eleventh grade, the differences between the groups were marginally significant, but only among those students who had not used alcohol at the commencement of sixth grade.

At the end of the intervention trial, a study of the trajectories of alcohol use between the treatment control groups was conducted for all three stages of Project Northland (Perry *et al.*, 2003). Consistent with the independent findings, the increase in alcohol use among the control group during the first stage was significantly greater than in the intervention group. However, during the interim stage, drinking trajectories appeared to level out between the groups, with significantly greater increases in alcohol use detected in the intervention group compared with the control group. The students in the intervention group appeared to return to the level of alcohol use that was normative among their peers. During the final stage this pattern was reversed, and the more intensive intervention was associated with significantly greater increases in alcohol use in the control group compared with the intervention group, demonstrating the positive impact of the final phase of the intervention.

In summary, Project Northland provides some support for primary prevention programs that systematically involve youth, parents, peers and the broader community. In particular, the finding that the most intensive stages of the program were associated with positive changes in adolescent drinking relative to the less intensive interim stage highlights the importance of multi-component programs that concurrently target multiple risk factors. Project Northland has recently been updated and adapted for a multi-ethnic urban population in Chicago (Komro *et al.*, 2004). The results of a randomized controlled trial to test the effectiveness of the revised Project Northland will be available in the near future, and should provide a clearer picture of the effectiveness of this program.

The Preparing for the Drug Free Years Program

The Preparing for the Drug Free Years program (PDFY; Kosterman *et al.*, 1997) is an American-based skills training program designed for parents of 8- to 14-year-old children. The program aims to reduce risks and enhance protection against early alcohol and drug use initiation through the improvement of parental behavior and family interaction patterns predictive of childhood substance use. The program focuses predominantly on parental intervention, consisting of four 2-hour parent sessions and one individual child session. The parent sessions involve instruction and skills training on parent–child bonding, enhancing positive child involvement, identifying risk factors, developing guidelines and expectations related to substance use, monitoring compliance, appropriate consequences, and managing anger and conflict. The child participates in a single session of peer-resistance skills training.

Spoth and colleagues (1996) evaluated the effectiveness of the PDFY among 220 families with sixth- or seventh-grade students. Families were selected from six school districts in Iowa, and were randomly assigned to either the intervention or the control group. At post-treatment, the PDFY program was associated with reduced adolescent favorable attitudes to alcohol use. By increasing protective factors, the program also made a small yet significant contribution to improved parent–adolescent bonding.

In a randomized control trial of the PDFY (Spoth *et al.*, 1998), positive effects on substance use were identified among 429 rural adolescents. Specifically, the intervention was delivered to adolescents with an average age of 11.35 years. Follow-up results at 3.5 years post-intervention indicated that, compared with the control group, adolescents who had participated in the intervention had lower rates of poly-substance use, including alcohol, tobacco, marijuana, inhalants and other illicit drug use. The PDFY intervention group was also found to have lower rates of delinquency. Park *et al.* (2000) specifically examined the trajectory of alcohol use from early to mid-adolescence in this sample. Results indicated that the PDFY intervention significantly reduced the growth of alcohol use and improved parental norms regarding adolescent alcohol use over time. Although the difference in mean alcohol use between the two groups was small, at the 3.5-year follow-up at age 15.5 years, 65 percent of the control group versus 52 percent of the PDYF group reported alcohol initiation; 42 percent versus 32 percent reported having been drunk; and 40 percent versus 24 percent said they had used alcohol in the past month.

Spoth and colleagues (1998) conducted a comparative study of the SFP and PDFY interventions using a randomized control design. At post-treatment, both programs were significantly associated with positive effects on parenting behaviors compared with the control group. The effects of the two programs were found to be comparable, with an intervention effect size for the SFP of 0.51, and an intervention effect size for the PDFY of 0.45. Thus, both programs appear to provide initial support for intervening in parenting behaviors. However, program effects on the child's behavior and alcohol use were not reported in these comparisons. In summary, the PDFY intervention has been shown to have positive effects on adolescent drinking attitudes and behavior and on substance use behavior more generally, as well as promising effects on parenting behaviors linked to youth drinking.

CLIMATE Schools

Climate Schools: Alcohol Module (CLIMATE; Vogl *et al.*, 2006) is a universal school-based alcohol prevention program recently developed in Australia. The program advocates a harm-minimization approach to adolescent drinking, and aims to prevent alcohol use, misuse and related harm. The intervention consists of six lessons, and utilizes a computerized cartoon-based teenage drama and interactive classroom activities to impart information and skills to young people. Content areas covered include alcohol guidelines, normative alcohol use information, short- and long-term harms of alcohol use, peer and media influences, drink refusal, harm minimization skills, and first aid.

A randomized control trial was conducted involving 1435 eighth-grade students from 16 schools in New South Wales and Australian Capital Territory (Vogl *et al.*, 2006). Schools were randomly allocated to receive the intervention or personal development, health and physical education classes, which included the usual alcohol prevention education delivered in each school. At the 12-month follow-up, students who received the CLIMATE intervention had significantly greater knowledge of information to aid in reducing alcohol-related harm and reduced expectancies regarding the benefits of consuming alcohol compared with students in the control group. Females who received the CLIMATE intervention also had lower average increases in alcohol consumption, frequency of binge drinking and alcohol-related harms compared with females in the control group; however, only minimal and transient changes in drinking behavior were detected for males. As the control schools received alcohol prevention education which was also based on a harm-minimization approach, the effects which were detected are a conservative measure of program success. This program is promising, because positive changes in both drinking attitudes and behavior were detected; however, it appears that the intervention has greater efficacy for reducing alcohol use and misuse in adolescent females than in males.

INTERVENTIONS FOR COLLEGE/UNIVERSITY POPULATIONS

Numerous interventions have been developed for alcohol use among college/university-age students. Unlike school-based interventions, which tend to focus on delaying the onset of alcohol use, programs in older adolescents and young adults focus predominantly on modifying individual levels and patterns of consumption, and especially on prevention of alcohol misuse and its consequences. As such, these programs tend to focus primarily (but not exclusively) on students whose drinking places them at risk of harm or has already created problems.

College-based intervention programs typically fall into one of three categories:

1. Educational or awareness programs
2. Cognitive behavioral skills training
3. Motivational enhancement programs.

As a considerable number of programs have been developed in each of these areas, the following section provides a brief overview of the effectiveness of the programs. For a more detailed review of this literature, readers are referred to two recent reviews by Larimer and Cronce (2002) and Saltz (2006), along with a synthetic report on this area complied by the National Advisory Council on Alcohol and Alcoholism (NIAAA) Task Force (NIAAA, 2002).

Educational or Awareness Programs

Educational or awareness interventions are the most widely disseminated programs in college/university settings (Moskowitz, 1989; Larimer and Cronce, 2002; Saltz, 2006). These programs typically focus on the provision of information about alcohol use and related harms; values-clarification programs designed to help students engage in goal-setting and responsible decision-making about alcohol; and provision of normative information to students on peer drinking prevalence and levels of drinking. Empirical research shows that changes in knowledge or attitudes can be achieved through these kinds of interventions, but that these changes typically do not translate into demonstrable changes in drinking behavior. In their review of this area, Larimer and Cronce (2002) appraised seven information-based interventions. While most of the programs were associated with significant changes in knowledge or attitudes, only one intervention (Kivlahan *et al.*, 1990) was associated with reductions in either alcohol consumption or problems. This randomized control trial evaluated intervention approaches for young adults ($n = 36$, mean age 23 years) at risk for alcohol problems. The 8-week curriculum-based intervention was associated with a reduction in alcohol consumption from 19.4 to 12.7 drinks per week among participants in the information-only intervention compared with participants in the control group, who reported a slight increase in consumption at the 12-month follow-up. The decrease in alcohol consumption was greatest among participants in the skills training condition (from 14.8 to 6.6 drinks per week), although most participants continued to report occasional heavy drinking.

Larimer and Cronce (2002) similarly found that only two of five programs based on values clarification, or a combination of values clarification and information provision, were associated with drinking reduction. However, the reviewers noted that each of the studies under review had methodological problems that hindered accurate assessment of their effectiveness. Finally, only two studies included in the review incorporated a normative re-education approach. In the first study (Barnett *et al.*, 1996), students participated in a norm-setting group, a values-clarification group, a combined intervention group or a control group. There were no differential effects of the interventions on drinking behavior over time; however, participants who received either of the norm-setting interventions reported significant changes in drinking norms compared with the values-clarification intervention and control groups. Changes in norms from baseline to post-intervention in turn predicted subsequent reductions in alcohol consumption irrespective of the treatment condition. In the second study (Schroeder and Prentice, 1998), the normative re-education component of the program was associated with a significant reduction in student drinking, but without detecting a change in perceived peer drinking norms. Inconsistency in the findings between these studies meant that clear conclusions could not be made about the effectiveness of the normative re-education approach.

Consistent with past reviews (see, for example, Moskowitz, 1989), the report by Larimer and Cronce (2002) concluded that the majority of studies on informational approaches have found no effect of these interventions on alcohol use and/or alcohol-related negative consequences. Values-clarification approaches may be efficacious, but are resource- and time-intensive to conduct and have not been evaluated in randomized trials. Normative re-education approaches are less costly and may hold more promise compared with other educational interventions, but have yet to be widely tested. Despite the lack of consistent empirical support for these approaches, education about alcohol may be an essential part of some interventions, especially programs that take a multi-component approach by combining information-giving with other complementary components and strategies (Saltz, 2006).

Based on the evidence available to date, the NIAAA Task Force therefore recommends that educational and awareness approaches be avoided *in isolation* unless new evidence of their value becomes available.

Cognitive Behavioral Skills Training

Cognitive behavioral skills training programs focus on teaching skills to modify beliefs or behaviors associated with high-risk drinking. The majority of programs are multimodal, including both specific alcohol-focused skills training (e.g., expectancy challenge procedures, self-monitoring of alcohol use and problems, blood-alcohol discrimination training) and general life skills (e.g., stress and time management training, assertiveness skills). Many of these programs also incorporate information, values-clarification and/or normative re-education components.

To date, the majority of studies evaluating the efficacy of cognitive behavioral interventions for drinking have utilized a multi-component skills training condition. Larimer and Cronce (2002) identified seven studies evaluating a total of ten multi-component skills training interventions. Of these, seven interventions demonstrated significant positive effects on alcohol consumption, harms, or both (Garvin *et al.*, 1990; Kivlahan *et al.*, 1990; Baer *et al.*, 1992; Miller, 1999).

Two of three alcohol-focused skills training programs reviewed by Larimer and Cronce (2002) showed statistically significant positive effects at short-term follow-up (Darkes and Goldman, 1993, 1998). These studies all incorporated an expectancy challenge component which aimed to assist drinkers to recognize how the subjective effects of alcohol are largely determined by a person's expectancies of those effects and not predominantly (if at all) by the alcohol itself. In the first study (Darkes and Goldman, 1993), heavy-drinking male participants were randomly assigned to traditional alcohol education, expectancy challenge or control conditions. Participants in the expectancy challenge condition were required to consume drinks in a social setting and then guess which participants had consumed alcohol and which a placebo. These participants also received information about placebo effects and expectancies, and students monitored their expectancies for a 4-week period. Two weeks post-treatment, participants in the expectancy challenge group reported a significant decrease in their alcohol consumption compared with participants in the other conditions. In a similar study (Darkes and Goldman, 1998), 54 heavy-drinking males were assigned to either a control group or one of two expectancy challenge conditions targeting (i) social expectancies using the procedure described above, or (ii) arousal expectancies using sedating cues or problem-solving tasks. Six weeks after treatment, participants in all three conditions had reduced their alcohol consumption; however, the largest reductions were demonstrated in the two expectancy conditions. In the third study, by Jones *et al.* (1995), students participated in an intervention that included didactic information and discussion about alcohol expectancies; self-monitoring of expectancies; and randomization to an expectancy challenge in which students were given an alcoholic or placebo beverage (but not in the presence of other students). Results showed an overall trend toward positive effects on drinking, but there was no effect by condition. Further analysis indicated that only those involved in the self-challenge component of the intervention had significantly reduced consumption. Taken together, findings from these three studies suggest that expectancy challenge procedures may decrease alcohol consumption among males. However, to evaluate this prevention approach more fully, larger-scale studies with longer follow-up periods are needed to replicate these findings in both men and women.

Larimer and Cronce (2002) reviewed three other studies that evaluated self-monitoring or self-assessment of alcohol use (Garvin *et al.*, 1990; Cronin, 1996; Miller, 1999). All three studies indicated significant positive effects of this strategy on either drinking levels, harms, or both. Cronin (1996) compared consumption rates and problems in students randomly assigned to a self-monitoring or control group. The intervention group was required to complete a diary anticipating alcohol consumption and problems for the upcoming semester break. Students who completed the diary reported significantly fewer negative consequences at the end of the semester break than did students in the control group. In another study by Garvin *et al.* (1990), students asked to record their daily alcohol consumption over a period of 7 weeks reported lower consumption at the 5-month follow-up than students in either an alcohol-education or assessment-only control group. Finally, Miller (1999) compared college students who participated in three computerized assessments of their drinking with students who also participated in a two-session peer-delivered alcohol skills training program, or in a two-session computerized peer-facilitated interactive group, or who were randomly allocated to a control group. At the 6-month follow-up, students in all three intervention groups reported decreases in drinking and consequences compared with students in the control group. Larimer and Cronce therefore concluded that current research provides support for the role of self-monitoring/assessment in promoting drinking change.

Taken together, several cognitive behavioral interventions, including specific, global and multi-component skills training, have demonstrated positive changes in drinking and related consequences. Larimer and Cronce (2002) noted that research designs evaluating these interventions have generally been more rigorous that those studies evaluating educational programs, but pointed out that methodological limitations were still evident in this research, primarily due to small sample sizes and relatively high attrition rates among some studies. In general, however, they concluded that that current research generally supports the efficacy of cognitive behavioral approaches.

Brief Motivational Enhancement Programs

Motivational enhancement programs generally aim to assist drinkers, particularly individuals who have suffered drinking-related harms and consequences, by increasing motivation to change their drinking patterns. These programs are generally brief (one or two sessions), individual or small-group focused, and incorporate alcohol information, skills training and feedback to enhance motivation to change. The feedback component of these interventions is usually derived from personalized assessment of individual drinking patterns and related consequences.

Larimer and Cronce (2002) reviewed eight motivational enhancement studies, of which four were conducted with college students (Baer *et al.*, 1992; Marlatt *et al.*, 1998; Borsari and Carey, 2000; Larimer *et al.*, 2001), three with college-age samples in mental health/medical settings (Dimeff, 1997; Aubrey, 1998; Monti *et al.*, 1999), and one with older high school students (D'Amico and Fromme, 2000). Each of these interventions demonstrated significant effects on drinking behavior, consequences, or both. For example, Baer *et al.* (1992) compared three formats of alcohol risk-reduction programming in heavy drinkers, and found that a single session of brief advice was comparable with a six-session discussion group and a six-session self-help manual in reducing alcohol use. Marlatt *et al.* (1998) extended these findings in a sample of 348 high-risk college students randomly assigned to a brief 45-minute personalized motivational feedback session or a control condition. Feedback incorporated discussion of personal drinking patterns and negative consequences, normative re-education including comparison of personal drinking patterns with campus norms, and advice/information regarding drinking-reduction techniques. Results indicated that participants in the intervention group reduced their alcohol consumption and negative consequences significantly, and maintained these reductions at the 2-year follow-up. These findings were replicated by Larimer and colleagues (2001) in a sample of 296 college students randomly assigned to a brief individual feedback program or a control condition. At 12 months after treatment, college students who had received the intervention reported a decrease in consumption from 15.5 to 12 standard drinks per week compared with an increase in the control group from 14.5 to 17 drinks per week. In another study, D'Amico and Fromme (2000) randomly assigned 300 high school students to risk skills training and personalized motivational feedback, a brief school-based alcohol intervention, or a control group. Post-treatment results indicated that participants in the risk skills training group reported significant reductions in the frequency of heavy drinking, drink driving, riding with an intoxicated driver, and drug use.

Research on brief motivational enhancement approaches has generally been methodologically rigorous, and while longer-term follow-up of these interventions is warranted, Larimer and Cronce (2002) concluded that there is strong support for the efficacy of brief, personalized motivational enhancement techniques, delivered individually or in combination with skills training information in small groups. Interestingly, some studies suggest that motivational enhancement and feedback might also be communicated effectively through other means, including an interactive computer program (see, for example, Dimeff, 1997) and personalized feedback delivered via post (see, for example, Walters, 2000). However, Larimer and Cronce pointed out that these studies were methodologically weaker than the face-to-face intervention studies due to small and poorly described samples and relatively short-term follow-ups.

Summary of Effective Interventions Among College Students

In their recent report on college drinking, the NIAAA Task Force (2002) identified the following interventions as having the best evidence for application with college students:

- a combination of cognitive behavioral skills with norm clarification and motivational enhancement interventions
- challenging alcohol expectancies
- brief motivational enhancement interventions.

The Task Force noted that these strategies are most effective when targeted toward individual problems, including at-risk or alcohol-dependent students, but that their effectiveness has not been adequately evaluated for broader campus-wide dissemination in the student population as a whole.

Campus-wide Strategies for the Prevention of Drinking

To target young adults in the student population as a whole, a range of prevention strategies was identified by the Task Force (NIAAA, 2002). These strategies complement individual-level interventions by focusing on legal, social, economic and physical environmental factors that can influence alcohol consumption and related harms. These strategies focus on influencing youth consumption and harms via two main mechanisms: (i) restricting the availability of alcohol, and (ii) creating conditions that support these restrictions. Six strategies were identified as effective for targeting alcohol use and problems among young people in college and community settings:

1. Increased enforcement of minimum drinking age laws
2. Implementation, increased publicity and enforcement of other laws to reduce alcohol-impaired driving
3. Restrictions on alcohol retail outlet density
4. Increased price and excise taxes on alcohol beverages
5. Responsible service beverage policies in social and commercial settings
6. The formation of a campus/community coalition to effectively implement strategies.

Nine other strategies were identified as promising by the Task Force. These strategies have both conceptual and theoretical appeal, but their effectiveness has not yet been comprehensively evaluated or replicated using rigorous evaluation designs. These strategies include:

1. Adopting campus-based policies to reduce high-risk use (e.g., reinforcing Friday classes and exams, eliminating keg parties, establishing alcohol-free activities and dormitories, controlling or reducing alcohol at sports events, and banning alcohol on campus – including faculty and alumni events)
2. Increasing enforcement at campus-based events that promote excessive drinking
3. Increasing publicity about enforcement of under-age drinking laws/eliminating "mixed" messages
4. Consistently enforcing campus disciplinary actions associated with policy violations
5. Conducting marketing campaigns to correct student misperceptions about alcohol use on campus
6. Provision of "safe rides" programs (i.e., providing students with access to alternative transportation to prevent alcohol-impaired driving)
7. Regulation of happy hours and sales
8. Enhancing awareness of personal liability
9. Informing new students and parents about alcohol policies and penalties.

INTERVENTIONS FOR SPECIAL AND HIGH-RISK POPULATIONS

Despite the emergence of comprehensive, multi-component approaches to alcohol prevention, school- and college-based interventions are not usually tailored for implementation in special or high-risk populations, such as individuals from ethnic or cultural minorities and children with a parental history of AUD. These groups require specially focused attention, as they are often exposed to unique factors (such as social, historical or cultural factors) that place them at increased risk for alcohol abuse and consequences). To date, these groups have been significantly neglected in past studies or programs (Sussman, 2006). The following section provides an overview of research that has been conducted on the prevention of alcohol use and misuse in a number of special or high-risk populations. For further information, readers are referred to recent reviews of these areas (e.g., Sussman, 2006; Zucker and Wong, 2006).

Gender

As described earlier in this chapter, males are more likely to initiate drinking early and to report alcohol misuse and related harms than females. Alcohol abuse and dependence are also more prevalent among males than in females. Interestingly, some research has indicated that males have poorer refusal skills, which are associated with an increased risk for alcohol use (Scheier *et al.*, 1999), whereas girls appear more likely to be pressured into drinking by their peers than boys (Bevitt-Mills, 2001). Despite these differences, most preventative interventions and strategies are delivered cross-gender, and evaluations of their effectiveness do not typically include separate assessments of outcome by gender. Indeed, gender is often not discussed at all, or it is only included as an adjustment-variable in program evaluations. Of those studies that have directly examined gender effects, some have revealed no difference in outcomes between males and females (see, for example, Sussman *et al.*, 2002b; Tobler *et al.*, 2000), whereas others, such as the CLIMATE schools intervention, identified differential outcomes as a function of gender (Vogl *et al.*, 2006). It is also notable that some interventions have only been delivered to either males or females (e.g., Darkes and Goldman, 1998), limiting the generalizability of these strategies to both genders. Given the documented gender differences between males and females in patterns of drinking initiation, consumption, problems, and related skills, it would be valuable for future studies to evaluate more rigorously the relationship between gender and intervention outcomes. This would provide justification for the cross-gender application and/or gender-based tailoring of specific intervention strategies, which may in turn improve program outcomes.

Ethnic and Indigenous Groups

Prevalence data indicate that youth in some ethnic and indigenous minority groups are at greater risk for alcohol misuse and AUD, yet these groups are under-represented in alcohol prevention research. At present, the most comprehensive data available on ethnic/indigenous minorities are derived from minorities based in the United States, including Native Americans, Hispanics and African-Americans. At least three comprehensive reviews of alcohol prevention in Native Americans have been written (May and Moran, 1995; Moran and Reaman, 2002; Parker-Langley, 2002). Across these three reviews 26 different studies were evaluated, with effects on alcohol use reported in 13 (Sussman, 2006). In his recent review, Sussman used "study" as a single, exchangeable unit, to explore intervention effects on alcohol use at 1-year follow-up. He reviewed seven interventions which included Native American youth. Of these programs, five reported behavioral data, all of which showed preventive effects.

Reviews of alcohol prevention in Native American groups have highlighted the importance of culturally derived interventions to enhance prevention efforts (Sussman, 2006). Cultural adaptation may involve adapting interventions to include traditional songs, ceremonies, dances and crafts and the involvement of community leaders and elders in prevention and decision-making. An intervention by Schinke and colleagues (2000) highlights the potential value of culturally focused programs. The study examined 1400 Native American youth from rural schools in the third to fifth grades (average age 10 years) and included a 3.5-year follow-up. The study used an experimental design (standard care, school based or school based plus community involvement). The skill condition included 15 weekly sessions on Native American legends, stories and values, and the community condition involved the school-based program plus community awareness efforts. Core learning activities were derived from LST, and included culturally adapted skills for problem-solving, coping, interpersonal communication and refusal assertion. Both the intervention conditions were effective, with participants in each condition reporting less drinking at follow-up than participants in the standard care condition (24% versus 30% drinking). It is noteworthy that in the Cochrane review of alcohol misuse prevention programs, Foxcroft and colleagues (2003) concluded that for every 17 individuals who received this intervention, 3.5 years later there would be one fewer person reporting greater than four drinks consumed in the last week. This program was one of only two prevention interventions judged by the review to show promise as an effective intervention for alcohol misuse over the longer-term.

Similar to Native Americans, African-American and Hispanic minorities have been demonstrated to suffer significant alcohol-related consequences (see, for example, Henderson *et al.*, 2002; Sussman *et al.*, 2002a). A number of prevention interventions have been evaluated in these minorities. In Sussman's (2006) review, 12 of 15 interventions among African-Americans reported behavioral data, of which 58 percent found preventive effects. Similarly, among Hispanic youth, 12 of 14 programs reported behavioral data. Of these 12 programs, 58 percent also found preventive effects. Most of the interventions reviewed comprised varying degrees of cultural adaptation and/or were delivered to multiple ethnic/indigenous groups. For example, Botvin and colleagues (1995b) developed a culturally tailored prevention program for Latino (37%) and African-American youth (49%) that was evaluated in 757 students (average age 12.7 years). The program used peer facilitators to assist adult leaders, and incorporated skills training through culturally relevant stories of myths, minority heros and a rap video. The program was compared with standard LST and an eight-session information-only control condition. Youth in the culturally sensitive intervention reported less drinking at the 2-year follow-up than youths in the LST condition, although both these groups reported less drinking and drunkenness than youth in the control condition. Botvin and colleagues (2001) followed this study with the development of a 25-session culturally-adapted LST program. The intervention was assessed in a sample of 3041 inner-city seventh-grade students (57%

African-American, 24% Latino, 8% Asian and 10% White or other background). The curriculum was adapted to include culturally relevant illustrations, language and role plays. The program was found to prevent binge drinking at the 2-year follow-up, with approximately 5.2 percent of controls compared with 2.2 percent of intervention youth reporting binge drinking.

Taken together, the findings indicate that approximately 60 percent of alcohol prevention programs demonstrate effects on drinking in ethnic minority groups in the United States, although there is evidence of somewhat higher preventive efficacy among Native Americans. Sussman (2006) concluded that programs which include culturally relevant education along with life-skills material appear to be particularly promising. However, he noted a number of significant limitations, including a paucity of rigorous research on alcohol prevention programs in both mixed and mono-ethnic group settings. The review also drew attention to the need to isolate effective components of prevention programs when applied to minority groups, particularly the effectiveness of specific cultural modifications versus generic program components. Finally, as the majority of research on prevention in minorities has focused on young adolescents, Sussman argued that more work is required with pre-adolescent youth, with longer-term follow-up, and with older adolescents and young adults.

Region

There is evidence that youth living in rural or other low population density areas are at greater risk for alcohol-related problems. To date, no tailored interventions for alcohol use prevention in rural populations have been identified; however, a number of generic prevention interventions have been evaluated in these communities (D'Onofrio, 1997; Sussman, 2006). Examples of generic programs that have been shown to have positive outcomes on drinking behavior in rural youth include the SFP and LST programs (Spoth *et al.*, 2002) and Project Northland (Perry *et al.*, 2002). Sussman identified a total of 13 programs that were conducted at least in part in rural regions. Of the 12 programs that reported behavioral outcomes, 58 percent showed preventive effects on alcohol use. While these programs appear to show some positive effects, it has not been tested whether these programs could be tailored to improve alcohol-related outcomes among youth living in rural or other low population density areas.

Children of Parents Suffering an AUD

Children of parents who suffer an AUD are at a significantly increased risk for early-onset drinking and the development of alcohol misuse and abuse. While a subset of these children move through childhood relatively trouble free, many develop externalizing and internalizing symptoms in early childhood (Sher, 1994). As described earlier in this chapter, parallel findings from community and clinical studies show that early externalizing and internalizing symptoms are strongly related to the later development of alcohol misuse (Jessor and Jessor, 1977; Sher, 1997; Harter, 2000). In a recent review of this arena, Zucker and

Wong (2006) showed that these prodromal symptoms to AUD can be identified in some children as early 3–5 years of age, providing identifiable targets for prevention programming in early childhood. Zucker and Wong argue that the etiologic data pertaining to externalizing and internalizing symptoms indicate a fairly stable continuity of risk over the course of childhood and adolescence. They therefore suggest that change in these risk behaviors achieved through prevention efforts should theoretically lead to change in alcohol-related behavior.

Despite well-documented risk pathways from externalizing/internalizing symptoms to later alcohol misuse, particularly among children with a parental history of AUD, there is a somewhat surprising lack of selective prevention efforts targeted toward early intervention in these trajectories. In their review of the literature, Zucker and Wong (2006) were only able to identify two intervention programs focusing on children with a parental history of AUD that had been subjected to rigorous evaluation through randomized clinical trial. The first used a population-based recruitment protocol to recruit families with current paternal AUD (Nye *et al.*, 1999). The intervention involved a 10-month parent training and marital problem-solving protocol, with a child focus on reducing conduct problems and increasing pro-social behavior. At the 6-month follow-up, positive changes in parenting style and child behavior were reported; however, later evaluation of child drinking was not conducted. The second intervention identified was a 14-session version of the SFP implemented among school-age children with an alcohol-abusing parent. Compared with the minimum attention control group, the SFP group produced significant improvements in child externalizing behavior (Maguin *et al.*, 1994) and family functioning (Safyer *et al.*, 2003). The longer-term follow-up will examine program effects on the delay of alcohol initiation and reduction in alcohol problems in the children.

Even fewer studies have evaluated prevention programs tailored specifically for college students with a parental family history of AUD. Only one study was identified (Roush and DeBlassie, 1989), which compared two informational/educational approaches and found no effect of either intervention on behavior. Interestingly, the responses of students with a parental history of AUD to interventions utilized in the general college population appear comparable to those of students without a family history of AUD. For example, Marlatt *et al.* (1998) reported similar responses to a brief motivational interview among high-risk college student drinkers, regardless of a student's family history of AUD. In addition, studies by Sammon *et al.* (1991) and Jack (1989) both indicated a trend toward students with parental history of AUD responding more positively to informational/values clarification/risk-reduction interventions than did students without a family history of AUD. However, the latter two studies were limited due to small sample sizes and non-random assignment of participants to the intervention condition.

Despite the elevated risk for alcohol use and abuse among children with a parental family history of AUD, there is a paucity of rigorous prevention research in this group. Parallel data from both clinical and community studies support the developmental view that prevention efforts which commence in the early childhood years may be more efficacious; however, important questions need to be addressed regarding the appropriate timing (i.e., early childhood versus elementary school) and dosing of interventions (i.e., multiple- or single-dose interventions; Zucker and Wong, 2006). Zucker and Wong also argue that, as externalizing and internalizing symptoms frequently co-occur with a range of other risks linked to later AUD (e.g., family conflict and violence, economic difficulties, parental psychiatric co-morbidity, trouble with the law, deviant peer friendships and low academic achievement), interventions that take a multi-component approach are more likely to be efficacious in this group, as well as with other high-risk children or adolescents (without a parental family history of AUD) who exhibit these prodromal symptoms.

SUMMARY

Our review has indicated that a high number of adolescents have had some experience with alcohol. The prevalence of alcohol use and AUD, however, varies across studies; this could be because of the following factors:

1. Differences in law regarding purchased and consumption of alcoholic beverages across countries. Furthermore, regulations that govern to whom alcohol may be sold, where and how they are sold may also have an influence on the rates of substance use.
2. Laws regarding advertising of alcoholic beverages also differ across countries, such as total bans on advertising in some countries, while in other countries there are regulations which govern the content of advertisement.
3. Cultural views about the use of alcohol may determine the accessibility and acceptance of its use. Furthermore, people in different countries differ in their drinking patterns.

All these factors, together with methodological differences such as the sampling procedure and assessment instruments, make it difficult to compare findings across studies.

Although it is illegal to sell alcoholic beverages to adolescents under a certain age, under-aged adolescents can buy alcohol without much difficulty. As shown by Bieleman *et al.* (2002), 73 percent of the 14- to 15-year-olds successfully bought strong alcoholic beverages in a liquor store. Among the 16- to 17-year olds, 98 percent obtained strong alcoholic beverages in restaurants, and 85 percent successfully bought such beverages from liquor stores. Therefore, a much stronger effort must be made to enforce the law on selling alcoholic beverages to the under-aged.

Considerable progress has been made over the last decade in the identification and evaluation of prevention and intervention strategies that aim to reduce alcohol use and misuse in young people. While many programs have had limited or no effect on drinking or drinking problems in the longer-term, several multi-component and novel approaches have demonstrated efficacy among elementary and high school students. College programs that comprise cognitive skills training, brief motivational enhancement and/or alcohol expectancy challenges have also demonstrated efficacy, particularly among high-risk and problem drinkers, and a number of campus-wide prevention strategies would appear to be promising for universal implementation in the student population as a whole. Comparatively few studies have been conducted on the prevention of youth alcohol use and misuse in special and high-risk groups, yet the literature does provide some direction for addressing these gaps – including ways in which generic programs and strategies may be adapted for implementation in these groups. Despite these promising developments, many interventions have not yet been subject to the rigorous level of evaluation required to ascertain efficacy. Furthermore, only few studies have completed follow-up over a sufficient period to demonstrate that short-term changes in alcohol use actually translate into subsequent reductions in harmful alcohol use and consequences. Given the high prevalence of youth drinking problems and harms in many communities worldwide, there is a strong need for improvements in research methodology and evaluations to build on the promising work conducted to date on interventions for youth alcohol use and misuse.

REFERENCES

Abel, E. (1998). *Fetal Alcohol Abuse Syndrome*. New York, NY: Plenum Press.

Adams, G., Cantwell, A.M. and Matheis, S. (2002). Substance use and adolescence. In: C.A. Essau (ed.), *Substance Abuse and Dependence in Adolescence*. London: Brunner-Routledge, pp. 1–20.

Australian Institute of Health and Welfare (2005). *2004 National Drug Strategy Household Survey*. Canberra: Australian Institute of Health and Welfare. Available at: http://www.aihw.gov.au/publications/phe/ndshs04/ndshs04.pdf.

Alati, R., Najman, J.M., Kinner, S.A. *et al.* (2005). Early predictors of adult drinking: a birth cohort study. *American Journal of Epidemiology*, 162, 1098–1107.

American Academy of Pediatrics (1995). Alcohol use and abuse: a pediatric concern. *American Academy of Pediatrics*, 95, 439–442.

American Psychiatric Association (1994). *Diagnostic and Statistical Manual of Mental Disorders*, 4th edn (DSM-IV). Washington, DC: American Psychiatric Association.

Andrews, J.A., Tildesley, E., Hops, H. *et al.* (2003). Elementary school age children's future intentions and use of substances. *Journal of Clinical Child and Adolescent Psychology*, 32(4), 556–567.

Anthony, J.C. and Petronis, K.R. (1995). Early-onset drug use and risk of later drug problems. *Drug and Alcohol Dependence*, 40, 9–15.

Armsden, G.C. and Greenberg, M.T. (1987). The Inventory of Parent and Peer Attachment: individual differences and their relationship to psychological well-being in adolescence. *Journal of Youth and Adolescence*, 16, 427–454.

Armstrong, T.D. and Costello, E.J. (2002). Community studies on adolescent substance use abuse or dependence and psychiatric comorbidity. *Journal of Consulting and Clinical Psychology*, 70, 1224–1239.

Ary, D.V., Duncan, T.E., Biglan, A. *et al.* (1999a). Development of adolescent problem behavior. *Journal of Abnormal Child Psychology*, 27, 141–150.

Ary, D.V., Duncan, T.E., Duncan, S.C. and Hops, H. (1999b). Adolescent problem behavior: the influence of parents and peers. *Behavior Research and Therapy*, 37, 217–230.

Aubrey, L.L. (1998). "Motivational interviewing with adolescents presenting for outpatient substance abuse treatment." Unpublished doctoral dissertation, University of New Mexico, Albuquerque.

Australian Bureau of Statistics (ABS). (2006). *Alcohol Consumption in Australia: A Snapshot, 2004–05* (cat. no. 4832.0.55.001). Canberra: ABS.

Baer, J., Marlatt, G.A., Kivlahan, D.R. *et al.* (1992). An experimental test of three methods of alcohol risk reduction with young adults. *Journal of Consulting and Clinical Psychology*, 60, 974–979.

Baer, J.S., Sampson, P.D., Barr, H.M. *et al.* (2003). A 21-year longitudinal analysis of the effects of prenatal alcohol exposure on young adult drinking. *Archives of General Psychiatry*, 60, 377–385.

Barnes, G.M. (1990). Impact of the family on adolescent drinking patterns. In: R.L. Collins, K.E. Leonard and J.S. Searles (eds), *Alcohol and the Family: Research and Clinical Perspectives*. New York, NY: Guilford Press, pp. 137–161.

Barnes, G.M. and Farrell, M.P. (1992). Parental support and control as predictors of adolescent drinking, delinquency, and related problem behaviors. *Journal of Marriage and the Family*, 54, 763–776.

Barnes, G.M., Farrell, M.P. and Windle, M. (1987). Parent–adolescent interactions in the development of alcohol abuse and other deviant behaviors. *Family Perspective*, 21, 321–335.

Barnes, G.M., Reifman, A.S., Farrell, M.P. *et al.* (1994). Longitudinal effects of parenting on alcohol misuse among adolescents. *Alcoholism: Clinical and Experimental Research*, 18, 507.

Barnes, G.M., Reifman, A.S., Farrell, M.P. and Dintcheff, B. A. (2000). The effects of parenting on the development of adolescent alcohol misuse: a six-wave latent growth model. *Journal of Marriage and the Family*, 62, 175–186.

Barnett, L.A., Far, J.M., Mauss, A.L. and Miller, J.A. (1996). Changing perceptions of peer norms as a drinking reduction program for college students. *Journal of Alcohol and Drug Education*, 41(2), 39–62.

Barr, H.M. and Streissguth, A.P. (2001). Identifying maternal self-reported alcohol use associated with fetal alcohol spectrum disorders. *Alcoholism: Clinical and Experimental Research*, 25(2), 283–287.

Barrera, M. Jr and Li, S.A. (1996). The relation of family support to adolescents' psychological distress and behavior problems. In: G.R. Pierce, B.R. Sarason and I.G. Sarason (eds), *Handbook of Social Support and the Family*. New York, NY: Plenum Press, pp. 313–343.

Beauvais, F. (1998). American Indians and alcohol. *Alcohol Research and Health*, 22, 253–259.

Bellis, M.A., Hughes, K., Morleo, M. *et al.* (2006). *Patterns of Risky Alcohol Consumption in North West Teenagers*. Liverpool, Merseyside: Centre for Public Health, Liverpool John Moores University.

Bevitt-Mills, J. (2001). "Gender Differences in Prevention Strategies Targeted to Female Adolescents." Paper presented at the 12th Annual Meeting of the APHA, Atlanta, Georgia.

Beyers, J.M., Toumbourou, J.W., Catalano, R.F. *et al.* (2004). A cross-national comparison of risk and protective factors for adolescent substance use: the United States and Australia. *Journal of Adolescent Health*, 35(1), 3–16.

Bieleman, B., Jetzes, M. and Kruize, F. (2002). *Alcoholverstrekking aan Jongeren: Naleving Leeftijdsgrenzen 16 en 18 Jaar uit de Dranken Horecawet: Metingen 1999 en 2001* {Alcohol Supply to Youths: Observance of Age Restrictions 16 and 18 Years from the Alcohol and Catering Law: Measures 1999 and 2001}. Rotterdam: Intraval.

Bjarnason, T., Andersson, B., Choquet, M. *et al.* (2003). Alcohol culture, family structure and adolescent alcohol use: multilevel modeling of frequency of heavy drinking among 15- to 16-year-old students in 11 European countries. *Journal of Studies on Alcohol*, 64, 200–208.

Bond, L., Thomas, L., Toumbourou, J. *et al.* (2000). *Improving the Lives of Young Victorians in our Community: A Survey of Risk and Protective Factors*. Melbourne: Centre for Adolescent Health.

Bonomo, Y., Coffey, C., Wolfe, R. *et al.* (2001). Adverse outcomes of alcohol use in adolescents. *Addiction*, 96, 1485–1496.

Borsari, B. and Carey, K.B. (2000). Effects of a brief motivational intervention with college student drinkers. *Journal of Consulting and Clinical Psychology*, 68, 728–733.

Botvin, G.J., Baker, E., Dusenbury, L. *et al.* (1990). Preventing adolescent drug abuse through a multimodal cognitive-behavioral approach: results of a 3-year study. *Journal of Consulting and Clinical Psychology*, 58, 437–466.

Botvin, G. J., Baker, E., Dusenbury, L. *et al.* (1995a). Long-term follow-up results of a randomized drug abuse prevention trial in a white middle-class population. *Journal of the American Medical Association*, 273, 1106–1112.

Botvin, G.J., Schinke, S.P., Epstein, J.A. *et al.* (1995b). Effectiveness of culturally focused and generic skills training approaches to alcohol and drug abuse prevention among minority adolescents: two-year follow-up results. *Psychology of Addictive Behaviors* 9, 183–194.

Botvin, G.J., Griffin, K.W., Diaz, T. and Ifill-Williams, M. (2001). Preventing binge drinking during adolescence: one- and two-year follow-up of a school-based preventive intervention. *Psychology of Addictive Behaviors*, 15, 360–365.

Bray, J.H., Adams, G.J., Getz, J.G. and Baer, P.E. (2001). Developmental, family, and ethnic Influences on adolescent alcohol usage: a growth curve approach. *Journal of Family Psychology*, 15, 301–314.

Brody, G.H. and Ge, X. (2001). Linking parenting processes and self-regulation to psychological functioning and alcohol use during early adolescence. *Journal of Family Psychology*, 15, 82–94.

Bukstein, O.G. (2000). Disruptive behavior disorders and substance use disorders in adolescents. *Journal of Psychoactive Drugs*, 32, 67–70.

Caetano, R., Clark, C.L. and Tam, T. (1998). Alcohol consumption among racial/ethnic minorities: theory and research. *Alcohol Research and Health*, 22, 233–241.

Caspi, A., Begg, D. and Dickson, N. (1997). Personality differences predict health-risk behaviors in young adulthood: evidence from a longitudinal study. *Journal of Personality and Social Psychology*, 73, 1052–1063.

Champion, H., Foley, K., Durant, R. *et al.* (2004). Adolescent sexual victimization, use of alcohol and other substances, and other health risk behaviors. *Journal of Adolescent Health*, 35, 321–328.

Chassin, L., Pitts, S.C., DeLucia, C. and Todd, M. (1999). A longitudinal study of children of alcoholics: predicting young adolescent substance use disorders, anxiety and depression. *Journal of Abnormal Psychology*, 108, 106–199.

Chassin, L., Carle, A.C., Nissim-Sabat, D. and Kumpfer, K.L. (2004). Fostering resilience in children of alcoholic parents. In: K.I. Maton, C.J. Schellenbach, B.J. Leadbeater and A.L. Solarz (eds), *Investing in Children, Families, and Communities: Strengths-based Research and Policy*. Washington, DC: American Psychological Association, pp. 137–155.

Clark, D.B. and Jacobs, R.G. (1992). Anxiety disorders and alcoholism in adolescents. A preliminary report. *Alcoholism: Clinical and Experimental Research*, 16, 371.

Clark, D.B., Bukstein, O.G., Smith, M.G. *et al.* (1995). Identifying anxiety disorders in adolescents hospitalized for alcohol abuse or dependence. *Psychiatric Services*, 46, 618–620.

Clark, E., Lutke, J., Minnes, P. and Ouellette-Kuntz, H. (2004). Secondary disabilities among adults with fetal alcohol spectrum disorder in British Colombia. *Journal of Fetal Alcohol Syndrome International*, 2, 1–12.

Colder, C.R. and Chassin, L. (1999). The psychosocial characteristics of alcohol users versus problem users: data from a study of adolescents at risk. *Development and Psychopathology*, 11, 321–348.

Cooper, M.L. (2002). Alcohol use and risky sexual behavior among college students and youth: evaluating the evidence. *Journal of Studies in Alcohol*, Suppl. No. 14, 101–117.

Cronin, C. (1996). Harm reduction for alcohol-use-related problems among college students. *Substance Use and Misuse*, 31, 2029–2037.

Curran, P.J., Stice, E. and Chassin, L. (1997). The relation between adolescent and peer alcohol use: a longitudinal random coefficients model. *Journal of Consulting and Clinical Psychology*, 65, 130–140.

D'Amico, E. and Fromme, K. (2000). Implementation of the risk skills training program: a brief intervention targeting adolescent participation in risk behaviors. *Cognitive and Behavioral Practice*, 7, 101–117.

D'Onofrio, C.N. (1997). The prevention of alcohol use by rural youth. In: *Rural Substance Abuse: State of Knowledge and Issues*. Rockville: MD: NIDA Research Monograph, No. 168.

Darkes, J. and Goldman, M. S. (1993). Expectancy challenge and drinking reduction: experimental evidence for a mediational process. *Journal of Consulting and Clinical Psychology*, 61, 344–353.

Darkes, J. and Goldman, M. S. (1998). Expectancy challenge and drinking reduction: process and structure in the alcohol expectancy network. *Experimental Clinical Psychopharmacology*, 6, 64–76.

De Zwart, W.M., Monshouwer, K. and Smit, F. (2000). Jeugd en Riskant Gedrag. Kerngegevens 1999. Roken, Drinken, Drugsgebruik en Gokken onder Scholieren vanaf Tien Jaar {Youth and Risky Behavior. Key Data 1999. Smoking, Drinking, Drug Use, and Gambling among Scholars Aged Ten Years and Older}. Utrecht: Trimbos-instituut.

Dimeff, L.A. (1997). "Brief intervention for heavy and hazardous college drinkers in a student primary health care setting." Unpublished doctoral dissertation, University of Washington, Seattle.

Dishion, T.J. and McMahon, R.J. (1998). Parental monitoring and the prevention of child and adolescent problem behavior: a conceptual and empirical formulation. *Clinical Child and Family Psychology Review*, 1, 61–75.

Dishion, T.J., Capaldi, D.M. and Yoerger, K. (1999). Middle childhood antecedents to progressions in male adolescent substance use: an ecological analysis of risk and protection. *Journal of Adolescent Research*, 14, 175–205.

Duncan, S.C., Duncan, T. E., Biglan, A. and Ary, D. (1998). Contributions of the social context to the development of adolescent substance use: a multivariate latent growth modeling approach. *Drug and Alcohol Dependence*, 50, 57–71.

Essau, C.A., Karpinski, N.A., Petermann, F. and Conradt, J. (1998). Häufigkeit und Komorbidität von Störungen durch Substanzkonsum. *Zeitschrift Kindheit und Entwicklung*, 7, 199–207.

Essau, C.A., Barrett, P. and Pasquali, K. (2002). Concluding remarks. In: C.A. Essau (ed.), *Substance Abuse and Dependence in Adolescence*. London: Brunner-Routledge, pp. 63–85.

Feehan, M., McGee, R., Nada-Raja, S. and Williams, S.M. (1994). DSM-III-R disorders in New Zealand 18-year-olds. *Australian and New Zealand Journal of Psychiatry*, 28, 87–99.

Famy, C., Streissguth, A.P. and Unis, A.S. (1998). Mental illness in adults with fetal alcohol syndrome or fetal alcohol effects. *American Journal of Psychiatry*, 155, 552–554.

Fergusson, D.M. and Horwood, L.J. (1996). The role of adolescent peer affiliations in the continuity between childhood behavioral adjustment and juvenile offending. *Journal of Abnormal Child Psychology*, 24, 205–221.

Fergusson, D.M. and Horwood, L.J. (1999). Prospective childhood predictors of deviant peer affiliations in adolescence. *Journal of Child Psychology and Psychiatry*, 40, 581–592.

Fergusson, D.M., Horwood, L.J. and Lynskey, M.T. (1993). Prevalence and comorbidity of DSM-III-R diagnoses in a birth cohort of 15 year olds. *Journal of the American Academy of Child and Adolescent Psychiatry*, 32, 1127–1134.

Fergusson, D.M., Lynskey, M. and Horwood, L.J. (1994). Childhood exposure to alcohol and adolescent drinking patterns. *Addiction*, 89, 1007–1016.

Fergusson, D.M., Horwood, L.J. and Lynskey, M.T. (1995). The prevalence and risk factors associated with abusive or hazardous alcohol consumption in 16-year-olds. *Addiction*, 90, 935–946.

Foxcroft, D.R. and Lowe, G. (1991). Adolescent drinking behavior and family socialization factors: a meta-analysis. *Journal of Adolescence*, 14, 255–273.

Foxcroft, D.R. and Lowe, G. (1997). Adolescents' alcohol use and misuse: the socializing influence of perceived family life. *Drugs: Education, Prevention and Policy*, 4, 215–229.

Foxcroft, D.R., Ireland, D., Lister-Sharp, D.J. *et al.* (2003). Longer-term primary prevention for alcohol misuse in young people: a systemic review. *Addiction*, 98, 397–411.

Galanter, M. (ed.). (2006). *Alcohol Problems in Adolescents and Young Adults: Epidemiology, Neurobiology, Prevention and Treatment.* New York, NY: Springer Science and Business Media.

Garvin, R.B., Alcorn, J.D. and Faulkner, K.K. (1990). Behavioral strategies for alcohol abuse prevention with high-risk college males. *Journal of Alcohol and Drug Education*, 36, 23–34.

Giaconia, R.M., Reinherz, H.Z., Silverman, A.B. *et al.* (1994). Ages of onset of psychiatric disorders in a community population of older adolescents. *Journal of the American Academy of Child and Adolescent Psychiatry*, 33, 706–717.

Grant, B.F. and Dawson, D.A. (1997). Age at onset of alcohol use and its association with DSM-IV alcohol abuse and dependence: results from the National Longitudinal Alcohol Epidemiologic Survey. *Journal of Substance Abuse*, 9, 103–110.

Grant, B.F., Stinson, F.S. and Harford, T.C. (2001). Age at onset of alcohol use and DSM-IV alcohol abuse and dependence: a 12-year follow-up. *Journal of Substance Abuse*, 13, 493–504.

Guo, J., Hawkins, J.D. and Hill, K.G. (2001). Childhood and adolescent predictors of alcohol abuse and dependence in young adulthood. *Journal of Studies on Alcohol*, 62, 754–762.

Hajema, K.J. and Knibbe, R.A. (1998). Changes in social roles as predictors of changes in drinking behavior. *Addiction*, 93, 1717–1727.

Harter, S.L. (2000). Psychosocial adjustment of adult children of alcoholics: A review of the recent empirical literature. *Clinical Psychology Review*, 20, 311–337.

Hawkins, J.D., Catalano, P. and Miller, J.Y. (1992). Risk and protective factors for alcohol and other drug problems in adolescence and early adulthood: implications for substance abuse prevention. *Psychological Bulletin*, 112, 64–105.

Hayes, L., Smart, D., Toumbourou, J.W. and Sanson, A. (2004). *Parenting Influences on Adolescent Alcohol Use*. Research Report No. 10. Melbourne: Australian Institute of Family Studies – Commonwealth of Australia.

Helzer, J.E. and Burnam, A. (1991). Epidemiology of alcohol addiction: United States. In: N.S. Miller (ed.), *Comprehensive Handbook of Drug and Alcohol Addiction*. New York, NY: Marcel Dekker Inc., pp. 9–38.

Henderson, G., Ma, G.X. and Shive, S.E. (2002). African-American substance users and abusers. In G.X. Ma and G. Henderson (eds), *Ethnicity and Substance Abuse: Prevention and Intervention*. Springfield, IL: Charles, C. Thomas.

Hill, E.M., Ross, L.T., Mudd, S.A. and Blow, F.C. (1997). Adulthood functioning: the joint effects of parental alcoholism, gender and childhood socio-economic stress. *Addiction*, 92, 583–596.

Holly, A., Türk, D., Nelson, B. *et al.* (1997). Prävalenz von Alkoholkonsum, Alkoholmissbrauch und -abhängigkeit bei Jugendlichen und jungen Erwachsenen. *Zeitschrift für Klinische Psychologie*, 26, 171–178.

Hovens, J.G., Cantwell, D.P. and Kiriakos, R. (1994). Psychiatric comorbidity in hospitalised adolescent substance misusers. *Journal of the American Academy of Child and Adolescence Psychiatry*, 33, 476–483.

Ilomäki, R., Hakko, H., Timonen, M. *et al.* (2004). Temporal relationship between the age of onset of phobic disorders and development of substance dependence in adolescent psychiatric patients. *Drug and Alcohol Dependence*, 75, 327–330.

Jack, L.W. (1989). The educational impact of a course about addiction. *Journal of Nursing and Education*, 28, 22–28.

Jackson, C. (2002). Perceived legitimacy of parental authority and tobacco and alcohol use during early adolescence. *Journal of Adolescent Health*, 31, 425–432.

Jacob, T. and Leonard, K. E. (1988). Alcoholic spouse interaction as a function of alcoholism subtype and alcohol consumption interaction. *Journal of Abnormal Psychology*, 97, 231–237.

Jacob, T. and Leonard, K. E. (1994). Family and peer influences in the development of adolescent alcohol abuse. In: R. Zucker, G. Boyd and J. Howard (eds), *Development of Alcohol Problems: Exploring the Biopsychosocial Matrix of Risk* {NIAAA Monograph No. 26}. Rockville, MD: National Institute on Alcohol Abuse and Alcoholism, pp. 123–156.

Jacob, T., Windle, M., Seilhamer, R.A. and Bost, J. (1999). Adult children of alcoholics: drinking, psychiatric, and psychosocial status. *Psychology of Addictive Behaviors*, 13, 3–21.

Jacob, T., Waterman, B., Heath, A. *et al.* (2003). Genetic and environmental effects on offspring alcoholism: new insights using an offspring-of-twins design. *Archives of General Psychiatry*, 60, 1265–1272.

Jacobson, J.L. and Jacobson, S.W. (2002). Effects of prenatal alcohol exposure on child development. *Alcohol Research and Health*, 26, 282–286.

Jessor, R. and Jessor, S.L. (1977). *Problem Behavior and Psychological Development: A Longitudinal Study of Youth*. New York, NY: Academic Press.

Johnston, L.D., O'Malley, P.M. and Bachman, J.G. (2002). *National Survey Results on Drug Use from the Monitoring the Future Study, 1975–2001*, Vols 1 and 2. Rockville, MD: US DHHS (NIH Publication Nos 02-5106 and 02-5107).

Jones, L.M., Silvia, L.Y. and Richman, C.L. (1995). Increased awareness and self-challenge of alcohol expectancies. *Substance Abuse*, 16, 77–85.

Kandel, D.B., Johnson, J.G., Bird, H.R. *et al.* (1997). Psychiatric disorders associated with substance use among children and adolescents: findings from the Methods for the Epidemiology of Child and Adolescent Mental Disorders (MECA) Study. *Journal of Abnormal Child Psychology*, 25, 121–132.

Kessler, R.C., Nelson, C.B., McGonagle, K.A. *et al.* (1996). The epidemiology of co-occurring addictive and mental disorders in the National Comorbidity Survey: implications for prevention and service utilization. *American Journal of Orthopsychiatry*, 66, 17–31.

Kivlahan, D., Marlatt, G.A., Fromme, K. *et al.* (1990). Secondary prevention with college drinkers: evaluation of an alcohol skills training program. *Journal of Consulting and Clinical Psychology*, 58, 805–810.

Kokkevi, A.E., Arapaki, A.A., Richardson, C. *et al.* (2007). Further investigation of psychological and environmental correlates of substance use in adolescence in six European countries. *Drug and Alcohol Dependence*, 88, 308–312.

Komro, K.A., Perry, C.L., Veblen-Mortenson, S. *et al.* (2004). Brief report: the adaptation of Project Northland for urban youth. *Journal of Pediatric Psychology*, 29, 457–466.

Kosterman, R., Hawkins, J.D., Spoth, R. *et al.* (1997). Effects of a preventive parent-training intervention on observed family interactions: proximal outcomes from preparing for the drug free years. *Journal of Community Psychology*, 25, 337–352.

Kosterman, R., Hawkins, J., Guo, J. *et al.* (2000). The dynamics of alcohol and marijuana initiation: patterns and predictors of first use in adolescence. *American Journal of Public Health*, 90, 360–366.

Kushner, M.G., Abrams, K. and Borchardt, C. (2000). The relationship between anxiety disorders and alcohol use disorders: a review of major perspectives and findings. *Clinical Psychology Review*, 20, 149–171.

Kypri, K., Voas, R.B., Langley, J.D. *et al.* (2006). Minimum purchasing age for alcohol and traffic crash injuries among 15- to 19-year-olds in New Zealand. *American Journal of Public Health*, 96, 126–131.

Larimer, M.E. and Cronce, J.M. (2002). Identification, prevention and treatment: a review of individual-focused strategies to reduce problematic alcohol consumption by college students. *Journal of Studies on Alcohol*, 14, 148–163.

Larimer, M.E., Turner, A.P., Anderson, B.K. *et al.* (2001). Evaluating a brief alcohol intervention with fraternities. *Journal of Studies on Alcohol*, 62, 370–380.

Lewinsohn, P.M., Hops, H., Roberts, R.E. *et al.* (1993). Adolescent psychopathology: I. Prevalence and incidence of depression and other DSM-III-R disorders in high school students. *Journal of Abnormal Psychology*, 102, 133–144.

Lewinsohn, P.M., Rohde, P. and Seeley, J.R. (1995). Adolescent psychopathology: III. The clinical consequences of comorbidity. *Journal of the American Academy of Child and Adolescent Psychiatry*, 34, 510–519.

Lewinsohn, P.M., Rohde, P. and Seeley, J.R. (1996). Alcohol consumption in high school adolescents: frequency of use and dimensional structure of associated problems. *Addiction*, 91, 375–390.

Locke, T.F. and Newcomb, M.D. (2003). Psychosocial outcomes of alcohol involvement and dysphoria in women: a 16-year prospective community study. *Quarterly Journal of Studies on Alcohol*, 64, 531–546.

Lowe, G., Foxcroft, D.R. and Sibley, D. (1993). *Adolescent Drinking and Family Life*, Vol. xi. England, PA: Harwood Academic Publishers/Gordon.

Lowry, R., Kann, L., Collins, J.L. and Kolbe, L. (1996). The effects of socio-economic status on chronic disease risk behaviors among US adolescents. *Journal of the American Medical Association*, 276, 792–797.

Loxley, W., Toumbourou, J. and Stockwell, T. *et al.* (2004). *The Prevention of Substance Use, Risk and Harm in Australia: A Review of the Evidence*. Canberra: National Drug Research Institute.

Maguin, E., Zucker, R.A. and Fitzgerald, H. E. (1994). The path to alcohol problems through conduct problems: a family based approach to very early intervention with risk. *Journal of Research on Adolescence*, 4, 249–269.

Mak, A.S. and Kinsella, C. (1996). Adolescent drinking, conduct problems, and parental bonding. *Australian Journal of Psychology*, 48, 15–20.

Marlatt, G.A., Baer, J.S., Kivlahan, D.R. *et al.* (1998). Screening and brief intervention for high-risk college student drinkers: results from a 2-year follow-up assessment. *Journal of Consulting and Clinical Psychology*, 66, 604–615.

May, P. and Moran, J. (1995). Prevention of alcohol misuse: a review of health promotion efforts among American Indians. *American Journal of Health Promotion*, 9, 288–298.

Milberger, S., Biederman, J., Faraone, S.V. *et al.* (1997). Further evidence of an association between attention-deficit/hyperactivity disorder and cigarette smoking. Findings from a high-risk sample of siblings. *American Journal of Addiction*, 6, 205–217.

Miller, E. T. (1999). "Preventing Alcohol Abuse and Alcohol-related Negative Consequences among Freshman College Students: Using Emerging Computer Technology to Deliver and Evaluate the Effectiveness of Brief Intervention Efforts." PhD Dissertation, University of Washington, Seattle.

Mitchell, P., Spooner, C., Copeland, J. *et al.* (2001). *The Role of Families in the Development, Identification, Prevention and Treatment of Illicit Drug Problems*. Canberra: NHMRC.

Monti, P.M., Colby, S.M., Barnett, N.P. *et al.* (1999). Brief intervention for harm reduction with alcohol-positive older adolescents in a hospital emergency department. *Journal of Consulting and Clinical Psychology*, 67(6), 989–994.

Moore, E.S., Ward, R.E., Jamison, P.L. *et al.* (2002). New perspectives on the face in fetal alcohol syndrome: what anthropometry tells us. *American Journal of Medical Genetics*, 109(4), 249–260.

Moran, J.R. and Reaman, J.A. (2002). Critical issues for substance abuse prevention targeting American Indian youth. *Journal of Primary Prevention*, 22, 201–233.

Morgan, M., Hibell, B., Andersson, B. *et al.* (1999). The ESPAD Study: implications for prevention. *Drugs: Education, Prevention and Policy*, 6, 243–256.

Moskowitz, J.M. (1989). The primary prevention of alcohol problems: a critical review of the research literature. *Journal of Studies on Alcohol*, 50, 54–88.

Myers, M.G., Stewart, D.G. and Brown, S.A. (1998). Progression from conduct disorder to antisocial personality disorder following treatment for adolescent substance abuse. *American Journal of Psychiatry*, 155, 479–485.

Neighbors, B.D., Clark, D.B., Donovan, J.E. and Brody, G.H. (2000). Difficult temperament, parental relationships, and adolescent alcohol use disorder symptoms. *Journal of Child and Adolescent Substance Abuse*, 10(1), 69–86.

Newcomb, M.D. (1994). Families, peers, and adolescent alcohol abuse: a paradigm to study multiple causes, mechanisms, and outcomes. In: R. Zucker, G. Boyd and J. Howard (eds), *Development of Alcohol Problems: Exploring the Biopsychosocial Matrix of Risk*. National Institute on Alcohol Abuse and Alcoholism (NIAAA) Research Monograph No. 26. Rockville, MD: NIAAA, pp. 157–168.

National Institute on Alcohol Abuse and Alcoholism (NIAAA) (2002). *A Call to Action: Changing the Culture of Drinking at US Colleges. Final Report of the Task Force on College Drinking*. NIH Publication No: 02-5010. Rockville, MD: National Institute on Alcohol Abuse and Alcoholism.

Nye, C.L., Zucker, R.A. and Fitzgerald, H.E. (1999). Early family-based intervention in the path to alcohol problems: rationale and relationship between treatment process characteristics and child parenting outcomes. *Journal of Studies on Alcohol Supplement*, 13, 10–21.

O'Leary, C. (2002). *Fetal Alcohol Syndrome: A Literature Review*. Canberra: Commonwealth Department of Health and Ageing.

O'Leary, C.M. (2004). Fetal alcohol syndrome: diagnosis, epidemiology, and developmental outcomes. *Journal of Paediatrics and Child Health*, 40, 2–7.

Oxford, M.L., Harachi, T.W., Catalano, R.F. and Abbott, R.D. (2001). Preadolescent predictors of substance initiation: a test of both the direct and mediated effect of family social control factors on deviant peer associations and substance initiation. *American Journal of Drug and Alcohol Abuse*, 27(4), 599–616.

Park, J., Kosterman, R., Hawkins, J.D. *et al.* (2000). Effects of the "Preparing for the Drug Free Years" curriculum on growth in alcohol use and risk for alcohol use in early adolescence. *Prevention Science*, 1(3), 125–138.

Parker-Langley, L. (2002). Alcohol prevention programs among American Indians: research findings and issues. In: P.D. Mail, S. Heurtin-Roberts, S.E. Martin and J. Howard (eds), *Alcohol Use Among American Indians and Alaska Natives*. NIAAA Research Monograph No. 37. Bethesda, MD: US DHHS.

Perry, C.L., Williams, C.L., Forster, J.L. *et al.* (1993). Background, conceptualization and design of a community-wide research program on adolescent alcohol use: Project Northland. *Health Education Research*, 8(1), 125–136.

Perry, C.L., Williams, C.L., Veblen-Mortenson, S. *et al.* (1996). Project Northland: outcomes of a community wide alcohol use prevention program during early adolescence. *American Journal of Public Health*, 86(7), 956–965.

Perry, C.L., Williams, C.L., Komro, K.A. *et al.* (2000). Project Northland high school interventions: community action to reduce adolescent alcohol use. *Health Education and Behavior*, 27(1), 29–49.

Perry, C.L., Williams, C.L., Komro, K.A. *et al.* (2002). Project Northland: long-term outcomes of community action to reduce adolescent alcohol use. *Health Education Research: Theory and Practice*, 17, 117–132.

Perry, C.L., Komro, K.A., Veblen-Mortenson, S. *et al.* (2003). A randomized control trial of the middle and junior high DARE and DARE plus programs. *Archives of Pediatrics and Adolescent Medicine*, 157(2), 178–184.

Poelen, E.A.P., Scholte, R.H.J., Engels, R.C.M.E. *et al.* (2005). Prevalence and trends of alcohol use and misuse among adolescents and young adults in the Netherlands from 1993 to 2000. *Drug and Alcohol Dependence*, 79, 413–421.

Poulton, R., Caspi, A., Milne, B.J. *et al.* (2002). Association between children's experience of socioeconomic disadvantage and adult health: a life-course study. *Lancet*, 360(9346), 1640–1645.

Premier's Drug Prevention Council (2003). *Victorian Youth Alcohol and Drug Survey 2003*. Melbourne: Victorian Government Department of Human Services.

Rai, A.A., Stanton, B., Wu, Y. *et al.* (2003). Relative influences of perceived parental monitoring and perceived peer involvement on adolescent risk behaviors: an analysis of six cross-sectional data sets. *Journal of Adolescent Health*, 33(2), 108–118.

Reboussin, B.A., Song, E.Y., Shrestha, A. *et al.* (2006). A latent class analysis of underage problem drinking: evidence from a community sample of 16-20 year olds. *Drug and Alcohol Dependence*, 83, 1999–2209.

Reifman, A., Barnes, G.M., Dintcheff, B.A. *et al.* (1998). Parental and peer influences on the onset of heavier drinking among adolescents. *Journal of Studies on Alcohol*, 59(3), 311–317.

Reifman, A., Watson, W.K. and McCourt, A. (2006). Social networks and college drinking: probing processes of social influence and selection. *Personality and Social Psychology Bulletin*, 32, 820–832.

Reinherz, H.Z., Giaconia, R.M., Lefkowitz, E.S. *et al.* (1993). Prevalence of psychiatric disorders in a community population of older adolescents. *Journal of the American Academy of Child and Adolescent Psychiatry*, 32, 369–377.

Richter, M., Leppin, A. and Gabhainn, S.N. (2006). The relationship between parental socio-economic status and episodes of drunkenness among adolescents: findings from a cross-national survey. *BMC Public Health*, 6, 289.

Roberts, C., Blakey, V. and Tudor Smith, C. (1999). The impact of "alcopops" on regular drinking by young people in Wales. *Drug Education Prevention Policy*, 6, 7–15.

Rohde, P., Lewinsohn, P.M. and Seeley, J.R. (1996). Psychiatric comorbidity with problematic alcohol use in high school adolescents. *Journal of the American Academy of Child and Adolescent Psychiatry*, 35, 101–109.

Rohde, P., Lewinsohn, P.M., Kahler, C.W. *et al.* (2001). Natural course of alcohol use disorders from adolescence to young adulthood. *Journal of the American Academy of Child and Adolescent Psychiatry*, 40, 83–90.

Rohde, P., Kahler, C.W., Lewinsohn, P.M. and Brown, R.A. (2004). Psychiatric disorders, familial factors, and cigarette smoking: II. Associations with progression to daily smoking. *Nicotine and Tobacco Research*, 6, 119–132.

Roush, K.L. and DeBlassie, R.R. (1989). Structured group counseling for college students of alcoholic parents. *Journal of College Student Development*, 30, 276–277.

Safyer, A., Maguin, E., Nochajski, T.H. *et al.* (2003). The impact of a family based alcohol prevention program on family functioning. *Alcoholism: Clinical and Experimental Research*, 27, 72A (No. 400).

Saggers, S. and Gray, D. (1998). *Dealing with Alcohol: Indigenous Usage in Australia, New Zealand and Canada*. New York, NY: Cambridge University Press.

Saltz, R.F. (2006). Prevention of college student drinking problems: a brief summary of strategies and degree of empirical support for them. In: M. Galanter (ed.), *Alcohol Problems in Adolescents and Young Adults: Epidemiology, Neurobiology, Prevention and Treatment*. New York, NY: Springer Science and Business Media, pp. 255–274.

Sammon, P., Smith, T., Cooper, T. and Furnish, G. (1991). On campus talking about alcohol and drugs (OCTAA). *Journal of Dental Education*, 55, 30–31.

SAMHSA (Substance Abuse and Mental Health Services Administration) (2007). *Results from the 2006 National Survey on Drug Use and Health: National Findings*. Office of Applied Studies, NSDUH Series H-32, DHHS Publication No. SMA 07-4293). Rockville, MD: Office of Applied Studies. Available at http://www.oas.samhsa.gov/nsduh/2k6nsduh/2k6Results.pdf.

Scheier, S., Botvin, G.J., Diaz, T. and Griffin, K.W. (1999). Social skills, competence, and drug refusal efficacy as predictors of adolescent alcohol use. *Journal of Drug Education*, 29, pp. 251–278.

Schinke, S.P., Tepavac, L. and Cole, K.C. (2000). Preventing substance use among Native American youth: three-year results. *Addictive Behaviors*, 25, 387–397.

Schroeder, C.M. and Prentice, D.A. (1998). Exposing pluralistic ignorance to reduce alcohol use among college students. *Journal of Applied Social Psychology*, 28(23), 2150–2182.

Sher, K. (1994). Individual-level risk factors. In: R. Zucker, G. Boyd and J. Howard (eds.), *Development of Alcohol Problems: Exploring the Biopsychosocial Matrix of Risk*. {NIAAA Monograph No. 26}. Rockville, MD: National Institute on Alcohol Abuse and Alcoholism, pp. 77–108.

Sher, K.J. (1997). Psychological characteristics of children of alcoholics. *Alcohol Health and Research World*, 21(3), 247–254.

Shults, R.A., Elder, R.W., Sleet, D.A. *et al.* (2001). Reviews of evidence regarding interventions to reduce alcohol-impaired driving. *American Journal of Preventive Medicine*, 21(4 Supplement), 66–88.

Smart, D., Richardson, N., Sanson, A. *et al.* (2005). *Patterns and Precursors of Adolescent Antisocial Behavior: Outcomes and Connections*. Melbourne: Australian Institute of Family Studies.

Spooner, C., Hall, W. and Lynskey, M. (2001). *Structural Determinants of Youth Drug Use*, ANCD Research Paper No. 2. Canberra: Australian National Council on Drugs.

Spoth, R., Redmond, C., Hockaday, C. and Yoo, S. (1996). Protective factors and young adolescent tendency to abstain from alcohol use: a model using two waves of intervention study data. *American Journal of Community Psychology*, 24(6), 749–770.

Spoth, R., Redmond, C. and Shin, C. (1998). Direct and indirect latent-variable parenting outcomes of two universal family-focused preventive interventions: extending a public health-oriented research base. *Journal of Consulting and Clinical Psychology*, 66(2), 385–399.

Spoth, R., Redmond, C. and Lepper, H. (1999). Alcohol initiation outcomes of universal family-focused preventative interventions: one- and two- year follow-ups of a controlled study. *Journal of Studies on Alcohol*, Special issue: *Alcohol and the Family: Opportunities for Prevention*, 13 (Suppl.), 103–111.

Spoth, R.L., Redmond, C. and Shin, C. (2001). Randomized trial of brief family interventions for general populations adolescent substance use outcomes 4 years following baseline. *Journal of Consulting and Clinical Psychology*, 69, 1–15.

Spoth, R.L., Redmond, C., Trudeau, L. and Shin, C. (2002). Longitudinal substance initiation outcomes for a universal preventive intervention combining family and school programs. *Psychology of Addictive Behaviors*, 16(2), 129–134.

Stanley, J., Tomison, A.M. and Pocock, J. (2003). *Child Abuse and Neglect in Indigenous Australian Communities*. National Child Protection Clearinghouse, Issue No. 19. Melbourne: Australian Institute of Family Studies.

Substance Abuse and Mental Health Services Administration (SAMHSA) (2006). *National Survey on Drug Use and Health (NSDUH)*. Rockville, MD: US Department of Health and Human Services.

Sussman, S. (2006). Prevention of adolescent alcohol problems in special populations. In: M. Galanter (ed.), *Alcohol Problems in Adolescents and Young Adults: Epidemiology, Neurobiology, Prevention and Treatment*. New York, NY: Springer Science and Business Media, pp. 225–253.

Sussman, S., Dent, C.W., Skara, S. *et al.* (2002a). Alcoholic liver disease (ALD): a new domain for prevention efforts. *Substance Use and Misuse*, 37, 1887–1904.

Sussman, S., Dent, C.W. and Stacy, A.W. (2002b). Project towards no drug abuse: a review of the findings and future directions. *American Journal of Health Behavior*, 26, 354–365.

Swahn, M.H., Simon, T.R., Hammig, B.J. and Guerrero, J.L. (2004). Alcohol-consumption behaviors and risk for physical fighting and injuries among adolescent drinkers. *Addictive Behaviors*, 29, 959–963.

Ter Bogt, T., van Dorsselaer, S. and Vollebergh, W. (2002). *Roken, Drinken en Blowen door Nederlandse Scholieren (11 t/m 17 jaar) 2001: Kerngegevens Middelengebruik uit het Nederlands HBSC-onderzoek.*{Smoking, Drinking, and Smoking Dope among Dutch Scholars (11–17 year) 2001: Key Data Substance Use from the Dutch HBSC study}. Utrecht: Trimbos-instituut.

Thomas, G., Reifman, A., Barnes, G.M. and Farrell, M. P. (2000). Delayed onset of drunkenness as a protective factor for adolescent alcohol misuse and sexual risk taking: a longitudinal study. *Deviant Behavior*, 21, 181–210.

Tobler, N.S., Roona, M.R., Ochshorn, P. *et al.* (2000). School-based adolescent drug prevention programs: 1998 meta-analysis. *Journal of Primary Prevention*, 20, 275–335.

Toumbourou, J.W., Williams, I.R., White, V.M. *et al.* (2004). Prediction of alcohol related harm from controlled drinking strategies and alcohol consumption trajectories. *Addiction*, 99, 498–508.

Vogl, L., Teesson, M. and Dillon, P. (2006). "The Efficacy of a Computerised School-based Prevention Program for Problems with Alcohol Use: Climate Schools Alcohol." Paper presented at the European Association for Behavioral and Cognitive Therapies (EABCT), Paris, France.

Wagenaar, A.C. and Toomey, T.L. (2002). Effects of minimum drinking age laws: review and analyses of the literature from 1960 to 2000. *Journal of Studies on Alcohol*, 14, 206–225.

Wagner, F.A. and Anthony, J.C. (2002). From first drug use to drug dependence: developmental periods of risk for dependence upon marijuana, cocaine, and alcohol. *Neuropsychopharmacology*, 26, 479–488.

Wagner, E.F. and Tarolla, S.M. (2002). Course and outcome. In: C.A. Essau (ed.), *Substance Abuse and Dependence in Adolescence*. London: Brunner-Routledge, pp. 119–142.

Wagner, F.A., Velasco-Mondragon, H.E., Herrera-Vazquezc, M. *et al.* (2005). Early alcohol or tobacco onset and transition to other drug use among students in the State of Morelos, Mexico. *Drug and Alcohol Dependence*, 77, 93–96.

Walters, S.T. (2000). In praise of feedback: an effective intervention for college students who are heavy drinkers. *Journal of American College Health*, 48(5), 235–238.

Weinberg, N.Z. (1997). Cognitive and behavioral deficits associated with parental alcohol use. *Journal of the American Academy of Child and Adolescent Psychiatry*, 36, 1177–1186.

Weitzman, E.R. and Ying-Yeh Chen, Y.Y. (2005). The co-occurrence of smoking and drinking among young adults in college: National survey results from the United States. *Drug and Alcohol Dependence*, 80, 377–386.

White, H. R., Xie, M. and Thompson, W. (2001). Psychopathology as a predictor of adolescent drug use trajectories. *Psychology of Addictive Behaviors*, 15, 210–218.

White, V. and Hayman, J. (2006). *Australian Secondary School Students' Use of Alcohol in 2005.* National Drug Strategy Monograph Series No. 58. Canberra: Australian Government Department of Health and Ageing.

White, H.R., Loeber, R., Stouthamer-Loeber, M. and Farrington, D.P. (1999). Developmental associations between substance use and violence. *Development and Psychopathology*, 11, 785–803.

Williams, B., Sanson, A., Toumbourou, J.W. and Smart, D. (2000). *Patterns and Predictors of Teenagers' Use of Licit and Illicit Substances in the Australian Temperament Project Cohort.* Melbourne: Report commissioned by the Ross Trust, Melbourne.

Williams, C.L. and Perry, C.L. (1998). Lessons from Project Northland: preventing alcohol problems during adolescence. *Alcohol Health and Research World*, 22(2), 107–116.

Williams, C.L., Perry, C.L., Farbakhsh, K. and Veblen-Mortenson, S. (1999). Project Northland: comprehensive alcohol use prevention for young adolescents, their parents, schools, peers, and communities. *Journal of Studies on Alcohol, Supplement*, 13, 112–124.

Williams, P.S. and Hine, D.W. (2002). Parental behavior and alcohol misuse among adolescents: a path analysis of mediating influences. *Australian Journal of Psychology*, 54, 17–24.

Windle, M. and Davies, P. T. (1999). Depression and heavy alcohol use among adolescents: concurrent and prospective relations. *Development and Psychopathology*, 11, 823–844.

Wittchen, H.-U., Nelson, C.B. and Lachner, G. (1998). Prevalence of mental disorders and psychosocial impairments in adolescents and young adults. *Psychological Medicine*, 28,109–126.

Wood, M.D., Read, J.P., Mitchell, R.E. and Brand, N.H. (2004). Do parents still matter? Parent and peer influences on alcohol involvement among recent high school graduates. *Psychology of Addictive Behaviors*, 18, 19–30.

Wu, L.T., Pilowsky, D.J. and Schlenger, W.E. (2005). High prevalence of substance use disorders among adolescents who use marijuana and inhalants. *Drug and Alcohol Dependence*, 78, 23–32.

Young, S.E., Corley, R.P., Stallings, M.C. *et al.* (2002). Substance use, abuse and dependence in adolescence: Prevalence, symptom profiles and correlates. *Drug and Alcohol Dependence*, 68, 309–322.

Zucker, R. and Wong, M.M. (2006). Prevention for children of alcoholics and other high risk groups. In: M. Galanter (ed.), *Alcohol Problems in Adolescents and Young Adults: Epidemiology, Neurobiology, Prevention and Treatment.* New York, NY: Springer Science and Business Media, pp. 299–330.

4

Cannabis Abuse and Dependence

Wayne Hall, Louisa Degenhardt and George Patton

In most developed countries cannabis is the illicit drug that is most often used by adolescents, and the one that adolescents are most likely to develop problems with that require treatment (Crowley, 2006; SAMHSA, 2006). Cannabis problems consequently predominate among young people seen in specialist addiction services, mental health services and criminal justice settings in Australia (Spooner *et al.*, 1996), Europe (EMCDDA, 2006) and the USA (Crowley *et al.*, 1998; Grella, 2006). Other illicit drugs, such as the psychostimulants, "party drugs" and inhalants, are less often used by adolescents (Essau, 2006). For these reasons, we focus on cannabis abuse and dependence in this chapter.

We first describe the epidemiology of cannabis use in developed societies such as Australia, Europe and the USA. Second, we summarize research on risk factors for the development of problem cannabis use in young people. Third, we describe the characteristics of adolescents who seek treatment for cannabis disorders and the results of the limited evaluations of approaches to treating adolescent cannabis abuse and dependence. We also discuss the special challenges in working with adolescents who are cannabis dependent – namely, the high rates of comorbid substance use and mental disorders, and the lack of motivation for treatment in this population, many of whom have been coerced by the legal system into seeking treatment. We conclude by discussing the prospects of preventing these disorders via educational and other interventions.

PATTERNS OF CANNABIS USE IN DIFFERENT COUNTRIES

THE UNITED STATES

In the United States in 2005, 46 percent of the adult population reported that they had tried cannabis at some time in their lives. Only 14 percent reported using cannabis in the past year, and 8 percent reported using it in the past month (SAMHSA, 2006). Lifetime use was 28 percent among those aged 12–17 years, and 59 percent among those aged 18–25 years. National Institute on Drug Abuse (NIDA) household surveys from 1974 to 1990 show that rates of monthly cannabis use among 18- to 25-year-olds increased throughout the 1970s and peaked in 1979. They then declined steadily throughout the 1980s to reach their lowest level in 1992, before increasing again in 1992 and throughout the 1990s until the early 2000s, when rates began to decline again (SAMHSA, 2006). Similar trends have been observed in the Monitoring the Future surveys of cannabis use among secondary school students, college students and young adults between 1975 and 2005 (Johnston *et al.*, 2006).

Bachman and colleagues have used Monitoring the Future data from 14 cohorts of high school seniors and college students who were followed from age 18 to 35 years to assess the effect of major life transitions (such as entering college or full-time employment, marrying and having children) on the use of cannabis in the past 30 days (Bachman *et al.*, 1997). They found a steady decline in monthly cannabis use from the early and mid-twenties to the early thirties. The pattern was very similar to that for alcohol, but less persistent than that for tobacco use. Big declines in cannabis use were seen in males and females after marriage, and during pregnancy in women. These findings have been confirmed in a detailed study of a single cohort that was followed from early adolescence into middle adulthood (Chen and Kandel, 1995, 1998).

AUSTRALIA

Cannabis is the most widely used illicit drug in Australia, with 34 percent of a household sample of adults aged 15 and older reporting that they had used it at some time in their lives (AIHW, 2005). Among 14- to 19-year-olds in 2004, the lifetime use of cannabis was 26 percent, increasing to 55 percent among 20- to 29-year-olds. Men were more likely to have used cannabis than women in all age groups, with 37 percent of males versus 30 percent of females reporting lifetime use in 2004.

The percentage of Australians aged between 20 and 29 years who have ever tried cannabis almost doubled between 1985 and 2004, from 28 percent to 55 percent (Donnelly and Hall, 1994; AIHW, 2005). In 2004, cannabis use was more common among males (14%) than females (8%), and among 14- to 19-year-olds (25%) and 20- to 29-year-olds (29%) than among those aged 30 to 39 years (16%) and those over 40 years (4%) (AIHW, 2005). During the 1990s, Australian adolescents initiated cannabis use at a progressively younger age: one in five cannabis users (21%) born between 1940 and 1949 had initiated cannabis use by age 18, compared with 43 percent of those born between 1950 and 1959, 66 percent of those born between 1960 and 1969, and 78 percent of those born between 1970 and 1979 (Degenhardt *et al.*, 2000).

The 2005 Australian School Students' Alcohol and Drugs Survey found that 18 percent of students aged 12–17 had ever used cannabis (White and Hayman, 2006), a decline from reported rates in the early 1990s of 25–30 percent (Donnelly and Hall, 1994; Lynskey and Hall, 1999). These surveys suggest that cannabis use increased among youth during the 1990s (Lynskey and Hall, 1999), before a decline that began in the late 1990s and has continued into the new millennium (White and Hayman, 2006). This mirrors trends in cannabis use among adults, which also increased during the 1980s until 1998, after which rates of use declined (AIHW, 2005).

EUROPE

Cannabis is the most widely used illicit drug among European adolescents, and its use is so common that it has been described as an "illegal everyday drug" (Essau, 2006). In the late 1990s and early 2000s, the median rates of lifetime cannabis use among European adults aged between 18 and 64 years was 15 percent, ranging from 31 percent in the Czech Republic to 2 percent in Romania (EMCDDA, 2006). Rates of lifetime use were higher among younger adults (aged between 15 and 34 years), with a median rate of 21 percent, ranging from 3 percent in Romania to 45 percent in Denmark (EMCDDA, 2006).

Smart and Ogborne (2000) have summarized data on illicit drug use among high school students in 36 European countries during the mid-1990s (*circa* 1995). The highest rates of lifetime cannabis use were in Scotland (53%), the United Kingdom (41%) and the Netherlands (22%). Increases in these rates during the 1990s have been observed in those countries that have undertaken a series of surveys over that time, namely the Netherlands, Switzerland and Norway (Harkin *et al.*, 1997).

CANNABIS USE AND DEPENDENCE

Edwards and Gross (1976) suggested that alcohol dependence should be distinguished from alcohol-related problems occurring in heavy drinkers, and thought of as a cluster of symptoms comprising seven facets:

1. Narrowing of the behavioral repertoire
2. Salience of drinking (alcohol use given priority over other activities)
3. Subjective awareness of a compulsion (experiencing loss of control over alcohol use, or an inability to stop using)

4. Increased tolerance (using more alcohol to get the same effects, or finding that the same amount of alcohol has less effect)
5. Repeated alcohol withdrawal symptoms
6. Relief or avoidance of withdrawal symptoms by further drinking
7. Reinstatement of dependent drinking after abstinence.

The concept of a dependence syndrome has since been extended to cannabis, and another category of problematic drug use, drug *abuse*, has also been added to classify persons who experience clinically significant problems associated with their drug use, but who are not drug dependent. There is now good clinical and epidemiological evidence for a cannabis-dependence syndrome much like that for alcohol and other drugs (Anthony, 2006; Babor, 2006; Budney, 2006). The most recent operationalization of the substance abuse and dependence syndromes is the *Diagnostic and Statistical Manual of Mental Disorders*, fourth edition (DSM-IV) (American Psychiatric Association, 1994) (see also Chapter 2 in this volume). DSM-IV Cannabis Abuse criteria require a pattern of substance use that causes clinically significant distress or impairment, as indicated by at least one of the abuse criteria (American Psychiatric Association, 1994). DSM-IV Cannabis Dependence criteria require a cluster of three or more indicators (of a possible total of seven) that a person continues to use the substance despite significant substance-related problems (American Psychiatric Association, 1994). These include: tolerance, indicators of impaired control over use, use despite problems, and the reduction of activities not related to substance use.

In epidemiological studies in the USA in the early 1980s (Robins and Reiger, 1991) and 1990s (Anthony *et al.*, 1994), around 4 percent of the US adult population had met DSM-III criteria for cannabis abuse or dependence at some time in their lives. Similar surveys in Australia, Canada and New Zealand have produced similar estimates of cannabis abuse and dependence (Wells *et al.*, 1992; Hwu and Compton, 1994; Russell *et al.*, 1994; Hall *et al.*, 1999).

The risk of developing dependence is about one in ten for those who have ever used cannabis (Anthony *et al.*, 1994), and perhaps as high as one in two for daily users (Chen *et al.*, 2005). The risk of developing dependence is higher for persons with a history of: poor academic achievement, deviant behavior in childhood and adolescence, non-conformity and rebelliousness, personal distress and maladjustment, poor parental relationships, and a parental history of drug and alcohol problems (Budney and Moore, 2002; Morral *et al.*, 2002; Coffey *et al.*, 2003; Macleod *et al.*, 2004).

Only a minority of those who meet the criteria for cannabis dependence in community surveys report seeking treatment. Among the minority of dependent users who do seek help after failing to quit unassisted (Kandel, 1975; Kandel and Yamaguchi, 2002), the detrimental effect of cognitive, mood and motivational impairments on work performance appears to be an important factor (Kandel, 1975; Stephens *et al.*, 1994).

CANNABIS DEPENDENCE AMONG ADOLESCENTS AND YOUNG ADULTS

Adolescents do experience problems related to cannabis use, and do present for treatment for their cannabis problems (which include dependence) (Crowley *et al.*, 1998; Tims *et al.*, 2002; Dennis *et al.*, 2004; Crowley, 2006). There is evidence for the validity of the dependence diagnosis in that those adolescents who present for treatment and are diagnosed as dependent have more severe drug problems and greater difficulties than those meeting criteria for abuse (Winters *et al.*, 1999).

There is less published population-based research exploring the symptom profile of cannabis dependence in adolescents and young adults. One of the first population-based studies was based upon an Australian cohort in the state of Victoria, which found that in a representative sample of young adults aged 20–21 years, the majority (60%) reported lifetime cannabis use. Overall, 12 percent of the cohort reported at least one symptom of DSM-IV-defined cannabis dependence. The prevalence of past-year DSM-IV cannabis dependence was 7 percent. The probability of dependence increased substantially with increasing frequency of cannabis use, from one in two among weekly users to almost three-quarters of daily users (Coffey *et al.*, 2002). Persistent desire or unsuccessful efforts to reduce or cease cannabis use were the most commonly reported symptoms. Tolerance and social consequences were the least reported symptoms.

Although withdrawal is not currently accepted as a criterion for cannabis dependence within DSM-IV (American Psychiatric Association, 1994), cannabis-dependent adolescents in substance abuse treatment do report withdrawal symptoms (Crowley *et al.*, 1998). The Victorian cohort study mentioned above found that among those using cannabis at least weekly in the past year, 46 percent reported symptoms of cannabis withdrawal (Coffey *et al.*, 2002). Of those meeting criteria for cannabis dependence and who reported withdrawal, over one-third reported that they used cannabis to alleviate such symptoms.

Anthony (2006) has summarized estimates of cannabis dependence among lifetime users derived from longitudinal studies of adolescents. In Australia, New Zealand and the United States, around one in six or seven young people who ever used cannabis developed dependence on it. The risk was much lower in German adolescents, one in fifty, for reasons that are unclear. Among adolescents with a history of near-daily cannabis use, Anthony estimated that the risk of dependence was one in three.

How Valid is Epidemiological Research on Adolescent and Adult Dependence?

There has been debate about the validity of large-scale epidemiological surveys in adolescents that use structured diagnostic interviews developed for adults (Caetano and Babor, 2006; Crowley, 2006). A recent review of epidemiological data on alcohol dependence among adolescents concluded that the rates of dependence may be inflated because of confusion over questions assessing tolerance and withdrawal symptoms (Caetano and Babor, 2006). Crowley (2006: 115) has argued, however, that substance use diagnoses "'work' in adolescents as they do in adults, showing good inter-rater reliability and validity".

Two possible solutions to this have been suggested: that alternative methods of assessment be developed by those conducting epidemiological studies with adolescents and young adults (Crowley, 2006), or that the results of existing surveys be considered as a manifestation of "adolescent dependence" that may be less severe (and more likely to remit) than adult dependence (Caetano and Babor, 2006). Future research will reveal which of these views is more appropriate.

RISK FACTORS FOR CANNABIS ABUSE AND DEPENDENCE

Epidemiological studies have identified a wide range of factors that predict an increased risk of substance use and dependence in general (for reviews of these factors, see Hawkins *et al.*, 1992a, Teesson *et al.*, 2005; Toumobourou and Catalano, 2005; for factors that predict cannabis abuse and dependence in particular, see Anthony, 2006). In general, these factors may be divided into the following broad categories: social and contextual factors, family factors, individual factors, and peer affiliations during adolescence (Hawkins *et al.*, 1992a).

SOCIAL AND CONTEXTUAL FACTORS

A broad range of social, ecological and contextual factors predicts early substance use and abuse by adolescents (Lascala *et al.*, 2005). Ready availability of drugs and alcohol is a moderate predictor of rates of tobacco, alcohol and cannabis use (Anthony, 2006). The use of these substances is also likely to be influenced by laws and norms concerning their use (Hawkins *et al.*, 1992a).

There have been continuing debates regarding whether the illegality of heroin, cocaine and cannabis use deters young people from using them, and whether law enforcement reduces drug supply, demand and use, and drug-related harm (Manski *et al.*, 2001). Proponents argue that law enforcement reduces the supply of cannabis and increases its price, and thereby reduces use. It is also plausible that the illegal status of cannabis deters some people from using it because it conveys the message that its use is socially unacceptable (Hawkins *et al.*, 1992a).

FAMILY FUNCTIONING AND FAMILY SUBSTANCE USE

An array of family factors is associated with increased rates of cannabis and other illicit drug use during adolescence (Hawkins *et al.*, 1992a; Brook *et al.*, 2006). These include poor quality of parent–child interaction and parent–child relationships (Jessor and Jessor, 1977; Brook *et al.*, 2006), parental divorce and conflict (Fergusson *et al.*, 1994a), and parental and sibling substance use (Barnes and Welte, 1986; Brook *et al.*, 1990; Bailey *et al.*, 1992; Lynskey *et al.*, 1994).

Two main aspects of the family environment appear to be associated with increased licit and illicit drug use among children and adolescents. These are the extent to which the child is exposed to a disadvantaged home environment, with parental conflict and poor discipline and supervision, and the extent to which the child's parents and siblings use alcohol and other drugs (Hawkins *et al.*, 1992a; Brook *et al.*, 2006).

INDIVIDUAL FACTORS

The personality traits of high novelty-seeking (Cloninger *et al.*, 1988) and sensation-seeking have been linked to greater youth alcohol and cannabis use (Thombs *et al.*, 1994). Early behavioral problems, particularly disruptive and troublesome behaviors during childhood, predict early and regular use of alcohol and other drugs (Anthony, 2006; Crowley, 2006). Poor school performance and low commitment to education also increase the risk of adolescent alcohol and drug use (Lynskey and Hall, 2000; Hall and Lynskey, 2005). Generally, the earlier that substance use begins, the higher the risk of an adolescent becoming a regular user (Fergusson *et al.*, 1994b; Toumobourou and Catalano, 2005).

PEER AFFILIATIONS DURING ADOLESCENCE

Affiliating with delinquent or drug-using peers is one of the strongest predictors of adolescent alcohol and other drug use (Kandel and Andrews, 1987; Brook *et al.*, 1990; Fergusson *et al.*, 1994b). The nature of this strong relationship between peer affiliations and adolescent substance use remains controversial, but the weight of evidence favors the view that peer affiliations during adolescence are an important determinant that operates independently of individual and family risk factors (Hawkins *et al.*, 1992a).

ASSOCIATIONS BETWEEN RISK FACTORS

Exposure to these risk factors is often highly correlated (Toumobourou and Catalano, 2005). That is, a young person who initiates substance use at an early age has often been exposed to multiple social and family disadvantages (Newcomb *et al.*, 1986), frequently comes from a family with problems and a history of parental substance use, and is often impulsive and has performed poorly at school. These young people also tend to affiliate with delinquent peers – a fact that is encouraged by ability streaming in schools, which places many children with poor school performance and family disadvantages in the same class. Consequently, although these factors individually make small contributions to the use of cannabis, a young person who has a number of these risk factors, as they often do, is at high risk of starting cannabis use at an early age, and of developing problems related to cannabis use (Toumobourou and Catalano, 2005).

CORRELATES OF CANNABIS DEPENDENCE

Assessment of the adult consequences of adolescent cannabis use has been hampered in various ways (Hall and Pacula, 2003; Anthony, 2006). Until relatively recently, there has been a paucity of longitudinal research on adolescent cannabis and other drug use and outcomes in young adulthood (Macleod *et al.*, 2004). Making causal inferences about the relationship between adolescent cannabis use and its putative psychosocial consequences is difficult. Young cannabis users are not a random sample of their peer group; they differ in their drug use and personal characteristics in ways that increase their likelihood of experiencing adverse outcomes that many parents attribute to cannabis use (Hall and Pacula, 2003; Macleod *et al.*, 2004). The greater the coincidence of these risk factors, the more likely a young person is to use cannabis, and to use it regularly.

IS CANNABIS A GATEWAY DRUG?

Surveys of adolescent drug use in the United States and elsewhere in the 1970s, 1980s and 1990s have consistently shown three types of association between cannabis use and the use of other illicit drugs, such as heroin and cocaine (Hall and Lynskey, 2005). First, almost all adolescents who tried cocaine and heroin had first used alcohol, tobacco and cannabis, in that order (Kandel, 2002). Second, there was a strong relationship between regular cannabis use and the later use of heroin and cocaine (Kandel, 1984; Donnelly and Hall, 1994). Third, the earlier the age at which any drug was first used, the more likely a user was to use the next drug in the sequence (McGee and Feehan, 1993; Fergusson and Horwood, 2000; Kandel, 2002).

Three explanations have been provided for these patterns of drug use (Hall and Lynskey, 2005). The first is that the relationship arises because cannabis and other illicit drugs are supplied by the same black market, so cannabis users have many more opportunities to try other illicit drugs than non-cannabis users. The second hypothesis is that the association is explained by characteristics of those who are early cannabis users that make them more likely to use other illicit drugs. The third hypothesis is that the relationship is causal, because the pharmacological effects of cannabis increase an adolescent's propensity to use other illicit drugs.

The Social Environmental Hypothesis

Wagner and Anthony (2002) found that young people who had used alcohol or tobacco were three times more likely to report an opportunity to use cannabis (75% vs 25%). They also found that opportunities to use cocaine were strongly related to cannabis, alcohol and tobacco use. Only 13 percent of young people who had not used alcohol, tobacco or cannabis reported an opportunity to use cocaine. This compared with 26 percent of alcohol and tobacco users, 51 percent of cannabis-only users, and 75 percent of those who had used alcohol, tobacco and cannabis. Fergusson and Horwood (2000), however, found that affiliation with drug-using peers only partially explained the relationship between cannabis and other illicit drug use. Statistical adjustment for peer drug use reduced but did not eliminate the relationship between cannabis and other illicit drug use.

Is the Gateway Pattern Explained by Personal Propensities to Use Drugs?

A plausible explanation for the association between cannabis and other illicit drug use is that socially deviant young people who have a predilection to use a variety of drugs are selectively recruited into cannabis use (Fergusson and Horwood, 2000). The sequence of drug involvement would simply reflect the differing availability and societal disapproval of different types of drugs (Donovan and Jessor, 1983). According to this hypothesis, cannabis use does not cause the use of other illicit drugs; rather, cannabis and heroin use are common consequences of pre-existing propensities to use all drugs (Newcomb and Bentler, 1988).

The selective recruitment hypothesis is supported by substantial correlations between non-conforming adolescent behaviors, such as dropping out of high school, early premarital sexual experience, delinquency, and early alcohol and illicit drug use (Jessor and Jessor, 1977). Regular cannabis users are more likely than their peers to have a history of such behavior (McGee and Feehan, 1993; Hawkins *et al.*, 1992a; Kandel and Davies, 1992).

The selective recruitment hypothesis has been tested in longitudinal studies by assessing whether cannabis use predicts the use of heroin and cocaine after statistically controlling for differences between cannabis users and non-users in personal characteristics that preceded their cannabis use (Fergusson and Horwood, 2000). Yamaguchi and Kandel (1984), for example, found that the relationship between cannabis use and "harder" illicit drug use was reduced but still persisted after statistically controlling for pre-existing adolescent behaviors and attitudes, interpersonal factors, and the age of initiation into drug use. The same finding has emerged in other studies (Kandel *et al.*, 1986; Fergusson and Horwood, 2000; Fergusson *et al.*, 2002).

A recent simulation study has provided some support for the common-cause hypothesis. Morral *et al.* (2002) asked whether a common-cause model would reproduce the three types of relationship between cannabis use and other illicit drug use described above. Morral and colleagues' common-cause model reproduced all three "gateway" patterns. Cannabis users were more likely to use other illicit drugs, cannabis use preceded the use of other illicit drugs, and there was a dose–response relationship between the frequency of cannabis use and the likelihood of using other illicit drugs.

A Shared Genetic Vulnerability to Drug Dependence

Behavior genetics studies suggest that the association between cannabis and other illicit drug use may be explained by a shared genetic vulnerability to develop dependence on a range of different drugs. Studies of identical and non-identical twins indicate that there is a genetic vulnerability to develop dependence on alcohol (Heath, 1995), cannabis (Kendler and Prescott, 1998) and tobacco (Han *et al.*, 1999). More recent studies suggest that a substantial part of the genetic vulnerability for these three drugs is shared (True *et al.*, 1999).

Lynskey and colleagues (2003) have recently used twin study methods to test this hypothesis. They examined the relationship between cannabis and other illicit drug use in 136 monozygotic and 175 dizygotic Australian twin pairs in which one twin had, and the other twin had not, used cannabis before the age of 17 years. If the association was attributable to a shared environment, then discordant twins raised together should not differ in the use of other illicit drugs. Similarly, if the association was attributable to shared genetic vulnerability to drug dependence, then there should be no difference in the use of other illicit drugs between monozygotic twins who did and did not use cannabis before the age of 17. Lynskey and colleagues found that the twin who had used cannabis before age 17 was more likely to have used sedatives, hallucinogens, stimulants and opioids than his or her co-twin who had not. These relationships persisted after controlling for other non-shared environmental factors that predicted an increased risk of developing drug abuse or dependence.

Pharmacological Explanations of the Gateway Pattern

Animal studies suggest a number of plausible ways in which the pharmacological effects of cannabis use could predispose regular cannabis users to use other illicit drugs (Hall and Lynskey, 2005). First, cannabis, cocaine, heroin and nicotine all act on the dopaminergic neurotransmitter systems that are involved in the "reward centers" in the midbrain, the nucleus accumbens (Gardner, 1999). Second, cannabinioid and opioid systems in the brain interact with one another, influencing each others' analgesic and euphoric effects, and producing similar effects on dopaminergic systems (Manzanares *et al.*, 1999).

Animal studies also potentially provide a way of directly testing whether these neural mechanisms may explain the relationship between cannabis and other illicit drug use in humans. Specifically, they can show whether self-administration of cannabinoids "prime" animals to self-administer other illicit drugs. Two recent studies in rats (Cadoni *et al.*, 2001; Lamarque *et al.*, 2001), for example, have provided some evidence for cross-sensitivity between cannabinoids and opioids, although in one study this was only observed in a strain of rats that were highly responsive to drug effects (Lamarque *et al.*, 2001).

There are a number of uncertainties about the relevance of these studies to gateway patterns of adolescent drug use. First, these effects were produced by injecting high doses of cannabinoids, and so may be most relevant to the minority of adolescents who expose themselves to similar high doses of THC (Lynskey, 2002). Second, the cross-sensitization between cannabinoids and opioids was symmetrical – that is, animals which were administered opioids were cross-sensitive to cannabinoids, and *vice versa* (Cadoni *et al.*, 2001). This suggests that if opioids were more readily available than cannabis, then opioids would be a gateway to cannabis use.

The Effects of Delaying Gateway Drug Use

If cannabis use "causes" the use of other illicit drugs, then we should be able to reduce the use of other illicit drugs by delaying adolescent cannabis use (e.g., Polich *et al.*, 1984). Most prevention studies have evaluated programs that aim to prevent tobacco use and to delay alcohol use, the most widely used drugs in adolescence. These studies have provided some suggestive evidence that preventing or delaying tobacco and alcohol use reduces rates of cannabis use (Botvin *et al.*, 2002), but no studies to date have demonstrated that delaying cannabis use reduces the use of other illicit drugs. Many preventive programs have not been evaluated, and those that have been have found it difficult to demonstrate that they have reduced the use of rarely used illicit drugs (Gerstein and Green, 1993; Manski *et al.*, 2001). Even if the gateway hypothesis is correct, the most effective prevention programs would produce very modest reductions in the use of other illicit drugs because their impacts on cannabis use are likely to be modest and other illicit drug use is a rarer event in representative samples of youth (Caulkins *et al.*, 1999).

An Overall Evaluation of the Gateway Hypothesis

The role of cannabis in the "gateway pattern" of drug use remains controversial because of the difficulty of excluding the hypothesis that the gateway pattern is due to the common characteristics of those who use cannabis and other drugs. The finding of a simulation study that supported the common causal explanation has to be weighed against (i) a number of well-controlled longitudinal studies which suggest that selective recruitment to cannabis use does not wholly explain the association between cannabis use and the use of other illicit drugs; and (ii) a discordant twin study which suggests that shared genes and environment do not wholly explain the association.

There is also a possibility that patterns of progression of substance use have altered in recent decades as a result of changing availability and social disapproval regarding different kinds of substance use (Robins, 1995). Patton and colleagues (2005) have recently found that weekly or more cannabis use during the teens and young adulthood was associated with an increased late initiation of tobacco use as well as greater progression to nicotine dependence. This study has raised a possibility that the relationship between cannabis and tobacco might now be reciprocal so that cannabis might be considered a "gateway" to tobacco use.

ADOLESCENT EDUCATIONAL PERFORMANCE

A major concern about adolescent cannabis use is that it impairs educational performance and increases the risk that a student discontinues education. This is a plausible outcome, because cannabis use impairs memory and attention and so could interfere with learning (Lynskey and Hall, 2000). Cross-sectional surveys typically find associations between cannabis use and poor educational attainment among schoolchildren and youth (see, for example, Lifrak *et al.*, 1997; see also Lynskey and Hall, 2000, for a review). A number of studies have also shown that cannabis use is higher among young people who either no longer attend school or who had high rates of school absenteeism (Fergusson *et al.*, 1996; Lynskey *et al.*, 1999).

Explaining the Relationship Between Cannabis Use and Educational Outcomes

The first explanation of the association is that cannabis use is one of the causes of poor educational performance (see, for example, Kandel *et al.*, 1986). A second alternative is that heavy cannabis use is a consequence of poor educational attainment because the latter is a risk factor for cannabis use (Hawkins *et al.*, 1992a; Duncan *et al.*, 1998). The first and second hypotheses could both be true (Krohn *et al.*, 1997) if poor school performance increases the risks of using cannabis, which in turn worsens school performance. A third hypothesis is that cannabis use and poor educational attainment reflect a common problem behavior syndrome (Jessor and Jessor, 1977; Donovan and Jessor, 1985) and/or results from factors that increase the risk of both early cannabis use and poor educational performance (see Hawkins *et al.*, 1992a; Newcomb and Bentler, 1989). These explanations can only be distinguished in prospective studies of young people who are assessed over time on their cannabis use, educational attainment, and potentially confounding factors (such as family and social circumstances, personality characteristics and delinquency) (Rutter, 1988). Such studies provide answers to the question: do young people who use cannabis have poorer educational outcomes than those who do not, when we allow for the fact that cannabis users are more likely to have a history of poor school performance and other characteristics before they used cannabis?

Longitudinal Studies of Cannabis Use and Educational Outcomes

Newcomb and Bentler (1988) followed 654 high school students over 8 years to examine the effects of early drug use on educational attainment at ages 19–24 years. They examined the extent to which cannabis, alcohol and drug use were associated with poor school performance in young adulthood, after taking account of the effects of confounding factors. Their analyses indicated that early substance use (which included cannabis use) predicted college dropout. Similar results were obtained by Fergusson and colleagues (1996), who examined the relationship between cannabis use before the age of 15 years and early school leaving at age 16 in nearly 1000 young people who had been followed from birth. The 10 percent of the sample who had used cannabis by the age of 15 had elevated risks of school problems at age 16; 22.5 percent left school before 16 compared with only 3.5 percent of those who had not used cannabis. Fergusson and colleagues also found that young people who used cannabis before age 15 differed from those who had not, even *before* they used cannabis. The relationship between early cannabis use and early school leaving persisted after statistical adjustment for these differences. Similar findings have been reported by other researchers (Krohn *et al.*, 1997; Duncan *et al.*, 1998; Ellickson *et al.*, 1998; Tanner *et al.*, 1999).

Explaining the Association Between Cannabis Use and Early School Leaving

A number of hypotheses may explain why cannabis use increases the risk of early school leaving and poor school performance. Some have suggested that heavy cannabis use may produce an "amotivational" syndrome (Smith, 1968), but the evidence reviewed elsewhere (Hall and Pacula, 2003: Chapter 7) suggests that this it is more prudent to see impaired motivation as a symptom of cannabis dependence. Secondly, chronic cannabis use causes cognitive impairment, which in turn increases the likelihood of leaving school early. Solowij (1998) has argued that daily cannabis use over 3 or more years produces more subtle impairment in selective attention and in the ability to ignore irrelevant sensory information. The adults in the studies reviewed by Solowij, for example, used cannabis daily for an average of 10 years. By contrast, in the study reported by Fergusson and Horwood (2000), the "heavy" cannabis use group included those who had smoked cannabis on at least 10 occasions. There is no evidence in the scientific literature on adults that such low levels of use are associated with any lasting cognitive impairment. A third explanation is simpler: the school performance of young persons who are intoxicated by cannabis every day is impaired, and furthermore, it was poor to begin with (Lynskey and Hall, 2000). A fourth hypothesis is that early cannabis use leads to the precocious adoption of adult roles, including leaving school early to join the workforce (Newcomb and Bentler, 1988). There is support for this hypothesis in that in addition to leaving school early, adolescent cannabis users are more likely to marry early and experience a teenage pregnancy and childbirth. A fifth hypothesis is that much of the influence of early cannabis use on later development can be attributed to the social setting in which adolescents use cannabis, namely within a delinquent and substance-using peer group (Fergusson and Horwood, 1997). In this hypothesis, the important causal factor is a peer group that rejects high educational achievement, and encourages a premature transition to adulthood.

These hypotheses are not mutually exclusive. Indeed, it is probable that the impaired educational performance of adolescent cannabis users is attributable to a combination of acute cognitive impairment, affiliation with peers who reject school, and a desire to make an early transition to adulthood (Lynskey and Hall, 2000).

CANNABIS USE AND DEPRESSION

In recent years, some authors have suggested that cannabis use may be a contributory cause of depression and suicidal behaviors (Holden and Pakula, 1998; Johns, 2001). Cross-sectional studies report associations between cannabis use and depression (Degenhardt *et al.*, 2003), but also suggest that much of the association can be explained by confounding factors (such as other drug use). Longitudinal studies are more informative about the relationship between cannabis use and depression (Caron and Rutter, 1991; Merikangas and Angst, 1995).

Does Cannabis Use Lead to Depression?

Among the earliest studies was one by Kandel and colleagues (1986), who followed up a cohort of adolescents in New York State. They found that cannabis use *per se* at age 15–16 years was *not* associated with depressive symptoms at age 24–25 years, but greater involvement with cannabis was associated with a lower degree of life satisfaction and with consulting a mental health professional or being hospitalized for a psychiatric disorder. A New Zealand birth cohort study also found that cannabis use by age 15 years was *not* associated with an increased risk of a mental disorder (depression, anxiety disorders, substance dependence or antisocial personality disorder) at age 18 years (McGee *et al.*, 2000).

The most comprehensive examination of the "common cause" hypothesis has been reported by Fergusson and Horwood (2001) using data on a wide range of possible confounding variables collected on a birth cohort studied from birth to young adulthood. In an early report, the use of cannabis 10 or more times by age 15–16 years was *not* associated with either major depression or suicide attempts at age 16–18 years, after controlling for the effects of confounding individual, familial, peer and socio-demographic variables (Fergusson and Horwood, 1997).

In contrast, Brook and colleagues found that early-onset cannabis use was associated with a slightly increased risk of major depressive disorder by the age of 27 years, in a longitudinal cohort study of American children (Brook *et al.*, 2002). After controlling for demographics, family history and child/adolescent depression, those who had used cannabis in adolescence had a small increase in the odds of major depressive disorder (1.17) compared with those who had not (95% CI 1.04, 1.33). Use at the earliest assessment point was more strongly related to the risk of major depression (OR 1.57; 95% CI 1.10, 2.22). Those who had first used cannabis in early adulthood did not have any increased risk of major depression by the age of 27 years.

The preceding studies have generally examined the consequences of low levels of cannabis use on risks for later depression. Where more frequent cannabis use has been examined, a different pattern of association with depressive symptoms has emerged. Fergusson and colleagues have more recently re-examined the association between cannabis use during adolescence and depression, suicidal ideation, and suicide attempts by age 21 years (Fergusson *et al.*, 2002). They examined the effects of heavier patterns of cannabis use than those in their earlier study (which used the low cut-off of 10 or more uses in a lifetime to define heavy use). They found that by age 20–21 years, 30 percent of those using cannabis weekly or more often met criteria for depression, compared with 15 percent of those who did not use cannabis at that age. When Fergusson and colleagues adjusted for socio-demographic and individual factors, adverse life events, peer affiliation, school and home-leaving age, and alcohol dependence, the associations were substantially reduced, but there remained an association between cannabis use and the risk of depression, suicidal ideation and suicide attempts in the same year. For suicidal ideation and suicide attempts, the association with weekly cannabis use was highest among those aged 14–15 years. This association declined with age, so that by the age of 20–21 years there was no association with weekly cannabis use.

Recently, similar results have been reported from an Australian cohort of adolescents who were followed into young adulthood to examine the link between early-onset *regular* cannabis use and early adulthood depressive and anxiety symptoms (Patton *et al.*, 2007). A clear dose–response relationship existed between the frequency of cannabis use and depressive and anxiety symptoms in young adults, with the clearest association in daily users even after adjusting for other substance use. This study found that weekly cannabis use in adolescence predicted a two-fold increase in depressive and anxiety symptoms in females at 20–21 years; daily use predicted a four-fold increase in risk. These relationships were adjusted for confounding factors, including socio-demographic variables, alcohol use, gender, and antisocial behavior.

Does Depression Lead to Cannabis Use?

Longitudinal studies that have examined the association between depression and later cannabis use have generally failed to find a significant association. Paton and colleagues found no significant relationship between depressive mood and cannabis use either at the same time point, or prospectively over 6 months of follow-up in a cohort of adolescents (16–17 years) from New York State (Paton *et al.*, 1977). They did find depressed mood was related to the *onset* of cannabis use among those who had not used it previously (Paton *et al.*, 1977). In a later analysis, Kandel and colleagues reported that depression at age 16–17 years was not associated with higher rates of cannabis use at age 24–25 years (Kandel and Davies, 1986).

The significance of these findings remains uncertain, because other studies have not found any relationships between cannabis use and depression. A cohort study of African-American students followed from sixth to tenth grades found that depression in sixth grade was *not* associated with subsequent cannabis use (Miller-Johnson *et al.*, 1998). Similarly, a study of a Dutch cohort of children found that depression did not predict later substance dependence (including cannabis) (Hofstra *et al.*, 2002). The Dunedin, New Zealand, cohort study analyzed the relationships between depression at age 15 years and alcohol or cannabis dependence at age 21 years in females in their birth cohort (Bardone *et al.*, 1998). There was no significant association between the early-onset depression and later cannabis dependence, with or without statistical controlling for covariates.

A longitudinal study of children with pre-pubertal major depression found that there was no significant association with drug abuse or dependence by the time they were in their mid- to late twenties (Weissman *et al.*, 1999). The same results were found by Brook and colleagues when they analyzed the association between adolescent depression and later cannabis use, after controlling for age and gender (Brook *et al.*, 1998). More recently, Patton and colleagues analyzed the strength of association between depression between ages 14 and 18, and use of cannabis either weekly or daily at age 20–21 years (Patton *et al.*, 2007). There was no significant relationship between adolescent depression and young adult weekly or daily cannabis use after adjusting for socio-demographic variables, alcohol use, gender, adolescent cannabis use and antisocial behavior.

Summary

Longitudinal studies have consistently indicated that among cohorts of adolescents and young adults, the "self-medication" hypothesis does *not* fit the evidence. There is more mixed evidence that heavy cannabis use increases the risk of depression during follow-up, and this relationship is partly but not *completely* explained by confounding variables.

CANNABIS USE AND PSYCHOSIS

Cannabis use and psychotic symptoms and disorders are associated in the general population (see, for example, Degenhardt and Hall, 2001; Tien and Anthony, 1990) and in clinical samples of patients with schizophrenia (Mueser *et al.*, 1992; Warner *et al.*, 1994; Hambrecht and Hafner, 1996). The major contending hypotheses to explain the association have been: (i) that cannabis use precipitates schizophrenia in persons who are otherwise vulnerable; (ii) cannabis use is a form of self-medication for schizophrenia; and (iii) that the association arises from uncontrolled residual confounding by variables that predict an increased risk of cannabis use and of schizophrenia (Macleod *et al.*, 2004).

To decide between these hypotheses, we need evidence that cannabis use preceded the psychosis; that plausible alternative explanations based on confounding can be excluded (Hall, 1987). The best evidence for answering these questions comes from longitudinal population-based studies that have assessed cannabis use before the onset of psychotic symptoms, followed the cohort over a substantial period and used statistical methods to assess the contribution of a variety of factors other than cannabis use that may explain the relationship (Macleod *et al.*, 2004).

The Swedish Conscript Study

Until very recently, the most convincing evidence that cannabis use precipitates schizophrenia came from a 15-year prospective study of cannabis use and schizophrenia in 50 465 Swedish conscripts (Andreasson *et al.*, 1987). This study investigated the relationship between self-reported cannabis use at age 18 and the risk of being diagnosed with schizophrenia in the Swedish psychiatric case register during the next 15 years. Andreasson and colleagues found a dose–response relationship between the risk of schizophrenia and the number of times cannabis had been used by age 18 (1.3 times higher for those who had used cannabis 1–10 times, 3 times higher for those who had used cannabis 1–50 times, and 6 times higher for those who had used cannabis more than 50 times). These risks were reduced after statistical adjustment for potentially confounding variables (a psychiatric diagnosis at age 18, and parental divorce), but the relationships remained statistically significant.

Zammit and colleagues (2002) reported a 27-year follow-up of the Swedish cohort study. This study improved on the earlier study in the following ways: the psychiatric register provided more complete coverage of cases diagnosed with schizophrenia; and there was better statistical control of more potentially confounding variables, including other drug use, IQ, known risk factors for schizophrenia and social integration. Cannabis use at baseline predicted a dose–response relationship between the frequency of cannabis use at age 18 and the risk of schizophrenia during the follow-up. The relationship persisted after statistically controlling for the effects of other drug use and other potential confounding factors, including a history of psychiatric symptoms at baseline. They estimated that 13 percent of cases of schizophrenia could be averted if all cannabis use were prevented.

Zammit and colleagues' findings were supported in a 3-year longitudinal study of the relationship between self-reported cannabis use and psychosis in a community sample of 4848 people in the Netherlands (van Os *et al.*, 2002). Van Os and colleagues reported that cannabis use at baseline predicted an increased risk of psychotic symptoms during the follow-up period in individuals who had not reported psychiatric symptoms at baseline. There was a dose–response relationship between frequency of cannabis use at baseline and risk of psychotic symptoms during the follow-up period. These relationships persisted when they statistically controlled for the effects of other drug use. The relationship between cannabis use and psychotic symptoms was also stronger for cases with more severe psychotic symptoms.

A study by Henquet and colleagues (2004) substantially replicated both the Swedish and Dutch studies in a 4-year follow-up of a cohort of 2437 adolescents and young adults between 1995 and 1999 in Munich. They found a dose–response relationship between self-reported cannabis use at baseline and the likelihood of reporting psychotic symptoms. As in the Dutch cohort, young people who reported psychotic symptoms at baseline were much more likely to experience psychotic symptoms at follow-up if they used cannabis than were cannabis-using peers without such a history.

The results of the three large European cohort studies have been confirmed in two smaller New Zealand birth cohorts. Arsenault and colleagues (2002) reported a prospective study of the relationship between adolescent cannabis use and psychosis in a New Zealand birth cohort ($n = 759$). They found a relationship between cannabis use by age 15 and an increased risk of psychotic symptoms by age 26. The relationship did not change when they controlled for other drug use, but it was no longer statistically significant after adjusting for psychotic symptoms at age 11. The latter probably reflected the small number of psychotic disorders observed in the sample. Fergusson *et al.* (2003) found a relationship between cannabis dependence at age 18 and later symptoms that included those in the psychotic spectrum reported at age 21 in the Christchurch birth cohort. Fergusson and colleagues adjusted for a large number of potential confounding variables, including self-reported psychotic symptoms at the previous assessment, other drug use and other psychiatric disorders, but whether the association represents a link between cannabis use and psychotic symptoms specifically, or more general psychiatric morbidity, remains unclear.

The Self-Medication Hypothesis

The self-medication hypothesis was not supported in either the van Os or Henquet studies. Both studies found that early psychotic symptoms did not predict an increased risk of using cannabis (as is required by the self-medication hypothesis). The direction of the relationships was from early cannabis use to psychosis. Their negative results have recently been supported by Verdoux *et al.* (2002), who examined the temporal relationship between cannabis use and psychotic symptoms using an experience sampling method. They asked 79 college students to report on their drug use and experience of psychotic symptoms at randomly selected time points, several times each day over 7 consecutive days. The sample included high cannabis users ($n = 41$) and an over-representation of students identified as vulnerable to psychosis ($n = 16$). Verdoux and colleagues found that in time periods when cannabis was used, users reported more unusual perceptions, and these relationships were stronger in vulnerable individuals. There was no temporal relationship between reporting unusual experiences and using cannabis use, as would be predicted by the self-medication hypothesis.

Summary

There is reasonable evidence from prospective epidemiological studies which suggests that cannabis use can precipitate schizophrenia in persons who are vulnerable because of a personal or family history of schizophrenia. There is also evidence that a genetic vulnerability to psychosis increases the risk that cannabis users will develop psychosis (McGuire *et al.*, 1995; Arseneault *et al.*, 2002; Verdoux *et al.*, 2002). A casual relationship also has biological plausibility in that the cannabinoid and dopaminergic neurotransmitter systems interact in animals. D'Souza and colleagues (1999) have shown in a provocation study that THC produces a dose-dependent increase in psychotic symptoms under double-blind placebo conditions; and Caspi and colleagues (2005) have shown an interaction between specific alleles of the COMT allele and psychotogenic effects of cannabis. If these results can be replicated and extended, they will increase the likelihood that cannabis can be a contributory cause of psychosis in vulnerable individuals.

THE TREATMENT OF ADOLESCENT CANNABIS DEPENDENCE

Although many cannabis-dependent adults quit without professional help, a minority who are unable to stop on their own seek assistance. Until recently, there has been a paucity of research on the best methods of assisting dependent cannabis users to stop. In the past decade a series of controlled studies of treatment for cannabis-dependent adults have been conducted on behavioral (Stephens *et al.*, 2006), contingency management (Budney, 2006), psychodynamic (Grenyer and Solowij, 2006) and cognitive behavioral treatments (Budney *et al.*, 2000; Copeland *et al.*, 2001). These studies have typically reported large reductions in cannabis use and cannabis-related problems, but rates of abstinence at the end of treatment have been modest (20–40%). Rates of subsequent relapse have been substantial, so rates of enduring abstinence have been very modest (Budney and Moore, 2002). These outcomes are not very different from those observed in the treatment for alcohol and other forms of drug dependence (Budney and Moore, 2002).

Cannabis-dependent adolescents present an even more challenging group to treat than adults. They have higher rates of other complicating problems, including problems at school (Lynskey and Hall, 2000), other substance-related problems (Anthony and Petronis, 1995; Fergusson *et al.*, 1996), and involvement in crime and the criminal justice system (Fergusson *et al.*, 1994b). Adolescents with cannabis abuse and dependence, especially males, have high rates of comorbid conduct disorder, high rates of disruptive behavior, and high rates of alcohol and other types of drug abuse and dependence (see, for example, Degenhardt *et al.*, 2001a; Swift *et al.*, 2001; Whitmore and Riggs, 2006). The more such disorders cannabis-dependent adolescents have, the more likely they are to continue to abuse cannabis and other drugs and to engage in antisocial behavior (Grella, 2006).

Persons with cannabis use disorders in community surveys also have higher rates of anxiety and affective disorders than persons who do not have this diagnosis, and comorbid anxiety and affective disorders are predictive of treatment-seeking (Degenhardt *et al.*, 2001b). In treating cannabis-dependent adolescents, we need to improve recognition and treatment of these comorbid anxiety and affective disorders (Hall and Farrell, 1997). Brief, valid and reliable screening tests can be used to detect anxiety and depressive disorders among drug-dependent persons (Dawes and Mattick, 1997).

The high rates of conduct disorder and of involvement in the juvenile justice system (Crowley *et al.*, 1998; Grella, 2006) mean that many cannabis-dependent adolescents are legally coerced into treatment. This presents major challenges in engaging them in their treatment, because they may not be motivated to change – they may not consider their cannabis use to be a problem or see the need to change, despite the concerns of parents and difficulties at school and with the law (Brown and Ramo, 2006). One promising approach to engaging them in treatment and motivating them to change their drug use that is currently being evaluated involves using a "check-up" approach to enhance motivation with this group (Berghuis *et al.*, 2006).

Research into the treatment of adolescent cannabis and other illicit drug abusers is a relatively recent phenomenon (Liddle and Rowe, 2006). Observational studies of the outcome of treatment of adolescents with cannabis and other drug use problems within adult treatment services in the USA in the 1970s and 1980s was "mixed at best" (Grella, 2006). There were modest reductions in alcohol and other substance use overall (Flanza, 2006), but there was a worsening of substance abuse problems in a substantial minority of younger adolescents, which was most pronounced in those with multiple comorbid substance use disorders and involved with the criminal justice system (Grella, 2006).

More recent follow-up studies have been reported of adolescents treated in 37 community-based adolescent treatment programs in the USA in the 1990s (the DATOS-A study) (Grella, 2006). These programs provided a mix of approaches, including short-term inpatient treatment, therapeutic communities, residential treatment, and outpatient drug-free counseling. Their results were also very mixed (Brown and Ramo, 2006). At the end of 12 months, 54 percent had substantially reduced rates of substance abuse from baseline, but 22 percent had increased their use and 18 percent had not changed. Only 6 percent were abstinent at the end of a year (Grella, 2006). A 4-year follow-up of two cohorts of adolescents enrolled in 12-step community treatment programs reported similarly discouraging outcomes (Brown and Ramo, 2006). At the 4-year follow-up, 48 percent had been continuous heavy users of cannabis and other drugs, 27 percent had slowly worsened with time after initially improving, 10 percent were slow improvers, 8 percent were non-problem drinkers, and 7 percent had been continuously abstinent (Brown and Ramo, 2006). A large study of adolescent treatment programs (Morral *et al.*, 2006), taking account of case mix differences between treatments, was not able to find any differences in treatment outcome between four long-term residential treatments, four short-term residential treatments, and four outpatient counseling programs for substance-dependent adolescents. The proportions adjudged recovered (living in the community and reporting no symptoms of substance abuse) at 12 months were 27 percent and 22 percent respectively.

Recently, two multicenter trials have used randomized controlled trials to evaluate the effects of varying combinations and durations of different treatment approaches that had promising evidence of efficacy. These included cognitive behavior therapy (CBT), motivational enhancement therapy (MET), family support network (FSN), adolescent community reinforcement approach

(ACRA), and multidimensional family therapy (MDFT). These trials involved 600 cannabis-abusing and -dependent adolescents (83% male) who were treated in four centers in the USA (Diamond *et al.*, 2006; Titus and Dennis, 2006). There were high rates of cannabis abuse and dependence and high rates of comorbidity – especially externalizing disorders such as conduct disorder, alcohol use disorders, and attention deficit hyperactivity disorder (ADHD) – and 62 percent were involved in the criminal justice system at intake (Titus and Dennis, 2006).

One set of trials at two sites compared 5 and 15 sessions of MET/CBT with 12 sessions of MET/CBT plus family support network. The other trial, at two separate sites, compared 5 sessions of MET/CBT with ACRA and MDFT. There were modest reductions in cannabis use (with the number of days of abstinence in the past 90 days increasing from 52 to 65), but 21 percent required additional treatment within 3 months of treatment. An abstinence rate of 24 percent was reported across four follow-up periods, with no differences between treatments. Adolescents with comorbid disorders, early age of onset and a family history of alcohol and drug problems had a poorer outcome (Diamond *et al.*, 2006).

THE PREVENTION OF ADOLESCENT CANNABIS ABUSE AND DEPENDENCE

Schools have been the setting for most trials of prevention, principally because schools provided a close-to-universal point of access to the age groups at greatest risk of initiation of cannabis use. The focus of interventions has varied from promotion of knowledge about drugs and their consequences, to enhancing refusal skills and, most recently, on aspects of emotional control implicated in substance use. Another recent development in the field of adolescent drug prevention has been a growing awareness of the limitations of school-based drug prevention strategies that try to influence individual drug use (Caulkins *et al.*, 1999; McBride, 2005). The field has seen a need for a broader perspective on what constitutes "drug prevention" – one that is based on an understanding of the underlying risk processes (Stockwell *et al.*, 2005; Toumobourou *et al.*, 2005).

Traditionally, school-based programs have aimed to affect young adolescents' decisions about whether to use drugs (McBride, 2005). Approaches that focus on knowledge have generally been shown to improve knowledge but are not to be effective in changing drug use (McBride, 2005; Robins, 1995). Programs teaching drug-resistance skills and norm setting, either alone or in combination with general personal and social skills, have generally been more effective, particularly where combined with booster sessions (Robins, 1995). School-based prevention programs that improve social competency are effective in preventing drug use and other problem behaviors: "self- control or social competency promotion instruction that makes use of cognitive-behavioral and behavioral instructional methods show consistently positive effects" (Coffey *et al.*, 2002).

A more recent promising approach to prevention looks beyond the individual student to promote a positive social environment at school and thereby enhance the protective effects of a positive school connection (Patton *et al.*, 2006). In an intervention that tied curriculum-based elements with those focused on whole-school change, substantial reductions were found in substance use and antisocial behaviors in early secondary school students.

Best-practice school-based drug education programs produce modest but behaviorally important reductions in drug use (Caulkins *et al.*, 1999), but best-practice school programs appear to be implemented rarely (McBride, 2005). School communities appear to prefer programs that reassure parents rather than ones that are likely to prevent drug use, and well-designed programs are often implemented poorly (McBride, 2005). In part, this may arise from a failure to establish programs that can both deliver an effective prevention dose and sit comfortably within normal school curricula. School-based drug prevention programs should: adopt best practice, create realistic expectations of their impact, sit as far as possible within usual school processes, and make clear that schools alone cannot prevent drug use among youth (Spooner and Hall, 2002; McBride, 2005). Such programs need to be part of a public policy that aims to create an environment for the healthy development of all children (Holder *et al.*, 2005).

There is an increasing awareness of the economic, socio-cultural and physical environmental influences on individual drug use. In part, this has arisen from an improved understanding of risk processes involved in substance use and substance use disorders. Some risk processes derived from the family setting, where risk factors such as family conflict, abuse and substance use suggest the potential for preventive interventions focused on family attachment and attitudes to substance use. So too risk factors such as early academic failure and childhood disruptive behavior suggest the potential for extending early successful approaches in the areas of intervention (Hawkins *et al.*, 1992b; Dolan *et al.*, 1993).

Spooner and colleagues concluded, after reviewing research on the structural determinants of youth drug use, that an even broader conceptualization was needed of the etiology of problem adolescent drug use and the type of interventions that were needed to reduce drug use and the harm that it causes (Spooner *et al.*, 2001). Macro-environmental factors (which include the economic environment, the social environment and the physical environment) have an influence from birth on risks of later drug use – long before young people are exposed to school-based drug prevention programs. A broader approach is needed – one that includes inter-sectoral collaboration and adopts a longer-term perspective – to replace uncoordinated, short-term, drug-specific prevention programs that focus only on changing the drug use of individuals.

Work in a variety of areas suggests the need to reorient efforts to prevent youth drug use in the following ways (Spooner *et al.*, 2001; Spooner and Hall, 2002; Stockwell *et al.*, 2005). We need to broaden our focus from individuals to environments that promote physical and mental health. This involves avoiding seeing drug prevention as an activity that addresses a number of co-occurring problem behaviors. It needs to join forces with crime prevention, mental health and suicide prevention programs that pay more attention to the earlier years of development and the role of families in these years (Toumobourou *et al.*, 2005). We need to encourage policy-makers to take a broader perspective on social investment in the developmental health of youth. This requires greater investment in research on adolescent drug use, mental health and criminology to improve our understanding of the causes and consequences of these behaviors, to better inform our efforts to prevent these disorders (Teesson *et al.*, 2005).

SUMMARY

Cannabis use has become very common among adolescents in many developed countries over the past several decades. The age of initiation has fallen steadily, while rates of regular use have risen. Both of these trends have been accompanied by increased rates of cannabis abuse and dependence among young people in specialist addiction and mental health services, in juvenile justice settings, and those under-performing at school.

Risks of developing dependence are around one in six to seven of adolescents who ever use cannabis in Australia, New Zealand and the USA. Cannabis dependence is correlated with being male and displaying disruptive and antisocial behavior and, to a lesser extent, with anxiety and depression. It is strongly predictive of alcohol and other forms of drug dependence, early school leaving, antisocial behavior and imprisonment.

Risk factors for problem cannabis use among adolescents include: initiating use at an early age; exposure to multiple social and family disadvantages; families with problems and a history of parental substance use; impulsivity and poor school performance; and affiliation with peers with a history of poor school performance, family disadvantage, and cannabis and other drug use. A young person who has a number of these risk factors – as many often do – is at high risk both of starting cannabis use at an early age, and of developing serious problems related to cannabis use.

Possible consequences of adolescent cannabis use include an increased risk of using of other illicit drugs, poor educational attainment, depression, and psychosis. There are relationships between cannabis dependence and all of these outcomes in longitudinal studies, the better ones of which have controlled for plausible alternative explanations of the associations. The case for cannabis playing some contributory causal role has increased in the case of poor educational attainment and psychosis, but some researchers remain skeptical because of the possibility of common causes explaining the associations. The same is true in the case of the relationships between cannabis and other drug use and depression, where common causal explanations also remain plausible.

Treatment for cannabis abuse and dependence in adolescents is largely behavioral and cognitive behavioral. Recent trials of these treatment approaches in adolescents show substantial reductions in cannabis use and problems in the short term, but no differences between different types of treatment in outcome at 12 months, high rates of relapse to cannabis use after treatment, and low rates of sustained abstinence. These modest outcomes reflect the special challenges in treating cannabis-dependent adolescents, namely their high rates of comorbid mental disorders, especially socially disruptive and antisocial behavior, and the low interest in and motivation for treatment among many young males who are legally coerced into seeking treatment.

The prevention of adolescent cannabis disorders must extend beyond the usual resort to school-based drug education and mass media campaigns that emphasize the risks of cannabis and other drug use. The best-practice educational programs that have modest effects on problem drug use are rarely implemented or implemented well. Broader preventive initiatives are required to address multiple risk factors for a range of co-occurring forms of problem behavior in young people, such as poor school performance, precocious sexual activity, early onset of alcohol and other drug use, and various forms of antisocial behavior. These include early childhood programs to support parents of at risk children, programs to support children entering school, programs in the early school years, programs to include engagement with school by adolescents and their parents, and parental effectiveness training in responding to problem behavior.

REFERENCES

AIHW (2005). 2004 National Drug Strategy Household Survey: detailed findings. *Drug Statistics Series* 16, Canberra: Australian Institute of Health and Welfare.

American Psychiatric Association (1994). *Diagnostic and Statistical Manual of Mental Disorders*, 4th edn. Washington, DC: American Psychiatric Association.

Andreasson, S., Engstrom, A., Allebeck, P. and Rydberg, U. (1987). Cannabis and schizophrenia: a longitudinal study of Swedish conscripts. *Lancet*, 2, 1483–1486.

Anthony, J.C. (2006). The epidemiology of cannabis dependence. In: R.A. Roffman and R.S. Stephens (eds.), *Cannabis Dependence: Its Nature, Consequences and Treatment*. Cambridge, Cambridgeshire: Cambridge University Press, pp. 58–105.

Anthony, J.C. and Petronis, K.R. (1995). Early-onset drug use and risk of later drug problems. *Drug and Alcohol Dependence*, 40, 9–15.

Anthony, J.C., Warner, L. and Kessler, R. (1994). Comparative epidemiology of dependence on tobacco, alcohol, controlled substances and inhalants: basic findings from the National Comorbidity Survey. *Experimental and Clinical Psychopharmacology*, 2, 244–268.

Arseneault, L., Cannon, M., Poulton, R. *et al.* (2002). Cannabis use in adolescence and risk for adult psychosis: longitudinal prospective study. *British Medical Journal*, 325, 1212–1213.

Babor, T. (2006). The diagnosis of cannabis dependence. In: R.A. Roffman and R.S. Stephens (eds), *Cannabis Dependence: Its Nature, Consequences and Treatment*. Cambridge, Cambridgeshire: Cambridge University Press, pp. 21–36.

Bachman, J.G., Wadsworth, K.N., O'Malley, P.M. *et al.* (1997). *Smoking, Drinking and Drug Use in Young Adulthood: The Impacts of New Freedoms and New Responsibilities*. Mahwah, NJ: Lawrence Erlbaum.

Bailey, S.L., Flewelling, R.L. and Rachal, J.V. (1992). Predicting continued use of marijuana among adolescents: the relative influence of drug-specific and social context factors. *Journal of Health and Social Behavior*, 33, 51–66.

Bardone, A.M., Moffitt, T.E., Caspi, A. *et al.* (1998). Adult physical health outcomes of adolescent girls with conduct disorder, depression and anxiety. *Journal of the American Academy of Child and Adolescent Psychiatry*, 37, 594–601.

Barnes, G.M. and Welte, J.W. (1986). Patterns and predictors of alcohol use among 7th–12th grade students in New York State. *Journal of Studies on Alcohol*, 47, 53–62.

Berghuis, J.P., Swift, W., Roffman, R. *et al.* (2006). The teen cannabis check-up: exploring strategies for reaching young cannabis users. In: R.A. Roffman and R.S. Stephens (eds), *Cannabis Dependence: Its Nature, Consequences and Treatment*. Cambridge, Cambridgeshire: Cambridge University Press, pp. 275–292.

Botvin, G.J., Scheier, L.M. and Griffin, K.W. (2002). Preventing the onset and developmental progression of adolescent drug use: implications for the gateway hypothesis. In: D.B. Kandel (ed.), *Stages and Pathways of Drug Involvement: Examining the Gateway Hypothesis*. New York, NY: Cambridge University Press., pp. 115–138.

Brook, D.W., Brook, J.S., Zhang, C. *et al.* (2002). Drug use and the risk of major depressive disorder, alcohol dependence and substance use disorders. *Archives of General Psychiatry*, 59, 1039–1044.

Brook, J.S., Brook, D.W., Gordon, A.S. *et al.* (1990). The psychosocial etiology of adolescent drug use: a family interactional approach. *Genetic, Social and General Psychology Monographs*, 116, 111–267.

Brook, J.S., Cohen, P. and Brook, D.W. (1998). Longitudinal study of co-occurring psychiatric disorders and substance use. *Journal of the American Academy of Child and Adolescent Psychiatry*, 37, 322–330.

Brook, J.S., Brook, D.W. and Pahl, K. (2006). The developmental context. In: H.A. Liddle and C.L. Rowe (eds), *Adolescent Substance Abuse: Research and Clinical Advances*. Cambridge, Cambridgeshire: Cambridge University Press, pp. 25–51.

Brown, S.A. and Ramo, D.E. (2006). Clinical course of youth following treatment for alcohol and drug problems. In: H.A. Liddle and C.L. Rowe (eds), *Adolescent Substance Abuse: Research and Clinical Advances*. Cambridge, Cambridgeshire: Cambridge University Press, pp. 79–103.

Budney, A.J. (2006). Are specific dependence criteria necessary for different substances: how can research on cannabis inform this issue? *Addiction*, 101(Suppl. 1), 125–133.

Budney, A.J. and Moore, B.A. (2002). Development and consequences of cannabis dependence. *Journal of Clinical Pharmacology*, 42, 28S–33S.

Budney, A.J., Higgins, S.T., Radonovich, K.J. and Novy, P.L. (2000). Adding voucher-based incentives to coping skills and motivational enhancement improves outcomes during treatment for marijuana dependence. *Journal of Consulting and Clinical Psychology*, 68, 1051–1061.

Cadoni, C., Pisanu, A., Solinas, M. *et al.* (2001). Behavioural sensitization after repeated exposure to {Delta}9-tetrahydrocannabinol and cross-sensitization with morphine. *Psychopharmacology*, 158, 259–266.

Caetano, R. and Babor, T.F. (2006). Diagnosis of alcohol dependence in epidemiological surveys: an epidemic of youthful alcohol dependence or a case of measurement error? *Addiction*, 101(Suppl. 1), 111–114.

Caron, C. and Rutter, M. (1991). Comorbidity in child psychopathology: concepts, issues and research strategies. *Journal of Child Psychology and Psychiatry*, 32, 1063–1080.

Caspi, A., Moffitt, T.E., Cannon, M. *et al.* (2005). Moderation of the effect of adolescent-onset cannabis use on adult psychosis by a functional polymorphism in the catechol-O-methyltransferase gene: longitudinal evidence of a gene X environment interaction. *Biological Psychiatry*, 57, 1117–1127.

Caulkins, J.P., Rydell, C.P., Everingham, S.M.S. *et al.* (1999). *An Ounce of Prevention, A Pound of Uncertainty: The Cost-effectiveness of School-based Drug Prevention Programs*. Santa Monica, CA: Rand Corporation.

Chen, C.Y., O'Brien, M.S. and Anthony, J.C. (2005). Who becomes cannabis dependent soon after onset of use? Epidemiological evidence from the United States: 2000–2001. *Drug and Alcohol Dependence*, 79, 11–22.

Chen, K. and Kandel, D.B. (1995). The natural history of drug use from adolescence to the mid-thirties in a general population sample. *American Journal of Public Health*, 85, 41–47.

Chen, K. and Kandel, D.B. (1998). Predictors of cessation of marijuana use: an event history analysis. *Drug and Alcohol Dependence*, 50, 109–121.

Cloninger, C.R., Sigvardsson, S. and Bohman, M. (1988). Childhood personality predicts alcohol abuse in young adults. *Alcoholism, Clinical and Experimental Research*, 12, 494–505.

Coffey, C., Carlin, J.B., Degenhardt, L. *et al.* (2002). Cannabis dependence in young adults: an Australian population study. *Addiction*, 97, 187–194.

Coffey, C., Carlin, J.B., Lynskey, M.T. *et al.* (2003). Adolescent precursors of cannabis dependence: findings from the Victorian Adolescent Health Cohort Study. *British Journal of Psychiatry*, 182, 330–336.

Copeland, J., Swift, W., Roffman, R. and Stephens, R. (2001). A randomized controlled trial of brief cognitive-behavioral interventions for cannabis use disorder. *Journal of Substance Abuse Treatment*, 21, 55–64.

Crowley, T.J. (2006). Adolescents and substance-related disorders: research agenda to guide decisions on *Diagnostic and Statistical Manual of Mental Disorders*, fifth edition (DSM-V). *Addiction*, 101(Suppl. 1), 115–124.

Crowley, T.J., Macdonald, M.J., Whitmore, E.A. and Mikulich, S.K. (1998). Cannabis dependence, withdrawal and reinforcing effects among adolescents with conduct symptoms and substance use disorders. *Drug and Alcohol Dependence*, 50, 27–37.

Dawes, S. and Mattick, R. (1997). *Review of Diagnostic and Screening Instruments for Alcohol and Other Psychiatric Disorders*. Canberra: Australian Government Publishing Service.

Degenhardt, L. and Hall, W.D. (2001). The association between psychosis and problematical drug use among Australian adults: findings from the National Survey of Mental Health and Well-being. *Psychological Medicine*, 31, 659–668.

Degenhardt, L., Lynskey, M.T. and Hall, W.D. (2000). Cohort trends in the age of initiation of drug use in Australia. *Australian and New Zealand Journal of Public Health*, 24, 421–426.

Degenhardt, L., Hall, W. and Lynskey, M. (2001a). The relationship between cannabis use and other substance use in the general population. *Drug and Alcohol Dependence*, 64, 319–327.

Degenhardt, L., Hall, W.D. and Lynskey, M. (2001b). The relationship between cannabis use, depression and anxiety among Australian adults: findings from the National Survey of Mental Health and Well-being. *Social Psychiatry and Psychiatric Epidemiology*, 36, 219–227.

Degenhardt, L., Hall, W.D. and Lynskey, M. (2003). Exploring the association between cannabis use and depression. *Addiction*, 98, 1493–1504.

Dennis, M., Godley, S.H., Diamond, G. *et al.* (2004). The Cannabis Youth Treatment (CYT) Study: main findings from two randomized trials. *Journal of Substance Abuse Treatment*, 27, 197–213.

Diamond, G., Leckrone, J., Dennis, M.L. and Godley, S.H. (2006). The Cannabis Youth Treatment Study: the treatment models and preliminary findings. In: R.A. Roffman and R.S. Stephens (eds), *Cannabis Dependence: Its Nature, Consequences and Treatment.* Cambridge, Cambrigeshire: Cambridge University Press, 247–274.

Dolan, L.J., Kellam, S.G., Brown, C.H. *et al.* (1993). The short-term impact of two classroom-based preventive interventions on aggressive and shy behaviors and poor achievement. *Journal of Applied Developmental Psychology*, 14, 317–345.

Donnelly, N. and Hall, W.D. (1994). Patterns of cannabis use in Australia. *National Drug Strategy Monograph* 27, Canberra: Australian Government Publishing Service.

Donovan, J.E. and Jessor, R. (1983). Problem drinking and the dimension of involvement with drugs: a Guttman scalogram analysis of adolescent drug use. *American Journal of Public Health*, 73, 543–552.

Donovan, J.E. and Jessor, R. (1985). Structure of problem behavior in adolescence and young adulthood. *Journal of Consulting and Clinical Psychology*, 53, 890–904.

D'Souza, D.C., Berman, R.M., Krystal, J.H. and Charney, D.S. (1999) Symptom provocation studies in psychiatric disorders. Scientific value, risks and future. *Biological Psychiatry*, 46, 1060–1080.

Duncan, S.C., Duncan, T.E., Biglan, A. and Ary, D. (1998). Contributions of the social context to the development of adolescent substance use: a multivariate latent growth modeling approach. *Drug and Alcohol Dependence*, 50, 57–71.

Edwards, G. and Gross, M.M. (1976). Alcohol dependence: provisional description of a clinical syndrome. *British Medical Journal*, 1, 1058–1061.

Ellickson, P., Bui, K., Bell, R. and McGuigan, K.A. (1998). Does early drug use increase the risk of dropping out of high school? *Journal of Drug Issues*, 28, 357–380.

EMCDDA (2006). *Annual Report* 2006*: The State of the Drugs Problem in Europe*. Lisbon: European Monitoring Centre for Drugs and Drug Addiction.

Essau, C. (2006). Epidemiological trends and clinical implications of adolescent substance abuse in Europe. In: H.A. Liddle and C.L. Rowe (eds), *Adolescent Substance Abuse: Research and Clinical Advances*. Cambridge, Cambridgeshire: Cambridge University Press, pp. 129–147.

Fergusson, D.M. and Horwood, L.J. (1997). Early onset cannabis use and psychosocial adjustment in young adults. *Addiction*, 92, 279–296.

Fergusson, D.M. and Horwood, L.J. (2000). Does cannabis use encourage other forms of illicit drug use? *Addiction*, 95, 505–520.

Fergusson, D.M. and Horwood, L.J. (2001). The Christchurch Health and Development Study: review of findings on child and adolescent mental health. *Australian and New Zealand Journal of Psychiatry*, 35, 287–296.

Fergusson, D.M., Horwood, J. and Swain-Campbell, N. "Cannabis Use and psychosocial adjustment in adolescence and young adulthood." Unpublished manuscript.

Fergusson, D.M., Horwood, L.J. and Lynskey, M.T. (1994a). Parental separation, adolescent psychopathology and problem behaviors. *Journal of the American Academy of Child and Adolescent Psychiatry*, 33, 1122–1131; discussion 1131–1123.

Fergusson, D.M., Horwood, L.J. and Lynskey, M.T. (1994b). The childhoods of multiple problem adolescents: a 15-year longitudinal study. *Journal of Child Psychology and Psychiatry*, 35, 1123–1140.

Fergusson, D.M., Lynskey, M.T. and Horwood, L.J. (1996). The short-term consequences of early onset cannabis use. *Journal of Abnormal Child Psychology*, 24, 499–512.

Fergusson, D.M., Horword, L.J. and Swain-Campbell, N. (2002). Cannabis use and psychosocial adjustment in adolescence and young adulthood. *Addiction*, 97, 1123–1135.

Fergusson, D.M., Horwood, J.L. and Swain-Campbell, N.R. (2003). Cannabis dependence and psychotic symptoms in young people. *Psychological Medicine*, 33, 15–21.

Flanza, J. P. (2006). Health services with drug abusing adolescents: the next frontier of research. In: H.A. Liddle and C.L. Rowe (eds), *Adolescent Substance Abuse: Research and Clinical Advances*. Cambridge, Cambridgeshire: Cambridge University Press, pp. 204–219.

Gardner, E. (1999). Cannabinoid interaction with brain reward systems. In: G. Nahas, K. Sutin, D. Harvey and S. Agurell (eds), *Marihuana and Medicine*. Towa, NJ: Humana Press, pp. 187–205.

Gerstein, D.R. and Green, L.W. (eds). (1993). *Preventing Drug Abuse: What Do We Know?* Washington, DC: National Academy Press.

Grella, C. (2006). The Drug Abuse Treatment Outcome Studies: outcomes with adolescent substance abusers. In: H.A. Liddle and C.L. Rowe (eds), *Adolescent Substance Abuse: Research and Clinical Advances*. Cambridge, Cambridgeshire: Cambridge University Press, 148–169.

Grenyer, B.F.S. and Solowij, N. (2006). Supportive-expressive therapy for cannabis dependence. In: R.A. Roffman and R.S. Stephens (eds), *Cannabis Dependence: Its Nature, Consequences and Treatment*. Cambridge, Cambridgeshire: Cambridge University Press, pp. 225–243.

Hall, W.D. (1987). A simplified logic of causal inference. *Australian and New Zealand Journal of Psychiatry*, 21, 507–513.

Hall, W.D. and Farrell, M. (1997). Comorbidity of mental disorders with substance misuse. *British Journal of Psychiatry*, 171, 4–5.

Hall, W.D. and Lynskey, M. (2005). Is cannabis a gateway drug? Testing hypotheses about the relationship between cannabis use and the use of other illicit drugs. *Drug and Alcohol Review*, 24, 39–48.

Hall, W.D. and Pacula, R.L. (2003). *Cannabis Use and Dependence: Public Health and Public Policy*. Cambridge, Cambridgeshire: Cambridge University Press.

Hall, W.D., Teesson, M., Lynskey, M.T. and Degenhardt, L. (1999). The 12-month prevalence of substance use and ICD-10 substance use disorders in Australian adults: findings from the National Survey of Mental Health and Well-being. *Addiction*, 94, 1541–1550.

Hambrecht, M. and Hafner, H. (1996). Substance abuse and the onset of schizophrenia. *Biological Psychiatry*, 40, 1155–1163.

Han, C., McGue, M.K. and Iacono, W.G. (1999). Lifetime tobacco, alcohol and other substance use in adolescent Minnesota twins: univariate and multivariate behavioral genetic analyses. *Addiction*, 94, 981–993.

Harkin, A., Anderson, P. and Goos, P. (1997). *Smoking, Drinking and Drug Taking in the European Region*. Copenhagen: WHO Regional Office for Europe.

Hawkins, J.D., Catalano, R.F. and Miller, J.Y. (1992a). Risk and protective factors for alcohol and other drug problems in adolescence and early adulthood: implications for substance abuse prevention. *Psychological Bulletin*, 112, 64–105.

Hawkins, J.D., Catalano, R., Morrison, D. *et al.* (1992b). The Seattle Social Development Project: effect of the first four years on protective and problem behaviors. In: J. McCord and R. Tremblay (eds), *Preventing Antisocial Behavior: Interventions from Birth through to Adolescence*. New York, NY: Guilford Press.

Heath, A.C. (1995). Genetic influences on alcoholism risk: a review of adoption and twin studies. *Alcohol Health and Research World*, 19, 166–171.

Henquet, C., Krabbendam, L., Spauwen, J. *et al.* (2004). Prospective cohort study of cannabis use, predisposition for psychosis and psychotic symptoms in young people. *British Medical Journal*, 330, 11.

Hofstra, M.B., van der Ende, J. and Verhulst, F.C. (2002). Child and adolescent problems predict DSM-IV disorders in adulthood: a 14-year follow-up of a Dutch epidemiological sample. *Journal of the American Academy of Child and Adolescent Psychiatry*, 41, 182–189.

Holder, H.D., Treno, A. and Levy, D. (2005). Community systems and ecologies of drug and alcohol problems. In: T. Stockwell, P.J. Gruenwald, J.W. Toumbourou and W. Loxley (eds), *Preventing Harmful Substance Use: The Evidence Base for Policy and Practice*. Chichester, Sussex: John Wiley & Sons, pp. 149–162.

Holden, R.J. and Pakula, I. (1998). Marijuana, stress and suicide: a neuroimmunological explanation. *Australian and New Zealand Journal of Psychiatry*, 32, 465–466.

Hwu, H.G. and Compton, W.M. (1994). Comparison of major epidemiological surveys using the Diagnostic Interview Schedule. *International Review of Psychiatry*, 6, 309–327.

Jessor, R. and Jessor, S.L. (1977). *Problem Behavior and Psychosocial Development: A Longitudinal Study of Youth*. New York, NY: Academic Press.

Johns, A. (2001). Psychiatric effects of cannabis. *British Journal of Psychiatry*, 178, 116–122.

Johnston, L.D., O'Malley, P.M., Bachman, J.G. and Schulenberg, J.E. (2006). *Monitoring the Future: National Survey Results on Drug Use 1975–2005*. Bethesda, MD: US Department of Health and Human Services, National Institutes of Health.

Kandel, D.B. (1975). Stages in adolescent involvement in drug use. *Science*, 190, 912–914.

Kandel, D.B. (1984). Marijuana users in young adulthood. *Archives of General Psychiatry*, 41, 200–209.

Kandel, D.B. (2002). *Stages and Pathways of Drug Involvement: Examining the Gateway Hypothesis*. New York, NY: Cambridge University Press.

Kandel, D.B. and Andrews, K. (1987). Processes of adolescent socialisation by parents and peers. *International Journal of the Addictions*, 22, 319–342.

Kandel, D.B. and Davies, M. (1986). Adult sequelae of adolescent depressive symptoms. *Archives of General Psychiatry*, 43, 255–262.

Kandel, D.B. and Davies, M. (1992). Progression to regular marijuana involvement: phenomenology and risk factors for near-daily use. In: M.D. Glantz (ed.), *Vulnerability to Drug Abuse*. Washington, DC: American Psychological Association, pp. 211–253.

Kandel, D.B. and Yamaguchi, K. (2002). Stages of drug involvement in the US population. In D.B. Kandel (ed.), *Stages and Pathways of Drug Involvement: Examining the Gateway Hypothesis*. New York, NY: Cambridge University Press, pp. 65–89.

Kandel, D.B., Davies, M., Karus, D. and Yamaguchi, K. (1986). The consequences in young adulthood of adolescent drug involvement: an overview. *Archives of General Psychiatry*, 43, 746–754.

Kendler, K.S. and Prescott, C.A. (1998). Cannabis use, abuse and dependence in a population-based sample of female twins. *American Journal of Psychiatry*, 155, 1016–1022.

Krohn, M.D., Lizotte, A.J. and Perez, C.M. (1997). The interrelationship between substance use and precocious transitions to adult statuses. *Journal of Health and Social Behavior*, 38, 87–103.

Lamarque, S., Taghzouti, K. and Simon, H. (2001). Chronic treatment with {Delta} 9-tetra hydrocannabinol enhances the locomotor response to amphetamine and heroin: implications for vulnerability to drug addiction. *Neuropharmacology*, 41, 118–129.

Lascala, E., Friesthler, B. and Gruenwald, P.J. (2005). Population ecologies of drug use, drinking and related problems. In: T. Stockwell, P.J. Gruenwald, J.W. Toumbourou and W. Loxley (eds), *Preventing Harmful Substance Use: The Evidence Base for Policy and Practice*. Chichester, Sussex: John Wiley & Sons.

Liddle, H. and Rowe, C.L. (2006). Treating adolescent substance abuse: state of the science. In: H.A. Liddle and C.L. Rowe (eds.), *Adolescent Substance Abuse: Research and Clinical Advances*. Cambridge, Cambridgeshire: Cambridge University Press, pp. 1–21.

Lifrak, P.D., McKay, J.R., Rostain, A. *et al.* (1997). Relationship of perceived competencies, perceived social support and gender to substance use in young adolescents. *Journal of the American Academy of Child and Adolescent Psychiatry*, 36, 933–940.

Lynskey, M. (2002). An alternative model is feasible, but the gateway hypothesis has not been invalidated: Comments on Morral *et al. Addiction*, 97, 1505–1507.

Lynskey, M.T. and Hall, W.D. (1999). *Cannabis Use among Australian Youth: Prevalence and Correlates of Use*. Sydney: National Drug and Alcohol Research Centre, University of New South Wales.

Lynskey, M.T. and Hall, W.D. (2000). The effects of adolescent cannabis use on educational attainment: a review. *Addiction*, 96, 433–443.

Lynskey, M.T., Fergusson, D.M. and Horwood, L.J. (1994). The effect of parental alcohol problems on rates of adolescent psychiatric disorders. *Addiction*, 89, 1277–1286.

Lynskey, M.T., White, V., Hill, D. *et al.* (1999). Prevalence of illicit drug use among youth: results from the Australian School Students' Alcohol and Drugs Survey. *Australian and New Zealand Journal of Public Health*, 23, 519–524.

Lynskey, M.T., Heath, A.C., Bucholz, K.K. and Slutske, W.S. (2003). Escalation of drug use in early-onset cannabis users vs co-twin controls. *Journal of the American Medical Association*, 289, 427–433.

Macleod, J., Oakes, R., Copello, A. *et al.* (2004). Psychological and social sequelae of cannabis and other illicit drug use by young people: a systematic review of longitudinal, general population studies. *Lancet*, 363, 1579–1588.

Manski, C.F., Pepper, J.V. and Petrie, C.V. (eds) (2001). *Informing America's Policy on Illegal Drugs: What We Don't Know Keeps Hurting Us*. Washington, DC: National Academy Press.

Manzanares, J., Corchero, J., Romero, J. *et al.* (1999). Pharmacological and biochemical interactions between opioids and cannabinoids. *Trends in Pharmacological Sciences*, 20, 287–294.

McBride, N. (2005). The evidence base for school drug education interventions. In: T. Stockwell, P.J. Gruenwald, J.W. Toumbourou and W. Loxley (eds), *Preventing Harmful Substance Use: The Evidence Base for Policy and Practice*. Chichester, Sussex: John Wiley & Sons, pp. 129–147.

McGee, R. and Feehan, M. (1993). Cannabis use among New Zealand adolescents. *New Zealand Medical Journal*, 106, 345.

McGee, R., Williams, S., Poulton, R. and Moffitt, T. (2000). A longitudinal study of cannabis use and mental health from adolescence to early adulthood. *Addiction*, 95, 491–503.

McGuire, P.K., Jones, P., Harvey, I. *et al.* (1995). Morbid risk of schizophrenia for relatives of patients with cannabis-associated psychosis. *Schizophrenia Research*, 15, 277–281.

Merikangas, K. and Angst, J. (1995). The challenge of depressive disorders in adolescence. In: M. Rutter (ed.), *Psychosocial Disturbances in Young People*. Cambridge, Cambridgeshire: Cambridge University Press, pp. 131–165.

Miller-Johnson, S., Lochman, J.E., Coie, J.D. *et al.* (1998). Comorbidity of conduct and depressive problems at sixth grade: substance use outcomes across adolescence. *Journal of Abnormal Child Psychology*, 26, 221–232.

Morral, A., McCaffrey, D.F. and Paddock, S.M. (2002). Reassessing the marijuana gateway effect. *Addiction*, 97, 1493–1504.

Morral, A., McCaffrey, D.F., Rideway, G. *et al.* (2006). *The Relative Effectiveness of 10 Adolescent Substance Abuse Treatment Programs in the United States*. Santa Monica, CA: RAND Drug Policy Research Center.

Mueser, K.T., Bellack, A.S. and Blanchard, J.J. (1992). Comorbidity of schizophrenia and substance abuse: implications for treatment. *Journal of Consulting and Clinical Psychology*, 60, 845–856.

Newcomb, M.D. and Bentler, P.M. (1988). *Consequences of Adolescent Drug Use: Impact on the Lives of Young Adults*. Thousand Oaks, CA: Sage.

Newcomb, M.D. and Bentler, P.M. (1989). Substance use and abuse among children and teenagers. *American Psychologist*, 44, 242–248.

Newcomb, M.D., Maddahian, E. and Bentler, P.M. (1986). Risk factors for drug use among adolescents: concurrent and longitudinal analyses. *American Journal of Public Health*, 76, 525–531.

Patton, G.C., Coffey, C., Carlin, J.B. *et al.* (2005). Reverse gateways? Frequent cannabis use as a predictor of tobacco initiation and nicotine dependence. *Addiction*, 100, 1518–1525.

Patton, G.C., Bond, L., Carlin, J.B. *et al.* (2006). Promoting social inclusion in schools: a group-randomized trial of effects on student health risk behavior and well-being. *American Journal of Public Health*, 96, 1582–1587.

Patton, G.C., Coffey, C., Carlin, J. *et al.* (2007). The mental health of young cannabis users: findings from the Victorian Adolescent Health Cohort Study. *British Medical Journal*, submitted.

Paton, S., Kessler, R. and Kandel, D. (1977). Depressive mood and adolescent illicit drug use: a longitudinal analysis. *Journal of Genetic Psychology*, 131, 267–289.

Polich, J.M., Ellickson, P.L., Reuter, P. and Kahan, J.P. (1984). *Strategies for Controlling Adolescent Drug Use*, Santa Monica, CA, Rand Corporation.

Robins, L. (1995). The natural history of substance use as a guide to setting drug policy. *American Journal of Public Health*, 85, 12–13.

Robins, L.N. and Reiger, D.A. (eds) (1991). *Psychiatric Disorders in America: The Epidemiological Catchment Area Study*. New York, NY: The Free Press.

Russell, J.M., Newman, S.C. and Bland, R.C. (1994). Drug abuse and dependence. *Acta Psychiatrica Scandinavica*, 89, 54–62.

Rutter, M. (1988). Longitudinal data in the study of causal processes: some uses and some pitfalls. In: M. Rutter (ed.), *Studies of Psychosocial Risk: The Power of Longitudinal Data*. Cambridge, Cambridgeshire: Cambridge University Press, pp. 12–19.

SAMHSA (2006). Treatment Episode Data Set (TEDS) 1994–2004. *National Admissions to Substance Abuse Treatment Services, DASIS Series S-* 33 *DHHS Publications No (SMA)* 06-4180, Rockville, MD: Substance Abuse and Mental Health Services Administration.

Smart, R.G. and Ogborne, A.C. (2000). Drug use and drinking among students in 36 countries. *Addictive Behaviors*, 25, 455–460.

Smith, D.E. (1968). Acute and chronic toxicity of marijuana. *Journal of Psychedelic Drugs*, 2, 37–47.

Solowij, N. (1998). *Cannabis and Cognitive Functioning*. Cambridge, Cambridgeshire: Cambridge University Press.

Spooner, C. and Hall, W.D. (2002). Preventing drug misuse by young people: we need to do more than "just say no". *Addiction*, 97, 478–481.

Spooner, C., Mattick, R. and Howard, J. (1996). The nature and treatment of adolescent substance abuse: final report of the adolescent treatment research project. *NDARC Monograph* 26, Sydney: National Drug and Alcohol Research Centre.

Spooner, C., Hall, W.D. and Lynskey, M. (2001). *The Structural Determinants of Youth Drug Use*. ANCD Research Paper 2, Canberra: Australian National Council on Drugs.

Stephens, R.S., Roffman, R.A. and Simpson, E.E. (1994). Treating adult marijuana dependence – a test of the relapse prevention model. *Journal of Consulting and Clinical Psychology*, 62, 92–99.

Stephens, R. S., Roffman, R.A., Copeland, J. and Swift, W. (2006). Cognitive behavioral and motivational enhancement treatments for cannabis dependence. In: R.A. Roffman and R.S. Stephens (eds), *Cannabis Dependence: Its Nature, Consequences and Treatment*. Cambridge, Cambridgeshire: Cambridge University Press, pp. 131–153.

Stockwell, T., Gruenwald, P.J., Toumbourou, J.W. and Loxley, W. (2005). Preventing risky drug use and related harms: the need for a synthesis of new knowledge. In: T. Stockwell, P.J. Gruenwald, J.W. Toumbourou and W. Loxley (eds), *Preventing Harmful Substance Use: The Evidence Base for Policy and Practice*. Chichester, Sussex: John Wiley & Sons.

Swift, W., Hall, W.D. and Teesson, C. (2001). Characteristics of DSM-IV and ICD-10 cannabis dependence among Australian adults: results from the National Survey of Mental Health and Well-being. *Drug and Alcohol Dependence*, 63, 147–153.

Tanner, J., Davies, S. and O'Grady, B. (1999). Whatever happened to yesterday's rebels? Longitudinal effects of youth delinquency on education and employment. *Social Problems*, 46, 250–274.

Teesson, M., Degenhardt, L., Proudfoot, H. *et al.* (2005). How common is comorbidity and why does it occur? *Australian Psychologist*, 40, 81–87.

Thombs, D.L., Beck, K.H., Mahoney, C.A. *et al.* (1994). Social context, sensation seeking and teenage alcohol abuse. *Journal of School Health*, 64, 73–79.

Tien, A.Y. and Anthony, J.C. (1990). Epidemiological analysis of alcohol and drug use as risk factors for psychotic experiences. *Journal of Nervous and Mental Disease*, 178, 473–480.

Tims, F.M., Dennis, M.L., Hamilton, N. *et al.* (2002). Characteristics and problems of 600 adolescent cannabis abusers in outpatient treatment. *Addiction*, 97, 46–57.

Titus, J.C. and Dennis, M.L. (2006). Cannabis Youth Treatment intervention: preliminary findings and implications. In: H.A. Liddle and C.L. Rowe (eds), *Adolescent Substance Abuse: Research and Clinical Advances*. Cambridge, Cambridgeshire: Cambridge University Press, pp. 104–126.

Toumobourou, J.W. and Catalano, R.F. (2005). Preventing developmentally harmful substance use. In: T. Stockwell, P.J. Gruenwald, J.W. Toumbourou and W. Loxley (eds), *Preventing Harmful Substance Use: The Evidence Base for Policy and Practice*. Chichester, Sussex: John Wiley & Sons.

Toumobourou, J.W., Williams, J. and Patton, G. (2005). What do we know about preventing drug-related harm through social developmental intervention with children and young people? In: T. Stockwell, P.J. Gruenwald, J.W. Toumobourou and W. Loxley (eds), *Preventing Harmful Substance Use: The Evidence Base for Policy and Practice*. Chichester, Sussex: John Wiley & Sons.

True, W.R., Heath, A.C., Scherrer, J.F. *et al.* (1999). Interrelationship of genetic and environmental influences on conduct disorder and alcohol and marijuana dependence symptoms. *American Journal of Medical Genetics*, 88, 391–397.

van Os, J., Bak, M., Hanssen, M. *et al.* (2002). Cannabis use and psychosis: a longitudinal population-based study. *American Journal of Epidemiology*, 156, 319–327.

Verdoux, H., Gindre, C., Sorbara, F. *et al.* (2002). Cannabis use and the expression of psychosis vulnerability in daily life. *European Psychiatry*, 17, 180S.

Wagner, F.A. and Anthony, J.C. (2002). Into the world of illegal drug use: exposure opportunity and other mechanisms linking the use of alcohol, tobacco, marijuana and cocaine. *American Journal of Epidemiology*, 155, 918–925.

Warner, R., Taylor, D., Wright, J. *et al.* (1994). Substance use among the mentally ill: prevalence, reasons for use and effects on illness. *American Journal of Orthopsychiatry*, 64, 30–39.

Weissman, M.M., Wolk, S., Wickramaratne, P. *et al.* (1999). Children with prepubertal-onset major depressive disorder and anxiety grown up. *Archives of General Psychiatry*, 56, 794–801.

Wells, J., Bushnell, J., Joyce, P.R. *et al.* (1992). Problems with alcohol, drugs and gambling in Christchurch, New Zealand. In: M. Abbot and K. Evans (eds), *Alcohol and Drug Dependence and Disorders of Impulse Control.* Auckland: Alcohol Liquor Advisory Council, pp. 3–13.

White, V. and Hayman, J. (2006). Australian secondary school students' use of over-the-counter and illicit substances in 2005. *National Drug Strategy Monograph* 60, Carlton, Victoria: The Cancer Council Victoria.

Whitmore, E.A. and Riggs, P.D. (2006). Developmentally informed diagnostic and treatment considerations in comorbid conditions. In: H.A. Liddle and C.L. Rowe (eds), *Adolescent Substance Abuse: Research and Clinical Advances.* Cambridge, Cambridgeshire: Cambridge University Press, pp. 264–283.

Winters, K.C., Latimer, W. and Stinchfield, R.D. (1999). The DSM-IV criteria for adolescent alcohol and cannabis use disorders. *Journal of Studies on Alcohol*, 60, 337–344.

Yamaguchi, K. and Kandel, D.B. (1984). Patterns of drug use from adolescence to young adulthood: III. Predictors of progression. *American Journal of Public Health*, 74, 673–681.

Zammit, S., Allebeck, P., Andreasson, S. *et al.* (2002). Self reported cannabis use as a risk factor for schizophrenia in Swedish conscripts of 1969: historical cohort study. *British Medical Journal*, 325, 1199–1201.

5

Tobacco Use and Dependence

Judith S. Brook, Kerstin Pahl and David W. Brook

Despite declining rates of smoking in the United States (DiFranza *et al.*, 2000; Centers for Disease Control and Prevention, 2005a), nicotine dependence, via its close association with heavy smoking, constitutes one of the most serious public health problems of our time (Centers for Disease Control and Prevention, 2001). Smoking has been linked to numerous adverse physiological outcomes, including heart disease, cancer, stroke, and respiratory disease (United States Department of Health and Human Services, 2004). It is estimated that 440 000 deaths a year (Centers for Disease Control and Prevention, 2005b) are attributable to tobacco use. In 2004, approximately 12.1 percent of the US population were considered to be heavy smokers (25+ cigarettes per day; CDC, 2005a). A substantial percentage, if not all, of these individuals are likely to suffer from nicotine dependence, a condition that constitutes a severe barrier to tobacco cessation (Hughes *et al.*, 2006).

Nicotine dependence is closely related to daily smoking (Breslau *et al.*, 2001). Breslau and colleagues (2001) report that it takes at least one year of smoking daily for individuals to become dependent on nicotine. Only about 5 percent of smokers become dependent on nicotine before smoking daily. These findings indicate that nicotine dependence represents an advanced stage of heavy smoking (Hu, *et al.*, 2006). Thus, unlike the initiation of smoking and daily smoking, which typically take place before age 25, the onset of nicotine dependence seems to continue into the 40s (Breslau *et al.*, 2001).

DEFINITION AND ASSESSMENT OF NICOTINE DEPENDENCE

Nicotine dependence is most commonly assessed with two classes of diagnostic tools: variants on either the Fagerström Tolerance Questionnaire (FTQ, see Fagerström, 1978), most often the Fagerström Test for Nicotine Dependence (FTND, see Heatherton *et al.*, 1991) and/or measures based on the criteria for nicotine dependence as a substance use disorder as delineated in the *Diagnostic and Statistical Manual of Mental Disorders* (currently DSM-IV-TR, American Psychiatric Association, 2000). With the former, nicotine dependence can be conceptualized as either a continuous (assessing degree of dependence) or a dichotomous construct (by employing a cut-off score). For example, Prokhorov and colleagues (2001), using a moderated seven-item version of the FTQ for use with adolescents, suggest that a score ≤ 2 indicates no dependence, scores >2 and ≤ 5 indicate moderate dependence, and scores >5 indicate substantial dependence. However, there is currently no consensus about what constitutes the best cut-off score to determine the presence of nicotine dependence, especially in adolescent populations (Colby *et al.*, 2000).

DSM-based measures produce a dichotomous score indicating the presence or absence of the disorder. Both types of measures tap physical symptoms of nicotine addiction (i.e., tolerance, withdrawal symptoms), but the DSM-based measures assess a broader range of symptoms. The Fagerström criteria for nicotine dependence are more limited, and focus directly on the behavioral components and indirectly on some physiological components (e.g., length of time between awakening and first cigarette of the day) of tolerance and withdrawal. In contrast, the DSM-based criteria for nicotine dependence assess the physiological symptoms of nicotine dependence, as well as the larger behavioral, psychological and cognitive patterns associated with compulsive substance use.

The FTND consists of six items with a possible score range of 0–10, and inquires about the following (Fagerström *et al.*, 1996):

1. How soon after waking up individuals smoke their first cigarette (shorter interval scored as higher)
2. Whether individuals find it difficult to refrain from smoking in places where it is forbidden
3. Which cigarette they would most hate to give up (the first one in the morning – higher score – or “all the others”)
4. How much individuals smoke
5. If they smoke more frequently during the first hours after getting up
6. If they smoke when they are so ill that they have to stay in bed for most of the day.

In order to receive a diagnosis of nicotine dependence according to the DSM-IV-TR, a person must meet a minimum of three out of seven criteria. These include: tolerance; withdrawal; greater intake of nicotine or use over a longer period of time than intended (e.g., going through a pack of cigarettes faster than planned); persistent desire or unsuccessful attempts to cut down; spending a great deal of time in activities related to obtaining or using nicotine (e.g., chain-smoking); giving up or reducing important social, occupational or recreational activities because of nicotine use (e.g., avoiding places where smoking is prohibited); and continued use of nicotine despite knowledge of its having persistent negative physiological or psychological effects (e.g., continued use despite health problems). Withdrawal can give rise to a host of physical and psychological symptoms, including depressed mood, anxiety, insomnia, irritability, frustration, anger, difficulty concentrating, restlessness, increased appetite and decreased heart rate (DSM). The DSM-based definition of nicotine dependence has not been validated with adolescents (Stanton, 1995).

Recent research reports have questioned the suitability of both DSM-based measures of nicotine dependence and the Fagerström Test of Nicotine Dependence for use with adolescents (see, for example, Stanton, 1995; DiFranza *et al.*, 2002b; Prokhorov *et al.*, 2005). It seems that many of the items used to establish nicotine dependence are not appropriate for assessing tobacco dependence in adolescents. For example, the FTND asks about morning smoking and smoking when staying in bed because of illness. Both behaviors may not be possible for adolescents, who typically reside with parents or guardians and may not be able to smoke cigarettes at home (DiFranza *et al.*, 2002a). The DSM-based diagnosis describes a syndrome of behaviors and cognitions associated with heavy prolonged substance use and does therefore not capture the early signs of dependence that typically characterize adolescent nicotine dependence (DiFranza *et al.*, 2002a). Thus, both measures may not be ideal for use with adolescent populations, especially when studying the onset and early manifestations of nicotine dependence.

In response to these theoretical and practical considerations, DiFranza and colleagues (2002a) have developed a measure, the ten-item "Hooked On Nicotine Checklist" (HONC), for use with adolescents, which reflects the idea that the single most important feature of dependence is impaired control or the loss of autonomy over the use of the substance (see Table 5.1): "In our autonomy theory, we propose that the onset of dependence can be defined as the moment when an individual loses full autonomy over the use of tobacco" (DiFranza *et al.*, 2002a: 399). Supporting this notion, their study found that endorsement of a single item on the HONC (indicating loss of autonomy over smoking) predicted failed quit attempts, continued smoking, and daily smoking at a statistically significant level (DiFranza *et al.*, 2002a). HONC scores also correlated with other smoking measures in this study and showed good psychometric properties. Thus, researchers who wish to assess nicotine dependence in adolescents may be well-advised to employ the HONC in addition to the more commonly used FTND and DSM-based measures.

TABLE 5.1 The Hooked on Nicotine Checklist

1. Have you ever tried to quit, but couldn't?
2. Do you smoke now because it is really hard to quit?
3. Have you ever felt like you were addicted to tobacco?
4. Do you ever have strong cravings to smoke?
5. Have you ever felt like you really needed a cigarette?
6. Is it hard to keep from smoking in places where you are not supposed to, like school?

When you tried to stop smoking . . . (or, when you haven't used tobacco for a while . . .):

7. Did you find it hard to concentrate because you couldn't smoke?
8. Did you feel more irritable because you couldn't smoke?
9. Did you feel a strong need or urge to smoke?
10. Did you feel nervous, restless, or anxious because you couldn't smoke?

From DiFranza *et al.* (2002b). Development of symptoms of tobacco dependence in youths: 30-month follow up data from the DANDY Study. *Tobacco Control*, 11, 229. ©2002 Joseph R. DiFranza, MD; reprinted with permission.

EPIDEMIOLOGY OF NICOTINE DEPENDENCE

The prevalence of nicotine dependence is not easily established. This is in part due to the different inclusion criteria researchers have employed to assess this construct (Hughes *et al.*, 2006). Some studies assess dependence only among those who report smoking daily (e.g., Cottler *et al.*, 1995), while other studies report prevalence in population samples (e.g., Breslau *et al.*, 2001). In addition, some studies report lifetime dependence (Robins *et al.*, 1985), while others focus on current nicotine dependence (e.g., Grant *et al.*, 2004). However, based on the limited epidemiological research on nicotine dependence, it seems that approximately 20–25 percent of the adult US population is nicotine dependent at some point in their lifetime (Hughes *et al.*, 2006). Breslau *et al.* (2001) reported a lifetime prevalence of nicotine dependence, as defined by DSM-III-R, of 24.1 percent in their representative population sample of approximately 4000 individuals. Hu and colleagues (2006) found that 21.7 percent of a sample of approximately 14 000 young adults met the criteria for lifetime nicotine dependence using a modified version of the FTND. Only Robins and colleagues (1985) found a substantially higher proportion of 37 percent of lifetime nicotine dependence in their epidemiological study of over 3000 adults. However, this study was conducted over 20 years ago, at a time when smoking rates in the US were substantially higher and few tobacco control policies were in place (Hughes *et al.*, 2006).

With regard to current nicotine dependence, a nationally representative study by Grant and colleagues (2004) of over 43 000 participants found that 13 percent of the US population was currently dependent on nicotine. This closely matches the estimates of 14 percent among young adults reported by Hu and colleagues (2006).

Cross-cultural research using DSM-based criteria show that lifetime nicotine dependence (for men and women) in the United States is similar to levels in Germany (21%, John *et al.*, 2004a) and Seoul, Korea (20%, Lee *et al.*, 1990), and higher than in Hong Kong (13%, Chen *et al.*, 1993) and Takayama, Japan (12%, Kawakami *et al.*, 1998). A comparison of mean scores on the FTND across six countries with nationally representative random samples of smokers revealed that the sample of American smokers (men and women) had higher dependence scores than samples in Austria, Denmark, Finland, France and Poland (Fagerström *et al.*, 1996). The authors suggest that these high levels of nicotine dependence in the US are due to selective quitting. Individuals who are less addicted to nicotine are more likely to quit smoking, leaving a remaining pool of more highly dependent smokers (Fagerström *et al.*, 1996). This interpretation is bolstered by the negative correlation found between smoking prevalence and degree of nicotine dependence found in this study across the six countries (Fagerström *et al.*, 1996). However, in some other countries, particularly in Asia, nicotine dependence levels tend to differ substantially by gender (see below).

NICOTINE DEPENDENCE IN ADOLESCENTS

Although more than 3 million adolescents in the US smoke (US Department of Health and Human Services, 1994), far fewer adolescent smokers than adult smokers receive a diagnosis of nicotine dependence (Colby *et al.*, 2000). With regard to prevalence levels of tobacco use among adolescents, much more is known about tobacco use than about tobacco dependence (Baker *et al.*, 2004). However, according to Colby and colleagues (2000), approximately one to three out of five adolescent smokers are dependent on nicotine. The latest wave of *Monitoring the Future* (Johnston *et al.*, 2006) showed that 4.0 percent of eighth-graders, 7.5 percent of tenth-graders and 13.6 percent of twelfth-graders smoke daily. Colby and colleagues (2000) estimate that adolescent smokers are classified as nicotine dependent at half the rate that adult smokers are.

Nevertheless, adolescents show similar symptoms of nicotine dependence as adults, though typically at lower rates (United States Department of Health and Human Services, 2004; Prokhorov *et al.*, 2005). For example, both groups report withdrawal, tolerance, and the wish to decrease their intake of tobacco (Stanton, 1995; Stanton *et al.*, 1996; Rojas *et al.*, 1998). Over 50 percent of adolescent smokers report attempts at cessation each year, but less than 20 percent succeed (defined as abstinence for more than 1 month) among those who smoke at least half a pack of cigarettes per day (Johnston *et al.*, 1989). One study found that approximately 20 percent of adolescents exhibited levels of dependence similar to those of adults (Prokhorov *et al.*, 1996). However, elsewhere Prokhorov and colleagues (2005) suggest that scales measuring nicotine withdrawal, which are designed for adults, may overestimate levels of actual withdrawal symptoms in adolescents. According to the authors, some of the typical symptoms (e.g., restlessness, irritability) may reflect "the cognitive and behavioral patterns often associated with the emotionally volatile and vulnerable life period known as adolescence" (Prokhorov *et al.*, 2005: 910) rather than nicotine withdrawal. Indeed, their study found that withdrawal symptoms only differentiated reliably between former heavy smokers and never smokers. Only a measure of "craving," a construct which is not included in the DSM-definition of withdrawal but is included in the HONC, increased in proportion to the number of cigarettes smoked.

Nevertheless, it seems that nicotine dependence may be more prevalent among adolescent and young adult smokers than among older adult smokers. For example, Kandel and Chen (2000) found that 28.5 percent of monthly smokers aged 12–17 years were considered nicotine-dependent according to a proxy measure for DSM-IV diagnoses. They also found that adolescents were more likely to be nicotine-dependent than adults who reported the same levels of nicotine intake. Breslau and colleagues (2001) found that the youngest group of participants who had ever smoked daily (15–24) in their study had a sevenfold increased risk of nicotine dependence vis-à-vis the oldest group of participants who had ever smoked daily (45–54). This was the case despite the fact that the younger participants were the least likely to be daily smokers, compared to older participants (aged 35–44 and 45–54, respectively).

In addition, it has been suggested that adolescents are more vulnerable to the addictive properties of nicotine (DiFranza *et al.*, 2000, 2002a, 2002b). Animal studies support this notion by showing that nicotine self-administration is adopted more readily by adolescent than by adult rats (e.g., Levin *et al.*, 2003), suggesting that adolescence is a sensitive period for developing nicotine addiction. Neurodevelopmental changes during adolescence may make this a period of particular risk for dependence (Chambers *et al.*, 2003; Barron *et al.*, 2005). This would explain why some adolescents seem to develop symptoms of dependence at a faster rate than adults (DiFranza *et al.*, 2000). For example, DiFranza and colleagues (2000) found that some adolescents who were less-than-daily smokers reported their first symptom of dependence (as measured by the HONC) within 2 weeks of smoking onset. In another study, DiFranza and colleagues (2002b) found that 70 percent of adolescents who had ever smoked developed symptoms of dependence (as measured by the HONC) before daily smoking. A similar finding was reported by Gervais, and colleagues (2006). Their study of the natural course of cigarette use among adolescents showed that symptoms of nicotine dependence (perceived mental addiction, perceived physical addiction, craving) developed soon after smoking initiation, and well before weekly or daily smoking. In sum, there is mounting evidence that nicotine dependence develops at a much faster rate than previously assumed, at least among some adolescents (DiFranza *et al.*, 2000, 2002a, 2002b; Gervais *et al.*, 2006).

In addition to neurodevelopmental explanations of why adolescents seem to develop nicotine dependence faster than adults, it is possible that the heritability of a vulnerability to the effects of tobacco, or a proneness to dependence, play a role in adolescents' tobacco dependence. Given the increasing public awareness regarding the dangers of smoking, and the increase in anti-tobacco policies targeting youths, it is possible that those adolescents who take up smoking despite these warnings have a genetic predisposition for dependence and/or are more deviant and sensation-seeking than those adolescents who abstain from tobacco use (Breslau *et al.*, 2001; Hughes, 2003).

DEMOGRAPHIC CORRELATES OF NICOTINE DEPENDENCE

Gender

Although the majority of epidemiological studies on nicotine dependence rates in the United States have found no significant gender difference in liability to nicotine dependence (Breslau *et al.*, 1993, 2001; Anthony *et al.*, 1994; Hu *et al.*, 2006), there have been some findings that women are more prone to developing nicotine dependence than men (Kandel *et al.*, 1997; Kandel and Chen, 2000; Young *et al.*, 2002).

Similarly, studies on nicotine dependence rates in an adolescent sample in New Zealand (Stanton, 1995) and a sample of 14- to 24-year-olds in Germany (Nelson and Wittchen, 1998) have found no significant gender differences in proneness to nicotine dependence among regular smokers. However, Fagerström and colleagues' (1996) cross-national comparative study found that, in each of the four countries in which data were recorded by gender (Austria, Denmark, Finland and Poland), nicotine dependence scores were higher in men than in women. Likewise, although Hu *et al.* (2006) reported no significant gender difference in the *risk* of developing lifetime nicotine dependence, among those *with* lifetime nicotine dependence a greater percentage of men are currently nicotine dependent than women. That is, men, once nicotine dependent, are more likely to remain dependent.

The reason for contradictory results regarding an existing gender difference (i.e., some researchers finding greater liability to nicotine dependence in men than in women, while others find the opposite) may be due to the different measures employed across studies. The studies finding evidence of greater liability to nicotine dependence in women than in men (Kandel *et al.*, 1997; Kandel and Chen, 2000; Young *et al.*, 2002) employ a DSM-based measure, while those ascertaining a greater likelihood of nicotine dependence in men than in women (Fagerström *et al.*, 1996; Hu *et al.*, 2006) utilize a Fagerström-based measure. It may be that women more typically fit the profile of a dependent smoker as defined by DSM, while men more often fit that as defined by Fagerström criteria.

Race/Ethnicity

There are considerable differences in smoking prevalence rates among ethnic groups in the United States. The 2004 National Survey on Drug Use and Health found that people of Asian and Latino origin reported the lowest rates of past-month cigarette use (13.4% and 21.9%, respectively), while American Indian/Alaska Natives reported the highest rates (34.8%, United States Department of Health and Human Services, 2004). Whites and Blacks reported

26.6 percent and 24.9 percent of past-month use, respectively (United States Department of Health and Human Services, 2004).

With regard to nicotine dependence, Breslau and colleagues (2001) found that among smokers who had ever smoked on a daily basis, Black smokers had a smaller likelihood of becoming dependent than White smokers, according to DSM-based criteria. There were no other ethnic differences found in this study. Similarly, Kandel and Chen (2000), using DSM-based criteria, found that Whites had the highest rate of nicotine dependence and Black smokers did not differ from Hispanic smokers. Hu *et al.* (2006), employing a revised version of the Fagerström Test for Nicotine Dependence, also found that Whites were most likely to meet criteria for lifetime nicotine dependence, along with Native Americans. Hispanics and Asians were least likely to meet criteria for lifetime nicotine dependence. However, while African-American smokers were less likely to initiate smoking, to smoke daily or to be lifetime dependent, they were more likely to be currently nicotine dependent than other ethnic groups.

Socioeconomic Status (SES)

Another factor that has been identified to play a role in smoking behavior is SES (DiFranza *et al.*, 2002a; Shenassa *et al.*, 2003). Research in industrialized countries has demonstrated an inverse association between SES and nicotine dependence (Siahpush *et al.*, 2006), and recent studies suggest that this effect extends to the offspring. That is, lower parental SES is linked with greater offspring smoking from adolescence through adulthood (Jefferis *et al.*, 2003; Najman *et al.*, 2004). In a community study by Fagan and colleagues (2005), for example, parental education, parental occupation and parental smoking independently predicted offspring smoking in the late twenties. As shown in Figure 5.1, however, these researchers found distinct pathways through which parental education, occupation and smoking each influenced offspring smoking in adulthood, with parental education having the greatest total effect.

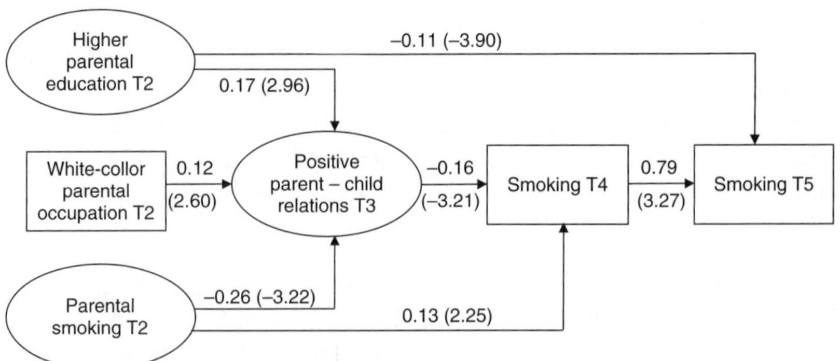

FIGURE 5.1 LISREL model predicting offspring smoking in late twenties (T5) from parental education, occupation, smoking, and child-rearing variables. Note: The participants' mean ages were 14.5 at T2, 17 at T3, 22 at T4, and 27 at T5.

RISK FACTORS FOR ADOLESCENT NICOTINE DEPENDENCE

While much is known regarding the predictors of smoking, less research has explicitly focused on the risk and protective factors for nicotine dependence. The literature is particularly scarce regarding the predictors of adolescent nicotine dependence. However, because the transition from smoking to dependence seems to occur rather quickly for at least some adolescents (DiFranza *et al.*, 2002a), we also summarize the literature on risk factors for adolescent smoking.

PERSONALITY ATTRIBUTES

Much research has linked personality attributes to adolescent smoking. In particular, personality characteristics representing a syndrome of unconventionality (e.g., rebelliousness, tolerance of deviance, delinquency) are predictive of adolescent smoking initiation and maintenance (Jessor and Jessor, 1977; Griesler *et al.*, 2002; Brook *et al.*, 2004). Identification with counter-cultural values and the desire to create a precocious adult-like social image may motivate such adolescents to take up smoking (Baker *et al.*, 2004). In addition, deviance-prone adolescents are more likely to affiliate with peers who smoke cigarettes – a well-established risk factor for adolescent tobacco use (see below) (Brook *et al.*, 1990, 2006; Kandel, 1996; Oetting and Donnermeyer, 1998).

Similarly, personality attributes and behaviors reflecting low levels of emotional and behavioral control (e.g., impulsivity, sensation seeking) have repeatedly been found related to adolescent smoking (Masse and Tremblay, 1997; Brook *et al.*, 2004). Adolescents who are sensation seekers are more prone to engaging in risk-taking behaviors, including tobacco use (Turbin *et al.*, 2000). It is less clear whether and how these personality factors relate to adolescent nicotine dependence. However, it is likely that personality attributes such as impulsivity and a proneness to sensation seeking share a genetic basis with a proneness to nicotine dependence. Supporting this notion, a recent study by Storr and colleagues (2005) found that problem behavior in first grade (e.g., breaking rules, starting fights) was moderately linked with a greater risk of belonging to a group of smokers characterized by higher levels of dependence as measured by the FTND in young adulthood. This relationship was more pronounced in females than in males.

MOTIVATIONAL FACTORS

Control of Negative Mood States

There is some evidence that smokers who are dependent on nicotine smoke in order to control negative mood states (Shiffman, 1989). In a multi-ethnic study of onset and persistence of smoking, Griesler and colleagues (2002) found that negative mood predicted persistence of smoking (not onset), but only among White participants. However, it is most likely that the relationship between tobacco use and psychological well-being is dynamic in nature (Windle and Windle, 2001;

Ellickson *et al.*, 2004; Orlando *et al.*, 2004). Orlando and colleagues (2001) suggest that smoking may initially be driven by psychological distress in an attempt to ameliorate negative affect, but that distress becomes exacerbated over time as a consequence of continued smoking and the resulting addiction to nicotine.

Weight Control

Smoking has been perceived as a weight-reduction and -management strategy, especially among adolescent girls and women (Klesges and Klesges, 1988; French *et al.*, 1994; Middleman *et al.*, 2001). Concerns about weight gain are also frequently cited by women contemplating smoking cessation or by those who relapse after quitting (Lissner *et al.*, 1992). Although the association of smoking cessation with weight gain has been well documented (Williamson *et al.*, 1991; Lissner *et al.*, 1992; Janzon *et al.*, 2004; Eisenberg and Quinn, 2006), the relationship of current smoking to body weight or body mass index (BMI) is less clear. While some investigations have found that smokers weigh less than non-smokers (Grunberg, 1990; Lissner *et al.*, 1992; Brook *et al.*, 2007), other studies do not support these findings (see, for example, Colditz *et al.*, 1992; French *et al.*, 1994; Klesges *et al.*, 1998). Moreover, research specifically on adolescents suggests there is often a positive relationship between smoking and weight or self-perception of weight (e.g., Gritz *et al.*, 1998; Winter *et al.*, 2002), especially among females. These results suggest that overweight youth are more like to turn to smoking as a weight reduction technique. However, decreased weight and BMI appear more related to lifetime smoking than smoking initiation (e.g., in youth), possibly because smoking mitigates age-related weight gain (United States Department of Health and Human Services, 2001).

PEER SMOKING

Peer smoking has long been established as one of the most powerful predictors of adolescent smoking (Kandel, 1996). However, it is not entirely clear whether the high correlations found between reports of self and peer smoking are due to social influence or to assortative peer selection (i.e., the tendency to select social groups that are similar to oneself; Kandel, 1996). In addition, adolescents tend to overestimate the similarity between their own smoking behavior and that of their peers (Baker *et al.*, 2004).

Peer influences seem to be most important for the initiation and maintenance of smoking, but not necessarily for developing nicotine dependence. While nicotine-dependent individuals tend to socialize with heavy smokers, peer smoking is not related to nicotine dependence as much as other factors are (e.g., biological vulnerabilities, parental smoking).

The influences of smoking by peers on smoking patterns seem to differ by ethnic group (Flay *et al.*, 1994; Unger *et al.*, 2001). Some research has explained lower levels of smoking among African-American youth by their having fewer friends who smoke in their peer networks (e.g., Ellickson *et al.*, 2004). Peer smoking also seems to be less influential among African-Americans than among youths of other ethnic groups. For example, Unger *et al.* (2001) found that the influences of friend smoking on smoking initiation were stronger among White adolescents than among African-American and Latino adolescents. A study by Griesler and Kandel (1998) found that peer pressure to smoke was influential among White and Latino adolescents, but not among African-Americans.

FAMILY SMOKING

Family smoking, and parental smoking in particular, have also been found to be related to adolescent smoking. The mechanisms underlying the relationship between family smoking and tobacco use may be due to genetic influences (Sullivan and Kendler, 1999) and/or social modeling (Bandura, 1986; Akers and Lee, 1996). Findings from studies of smoking trajectories over time show that parental smoking is related to offspring smoking trajectories characterized by early onset and escalation to high levels of use over time (Chassin *et al.*, 2000; Brook *et al.*, 2006). In addition, twin studies find more evidence for the heritability of tobacco dependence than tobacco use (Sullivan and Kendler, 1999). Thus, there seems to be a strong link between parental tobacco use and nicotine dependence. This link may be due to an underlying genetic vulnerability to the effects of nicotine or a proneness to particular personality characteristics (e.g., impulsivity) which make individuals more likely to become dependent on nicotine.

Another explanation for parental influence is social modeling, though this mechanism is more likely to influence smoking initiation than smoking persistence or nicotine dependence. This notion is supported by findings from Griesler and colleagues' (2002) study, which showed that maternal smoking was related to smoking initiation among adolescents but not to smoking persistence.

There is also increasing evidence of a link between maternal smoking during pregnancy and both offspring smoking in adolescence as well as progression to nicotine dependence (Buka *et al.*, 2003). At present, the mechanisms that underlie this relationship are not completely understood. One possibility is that nicotine exerts a direct effect on the nicotine receptors of the fetal brain (Ernst *et al.*, 2001) or increases the likelihood of behavioral dysregulation (e.g., ADHD, Braun *et al.*, 2006), which in turn predicts later offspring smoking and nicotine dependence (Shenassa *et al.*, 2003). Alternatively, mothers who smoke may have high rates of psychopathologies associated with smoking (e.g., depression), which are passed on to the child and make him or her more susceptible to nicotine dependence (Shenassa *et al.*, 2003).

MACRO-CONTEXTUAL FACTORS

One of the most important macro-environmental influences on adolescent smoking and nicotine addiction may be the media (Colby *et al.*, 2000). Representations of smoking in TV shows and movies abound (McCool *et al.*, 2001), and the presence of cigarette smoking in films has increased over the past decade (see, for example, Stockwell and Glantz, 1997; Teti and Glantz, 1998; Kacirk and

Glantz, 2001; Glantz *et al.*, 2004). Adolescents who are younger than 18 years seem to be particularly vulnerable to tobacco product placement, as their recall of tobacco products, including of specific cigarette brands, has been shown to be superior to that of other age groups (Mekemson and Glantz, 2002). Adolescents' exposure to such positive images of smoking may have a particularly powerful effect on their smoking behavior because they are in the process of developing personal identities and are searching for behavioral role models (Erikson, 1968; Chen *et al.*, 2002).

Several studies conducted in the United States have linked exposure to media models of smoking with smoking initiation (Sargent *et al.*, 2001; Dalton *et al.*, 2003) and greater frequency of smoking (Tickle *et al.*, 2001). For example, a recent study by Distefan and colleagues (2004) found that, among US American adolescents, having a favorite movie star who had appeared smoking on-screen in the previous 2 years was independently related to higher odds of smoking initiation. However, it is less clear how exposure to media images of smoking influences tobacco dependence among adolescents.

PSYCHOPATHOLOGY

Several investigators have reported high rates of smoking among psychiatric outpatients and inpatients (Gonzalez-Pinto *et al.*, 1958; Breslau, 1995; Brook *et al.*, 2000; de Leone *et al.*, 2002). Community studies examining smoking rates and psychiatric disorders have also been conducted (Lasser *et al.*, 2000). In these studies, high rates of smoking have been found among adults with psychiatric disorders. A limited number of studies focused on the relationship of smoking during adolescence and young adulthood and both alcohol and illicit drug dependence in young adulthood (Lewinsohn *et al.*, 1999; Brook *et al.*, 2002). In general, the findings indicate that current daily smoking significantly heightens the risk for substance use disorders.

While the above studies have examined rates of smoking, they have not focused their attention on the issue of nicotine dependence. In the recent past, there have been studies of nicotine dependence and psychiatric disorders using samples of specific populations. Data exist for regional samples or individuals attending health maintenance organizations (Breslau *et al.*, 1991, 1994; Breslau, 1995), as well as samples in Germany (Ulrich *et al.*, 2003). In these studies, nicotine dependence was found to be linked with several psychiatric disorders such as substance use disorders, mood disorders and anxiety disorders.

In a nationally representative study of the US, Grant and colleagues (2004) focused on the co-occurrence of nicotine dependence and several psychiatric disorders, including personality disorders, among adults. Their findings supported the co-occurrence of nicotine dependence and Axis I disorders such as alcohol and drug use disorders, major depression, dysthymia, mania, panic disorder, social phobia, and generalized anxiety disorder. In addition, Grant *et al.* (2004) reported an association between nicotine dependence and Axis II disorders, such as obsessive-compulsive personality disorder and antisocial personality disorder. Of interest is their finding that the relationships between nicotine dependence and Axis I and Axis II disorders were similar in males and females. Similar findings were reported by Xian and colleagues (2007). The investigators hypothesized a reciprocal relationship between nicotine dependence and other dependence on psychoactive substances through shared physiological effects, cross-tolerance or cueing (Collins *et al.*, 1993; Luo *et al.*, 1994; Gulliver *et al.*, 1995; Madden *et al.*, 1995). With respect to the physiological effects, substance abusers may smoke to decrease some of the negative effects of alcohol or other drugs. Furthermore, the use of nicotine may serve as a cue for the use of other substances, creating a learned association between the two behaviors.

It has also been proposed that nicotine and alcohol exert their effects through shared neuroregulatory pathways. Thus, the use of one of these substances might stimulate desire or craving for the other (Gulliver *et al.*, 1995), or lead to cross-tolerance. The relationship between nicotine dependence and Axis II disorders is consistent with earlier research, especially the investigations incorporating aspects of neuroticism and extroversion (Grant *et al.*, 2004; John *et al.*, 2004b). Neuroticism has been found to underlie the relationship between nicotine dependence and depression by acting as a common genetic or environmental predisposition. Genetic factors may make some people more susceptible to dependence on both alcohol and nicotine (Barron *et al.*, 2005; Rende *et al.*, 2005). There may be some overlap in the genetic factors that contribute to dependence on these two substances (e.g., nicotine and alcohol dependence; see Wilhelmsen *et al.*, 2005). In addition, those with an inherited predisposition are more likely to have had family members who modeled substance use behaviors.

In order to obtain a more accurate picture of individual smoking histories than that given by smoking frequencies at one or more points in time, several investigators have analyzed developmental trajectories or historical patterns of cigarette smoking from adolescence through young adulthood (Chassin *et al.*, 2000; Orlando *et al.*, 2004; Fergus *et al.*, 2005; Brook *et al.*, 2007). In a recent study by Brook and colleagues (2007), early-starting continuous smokers showed a significantly higher risk for both alcohol and drug dependence than each of the other trajectory groups (non-smokers and late starters). Thus, the early-starting continuous smokers group appeared to be more vulnerable to substance dependence in general than the other groups (Brook *et al.*, 2007).

It has also been suggested that smoking may be reinforced by a pre-existing psychiatric disorder. Thus, individuals may use nicotine as a form of self-medication for a number of psychiatric disorders (Upadhyaya *et al.*, 2002). In the case of individuals with depressive disorders, self-medication may function via a MAO inhibitory effect of smoking. This, in turn, may be related to serotonin and dopamine metabolism. In addition to the possible genetic and neuroregulatory explanations, some personality characteristics may be associated with the heightened risk for substance dependence shown by heavy smokers. Common environmental factors such as family stress may underlie both nicotine dependence and the onset of psychiatric symptoms. It is also possible that smoking in adolescence occurs prior to the onset of psychiatric disorders (Upadhyaya *et al.*, 2002). Research that focuses on the nature of the association between nicotine dependence and psychiatric disorders should follow up a large sample of adolescents into adulthood so that any underlying personality factors can be assessed prior to longitudinal follow-up. This approach will facilitate our gaining a more complete understanding of the personality traits underlying both nicotine dependence and psychiatric disorders. In general, the findings from the above investigations suggest that nicotine dependence and psychiatric disorders may reinforce one another, making it very difficult for people with psychiatric disorders to give up smoking. Thus, treatment for smoking could be hindered by the co-occurrence of psychiatric disorders and smoking, since both psychiatric disorders and smoking may have resulted in a system of mutually reinforcing conditions (Buka *et al.*, 2003).

PREVENTION AND TREATMENT

PREVENTION OF SMOKING

Because nicotine is so highly addicting and the effects of smoking are so deleterious to health (see, for example, Ezzati *et al.*, 2005; Teo *et al.*, 2006), the role of the primary prevention of smoking is extremely important. It is preferable, and more effective and cost-effective, to prevent the initiation of smoking than to treat smoking with the goal of achieving smoking cessation.

Because of the complex biopsychological factors and their interactions involved in the initiation of smoking, efforts at smoking prevention should begin early in life, even during the mother's pregnancy. Helping pregnant females to stop smoking is the first step on the road to preventing smoking by the offspring. Because of the adverse effects of second-hand smoke (SHS), it is also an important step to help other family members, including the father, stop smoking (Bricker *et al.*, 2005). These pre-natal efforts, if successful, will set the stage for the child to be born into a smoke-free home, which will play a role in the prevention of smoking by the child.

After birth, the maintenance of a smoke-free environment continues to be of great importance, both in terms of the effects of SHS upon the child, and also in terms of the adverse effects of smoking on the parents' functioning, well-being and marital relationship. As the child enters school, the inclusion of smoking prevention efforts and education about smoking early on in the school years may have an effective and positive role in preventing later smoking (Jackson and Dickinson, 2003).

Education of teachers and the public at large about the addictive nature of nicotine and the adverse psychosocial and health effects of smoking is an important public health goal. There is an extensive literature about these efforts, which include such components as anti-smoking advertising (Pechmann and

Reibling, 2000; Biener *et al.*, 2006), the use of taxes as a deterrent to smoking (Ross and Chaloupka, 2003; Frieden *et al.*, 2005), and legislative and administrative efforts to strengthen the legal regulation or control of smoking (Jason *et al.*, 1999; Levy and Friend, 2003). The institutionalization of rules against smoking may motivate people to refrain from smoking initiation, or to stop smoking.

In addition to these (and other) public health efforts to deter adolescents and adults from smoking, reaching out to individuals, especially those at risk for smoking, can also be effective. For example, pediatricians and internists (and other medical specialists), as well as other healthcare personnel, should make active efforts, whenever they have clinical contact with children, adolescents and their parents, to warn children and adolescents against beginning to smoke. The timing of such interventions by individual practitioners may play a role in their effectiveness, and such interventions should be linguistically and culturally appropriate. Such interventions may include training in the development of problem-solving skills, life skills, cognitive restructuring, behavioral self-management and refusal skills.

There are a number of strategies for the prevention of adolescent smoking, which are similar to those for the prevention of other adolescent substance use. Strategies for preventing adolescent tobacco and drug use have been summarized by Dierker and colleagues (1997), and are listed in Table 5.2.

TABLE 5.2 Preventive Programs for Tobacco and Drug Use

Preventive programs	Strategies/target behavior
1. Early childhood and family support programs	Focus on the prenatal and early infancy periods. Interventions provide social support for mothers, health care, etc. The programs help buffer the effects of poverty by reducing the following risk factors: tobacco and drug use, behavior problems, family management problems, and academic failure.
2. Programs for parents and children of adolescents	Parenting skills training: Parents are taught to monitor their children's behavior, to use contingent discipline for undesired behavior, and to consistently reward prosocial behavior. The training helps buffer the risk of tobacco and drug use by decreasing family conflict.
3. Social competence and skills training	Teaching adolescents behavioral skills to deal with interpersonal problems. Social competence promotion may affect the adolescent's willingness to refrain from tobacco use when confronted with problem situations.
4. The promotion of academic achievement	Smoking and other drug abuse may be prevented by reducing a low academic achievement and problem behavior in school. The strategies to reduce these risk factors include early childhood education, changes in the classroom teacher's institutional practices, and academic tutoring of adolescents with low grades.

(*Continues*)

TABLE 5.2 (*Continued*)

Preventive programs	Strategies/target behavior
5. Organizational changes in school	Changes in school organization may reduce smoking and other drug use risk factors through such activities as curriculum restructuring and greater school-faculty-community integration.
6. Youth involvement in alternative activities	Providing adolescents with the opportunities to be involved in school activities to help reduce the likelihood of violating school rules such as proscription against tobacco and other drug use.
7. Comprehensive risk-focused programs	Consists of a combination of interventions that focus on different sources of social influence. Such interventions may include training parents in positive parent–child communication skills, and training of community leaders to organize smoking and other drug use prevention task forces.

Adapted from Dierker *et al.* (1997).

SMOKING CESSATION TREATMENT

This section will discuss briefly a number of methods currently used for the treatment of tobacco dependence. This brief review can only touch on aspects of treatment, which are discussed in great detail in an abundant professional literature on this topic. Nevertheless, this summary may provide a useful, if abbreviated, overview. Although the term tobacco dependence is commonly used, it is evident that the addicting nature of tobacco use is to be found in its nicotine content, although the psychosocial concomitants of smoking contribute to dependence. Nicotine is a central nervous system stimulant, which is highly addicting. Nicotine acts on nicotinic acetylcholine receptors, particular in the nucleus accumbens, which release the neurotransmitor dopamine, thought to be the primary component of the brain reward system that leads to reinforcement of smoking behavior and relief of craving and withdrawal symptoms.

Although the goal of treatment ideally should be smoking cessation, this goal is difficult for many adolescents to achieve. Many adolescents require a number of repeated attempts at stopping smoking before achieving total abstinence, and for some adolescents an interim goal of reducing the number of cigarettes smoked (a harm-reduction approach) may serve during the often-lengthy process of giving up smoking completely.

There are two primary methods of treatment of tobacco dependence: psychosocial treatment techniques, and psychopharmacological treatments. Research has shown that these two treatment methods work most effectively when used together (Ingersoll and Cohen, 2005).

Psychosocial Treatments

There is a variety of psychosocial methods for the treatment of smoking. Methods to achieve cessation may involve the use of educational materials, as well as advice given by physicians and other healthcare professionals. There are several self-help programs that provide education and support for cessation. One example is Nicotine Anonymous, which uses a 12-step approach. Many programs use a group treatment approach to help smokers become motivated to quit (e.g., SmokeEnders). Formal smoking cessation programs may use a combination of psychosocial treatment methods in addition to psychopharmacologic interventions. Such treatment methods may consist of individual or group sessions, often using a cognitive-behavioral approach. Smoking cessation groups for adolescents may be effective, although many adolescents are initially resistant to stopping smoking. Groups can provide mutual support, education about smoking and the cessation process, and training in the behavioral skills necessary to quit smoking and remain abstinent (Carmody, 2002). Unfortunately, most smokers who want to quit do not participate in smoking cessation treatment programs. However, many smokers become members of smoking cessation groups after a number of unsuccessful attempts at quitting without help.

Psychosocial treatments may be given as individual therapy or as group therapy. In all cases, behavioral treatment for smoking cessation is built on an understanding of the "five As":

1. *Ask*, which involves the regular identification of tobacco use by questioning patients at each opportunity.
2. *Advise*, which refers to strongly urging tobacco users to stop smoking; such advice should be given, clearly, emphatically, and in an individualized fashion.
3. *Assess*, which refers to evaluating the patient's wish to stop smoking.
4. *Assist*, which refers to helping the patient in stopping smoking, and includes setting a quit date, and helping the patient understand possible obstacles to quitting. It may include practical counseling, with a review of cues and triggers that may interfere with cessation. It may also include social support, both professional and in the patient's social environment. This phase may also include the prescription of appropriate pharmaceutical therapies to help the patient stop.
5. *Arrange*, which refers to scheduling the patient for follow-up contact in order to evaluate his or her success in quitting, and to reinforce the need to persevere.

For those adolescents who are unwilling to stop smoking, the therapist may provide a motivational intervention, the "five Rs". These comprise relevance, risk, rewards, roadblocks and repetition. *Relevance* refers to helping adolescents to understand the importance of cessation in their lives. Its specific importance is in terms of *risks*; the adolescents should be helped to assess the adverse health and social consequences of smoking, including a discussion of acute risks, long-term risks and environmental risks. *Rewards* refers to asking the adolescents to evaluate the potential positive results of stopping smoking. *Roadblocks* includes the discussion with the patient of barriers to smoking cessation, as well as ways of dealing with such barriers. Common barriers include weight gain, withdrawal symptoms and depression. *Repetition* refers to the need to repeat the motivational intervention at every contact with the patient. Adolescents should learn that many people make several attempts at stopping smoking before achieving success.

Although psychosocial interventions for smoking cessation with adolescents may be given individually by a variety of healthcare providers, the use of group-therapy approaches with adolescents to provide smoking cessation treatment has been increasing. Smoking cessation groups are used to provide the elements of the five As and the five Rs noted above. Many groups for adolescents and adults are offered by a number of public and private agencies, including the American Cancer Society, and the American Lung Association. Commercial smoking cessation programs, including SmokeEnders, offer groups utilizing group support and education. Patients come to smoking cessation groups on their own, but many come after referral by a healthcare professional.

In setting up groups, the appropriate evaluation of adolescent patients for each group is important, and includes a history of smoking and prior efforts to stop smoking, as well as past treatment history. In evaluating adolescent patients for treatment, the Stages of Change Model (Prochaska and DiClemente, 1992) offers a framework to utilize methods of behavioral change, and has been used in developing smoking cessation treatments. The five stages of change included in this model are pre-contemplation, contemplation, preparation, action and maintenance. The action stage is when the smoker attempts to quit.

Smoking Cessation Group Processes

Smoking cessation groups utilize many of the techniques used in group therapy for other difficulties. These techniques include mutual introductions, a discussion of the adolescent members' motivation for joining the group and wanting to quit, and a discussion of each adolescent's smoking history. The development of group cohesion is important in helping group members to maintain their motivation to stop smoking. Group members assess whether a particular group can be helpful. As the group sessions progress, and group members get to know one another better, they work on creating a plan to stop smoking, which includes setting a "quit date" and a discussion of ways of coping with nicotine withdrawal symptoms, craving for cigarettes, and the possibility of weight gain. Group members may all select the same "quit date", or they may decide to select individual "quit dates". Group members discuss their own experiences with stopping smoking and with coping with withdrawal symptoms, and not giving in to the wish to smoke. Many group members may need additional support and contact with other group members at the time of the "quit date" and immediately afterwards. Some therapists use telephone contacts in addition to an increased frequency of group sessions to help group members get through this difficult time. More successful group members encourage and support less successful group members, and act as models that provide successful coping methods for less successful members.

Many smoking cessation groups use a psychoeducational approach, and present some of the material mentioned above in order to help adolescent smokers develop the skills needed to stop smoking, and prevent relapse. In any smoking cessation group, the group leader's ability to utilize the group process is of great importance, even in coping skills groups, or groups for the provision of information about smoking and smoking cessation. In accordance with the principles noted above, groups may be organized to provide preparation for quitting, the quit date, and relapse prevention. Group cohesion helps group members renew their commitment to smoking cessation. Goals and aspects of treatment are discussed in all groups. In cognitive-behavioral groups, group members may be assigned homework in order to practice the skills needed to stop smoking. In later group phases, the group discussion focuses on resisting the urge to smoke, coping with withdrawal symptoms, and the commitment to maintaining abstinence. Follow-up groups used for relapse prevention help adolescent group members identify high-risk situations, and specific methods of coping without smoking. Social support is emphasized as a significant aspect of relapse prevention. The concurrent treatment of depression is essential for success in achieving smoking cessation. Group support is useful for this purpose, and antidepressant medication, such as bupropion, is also of great value.

The process of stopping smoking is generally considered to have three phases. These include preparing to stop smoking, stopping smoking on a specific date, and relapse prevention to maintain abstinence commencing with initial cessation on the date of stopping. Preparing to stop smoking involves assessing and enhancing motivation to stop smoking. Sometimes this process is addressed through the use of motivational enhancement techniques. Methods of stopping smoking are discussed by group members, and a specific "quit date" is determined. On the date of stopping (the quit date), the group helps members by offering support and techniques for coping and getting through the day without a cigarette.

After cessation, relapse prevention sessions are useful in helping adolescent group members to maintain abstinence from smoking. Cognitive-behavioral techniques and coping skills training may be particularly useful for adolescents during this time. Relapse prevention methods identify risky people, places and things, and help adolescent members to cope with these risks. Examples of risky situations include the presence of other people smoking, being in a place (such as a bar) where smoking is common, or being in a store where cigarettes are offered for sale.

Most adult smoking cessation group members are able to stop smoking initially but, over the long term, only 30–40 percent remain abstinent. At the current time, there is not sufficient data to estimate the percent of adolescents who will remain abstinent over the long term. Future longitudinal studies are warranted to provide such data. Adolescents people may be more successful in further attempts at smoking cessation in other group settings. The provision of social support for stopping smoking by family members and friends plays a significant role in preventing relapse to smoking.

It should be noted that many adolescent smokers are dependent on or abuse alcohol or other drugs (Everett *et al.*, 1998; Ramsey *et al.*, 2005). For such adolescents, the concurrent treatment of substance abuse/addiction and smoking is likely to be helpful, although there is some evidence that the treatment of substance abuse prior to attempting smoking cessation may be more effective.

Psychopharmacological Treatments

The medications now available for the treatment of tobacco dependence include various forms of nicotinic receptor agonists, the dopaminergic-noradrenergic reuptake inhibitor (DNRI), bupropion, and the nicotinic receptor partial agonist, *Varenicline.*

- *Nicotinic receptor agonists* are available in a number of forms. These include a nicotine oral inhaler and a nicotine nasal spray, marketed under the brand name *Nicotrol.* Also available is nicotine polacrilex gum, both a generic form and gum marketed under the brand name *Nicorette*, in two doses. Nicotine polacrilex is also available as a lozenge, marketed under the brand name *Commit*, in two dosage forms. There is also a nicotine transdermal patch, both a generic form and a patch marketed under the brand name *NicoDerm CQ*, in three dosage forms. All of these types of nicotinic receptor agonists work in the same way, by providing a source of nicotine other than that from the use of tobacco products, thereby relieving the craving and withdrawal symptoms commonly experienced by people who are addicted to nicotine. They work on the principle that becoming accustomed to a non-tobacco source of nicotine will wean the user away from tobacco, and eventually permit the gradual decrease in the dose of nicotine needed to prevent craving and withdrawal symptoms. The various forms of nicotine are provided to cater to individual preference. The duration of treatment using these medications varies depending on the degree of addiction present. Each form has its own particular common side effects, and all the forms listed are about equally effective.
- *The dopaminergic-noradrenergic reuptake inhibitor, bupropion,* is commonly used for its antidepressant effects as well as for its specific effects for the treatment of tobacco dependence. Bupropion is marketed under the brand names *Wellbutrin* and *Zyban*, as well as a generic form. There are a number of side effects commonly seen with the use of bupropion, ranging from insomnia, headache, dizziness and anxiety to Stevens-Johnson syndrome, which is a rare occurrence.
- *The nicotinic receptor partial agonist, varenicline*, is quite new. Varenicline is a partial agonist binding selectively to the $\alpha4\beta2$ nicotinic acetylcholine receptors more tightly than nicotine, thereby blocking nicotine from binding to them. Varenicline stimulates receptor-mediated activity, but less than nicotine, thereby reducing the availability of nicotine binding sites.

SUMMARY

Tobacco use and dependence among adolescents constitute a serious problem for public health. By age 13, a significant number of adolescents smoke daily (Johnston *et al.*, 2006). The percentage of adolescents who smoke on a regular basis increases throughout the high-school years (Johnston *et al.*, 2006). Thus, a substantial number of adolescents can be considered dependent on nicotine by the age of 17. Recent research suggests that nicotine dependence may develop more rapidly in adolescent smokers than in adult smokers (DiFranza *et al.*, 2000). It is possible that this rapid development of addiction to nicotine is due to the fact that adolescence, in contrast to adulthood, is a sensitive period of neurodevelopment (Chambers *et al.*, 2003; Barron *et al.*, 2005). Additionally, adolescence is characterized by marked changes in social and emotional development, which may make adolescents vulnerable to social influences that promote tobacco use (e.g., peer influences, media influences).

The seriousness of adolescent nicotine dependence takes further weight from the fact that substance dependence may adversely affect adolescents' social-emotional development, interpersonal relationships and physical maturation. Essential adolescent tasks, including separation from parents, achieving educational goals, and the development of positive relationships with peers may be interfered with by a dependence on nicotine. Healthy adolescent development is the foundation for a smooth transition into adaptive functioning in young adulthood.

There is a considerable amount of research focused on identifying the predictors of smoking initiation and smoking maintenance. Less research has examined the risk factors for developing nicotine dependence. However, several domains of risk factors, which may play a role in the development of nicotine dependence, have been suggested. These include genetic factors (see, for example, Sullivan, 1999), personality attributes (e.g., Griesler *et al.*, 2002), attitudes (e.g., Baker *et al.*, 2004), psychopathology (e.g., de Leon *et al.*, 2002), family smoking (e.g., Chassin *et al.*, 2000), peer influences (e.g., Kandel, 1996), and the media (e.g., Mekemson and Glantz, 2002). Future research should aim to identify the mechanisms that operate between these domains of psychological risk factors and the development of nicotine dependence in adolescents. Recent research on the longitudinal trajectories of smoking suggests that there are different classes of smokers, which are characterized by differential developmental patterns of tobacco use over time. Identification of some of the antecedents of membership in classes of smoking characterized by early initiation and high frequency of use (e.g., parental smoking, unconventional personality attributes) also points to some of the underlying causes of nicotine dependence.

In addition, other research which focuses on the interaction of nicotine dependence with psychiatric disorders and substance use disorders will lead to a greater comprehension of the etiology and treatment of nicotine dependence. At the present time, large controlled clinical trials to assess the underlying genetic predisposition for nicotine dependence and other psychiatric disorders are needed. Studies that incorporate predictor (e.g., sensation-seeking), moderator (e.g., age) and mediator (e.g., self-medication) variables relevant to comorbidity of tobacco dependence and other psychiatric disorders are needed. A greater comprehension of the etiology and consequences of comorbid psychiatric disorders and nicotine dependence is essential for the development of more effective treatments.

Because of the high morbidity and mortality associated with smoking, prevention and treatment efforts for adolescent smokers are imperative. Although some adolescent smokers who stop do so without help, relapse is very common. For most smokers, a combination of psychosocial interventions and psychopharmacological treatment is most effective. It is important to remember that repeated attempts at cessation may be necessary for a patient to achieve success. Social support, in the treatment setting and in the home environment, is necessary for successful treatment. This is of vital importance for adolescent smokers, who are particularly vulnerable to social influences. Patients need to learn about aspects of their own smoking practices in order to use this knowledge successfully. Treatment must be individualized for each patient, whatever methods are used; effective follow-up and relapse prevention efforts are often necessary for patients to maintain abstinence from smoking. Newer psychopharmacological treatments may be of great effectiveness, especially when used in conjunction with psychosocial interventions.

In sum, future research into the biological and psychosocial etiology and consequences of nicotine dependence is needed using a biobehavioral approach. Both pharmacological and psychosocial approaches to prevention and treatment focused on smoking cessation deserve research and clinical attention.

ACKNOWLEDGMENT

The research has been supported through NIDA grants DA003188, DA00572 and DA12374, NCI grants CA094845 and CA84063, and Research Scientist Award KO8DA00244 awarded to Judith S. Brook.

We greatfully acknowledge the support of Elizabeth Rubenstone, who provided insightful feedback, and gave thoughtful comments on several drafts of the article. We also extend thanks to Jonathan Koppel, who performed the literature searches, and Patricia Contino, who prepared the manuscript.

REFERENCES

Akers, R.L. and Lee, G. (1996). A longitudinal test of social learning theory: adolescent smoking. *Journal of Drug Issues*, 26, 317–343.

American Psychiatric Association. (2000). *Diagnostic and Statistical Manual of Mental Disorders*, revised 4th edn. Washington, DC: American Psychiatric Association.

Anthony, J.C., Warner, L.A. and Kessler, R.C. (1994). Comparative epidemiology of dependence on tobacco, alcohol, controlled substances and inhalants: Basic findings from the National Comorbidity Survey. *Experimental and Clinical Psychopharmacology*, 2, 244–268.

Baker, T.B., Brandon, T.H. and Chassin, L.A. (2004). Motivational influences on cigarette smoking. *Annual Review of Psychology*, 55, 463–491.

Bandura, A. (1986). *Social Foundations of Thought and Action: A Social Cognitive Theory*. Englewood Cliffs, NJ: Prentice Hall.

Barron, S., White, A., Swartzwelder, H.S. *et al.* (2005). Adolescent vulnerabilities to chronic alcohol or nicotine exposure: findings from rodent models. *Alcoholism: Clinical and Experimental Research*, 29, 1720–1725.

Biener, L., Reimer, R.L., Wakefield, M. *et al.* (2006). Impact of smoking cessation aids and mass media among recent quitters. *American Journal of Preventive Medicine*, 30, 217–224.

Braun, J., Kahn, R.S., Froelich, T. *et al.* (2006). Exposure to environmental toxicants and Attention Deficit Hyperactivity Disorder in US children. *Environmental Health Perspectives*, 114, 1904–1909.

Breslau, N. (1995). Psychiatric comorbidity of smoking and nicotine dependence. *Behavior Genetics*, 25, 95–101.

Breslau, N., Kilbey, M.M. and Andreski, P. (1991). Nicotine dependence, major depression and anxiety in young adults. *Archives of General Psychiatry*, 48, 1069–1074.

Breslau, N., Fenn, N. and Peterson, E.L. (1993). Early smoking initiation and nicotine dependence in a cohort of young adults. *Drug and Alcohol Dependence*, 33, 129–137.

Breslau, N., Kilbey, M.M. and Andreski, P. (1994). DSM-III-R nicotine dependence in young adults: pevalence, correlates and associated psychiatric disorders. *Addiction*, 89, 743–754.

Breslau, N., Johnson, E.O., Hiripi, E. and Kessler, R.C. (2001). Nicotine dependence in the United States: pevalence, trends and smoking persistence. *Archives of General Psychiatry*, 58, 810–816.

Bricker, J.B., Peterson, A.V., Robyn Andersen, M. *et al.* (2005). Friends', parents' and older siblings' smoking: reevaluating their influence on children's smoking. *Nicotine and Tobacco Research*, 8, 217–226.

Brook, D.W., Brook, J.S., Zhang, C. *et al.* (2002). Drug use and the risk of major depressive disorder, alcohol dependence and substance use disorders. *Archives of General Psychiatry*, 59, 1039–1044.

Brook, D.W., Zhang, C. and Brook, J.S. (2007). Trajectories of cigarette smoking from adolescence to young adulthood as predictors of obesity in the late twenties and early thirties. Unpublished manuscript.

Brook, J.S., Brook, D.W., Gordon, A. *et al.* (1990). The psychosocial etiology of adolescent drug use: a family interactional approach. *Genetic*, *Social* and *General Psychology Monographs*, 116, 111–267.

Brook, J.S., Richter, L. and Rubenstone, E. (2000). Consequences of adolescent drug use on psychiatric disorders in early adulthood. *Annals of Medicine*, 32, 401–407.

Brook, J.S., Pahl, K., Balka, E.B. and Fei, K. (2004). Smoking among New Yorican adolescents: time 1 predictors of time 2 tobacco use. *Journal of Genetic Psychology*, 165, 310–323.

Brook, J.S., Pahl, K. and Ning, Y. (2006). Peer and parent influences on longitudinal trajectories of smoking among African Americans and Puerto Ricans. *Nicotine and Tobacco Research*, 8, 639–651.

Brook, J.S., Balka, E.B., Ning, Y. and Brook, D.W. (2007). Trajectories of cigarette smoking among African-Americans and Puerto Ricans from adolescence to young adulthood: associations with dependence on alcohol and illegal drugs. *American Journal on Addictions*, 16, 195–201.

Buka, S.L., Shenassa, E.D. and Niaura, R. (2003). Elevated risk of tobacco dependence among offspring of mothers who smoked during pregnancy: a 30-year prospective study. *American Journal of Psychiatry*, 160, 1978–1984.

Carmody, T.P. (2002). Smoking cessation treatment groups. In: D.W. Brook and H.I. Spitz (eds), *The Group Therapy of Substance Abuse*. New York, NY: Haworth Press: 351–368.

Centers for Disease Control and Prevention (2001). Targeting tobacco use: the nation's leading cause of death. *At A Glance*, available at http://www.cdc.gov/nccdphp/publications/aag/osh.htm (accessed 15 September 2007).

Centers for Disease Control and Prevention. (2005a). Cigarette smoking among adults – United States 2004. *Morbidity and Mortality Weekly Report*, 54, 1121–1124.

Centers for Disease Control and Prevention. (2005b). Annual smoking-attributable mortality, years of potential life lost and productivity losses – United States, 1997–2001. *Morbidity and Mortality Weekly Report*, 54, 625–628.

Chambers, R.A., Taylor, J.R. and Potenza, M.N. (2003). Developmental neurocircuitry of motivation in adolescence: a critical period of addiction vulnerability. *American Journal of Psychiatry*, 160, 1041–1052.

Chassin, L.C.P.C., Pitts, S.C. and Sherman, S.J. (2000). The natural history of cigarette smoking from adolescence to adulthood in a Midwestern community sample: multiple trajectories and their psychosocial correlates. *Health Psychology*, 19, 223–231.

Chen, C., Wong, J., Lee, N. *et al.* (1993). The Shatin Community Mental Health Survey in Hong Kong: II. Major findings. *Archives of General Psychiatry*, 50, 125–133.

Chen, X., Cruz, T.S., Schuster, D.V. *et al.* (2002). Receptivity to pro-tobacco media and its impact on cigarette smoking among ethnic minority youth in California. *Journal of Health Communication*, 7, 95–111.

Colby, S.M., Tiffany, S.T., Shiffman, S. and Niaura, R.S. (2000). Are adolescent smokers dependent on nicotine? A review of the evidence. *Drug and Alcohol Dependence*, 59(Suppl. 1), S83–S95.

Colditz, G.A., Segal, M.R., Meyers, A.H. *et al.* (1992). Weight change in relation to smoking cessation among women. *Journal of Smoking-Related Disorders*, 3, 145–153.

Collins, A.C., Romm, E., Selvaag, S. *et al.* (1993). A comparison of the effects of chronic nicotine infusion on tolerance to nicotine and cross-tolerance to ethanol in long- and short-sleep mice. *Journal of Pharmacology and Experimental Therapeutics*, 266, 1390–1397.

Cottler, L.B., Schuckit, M.A., Helzer, J.E. *et al.* (1995). The DSM-IV field trial for substance use disorders; major results. *Drug and Alcohol Dependence*, 38, 59–69.

Dalton, M.A., Sargent, J.D., Beach, M.L. *et al.* (2003). Effect of viewing smoking in movies on adolescent smoking initiation: a cohort study. *Lancet*, 362, 281–285.

de Leone, J., Diaz, F.J., Rogers, T. *et al.* (2002). Initiation of daily smoking and nicotine dependence in schizophrenia and mood disorders. *Schizophrenia Research*, 56, 47–54.

Dierker, L., Merikangas, K.R. and Essau, C.A. (1997). Substance use disorders. In: C.A. Essau and F. Petermann (eds.) *Developmental Psychopathology: Epidemiology, Diagnostics and Treatment*. Melbourne: Harwood Academic Publishers, pp. 311–344.

DiFranza, J.R., Rigotti, N.A., McNeill, A.D. *et al.* (2000). Initial symptoms of nicotine dependence in adolescents. *Tobacco Control*, 9, 313–319.

DiFranza, J.R., Savageau, J.A., Fletcher, K. *et al.* (2002a). Measuring the loss of autonomy over nicotine use in adolescents: the DANDY (Development and Assessment of Nicotine Dependence in Youths) study. *Archives of Pediatrics and Adolescent Medicine*, 156, 397–403.

DiFranza, J.R., Savageau, J.A., Rigotti, N.A. *et al.* (2002b). Development of symptoms of tobacco dependence in youths: 30 months follow up data from the DANDY study. *Tobacco Control*, 11, 228–235.

Distefan, J.M., Pierce, J.P. and Gilpin, E.A. (2004). Do favorite movie stars influence adolescent smoking initiation? *American Journal of Public Health*, 94, 1239–1244.

Eisenberg, D. and Quinn, B.C. (2006). Estimating the effect of smoking cessation on weight gain: an instrumental variable approach. *Health Services Research*, 41, 2255–2266.

Ellickson, P.L., Orlando, M., Tucker, J.S. and Klein, D.J. (2004). From adolescence to young adulthood: Racial/ethnic disparities in smoking. *American Journal of Public Health*, 94, 293–299.

Erikson, E.H. (1968). *Identity: Youth and Crisis*. Oxford, Oxfordshire: Norton & Company.

Ernst, M., Moolchan, E. and Robinson, M. (2001). Behavioral and neural consequences of prenatal exposure to nicotine. *Journal of the American Academy of Child and Adolescent Psychiatry*, 40, 630–641.

Everett, S.A., Giovino, G.A., Warren, C.W. *et al.* (1998). Other substance use among high school students who use tobacco. *Journal of Adolescent Health*, 23(5), 298–296.

Ezzati, M., Henley, S.J., Thun, M.J. and Lopez, A.D. (2005). Role of smoking in global and regional cardiovascular mortality. *Circulation*, 112(4), 489–497.

Fagan, P., Brook, J.S., Rubenstone, E. and Zhang, C. (2005). Parental occupation, education and smoking as predictors of offspring tobacco use in adulthood: a longitudinal study. *Addictive Behaviors*, 30, 514–529.

Fagerström, K.O. (1978). Measuring degree of physical dependence to tobacco smoking with reference to individualization of treatment. *Addictive Behaviors*, 3, 235–241.

Fagerström, K.O., Kunze, M., Schoberberger, R. *et al.* (1996). Nicotine dependence versus smoking prevalence: comparisons among countries and categories of smokers. *Tobacco Control*, 5, 52–56.

Fergus, S., Zimmerman, M.A. and Caldwell, C.H. (2005). Psychosocial correlates of smoking trajectories among urban African-American adolescents. *Journal of Adolescent Research*, 20, 423–452.

Flay, B.R., Hu, F.B., Siddiqui, O. *et al.* (1994). Differential influence of parental smoking and friends' smoking on adolescent initiation and escalation of smoking. *Journal of Health and Social Behavior*, 35, 248–265.

French, S.A., Perry, C.L., Leon, G.R. and Fulkerson, J.A. (1994). Weight concerns, dieting behavior and smoking initiation among adolescents: a prospective study. *American Journal of Public Health*, 84, 1818–1820.

Frieden, T.R., Mostashari, F., Kerker, B.D. *et al.* (2005). Adult tobacco use levels after intensive tobacco control measures: New York City, 2002–2003. *American Journal of Public Health*, 95, 1016–1023.

Gervais, A., O'Loughlin, J., Meshefedjian, G. *et al.* (2006). Milestones in the natural course of onset of cigarette use among adolescents. *Canadian Medical Association Journal*, 175, 255–263.

Glantz, S.A., Kacirk, K.W. and McCulloch, C. (2004). Back to the future: smoking in movies in 2002 compared with 1950 levels. *American Journal of Public Health*, 94, 261–263.

Gonzalez-Pinto, A., Gutierrez, M., Ezcurra, J. *et al.* (1958). Tobacco smoking and bipolar disorder. *Journal of Clinical Psychiatry*, 59, 225–228.

Grant, B.F., Stinson, F.S., Dawson, D.A. *et al.* (2004). Co-occurrence of 12-month alcohol and drug use disorders and personality disorders in the United States: results from the National Epidemiologic Survey on Alcohol and Related Conditions. *Archives of General Psychiatry*, 61, 361–368.

Griesler, P.C. and Kandel, D.B. (1998). Ethnic differences in correlates of adolescent cigarette smoking. *Journal of Adolescent Health*, 23, 167–180.

Griesler, P.C., Kandel, D.B. and Davies, M. (2002). Ethnic differences in predictors of initiation and persistence of adolescent cigarette smoking in the National Longitudinal Survey of Youth. *Nicotine and Tobacco Research*, 4, 79–93.

Gritz, E.R., Prokhorov, A.V., Hudmon, K.S. *et al.* (1998). Cigarette smoking in a multiethnic population of youth: methods and baseline findings. *Preventive Medicine*, 27, 365–384.

Grunberg, N.E. (1990). The inverse relationship between tobacco use and body weight. In: L.T. Kozlowski, H.M. Annis, H.D. Chappel *et al.* (eds), *Research Advances in Alcohol and Drug Problems*, Vol. 10. New York, NY: Plenum Press, pp. 270–315).

Gulliver, S.B., Rohsenow, D.J., Colby, S.M. *et al.* (1995). Interrelationships of smoking and alcohol dependence, use and urges to use. *Journal of Studies on Alcohol*, 56, 202–206.

Heatherton, T.F., Kozlowski, L.T., Frecker, R.C. and Fagerström, K.O. (1991). The Fagerström Test for Nicotine Dependence: a revision of the Fagerström Tolerance Questionnaire. *British Journal of Addictions*, 86, 1119–1127.

Hu, M.C., Davies, M. and Kandel, D.B. (2006). Epidemiology and correlates of daily smoking and nicotine dependence among young adults in the United States. *American Journal of Public Health*, 96, 299–308.

Hughes, J.R. (2003). *The Case for Hardening the Target. Those who Continue to Smoke: Is Achieving Abstinence Harder and Do We Need to Change our Interventions?* NIH Publication No. 03-5370.

Bethesda, MD: Department of Health and Human Services, National Institutes of Health, National Cancer Institute.

Hughes, J.R., Helzer, J.E. and Lindberg, S.A. (2006). Prevalence of DSM/ICD-defined nicotine dependence. *Drug and Alcohol Dependence*, 85, 91–102.

Ingersoll, K.S. and Cohen, J. (2005). Combination treatment for nicotine dependence: state of the science. *Substance Use and Misuse*, 40, 1923–1943.

Jackson, C. and Dickinson, D. (2003). Can parents who smoke socialise their children against smoking? Results from the Smoke-free Kids intervention trial. *Tobacco Control*, 12, 52–59.

Janzon, E., Hedblad, B., Berglund, G. and Engstrom, G. (2004). Changes in blood pressure and body weight following smoking cessation in women. *Journal of Internal Medicine*, 255, 266–272.

Jason, L.A., Berk, M., Schnopp-Wyatt, D.L. and Talbot, B. (1999). Effects of enforcement of youth access laws on smoking prevalence. *American Journal of Community Psychology*, 27, 143–160.

Jefferis, B., Graham, H., Manor, O. and Power, C. (2003). Cigarette consumption and socio-economic circumstances in adolescence as predictors of adult smoking. *Addiction*, 98, 1756–1772.

Jessor, R. and Jessor, S.L. (1977). *Problem Behavior and Psychosocial Development*. New York, NY: Academic Press.

John, U., Meyer, C., Hapke, U. and Rumpf, H.-J. (2004a). Nicotine dependence and lifetime smoking in a population sample. *European Journal of Public Health Research*, 14, 182–185.

John, U., Meyer, C., Rumpf, H.-J. and Hapke, U. (2004b). Smoking, nicotine dependence and psychiatric comorbidity – a population-based study including smoking cessation after three years. *Drug and Alcohol Dependence*, 76, 287–295.

Johnston, L.D., O'Malley, P.M. and Bachman, J.G. (1989). *Drug Use, Drinking and Smoking: National Survey Results from High School, College and Young Adult Populations 1975–1988*. Rockville, MD: National Institute on Drug Abuse.

Johnston, L.D., O'Malley, P.M., Bachman, J.G. and Schulenberg, J.E. (2006). *Monitoring the Future: National Survey Results on Drug Use, 1975–2005*. NIH Publication No. 04-5507, Vol. 1: *Secondary School Students*. Bethesda, MD: National Institute on Drug Abuse.

Kacirk, K. and Glantz, S.A. (2001). Smoking in movies in 2000 exceeded rates in the 1960s. *Tobacco Control*, 10, 397–398.

Kandel, D.B. (1996). The parental and peer contexts of adolescent deviance: an algebra of interpersonal influences. *Journal of Drug Issues*, 26, 289–315.

Kandel, D.B. and Chen, K. (2000). Extent of smoking and nicotine dependence in the United States: 1991–1993. *Nicotine and Tobacco Research*, 2, 263–274.

Kandel, D.B., Chen, K., Warner, L.A. *et al.* (1997). Prevalence and demographic correlates of symptoms of last year dependence on alcohol, nicotine, marijuana and cocaine in the US population. *Drug and Alcohol Dependence*, 44, 11–29.

Kawakami, N., Takatsuka, N., Shimzu, H. and Takai, A. (1998). Life-time prevalence and risk factors of tobacco/nicotine dependence in male ever- smokers in Japan. *Addiction*, 93, 1023–1032.

Klesges, R.C. and Klesges, L.M. (1988). Cigarette smoking as a dieting strategy in a university population. *International Journal of Eating Disorders*, 7, 413–419.

Klesges, R.C., Zbikowski, S.M., Lando, H.A. *et al.* (1998). The relationship between smoking and body weight in a population of young military personnel. *Health Psychology*, 17, 454–458.

Lasser, K., Boyd, J.W., Wollhandler, S. *et al.* (2000). Smoking and mental illness. *Journal of the American Medical Association*, 284, 2606–2610.

Lee, C.K., Kwak, Y.S., Yamamoto, J. *et al.* (1990). Psychiatric epidemiology in Korea: 1. Gender and age differences in Seoul. *Journal of Nervous and Mental Disease*, 178, 242–246.

Levin, E.D., Rezvani, A.H., Montoya, D. *et al.* (2003). Adolescent-onset nicotine self-administration modeled in female rats. *Psychopharmacology*, 169, 141–149.

Levy, D.T. and Friend, K.B. (2003). The effects of clean indoor air laws: what do we know and what do we need to know? *Health Education Research*, 18, 592–609.

Lewinsohn, P.M., Rohde, P. and Brown, R.A. (1999). Level of current and past adolescent cigarette smoking as predictors of future substance use disorders in young adulthood. *Addiction*, 94, 913–921.

Lissner, L., Bengtsson, C., Lapidus, L. and Bjorkelund, C. (1992). Smoking initiation and cessation in relation to body fat distribution based on data from a study of Swedish women. *American Journal of Public Health*, 82, 273–275.

Luo, Y., Marks, J.M. and Collins, A.C. (1994). Genotype regulates the development of tolerance to ethanol and cross-tolerance to nicotine. *Alcohol*, 11, 167–176.

Madden, P.A.F., Heath, A.C., Starmer, G.A. *et al.* (1995). Alcohol sensitivity and smoking history in men and women. *Alcoholism: Clinical and Experimental Research*, 19, 1111–1120.

Masse, L. and Tremblay, R. (1997). Behavior of boys in kindergarten and onset of substance use during adolescence. *Archives of General Psychiatry*, 54, 62–68.

McCool, J.P., Cameron, L.D. and Petrie, K.S. (2001). Adolescent perceptions of smoking imagery in film. *Social Science and Medicine*, 52, 1577–1587.

Mekemson, C. and Glantz, S.A. (2002). How the tobacco industry built its relationship with Hollywood. *Tobacco Control*, 11(Suppl 1), 181–191.

Middleman, A.B., Vazquez, I. and DuRant, R.H. (1998). Eating patterns, physical activity and attempts to change weight among adolescents. *Journal of Adolescent Health*, 22, 37–42.

Najman, J.M., Aird, R., Bor, W. *et al.* (2004). The intergenerational transmission of socioeconomic inequalities in child cognitive development and emotional health. *Social Science and Medicine*, 58, 1147–1158.

Nelson, C.B. and Wittchen, H.U. (1998). Smoking and nicotine dependence: results from a sample of 14- to 24-year-olds in Germany. *European Addiction Research*, 4, 42–49.

Oetting, E.R. and Donnermeyer, J.F. (1998). Primary socialization theory: the etiology of drug use and deviance. I. *Substance Use and Misuse*, 33, 995–1026.

Orlando, M., Ellickson, P.L. and Jinnett, K. (2001). The temporal relationship between emotional distress and cigarette smoking during adolescence and young adulthood. *Journal of Consulting and Clinical Psychology*, 69, 959–970.

Orlando, M., Tucker, J.S., Ellickson, P.L. and Klein, D.J. (2004). Developmental trajectories of cigarette smoking and their correlates from early adolescence to young adulthood. *Journal of Consulting and Clinical Psychology*, 72, 400–410.

Pechmann, C. and Reibling, E.T. (2000). Anti-smoking advertising campaigns targeting youth: Case studies from USA and Canada. *Tobacco Control*, 9 (Suppl II), ii18–ii31.

Prochaska, J.O. and DiClemente, C.C. (1992). Stages of change in the modification of problem behaviors. *Progressive Behavior Modificiation*, 28, 183–218.

Prokhorov, A.V., Pallonen, U.E., Fava., J.L. *et al.* (1996). Measuring nicotine dependence among high-risk adolescent smokers. *Addictive Behaviors*, 21, 117–127.

Prokhorov, A., Hudmon, K.S., de Moor, C.A. *et al.* (2001). Nicotine dependence, withdrawal symptoms and adolescents' readiness to quit smoking. *Nicotine and Tobacco Research*, 3, 151–155.

Prokhorov, A.V., Hudmon, K.S., Cinciripini, P.M. and Marani, S. (2005). "Withdrawal symptoms" in adolescents: a comparison of former smokers and never-smokers. *Nicotine and Tobacco Research*, 7, 909–913.

Ramsey, S.E., Brown, R.A., Strong, D.R. *et al.* (2005). Cigarette smoking and substance use among adolescents in psychiatric treatment. *Journal of Child and Adolescent Substance Abuse*, 14, 1–13.

Rende, R., Slomkowski, C., McCaffery, J. *et al.* (2005). A twin sibling study of tobacco use in adolescence: Etiology of individual differences and extreme scores. *Nicotine and Tobacco Research*, 7, 413–419.

Robins, L.E., Helzer, J.E. and Przybeck, T. (1985). *Substance Abuse in the General Population.* New York, NY: Guilford Press.

Rojas, N.L., Killen, J.D., Haydel, K.F. and Robinson, T.N. (1998). Nicotine dependence among adolescent smokers. *Archives of Pediatrics and Adolescent Medicine*, 152, 51–56.

Ross, H. and Chaloupka, F.J. (2003). The effect of cigarette prices on youth smoking. *Health Economics*, 12, 217–230.

Sargent, J.D., Tickle, J.J., Beach, M.L. *et al.* (2001). Brand appearance in contemporary cinema films and contribution to global marketing of cigarettes. *Lancet*, 357, 29–32.

Shenassa, E.D., McCaffery, J.M., Swan, G.E. *et al.* (2003). Intergenerational transmission of tobacco use and dependence: a transdisciplinary approach. *Nicotine and Tobacco Research*, 5(Suppl. 1), S55–S69.

Shiffman, S. (1989). Tobacco "chippers" – individual differences in tobacco dependence. *Psychopharmacology*, 97, 539–547.

Siahpush, M., McNeill, A., Borland, R. and Fong, G. T. (2006). Socioeconomic variations in nicotine dependence, self-efficacy and intention to quit across four countries: findings from the International Tobacco Control (ITC) Four Country Survey. *Tobacco Control*, 15(Suppl. III), iii71–iii75.

Stanton, W.R. (1995). DSM-III-R tobacco dependence and quitting during late adolescence. *Addictive Behaviors*, 20, 595–603.

Stanton, W.R., Lowe, J.B. and Gillespie, A.M. (1996). Adolescents' experiences of smoking cessation. *Drug and Alcohol Dependence*, 2, 63–70.

Stockwell, T.F. and Glantz, S.A. (1997). Tobacco use is increasing in popular films. *Tobacco Control*, 6, 282–284.

Storr, C.L., Reboussin, B.A. and Anthony, J.C. (2005). The Fagerström Test for Nicotine Dependence: a comparison of standard scoring and latent class analysis approaches. *Drug and Alcohol Dependence*, 80, 241–250.

Strauss, R.S. and Mir, H.M. (2001). Smoking and weight loss attempts in overweight and normal-weight adolescents. *International Journal of Obesity and Related Metabolic Disorders*, 25, 1381–1385.

Sullivan, P.F. and Kendler, K.S. (1999). The genetic epidemiology of smoking. *Nicotine and Tobacco Research*, 1, S51–S57.

Teo, K.K., Ounpuu, S., Hawken, S. *et al.* (2006). Tobacco use and risk of myocardial infarction in 52 countries in the INTERHEART study: a case–control study. *Lancet*, 368, 647–658.

Teti, T.S. and Glantz, S.A. (1998). Smoking in movies remained high in 1997. *Tobacco Control*, 7, 441.

Tickle, J.J., Sargent, J.D., Dalton, M.A. *et al.* (2001). Favourite movie stars, their tobacco use in contemporary movies and its association with adolescent smoking. *Tobacco Control*, 10, 16–22.

Turbin, M., Jessor, R. and Costa, F. (2000). Adolescent cigarette smoking: health-related behavior or normative transgression? *Prevention Science*, 1, 115–124.

Ulrich, J., Meyer, C., Rumpf, H.-J. and Hapke, U. (2003). Probabilities of alcohol high risk drinking, abuse, or dependence estimated on grounds of tobacco smoking and nicotine dependence. *Addiction*, 98, 805–814.

Unger, J.B., Rohrbach, L.A., Cruz, T.B. *et al.* (2001). Ethnic variation in peer influences on adolescent smoking. *Nicotine and Tobacco Research*, 3, 167–176.

United States Department of Health and Human Services (1994). *Preventing Tobacco Use among Young People: A Report of the Surgeon General.* Atlanta, GA: US Department of Health and Human Services, Public Health Service, Centers for Disease Control and Prevention, National Center for Chronic Disease Prevention and Health Promotion, Office on Smoking and Health.

United States Department of Health and Human Services (2001). *Women and Smoking: A Report of the Surgeon General.* Atlanta, GA: US Department of Health and Human Services, Public Health Service, Centers for Disease Control and Prevention, National Center for Chronic Disease Prevention and Health Promotion, Office on Smoking and Health.

United States Department of Health and Human Services (2004). *Results from the* 2004 *National Survey on Drug Use and Health: Detailed Tables.* Available at www.oas.samhsa.gov.nsduh (accessed 4 December 2006).

Upadhyaya, H.P., Deas, D., Brady, K.T. and Kruesi, M. (2002). Cigarette smoking and psychiatric comorbidity in children and adolescents. *Journal of the American Academy of Child and Adolescent Psychiatry*, 41, 1294–1305.

Wilhelmsen, K.C., Swan, G.E., Chang, L.S. *et al.* (2005). Support for previously identified alcoholism susceptibility loci in a cohort selected for smoking behavior. *Alcoholism: Clinical and Experimental Research*, 29, 2108–2115.

Williamson, D.F., Madans, J., Anda, R.F. *et al.* (1991). Smoking cessation and severity of weight gain in a national cohort. *New England Journal of Medicine*, 324, 739–745.

Windle, M. and Windle, R.C. (2001). Depressive symptoms and cigarette smoking among middle school adolescents: prospective associations and intrapersonal and interpersonal influences. *Journal of Consulting and Clinical Psychology*, 69, 215–226.

Winter, A.L., de Guia, N.A., Ferrence, R. and Cohen, J.E. (2002). The relationship between body weight perceptions, weight control behaviours and smoking status among adolescents. *Canadian Journal of Public Health*, 93, 362–365.

Xian, H., Scherrer, J.F., Eisen, S.A. *et al.* (2007). Nicotine dependence subtypes: association with smoking history, diagnostic criteria and psychiatric disorders in 5440 regular smokers from the Vietnam Era Twin Registry. *Addictive Behaviors*, 32, 137–147.

Young, S.E., Corley, R.P., Stallings, M.C. *et al.* (2002). Substance use, abuse and dependence in adolescence: prevalence, symptom profiles and correlates. *Drug and Alcohol Dependence*, 68, 309–322.

6

EATING ADDICTION

DAVID H. GLEAVES AND JANET D. CARTER

The possible association between the eating disorders (EDs) and addictions has a long history, both in the EDs and substance abuse literature (Vandereycken, 1990). Whether or not disordered eating should be conceptualized as a form of addictive behavior has been a matter of vigorous debate and the answer to the question probably depends on what form of disordered eating is being considered, as well as what definition of addiction is used.

Regarding the former issue, numerous different behaviors associated with ED have, in one form or another, been conceptualized as addictive. Most addictive models of EDs (Gold *et al.*, 2003) focus mainly on compulsive binge eating, such as that associated with bulimia nervosa (BN) or binge eating disorder (BED). With such a conceptualization, it would be hard to envision restricting anorexia nervosa (AN) as an addiction given that it is a disorder characterized by *not* eating. However, other researchers have proposed addiction models of anorexia based on the idea that individuals become addicted to endogenous opioids created by starvation (Marrazzi and Luby, 1986). Other conceptualizations of EDs as addictions have focused on an alleged addiction to exercise (Epling and Pierce, 1988), purging (Abraham and Joseph, 1986–1987), or even to rumination (Blinder *et al.*, 1986). Thus, according to addiction perspectives on EDs, it is possible to become addicted for virtually any aspect of eating, including not eating.

Regarding the issue of how addiction is defined, if a fairly broad definition of addiction is used – for example, as compulsive behaviors, perceived as out-of-control, that persist in spite of negative consequences (Garner and Gerborg, 2004) – then it is fairly easy to see that EDs would qualify. There is also no mistaking the similarity between disordered eating and the addictions. Persons with EDs experience preoccupations with food in general, with specific foods, or even with the avoidance of food. Such persons at times perceive their eating behavior as compulsive and out of control. Eating-related activities may consume the majority of their day, may be secretive in nature and may be associated with shame and guilt. Persons with EDs may also appear to use substances to help cope with stress and negative emotions and the pattern continues despite negative and even life-threatening effects.

Gold and colleagues are recent proponents of the addiction model of EDs (Gold *et al.*, 2003). They cite the phenomenological overlap of disordered eating and substance abuse, noting the common-sense adage that "if it looks like a duck, acts like a duck and quacks like a duck, it must be a duck" (Gold *et al.*, 2003: 121). However, they also cite a wealth of physiological data that point to a relationship between food intake and the activity of the mesolimbic dopaminergic system (MDS), which is similar to the relationship between reward, illicit drug reinforcement, self-stimulation and sexual behavior and MDS activity. Different physiological data (the action of endogenous opioids) have been studied by Marrazzi and colleagues (1997), who suggest that the data support their auto-addiction model of anorexia and BN.

Other researchers have studied EDs and addictions from a psychological, psychometric or psychodynamic perspective. Worthington and colleagues (2002) argued that both EDs and addictions may be considered maladaptive coping responses that can result in part from unresolved trauma. Thus, both drug abuse and disordered eating may be means of managing negative affect. Psychometric (i.e., factor analysis) research sometimes suggests that disordered eating seems to factor along with other addictive behavior, including compulsive shopping and substance use (Rodríguez-Villarino *et al.*, 2005), suggesting that there may be a single underlying construct that explains all of these behaviors.

Conversely, other researchers, such as Wilson (2000; Wilson and Latner, 2001), have concluded that the bulk of the evidence suggests that, particularly when a more restrictive definition of addiction is used (one requiring the presence of tolerance, physical dependence and withdrawal), disordered eating does not qualify as an addiction. They argued that there is no credible evidence that these phenomena apply to EDs, and reached the overall conclusion that "the available evidence argues against viewing EDs as a form of addiction. Furthermore, the addiction model fails in conceptualizing the clinical features of EDs and in accounting for the important differences among anorexia, bulimia nervosa and BED" (Wilson and Latner, 2001: 598).

Other researchers also do not deny the conceptual similarity of EDs and addictions, but argue that we are dealing with an issue of partial similarity (Vandereycken, 1990; Garner and Gerborg, 2004). That is, although the problems are similar in many ways, the comparison breaks down at a critical point. The biggest problem with the model has to do with treatments derived from it. Specifically, most treatments that stem from addiction models involve abstinence from the addictive substance. With substances such as alcohol, narcotics or cocaine, this is possible; with food it is not possible to abstain completely, and, in fact, when an individual tries to do so, it is considered an ED. So instead of endorsing complete abstinence, proponents of an addiction model suggest that persons need to abstain from certain foods, specifically those with which the person may lose control. However, such restrictive rules regarding eating are believed to be part of the cognitive styles that actually maintain most EDs. Furthermore, an addiction/abstinence-based approach to treatment communicates to the individual the belief that he or she is powerless over food, which again is counter to the cognitive-behavioral treatments that have been found to be effective for treating at least some EDs (Wilson, 2000; Wilson and Latner, 2001; Garner and Gerborg, 2004).

Overall, it is clear that conceptualizing EDs as addictions is a controversial and even contentious topic. Other than this brief introduction to the different perspective on the issue, it is not the purpose of this chapter to attempt to resolve the debate. Regardless of their relationship with addictive behaviors, EDs are unquestionably significant problems among adolescents, particularly girls. Thus, for the remainder of this chapter we will focus on EDs. We will review the literature on the definitions, scope and treatment of the various EDs. For all intents and purposes we are thus using the terms *eating addiction* and *eating disorder* synonymously, although doing so should not be assumed to imply that they are necessarily best characterized as forms of addiction.

DEFINITION OF EATING DISORDERS

The EDs are in general characterized by gross disturbances in eating behavior as well as extreme and distorted concerns about body shape and/or weight. The current *Diagnostic and Statistical Manual of Mental Disorders* (DSM-IV-TR; American Psychiatric Association, 2000) distinguishes between three primary types of EDs: AN, BN and Eating Disorder Not Otherwise Specified (EDNOS). The latter refers to instances in which an individual meets some but not all the criteria required for the diagnosis of either AN or BN. BED is a more recently recognized disorder that technically falls into the EDNOS category (although research criteria have been developed). There are, however, numerous possible manifestations of EDNOS other than BED.

In earlier versions of the DSM-IV-TR (up to and including the third edition – revised), the EDs were listed within the "Disorders usually first evident in infancy, childhood, or adolescence" section. Given their prominence among adults, they were moved to their own section in the most recent edition. However, it is important to not lose sight of the fact that these are in many ways disorders of adolescence.

ANOREXIA NERVOSA (AN)

The central feature of AN is a "refusal to maintain a minimally normal body weight" (APA, 2000: 583), with the minimum weight threshold set at 85 percent of the person's expected weight for his or her age and height. The weight criterion may also be expressed in terms of a body mass index (BMI), which is calculated as (weight in kilograms)/(height in meters^2). A BMI of 17.5 or lower is generally adopted as indicative of AN, although some flexibility is needed and BMIs are often difficult to interpret with children and adolescents. A percentage of expected weight may be more appropriate for this age group (Fisher *et al.*, 1995). An individual may be at a minimal body size through having lost weight or through never having gained the weight that would be expected with normal development. Mechanisms of weight control may include intentional restriction of food-intake (dieting, fasting), excessive exercising, or purging behaviors (self-induced vomiting and misuse of laxatives, diuretics or enemas).

In addition to the intentional low weight, individuals with AN also experience an intense fear of gaining weight and becoming fat (APA, 2000). This fear does not seem to lessen as the individual loses weight (Walsh and Garner, 1997). Individuals with AN may experience their bodies in a distorted way, feeling "fat" and chronically dissatisfied with their body shape. Such individuals may monitor their own weight and body size closely and experience intense shame, disillusionment and frustration if they gain weight. Conversely, weight losses are experienced as important achievements and exemplars of self-discipline. That is, weight and body shape exerts a disproportional influence on the self-esteem of individuals with AN (APA, 2000). Another criterion of AN is the presence of amenorrhea in post-menarchal females. In young anorexic adolescents, the onset of menstruation may be delayed.

The DSM-IV-TR distinguishes between two types of AN, based on the principal method of weight control. Restricting anorexics do not engage in regular binge eating and purging, whereas binge-eating/purging anorexics do. However, excessive dieting and exercising is not unique to either type of anorexia (APA, 2000). There is a wealth of evidence supporting the validity of this distinction (see, for example, DaCosta and Halmi, 1992; Gleaves *et al.*, 2000).

Recognizing AN in adolescents presents many challenges. First, in a prepubescent female (or a male), the amenorrhea criterion is not applicable. Second, there may not be a noticeable weight loss, but rather a failure to achieve normal weight or to gain weight at a normal rate. Related to this challenge, normal weight is also sometimes difficult to determine and quantify. A related concern is that severe anorexia may inhibit normal skeletal development, and thus height may be affected. See Netemeyer and Williamson (2001) for a more detailed discussion of assessment of AN among children and adolescents.

BULIMIA NERVOSA (BN)

According to the current DSM-IV, BN is characterized by repeated (at least twice a week for 3 months) episodes of binge eating followed by inappropriate compensatory responses to prevent weight gains (APA, 2000), plus some form of body image disturbance. DSM-IV defines a binge as "eating in a discrete period of time an amount of food that is definitely larger than most individuals would eat under similar circumstances" (APA, 2000: 589), although there is some debate in the field regarding whether or not the size criterion is necessary (Rossiter and Agras, 1990). There is also by definition a subjective sense of loss of control during the binge episodes. Binges are often triggered by the intense hunger felt after dieting, dysphoric mood states, stress, and feelings and thoughts associated with body image and food cravings (Schlundt and Johnson, 1990; Walsh and Garner, 1997).

The compensatory behaviors referred to in the criteria may be purging through self-induced vomiting or use of laxatives, but may also be simply excessive exercise or starvation (or other methods). These latter behaviors are not, according to the DSM-IV, considered purging, although their goal is still to *undo* the effects of the binge. Thus, DSM-IV classifies BN into Purging Type and Non-purging Type according to the presence or absence of regular use of purging behaviors, respectively. There is less support for this distinction (Gleaves *et al.*, 2000) than there is for the subtypes of AN described above, although it is generally believed that the purging type is associated with more pathology than the non-purging type (see, for example, Willmuth *et al.*, 1988). As with the bingeing criterion, the compensatory behaviors need to occur on average at least twice a week for 3 months to meet the threshold for diagnosis.

The DSM body image criterion for BN is somewhat vague, and worded only as "Self-evaluation is unduly influenced by body shape and weight". There is, however, evidence that women with BN overestimate their current size, and desire to be excessively thin, relative to same-sized women without BN (Williamson *et al.*, 1989). When controlling for actual body size, persons with BN seem indistinguishable from those with AN in terms of these phenomena (Williamson, Cubic and Gleaves, 1993).

BINGE EATING DISORDER (BED)

As noted above, BED is not currently accepted as a formal diagnosis in DSM-IV but rather is listed in the "Criteria sets and axes provided for further study" section (APA, 2000: 759). The core feature of the disorder is the presence of recurrent binge eating (as seen with BN) but in the absence of the compensatory behaviors that occur with BN. Persons with BED may not be as restrictive in their eating as persons with BN, and a large percentage of BED individuals are obese. Because of their obese status, persons with BED are very often dissatisfied with their bodies; however, the body image distortion sometimes seen among persons with AN or BN may not occur with BED.

Before the coining of the term BED, the disorder was known by other names. Williamson (1990), for example, referred to this group of individuals as compulsive overeaters. Some researchers (e.g., Hay and Fairburn, 1998) have conceptualized BED as being less severe than BN. However, the range and frequency of comorbid psychopathology for BED is similar to that with BN. Furthermore, the mortality rates for BED may actually be higher than with BN because of the associated obesity (Agras, 2001).

EATING DISORDER NOT OTHERWISE SPECIFIED (EDNOS)

We believe that EDNOS warrants its own section here because it appears to be the most common ED encountered in clinical practice (Fairburn and Bohn, 2005). There are no positive criteria for EDNOS, and DSM-IV-TR defines these only as "disorders of eating that do not meet the criteria for any specific eating disorder" (APA, 2000: 594). Although the DSM lists six possible presentations of EDNOS (with one being BED), Fairburn and Bohn described two subtypes as particularly common. The first are instances where the individual's presentation closely resembles AN or BN nervosa, but he or she just fails to meet the diagnostic thresholds (body weight or frequency of bingeing). However, these cases should not be thought of as non-severe. The fact that they appear in clinical practice suggests that they warrant clinical attention. The second subtype are cases in which the clinical features of AN and BN are combined in ways other than in the two recognized syndromes. These cases might be described as "mixed". Williamson *et al.* (1992) provided empirical support for the existence of these clusters, in addition to BED. Another subtype described specifically in the adolescent literature is that of individuals who purge but do not binge (Binford and Le Grange, 2005).

EPIDEMIOLOGY, COMORBIDITY, USE OF MENTAL HEALTH SERVICES

EPIDEMIOLOGY

Prevalence

Hoek and van Hoeken (2003) reviewed the ED prevalence research and reported an average prevalence rate of 0.3 percent for AN among young females. The prevalence rates for BN were 1 percent and 0.1 percent for young women and men, respectively. Those authors estimated the prevalence of binge eating disorder to be at least 1 percent, although some published estimates are considerably higher. The research incorporated in the Hoek and van Hoeken review typically included adolescents, but the averages were not specific to adolescence.

The authors also did not report the prevalence of EDs in general, or EDNOS. In one recent study specific to adolescents, Kjelsås and colleagues (2004) examined a sample of 1960 adolescent girls and boys ages 14–15 in Norway. Lifetime prevalence of any ED among girls was 17.9 percent. Consistent with the clinical data, the most prevalent single disorder was EDNOS (lifetime prevalence = 14.6 percent, not including BED). Respective lifetime prevalence rates for AN, BN and BED were 0.7, 1.2 and 1.5 percent. For boys, lifetime prevalence for any ED was 6.5 percent, and respective rates for EDNOS, AN, BN and BED were 5.0, 0.2, 0.4 and 0.9 percent. Thus, as with girls, EDNOS was also most common. In one prevalence study among obese adolescents seeking weight-loss treatment, Decaluwe and Braet (2003) found that 1 percent met criteria for BED. Binge-eating was more common among girls than boys.

In addition to studies of the prevalence of specific ED diagnoses *per se*, there has been research on the prevalence of eating disordered behaviors among adolescents. In some studies, as many as 50 percent of participants report binge eating or self-induced vomiting (Fisher *et al.*, 1995), although the research is mixed regarding whether boys or girls report these behaviors more frequently (Marcus and Kalarchian, 2003). In practice, recognizing and detecting EDs may often be difficult due to the secrecy associated with the behaviors of binge eating and purging. Furthermore, some researchers have hypothesized that the prevalence of some EDs (particularly BN) may be lower among children and adolescents than among adults for logistical reasons – that is, most children do not have the money and privacy to allow for frequent binge eating (Netemeyer and Williamson, 2001). This may be less of an issue for adolescents, but depends on their age. AN is also more obvious because of the extreme low weight. However, when the low weight is a manifestation of a failure to gain weight, such detection can be much more difficult.

Gender Differences

As the above data suggest, EDs in general and both AN and BN occur at a lower rate among males than among females. It is possible that the prevalence of AN in boys is higher than it seems to be, but is not readily recognized because of its reputation as a female disorder. There is some evidence indicating that males who become anorexic do so at an earlier age than females. Another apparent difference between male and female anorexics is that males tend to be obese prior to dieting (Andersen and Holman, 1997). Regarding BN, males usually have a later onset. A subgroup of boys with a higher risk of developing BN includes athletes that need to maintain their weight below specific thresholds (e.g., wrestlers, runners) or for whom physical appearance and body shape is particularly important (e.g., body-builders) (Carlat *et al.*, 1997). Homosexuality and bisexuality also seem to be a risk factor for BN in males, as the prevalence of homosexuality and bisexuality is higher in men with BN than in the general population (10% versus 43%; Carlat *et al.*, 1997). However, whether or not this applies to adolescents is not clear.

Social Class and EDs

Researchers have often reported that EDs, specially AN, are more common among females of middle to high social classes (see, for example, Crisp *et al.*, 1976). However, more recent studies also show that ED cases can be found across all social classes. If EDs are more common among the higher social classes, the effect seems specific to AN; BN may actually be more common among lower socio-economic groups (Hoek *et al.*, 2003).

Incidence

According to Hoek and van Hoeken's (2003) review, the incidence of AN is 8 cases per 100 000 population per year and incidence rates for AN are the highest for females in the 15–19 age group. This age group constitutes approximately 40 percent of all identified cases. The authors estimated the incidence of BN to be 12 cases per 100 000 population per year. We are unaware of incidence data specifically on BED.

In terms of time trends, the incidence of AN appears to have increased over the last century, until the 1970s. The incidence and prevalence of bulimia no doubt increased up until the 1970s or 1980s, although this is difficult to document, given that the syndrome wasn't included in the DSM before 1980. There is also now some evidence that the prevalence of bulimia has actually decreased since the 1980s (Keel *et al.*, 2006).

COMORBIDITY

All of the EDs appear to have an elevated risk of medical complications or additional psychopathology. We only touch on the medical complications here; see Brambilla and Monteleone (2003) for a more comprehensive review. Regarding AN, comorbid medical problems include osteoporosis and osteopenia, cardiovascular problems, and orthopedic problems caused by excessive exercise along with nutritional deficiencies (Agras, 2001; Brambilla and Monteleone, 2003). In terms of comorbid psychopathology, there appears to be a high prevalence of depression, anxiety, obsessive-compulsive behavior, post-traumatic stress disorder and substance use. Interpersonal and family problems and personality disorders are also common (Agras, 2001; Gleaves and Eberenz, 1993).

For BN, there may be less medical comorbidity, but medical complications do occur. These include electrolyte imbalances, dental problems and cardiovascular problems (Agras, 2001, Brambilla and Monteleone, 2003). In terms of comorbid psychopathology, persons with BN also frequently exhibit depression, anxiety, substance abuse and personality disorders (Agras, 2001; Gleaves and Eberenz, 1995).

Given the focus of this chapter, the issue of ED and substance use warrants additional attention. EDs, particularly those involving binge eating (BN, BED and the bulimic subtype of AN), appear to have a high degree of comorbidity with substance use (Bulik *et al.*, 2004). Between 20 percent and 46 percent of women with such disorders report a history of problems with alcohol and/or drugs (Bulik *et al.*, 2004; Conason *et al.*, 2006). Some researchers have also studied adolescents specifically. For example, Wiederman and Pryor (1991) reported that approximately one-third of a sample of adolescents with BN reported smoking tobacco and marijuana and were drinking alcohol *at least* weekly. A much lower percentage of girls with AN reported such use, with only 1.7 percent reporting drinking on a weekly basis. Similar results were reported by Stock and colleagues (2002), who found that restricting anorexics actually reported less substance use than the general (non-clinical) population. In their sample, individuals who purged reported a higher rate of substance use, but not higher than in the general adolescent population. However, this group was small, and the authors did not specifically examine adolescents who binged.

USE OF MENTAL HEALTH SERVICES

The research on use of mental health services by persons with EDs is quite limited, particularly for adolescents. However, Simon and colleagues (2005) recently reviewed the available research on health-service use and costs. Findings are also somewhat variable, and dependent on the location of the research (i.e., the country) and how the data were collected. Published research has been conducted in the UK, Germany, Australia, the USA, Austria, Denmark and the Netherlands. A general conclusion of Simon *et al.* (2005) was that EDs are underdetected and undertreated. Detection and treatment at the primary-care level is particularly low. At least in the USA and Europe, only a fraction of persons with EDs are recognized or treated at the primary-care level. Poor detection does not seem to be due to persons with EDs visiting practitioners at a lower rate; these individuals actually visit doctors more frequently. Turnbull *et al.* (1996) also found that, prior to patients receiving ED diagnoses, many general practitioners had prescribed laxatives or diuretics (which should be regarded as contraindicated). Moreover, EDs are too often treated in non-specialist units. For example, the National (UK) Inpatient Child and Adolescent Psychiatry Study (NICAPS; O'Herlihy *et al.*, 2001) reported that more hospital beds were occupied by young people with EDs than any other mental disorder.

In a fairly large-scale study (involving insurance claims from just under 4 million patients) of service use in the US for the year 1995, Striegel-Moore and colleagues (2000) found that outpatient treatment was the norm across all EDs for males and females. Only 21.5 percent of females and 18.4 percent of males were hospitalized for AN. For BN, 12 percent and 22 percent of females and males, respectively, received inpatient treatment. The (average) numbers were even lower for EDNOS (12.3% of females and 6.8% of males). This study was not specific to adolescents, but they were included in the sample. For females that required inpatient treatment, the average numbers of days were 26.0, 14.7 and 19.9 for AN, BN and EDNOS respectively. For females and outpatient treatment, the average numbers of days were 17.0, 15.6 and 13.7 respectively. For males, service use was slightly less, averaging 9.2, 9.1 and 10.6 days respectively for AN, BN and EDNOS. It is noteworthy that these averages (particularly for males) are considerably lower than the 20 or so treatment sessions that are used in most empirically-based treatments. Of course, a limitation of the data is that they are based on insurance claims and do not take into consideration treatments paid as an out-of-pocket expense.

In terms of the treatment costs reviewed by Simon *et al.* (2005), the UK study reported that the health care costs of AN in 1990 were £4.2 million. However, the study did not attempt to estimate outpatient treatment or that from private ED services, and did not consider BN, BED or EDNOS. In Germany during 1998, the estimated healthcare cost for AN was €65 million, with an estimate of €10 million for BN. However, the figures did not include costs of primary care, outpatient care or pharmacological treatments; also, BED and EDNOS were not examined. In the Australian study, the costs were estimated to be Aus$22 million for the year 1993/1994.

In the US study by Striegel-Moore *et al.* (2000), the authors calculated the average yearly costs for treating (inpatient and outpatient combined) AN, BN or EDNOS. Respective costs for women were $6045, $2962 and $3207. Comparative costs for treatment of schizophrenia and OCD were $4824 and $1930. For men, costs were $2746, $3885 and $2165 for AN, BN and EDNOS, respectively, and $5093 and $1803 for schizophrenia and OCD respectively. Thus, overall, AN costs are similar to those of schizophrenia and, again, out-of-pocket expenses were not included. These expenses are often enormous, particularly in the US, where there is no nationalized healthcare. Bernstein (2007) recently described one fairly typical instance where an adolescent girl was hospitalized for 16 months but the insurance company would pay for only 10 days, leaving the father with a bill for over US$1 million. Although 16 months is well above the mean reported by Striegel-Moore and colleagues, they also reported a large range, and it appears that they only reported what was covered by insurance companies.

COURSE AND OUTCOME

The course and outcome for EDs depend on the particular disorder, as well as a variety of other predictive factors. Of all psychiatric disorders, AN appears to have the highest mortality rate, at approximately 5.6 percent per decade (Agras, 2001). Deaths are either due to physical complications or to suicide. In terms of the course and outcome, in one early review of follow-up studies averaging approximately 10 years, Schwartz and Thompson (1981) concluded that between 25 percent and 50 percent of patients had recovered and perhaps 20 percent were much improved. More recently, Steinhausen (2002) reviewed 119 patient samples with follow-ups of greater than 10 years, and found mean values of 73.2 percent recovery, 8.5 percent improvement, 13.7 percent chronicity and 9.4 percent mortality.

For BN, longer-term outcome is better than for AN, but is still associated with a considerable degree of relapse and chronicity (Agras, 2001). In Agras's review, he concluded that follow-up studies suggest that only 10 percent of bulimic subjects continue to experience the full syndrome at 10-year follow-up, with AN developing in less than 1 percent. Some 60 percent of subjects are in full or partial remission from the disorder at 10-year follow-up; however, between 30 percent and 50 percent continue to have a clinical ED (Agras, 2001). Diagnostic crossover to AN and BED is low. Mortality in BN is considerably lower than in AN. Social adjustment and sexuality apparently normalizes in quite a few bulimic women over the course of time. A large group of bulimic patients, however, become chronic and suffer from severe bulimic symptoms and social and sexual impairment. In one recent 12-year follow-up study, Fichter and Quadflieg (2004) followed a sample of 196 women diagnosed with BN (purging type). After 12 years, the majority of patients (70.1%) showed no major DSM-IV ED, 13.2 percent had EDNOS, 10.1 percent had BN-P and 2 percent had died.

Less is known about the course and outcome of EDNOS. However, Grilo *et al.* (2003) found that the 2-year course for EDNOS was better than for BN (40% remitted for BN versus 59% for EDNOS). Of course, such a finding would depend on the nature of the EDNOS sample. Also of interest, Grilo and colleagues found that the course for both BN and EDNOS seemed unrelated to the presence, severity or change in comorbid personality disorder or other Axis I disorder.

The course and outcome for BED may be the most positive of the EDs. Fairburn and colleagues (2000) followed (for 5 years) a sample of young women diagnosed as having either BN or BED. Whereas the outcome of those with BN was relatively poor, that of the BED group was relatively good, with the great majority making a full recovery even though they had not received treatment.

RISK AND PROTECTIVE FACTORS

RISK FACTORS

Despite being a serious cause of morbidity and mortality in adolescents, our understanding of the factors that lead to the development of EDs is deficient. A variety of approaches have been used to investigate risk factors for EDs. Some research has been informed by one specific etiological approach (e.g., biological, cognitive-behavioral, psychodynamic), whereas other research has used integrative perspectives (e.g., biopsychosocial). Whatever the case, the underlying model has lead to the investigation of a (few or large) range of risk factors believed to be important in the development of EDs. Due to the enormous time and cost requirements associated with investigating risk factors in prospective longitudinal studies, the majority of such research has occurred within case–control studies, retrospective studies or cross-sectional designs (typically comparing affected versus non-affected individuals). A consequence of the differing theoretical and methodological approaches is that a large number of putative societal, familial, individual/psychological and biological variables have been identified, many of which require further validation.

Sociocultural Risk Factors

The fact that EDs do not occur uniformly in all cultures at all times has led some researchers to focus on the contribution of sociocultural factors (Stice *et al.*, 1998; Warren *et al.*, 2005). An obsession with slimness is concentrated in Western cultures and countries that have become more Westernized. In contrast, EDs are rare in underdeveloped countries. The media are often blamed for promulgating the idealization of thinness, the derogation of fatness and the subsequent development of eating pathology in children and adolescents. The emphasis on women's appearance and on the virtue of a thin and toned body has been found in all forms of media (Streigel-Moore *et al.*, 1986). The research in this area suggests that internalization of social and cultural messages about the importance of a thin body is related to ED symptomatology and body dissatisfaction (Groesz *et al.*, 2002). Similarly, peer influence is also often cited as a contributor to EDs, via the transmission of certain adolescent attitudes (e.g., the importance of thinness) and behaviors (e.g., dieting, purging). Some studies suggest that the influence of peers and family may be more potent than that of the media (Stice, 1998), although other studies report the reverse (Wertheim *et al.*, 1997). Not all individuals in Western cultures develop EDs, suggesting other factors influence the degree to which an individual internalizes social messages about the importance of body shape and weight, etc.

Familial Risk Factors

The family environment has also been implicated in the development of EDs. Parental attitudes, whether explicit or subtle, are thought to be a primary transmission pathway. A few empirical studies support this notion. A strong relationship has been found between family weight-control behaviors and the encouragement of daughters to diet (Striegel-Moore and Kearney-Cooke, 1994), and the internalization of thinness norms (Tester and Gleaves, 2005). Further, the children of mothers who themselves have an ED appear to be at more risk of developing an ED (Agras *et al.*, 1999). Family dynamics have also been associated with the development of EDs. Research in this area has reported that families of eating-disordered individuals are more likely to be overly concerned with parenting (Shoebridge and Gowers, 2000) and to have a highly critical family environment (Haworth-Hoeppner, 2000), and also an insecure attachment is common (Ward *et al.*, 2000a). Overall, however, it is not clear that family factors precede the eating pathology and have a causative role. It is also possible that family dysfunction is secondary to the presence of the illness, or that some common factor contributes to both.

Individual/Psychological Risk Factors

Many factors have been postulated to account for individual vulnerability to EDs. Low self-esteem (Fairburn *et al.*, 1997), perfectionism (Bardone *et al.*, 2000) and body dissatisfaction (Vitousek and Hollon, 1990) are all common findings in the literature. Numerous studies have also linked dieting to the genesis of EDs. Dietary restraint has been associated with a sense of control and autonomy, and also with being a precursor to binge eating, which in turn can lead to purging (Polivy and Herman, 1986; Striegel-Moore *et al.*, 1986). A variety of cognitive factors have also been identified as risk factors for EDs. These cognitive risk factors have included abnormal information processing (e.g., impulsivity) (Kaye *et al.*, 1995) and cognitive biases towards weight, shape and food (Green *et al.*, 1999). Adverse interpersonal experiences have also been linked to the development of EDs. Teasing about the appearance of an individual's body shape (Lunner *et al.*, 2000), high levels of life-stressors and difficulties (Raffi *et al.*, 2000), and childhood abuse and trauma (Everill and Waller, 1995) have all been implicated in the development of eating pathology. The influence of childhood abuse is complicated. As childhood abuse has also been linked with other psychiatric disorders, including depression and anxiety, it has been suggested that childhood abuse contributes to the development of EDs indirectly, possibly through its influence on self-esteem and anxiety (Kent and Waller, 2000). It has also been reported that EDs result from deficits in the ability to cope with emotional difficulties, identity problems or negative affect. The focus on weight, shape and food provides a means to gain some sense of control and emotional relief (Serpell *et al.*, 1999). Understanding how individual risk factors contribute to the development of EDs is complex. It is unlikely that one factor will be causal or of the same importance for all individuals.

Biological Risk Factors

A number of biological abnormalities have been linked with EDs. Disentangling the relationship between biological anomalies and EDs is complex. EDs may disrupt biological processes and, conversely, biological processes may contribute to the development of eating pathology. Twin and family studies have provided some evidence for the genetic transmission of EDs. Klump and colleagues (2000) concluded that 50–83 percent of the variance in AN and BN is genetic. They also suggested that not only is the disorder heritable, but also associated attitudes are highly heritable. It is commonly accepted that genes have an influence on EDs; however, how much liability genes account for and the nature of gene–environment interactions are not clear (Bulik *et al.*, 2000). A link between neuroendocrine factors, appetite and EDs, also between neurochemical imbalance and EDs, has also been found (Brewerton, 1995). Neuroendocrine abnormalities are thought to affect appetite either directly through hormonal dysfunction or by being mediational – i.e., an environmental factor disrupting hormonal functioning, which in turn affects eating. Multiple neurotransmitters have also been implicated in the development of EDs. However, for the most part endocrine and neurotransmitter abnormalities appear to be state-related and tend to normalize after recovery from EDs (Ward *et al.*, 2000b). The one exception may be serotonin. Serotonin modulates feeding by producing the sensation of fullness or satiety, and may remain elevated in females with EDs. Neuroimaging studies have also demonstrated subtle alterations in brain function and structure in girls with AN (Strober and Katz, 1988). While it seems that hormonal and neurochemical abnormalities and brain changes are implicated in EDs, there is not clear evidence for their causal affect.

Overall, our knowledge about the risk factors most necessary for the development of EDs is lacking. Some factors have received substantially more research attention than others, and it is likely that other important risk factors are yet to be discovered. The majority of studies examining risk factors are retrospective case–control studies or employ a cross-sectional design, and as such generate preliminary or putative risk factors. More large-scale prospective longitudinal studies are needed to identify definitive risk factors.

In an attempt to bring some clarity to this area and identify definitive risk factors, Stice (2002) conducted a meta-analysis of prospective and experimental studies examining both risk and maintenance factors for eating pathology. The risk factors examined in the studies reviewed by Stice were sociocultural, familial and individual. These factors included body mass, sociocultural pressure to be thin, modeling, thin-ideal internalization, body dissatisfaction, dieting, negative affect, perfectionism, early menarche, impulsivity and childhood sexual abuse. Due to a lack of methodological sound prospective or experimental studies on risk factors for anorexic symptoms, the Stice meta-analyses only included studies that examined bulimic symptoms, binge eating and composite ED symptom outcomes. He found that elevated body mass was a risk factor for perceived pressure to be thin, body dissatisfaction and dieting; however, body mass index did not appear to be a risk factor for eating pathology. This finding suggests that body mass may play a role in promoting risk factors for eating pathology, rather than directly fostering or maintaining eating disturbances. Stice also reported that body dissatisfaction was a risk factor for dieting and negative affect and, in contrast with elevated body mass index, body dissatisfaction was also a direct risk factor for eating pathology. Further, modeling of body image and eating disturbances by family members and peers, negative affect, perfectionism, impulsivity and substance use were all found to be risk factors for eating pathology. Another finding was that perceived pressure to be thin and internalization of the thin ideal were causal risk factors for body dissatisfaction, dieting, negative affect and eating pathology.

Although it has been accepted that dieting increases the risk for the onset of eating pathology, Stice (2002) reported that whereas the prospective studies suggested that self-reported dieting was a risk factor for negative affect and eating pathology, results from experimental studies were not supportive of this assumption. Stice concluded that dieting is not a specific risk factor for eating pathology, but rather attenuates overeating tendencies. Stice also found that childhood sexual abuse did not emerge as a risk factor for eating pathology; however, only one study (Vogeltanz-Holm *et al.*, 2000) included in the meta-analyses examined this putative risk factor. With regard to other potential risk factors, Stice reported that there was no empirical support for the notion that stress, control issues, dysfunctional family systems and deficits in parental affection were risk factors for eating pathology. Stice did note that there was some indication across review studies that perceived pressure to be thin, thin-ideal internalization and body dissatisfaction were potentiating factors that amplify the effects of other risk factors.

It is unlikely that a single risk factor can account for the development of EDs. In fact, most models of EDs involve multiple risk factors. Stice (2002) reviewed a number of the multivariate models that have been proposed to account for how risk factors work together to promote eating pathology. He concluded that the findings support a cumulative stressor model (Smolak *et al.*, 1993), a perfectionism × body dissatisfaction × low self-esteem model (Vohs *et al.*, 1999), and a dual pathway model of bulimic pathology (Stice *et al.*, 1996). Stice also noted, however, that most of these models have not been independently tested, and some models only accounted for a modest amount of variance in ED symptomatology.

PROTECTIVE FACTORS

Much less research has focused on identifying protective factors that might insulate children and adolescents from developing EDs. One factor that has received research attention and empirical support is positive family relationships. Two longitudinal studies indicate that spending time with parents, perceiving one's parents as friendly, and feeling closer to parents may protect against the development of body dissatisfaction and disordered eating (Swarr and Richards, 1996; Byley *et al.*, 2000). McVey *et al.* (2002) also found that adolescent girls who reported higher levels of paternal support were less likely to develop disordered eating when under stress. There is also some indication that social support is a protective factor that may mitigate the effects of other risk factors (Stice and Shaw, 2004), and that positive self-deception (i.e., a positive image about body appearance) may serve as a protective factor against internalization of sociocultural messages about the thin ideal (Tester and Gleaves, 2005). It is clear that a great deal more research is needed to investigate factors that decrease the probability that EDs will develop by improving resistance and resilience.

PREVENTION AND INTERVENTION

PREVENTION

Prevention programs for EDs have typically taken a primary or secondary approach. Primary prevention programs aim to lower the incidence of new cases of EDs and enhance protective factors, and as such tend to be universal – i.e., targeting all available adolescents. Early primary prevention programs provided psychoeducational material related to EDs; however, latterly these programs have incorporated components aimed at creating resistance to sociocultural pressures for thinness and encouraging healthy weight-control behaviors. The aim of secondary prevention programs is early identification and intervention to prevent the development of a full-blown disorder (Stice and Shaw, 2004). Secondary prevention programs are selective in that they target individuals who are at high risk of developing an ED; thus the focus is individuals with risk factors that have been shown to predict the onset of eating pathology (see risk factors above).

Historically, the findings for prevention programs have been mixed, with some researchers reporting marked effects (Stice *et al.*, 2006) and others no effects (Killen *et al.*, 1993; Paxton, 1993), or deterioration in ED pathology (Carter *et al.*, 1997). These latter results have raised concerns about the iatrogenic or harmful effect of prevention programs (Fingeret *et al.*, 2006). A Cochrane systematic review published in 2002 reported finding only one positive effect from a review of eight RCTs of prevention programs. Very similarly, in a recent update of the Cochrane review that included 12 RCTs that had investigated prevention programs, Pratt and Woolfenden concluded that, based on the available studies, firm conclusions about the efficacy of prevention programs in children and adolescents could not be made.

Recent meta-analyses have reported more positive findings (Stice and Shaw, 2004; Fingeret *et al.*, 2006). In their 2004 meta-analysis, Stice and Shaw categorized prevention programs that had been evaluated in controlled trials as either universal (primary programs) or selective (secondary programs). This meta-analysis included 51 published and unpublished studies evaluating 38 ED prevention programs; 25 percent of prevention studies were excluded from the meta-analysis because they did not include a control group.

Stice and Shaw (2004) reported that a number of promising ED prevention programs had been conducted. Of the programs, 53 percent ($n = 32$) resulted in significant reductions in at least one established risk factor, and 25 percent ($n = 15$) resulted in significant reduction in eating pathology. The authors reported that some prevention programs demonstrated persistent effects as long as 2 years from the initial intervention. Overall, however, average effect sizes were small to medium, with a wide variety of intervention effects being evident, ranging from no effects to those that produced significant effects for all outcomes. Stice and Shaw identified a number of factors that were associated with larger effects which included selective, interactive and multi-session prevention programs. They also reported that larger effects were evident for programs offered solely to females, to participants over the age of 15 years, and for programs that did not incorporate psychoeducational content.

Fingeret and colleagues (2006) also recently conducted a meta-analysis with the aim of establishing whether or not ED-related psychoeducational material produces iatrogenic effects, and also to investigate whether or not the type of intervention strategy employed and the population targeted impacted on the efficacy of prevention programs. The Fingeret *et al.* meta-analytic review included 57 separate studies; 9 studies were excluded because effect sizes could not be calculated and/or because they studies did not report independent effects for females. Fingeret and colleagues examined the effect of the prevention programs on five outcome variables – general eating pathology, dieting, body dissatisfaction, thin-ideal internalization and knowledge. These researchers reported that the outcome variable most affected by prevention programs was the accumulation of knowledge related to EDs. Small improvements in general eating pathology and dieting behaviors were evident across a range of intervention strategies and populations. Fingeret *et al.* could not find any evidence to support the notion that prevention programs produced harmful effects when psychoeducation was incorporated. Psychoeducation programs appeared to be as effective as other intervention strategies in influencing attitudinal and behavioral outcome variables, and selective prevention programs – i.e., those that targeted individuals at high risk for developing an ED – produced larger effects sizes than universal programs.

The results of these two meta-analyses suggest that continued development and investigation of prevention programs could be fruitful. Current prevention strategies focus on facilitating changes in attitudinal and behavioral risk factors, and it is assumed such changes result in the prevention of EDs. Rather than making this assumption, Stice and Shaw (2004) and Fingeret *et al.* (2006) recommend that future prevention studies should directly measure clinically significant symptoms indicative of EDs.

INTERVENTION/MANAGEMENT

Many of the current treatment recommendations for children and adolescents with EDs are based on uncontrolled and case–control studies, experience and anecdote, and protocols initially developed for older patients. Practice guidelines have been published by the National Institute for Clinical Excellence (NICE, 2004) in the UK. These guidelines are based on a systematic and rigorous review of available research on the management of EDs across the age ranges, and are also supported by consultation with experts in the field. All NICE guidelines have been graded from A (strong empirical support from well-conducted trials) to C (expert opinion with strong empirical support). Similarly, the American Psychiatric Association (APA; 2006) has also published practice guidelines, which are keyed according to the level of confidence of each recommendation (I, substantial confidence; II, moderate confidence; III, may be recommended on an individual basis). As such, the NICE and the APA practice guidelines are based on the best *available* data, and also represent a clinical consensus about best practice.

Inpatient Treatment

Most children and adolescents with EDs are treated on an outpatient basis; however, a minority require inpatient psychiatric or pediatric care. Indications for hospitalization have been outlined by others (Andersen *et al.*, 1997), and include the following:

- Evidence of malnutrition (under 75% of expected body weight) or dehydration
- Serious medical complications (e.g., metabolic abnormalities, cardiac dysrhythmia)
- Psychiatric emergencies (e.g., suicidal ideation, acute psychosis)
- Non-responsiveness to outpatient treatment.

Most hospitalization programs are multidisciplinary, and include a variety of treatment components. The first and most important goals are to achieve medical and nutritional stabilization, weight gain and regular eating. Nasogastric feeding is infrequently required, but may be needed when the patient is unable to tolerate food orally to gain sufficient weight. Treatment also focuses on facilitating fundamental change to attitudes about weight, shape and appearance, and also on disrupting the binge–purge cycle. In addition to focusing on specific ED symptoms, inpatient treatment promotes individual change and growth (affect regulation, self-identity) and assists with the acquisition of skills needed to deal with life issues (e.g., communication, conflict resolution).

There has been very little investigation into the efficacy of inpatient treatment for EDs in adolescents. One naturalistic study that compared the outcome for 21 adolescents with AN who received inpatient treatment with the outcome for 51 who received treatment as outpatients, the outpatients showed a better outcome after 2–7 years (Gowers *et al.*, 2000). The NICE guidelines recommend that the aim of inpatient treatment should be re-feeding and physical monitoring, in combination with psychosocial interventions. This recommendation carries the lowest grade of C, indicating expert opinion in the absence of empirical data.

Partial Hospitalization/Day Hospitalization

Day hospital programs have become an increasingly popular method for treatment provision. Day programs provide a treatment that is less intensive and less costly than inpatient care. Day programs also have the advantage of enabling the individual to transition to a situation that more closely resembles their natural environment. Individuals are able to continue some of their normal functional activities and engage in family and social roles. The goals of day programs are similar to those of inpatient treatment, with a focus on gradually decreasing the level of supervision, continuing and maintaining improvement, and generally restoring healthy mental, physical and social functioning (Zipfel *et al.*, 2002). As is the case with inpatient programs, there has been hardly any research on the efficacy of day programs. Two uncontrolled studies with adults indicate that day programs may be effective (Gerlinghoff *et al.*, 1998) and more cost-efficient than inpatient programs (Williamson *et al.*, 2001).

Outpatient Treatment

Intensive multicomponent outpatient treatment has also become increasing popular, particularly for the management of EDs in children and adolescents (Agras *et al.*, 1994). These programs typically consist of psychoeducation (including nutritional counseling) for individuals and their families, psychotherapy, and psychopharmacology. The comparative efficacy of inpatient, day programs and outpatient treatments is not yet known. In one study, Crisp *et al.* (1991) directly compared inpatient treatment, and two types of outpatient psychotherapy (individual and family therapy plus dietary counseling, or group psychotherapy plus dietary counseling), with no treatment. Crisp and colleagues reported that all three treatment regimes were significantly more effective than no treatment at 1 year in terms of weight gain, return of menstruation, and aspects of social and sexual adjustment.

Most psychotherapy models have been advocated for the treatment of EDs. Research specifically examining the efficacy of these treatments for children and adolescents is very sparse; consequently, there is insufficient support for any one treatment approach over another.

Family Therapy

Family therapy has shown promising results for the treatment of AN. The APA (2006) practice guidelines state that family therapy for AN is the most effective treatment for children and adolescents. Similarly, family therapy is also recommended in the NICE (2004) guidelines (grade B, indicating support from well-conducted clinical trials). No randomized controlled trials (RCT) have examined the efficacy of family therapy for BN; however, there is some indication from uncontrolled and case-series studies that family therapy may be effective (Dodge *et al.*, 1995; Le Grange *et al.*, 2003).

A variety of family therapy approaches have been developed. Family therapy focuses on the entire family unit, and has been used as a treatment by itself (Lock *et al.*, 2001) and also as a component in a multi-component treatment package (Strober and Yager, 1985). Although schools of family therapy vary with regard to the underlying theoretical principles and treatment goals, most strive to facilitate change within the family to reduce or eliminate problematic interactions and behaviors (Michel and Willard, 2004).

Cognitive Behavior Therapy (CBT)

A large number of well-conducted outcome studies have examined the efficacy of CBT for BN. Very few studies have examined CBT for AN in adults, and no RCTs of CBT for AN have been conducted with children or adolescents. CBT is based on a model that emphasizes the critical role of both cognitions and behavioral processes in the maintenance of EDs. CBT has been manualized and described in detail by others (for example, Fairburn *et al.*, 1993). The therapeutic focus in CBT includes the extreme value attached to an idealized body shape and weight, associated low self-esteem, restriction of food intake, loss of control over eating (i.e., binges), and compensatory behaviors (e.g., purging, excessive exercise).

Wilson and Fairburn (2002) have reviewed the empirical research comparing the efficacy of CBT and other psychological treatments for BN. They concluded that CBT is more effective than behavioral treatments alone, more effective than or at least as effective as other psychotherapies, produces a clinical significant degree of improvement, is comparatively quick-acting, and affects both the specific and general psychopathology of BN. They also concluded that CBT is associated with good maintenance of change at follow-up, although studies of long-term effectiveness are lacking. CBT has been recommended by others as the first-line treatment of choice for BN in adults (Chambless *et al.*, 1998; Thompson-Brenner *et al.*, 2003).

The literature on CBT for AN largely consists of a number of uncontrolled studies across a variety of clinical settings; consequently, the efficacy of CBT for AN is not clear. The few studies that have been conducted indicate potential efficacy, and there is also some evidence indicating that CBT for AN is associated with greater treatment compliance – i.e., reduced drop-out – compared with other treatments. In the absence of controlled trials for BN in adolescents, the NICE (2004) guidelines recommend that CBT be used with age-related modifications to suit the individual's level of development and circumstances, and that the family be included as appropriate (grade C; expert opinion in absence of empirical research).

Interpersonal Psychotherapy (IPT)

IPT focuses on assisting the individual to identify and change problematic interpersonal interactions maintaining the ED symptoms. Typically, treatment focuses on one of four main problem areas: interpersonal disputes, role transitions, grief, and interpersonal deficits. A limited number of studies have examined the efficacy of IPT for EDs, and currently no RCTs have been conducted with the adolescent population. Some current research indicates that IPT may be effective for EDs, but that it may work more slowly than CBT (Agras *et al.*, 2000). Given the insufficient number of studies, this is by no means conclusive. The only RCT to compare IPT with other psychotherapies, in a group of adult women, reported that IPT was less effective than CBT and non-specific clinical management (McIntosh *et al.*, 2005). There is also some support for the efficacy of IPT for patients with binge-eating who have not benefited from initial CBT (Whilfley *et al.*, 2002).

Psychodynamic Therapy

Psychodynamic therapy has a long history in the treatment of EDs, particularly AN. Psychodynamic models vary considerably; however, the goals of most are to assist individuals to develop modes of feeling and expressing power and dependency; to attenuate the severe superego along with primitive guilt; to develop more adaptive strategies for coping than the current eating behaviors; and to return the individual back to a healthy nutritional, physical, emotional and cognitive state (Herzog, 1995). There have been very few empirical studies examining the efficacy of psychodynamic treatments. In studies that have examined time-limited psychodynamic therapy for EDs, the results have been disappointing (Dare *et al.*, 2001).

Pharmacological Treatment

A variety of psychopharmacological options have been advocated for the treatment of EDs. In the main these have been utilized in adult populations and, overall, the effectiveness of psychotropics has been unsatisfactory. Medications used for AN have included antidepressants and anti-anxiety medications, which are usually prescribed within the context of a comprehensive treatment program. There is some evidence that Olanzapine (an atypical neuroleptic) may promote weight gain among individuals with AN, though the findings are very preliminary (Powers *et al.*, 2002). It is also possible that psychotropics may help to prevent relapse in adolescent and adult patients after weight restoration has occurred (Kotler and Walsh, 2000).

Pharmacological treatments for BN have been more promising, with various types of antidepressants and anticonvulsants explored; however, in the main these studies have been in adult populations. Fluoxetine, a serotonin reuptake inhibitor (SSRI), and tricyclics antidepressants (e.g., desipramine) have demonstrated short-term improvements in binge eating and purging (Casper, 2002). There are no published controlled treatment studies of adolescents with BN. One open trial for adolescents with bulimia nervosa ($n = 10$) has provided some preliminary evidence that fluoxetine (60 mg) may also decrease binges and purges in this population (Kotler *et al.*, 2003).

Monoamine oxidase inhibitor (MAOI) antidepressants have also been used in the treatment of BN; however, the results have been mixed (Mitchell *et al.*, 1993). Treatment success rates as high as 90 percent have been reported for anticonvulsant medication (e.g., phenytoin sodium) (Green and Rau, 1974), although a lack of response has also been reported (Green and Rau, 1977). Overall, although pharmacological treatments have shown some short-term use in the treatment of BN, they have also been associated with considerable relapse and there is some indication that medication alone may not be as effective as CBT (Casper, 2002). Importantly, the majority of psychopharmacological treatment studies have been conducted in adults: the results of these studies may not be generalizable to children and adolescents with eating disorders.

Although eating disorders are often viewed as disorders of adolescence, studies focusing on the treatment of eating disorders in adolescents are sorely lacking. Much more work needs to be done to determine the role of psychopharmacological agents, and to establish evidence-based, effective psychosocial interventions for adolescent eating disorders.

SUMMARY

EDs are characterized by compulsive behaviors that are perceived as being out-of-control and that persist in spite of the adverse consequences. Thus, they share many features with the other addictive behaviors covered in this volume. Whether or not they meet strict definitions of an addition is a different issue, and most likely they do not. However, EDs among adolescents are relatively common and are potentially life-threatening. They are also potentially treatable, and early detection and intervention during adolescence seems to be critical. However, far more research needs to be done with children and adolescents before we can make firm extrapolations from the adult treatment literature.

REFERENCES

Abraham, H.D. and Joseph, A.B. (1986–1987). Bulimic vomiting alters pain tolerance and mood. *International Journal of Psychiatry in Medicine*, 16, 311–316.

Agras, W.S. (2001). The consequences and costs of the eating disorders. *Psychiatric Clinics of North America*, 24, 371–379.

Agras, W.S., Telch, C., Arnow, B. *et al.* (1994). Weight loss, cognitive-behavioral and desipramine treatment in binge eating disorders: an additive design. *Behavior Therapy*, 25(2), 225–238.

Agras, W.S., Hammer, I. and McNicholas, F. (1999). A prospective study of the influences of eating disordered mothers on their children. *International Journal of Eating Disorders*, 25, 225–262.

Agras, W.S., Walsh, T., Fairburn, C.G. *et al.* (2000).A multicenter comparison of cognitive-behavioral therapy and interpersonal psychotherapy for bulimia nervosa. *Archives of General Psychiatry*, 57, 459–466.

American Psychiatric Association. (2000). *Diagnostic and Statistical Manual of Mental Disorders*, (revised 4th edn). Washington, DC: APA.

American Psychiatric Association. (2006). *Practice Guidelines for the Treatment of Patients with Eating Disorders*, 3rd edn. Available at http://www.psych.org/psych_pract/treatg/pg/EatingDisorders3ePG_04-28-0 (accessed 10 December 2006).

Andersen, A.E. and Holman, J.E. (1997). Males with eating disorders: challenges for treatment and research. *Psychopharmacology Bulletin. Special Issue: Research Priorities in Eating Disorders*, 33, 391–397.

Andersen, A.E., Bowers, W. and Evans, K. (1997). Inpatient treatment of anorexia nervosa. In: D.M. Garner and P.E. Garfinkel (eds.), *Handbook of Treatment for Eating Disorders*, 2nd edn. New York, NY: Guilford Press, pp. 327–353.

Bardone, A.M., Vohs, K.D., Abramson, L.Y. *et al.* (2000). The confluence of perfectionism, body dissatisfaction and low self-esteem predicts bulimic symptoms: clinical implications. *Behavior Research and Therapy*, 31, 265–280.

Bernstein, E. (2007). Eating disorders: families fight back; insurers have long covered only a fraction of huge costs; now, pressure to pay more. *Wall Street Journal*, 2 January, p. D1.

Binford, R.B. and Le Grange, D. (2005). Adolescents with bulimia nervosa and eating disorder not otherwise specified purging only. *International Journal of Eating Disorders*, 38, 157–161.

Blinder, B.J., Bain, N. and Simpson, R. (1986). Evidence for an opioid neurotransmission mechanism in adult rumination. *American Journal of Psychiatry*, 143, 255.

Brambilla, F. and Monteleone, P. (2003). Physical complications and physiological abberations in eating disorders. In: M. Maj, K. Halmi, J.J. Lopez-Ibor and N. Sartorius (eds), *Evidence and Experience in Psychiatry*, Vol. 6, *Eating Disorders*. Chichester, Sussex: Joh Wiley & Sons, pp. 139–192.

Brewerton, T.D. (1995). Review: toward a unified theory of serotonin dysregulation in eating and related disorders. *Psychoenuroendocrinology*, 20, 561–590.

Bulik, C.M., Sullivan, P.F., Wade, T.D. and Kendler, K.S. (2000). Twin studies of eating disorders: a review. *International Journal of Eating Disorders*, 27, 1–20.

Bulik, C.M., Klump, K.L., Thornton, L. *et al.* (2004). Alcohol use disorder comorbidity in eating disorders: a multicenter study. *Journal of Clinical Psychiatry*, 65, 1000–1006.

Byley, L., Archibald, A., Graber, J. and Brooks-Gunn, J. (2000). A prospective study of familial and social influences of girls' body image and dieting. *International Journal of Eating Disorders*, 28, 155–163.

Carlat, D.J., Camargo, C.A. and Herzog, D.B. (1997). Eating disorders in males: a report on 135 patients. *American Journal of Psychiatry*, 154, 1127–1132

Carter, J.C., Stewart, D.A., Dunn, V.J. and Fairburn, C.G. (1997). Primary prevention of eating disorders: might it do more harm than good? *International Journal of Eating Disorders*, 22, 167–172.

Casper, R. (2002). How useful are pharmacological treatments in eating disorders? *Psychopharmacology Bulletin*, 36(2), 88–104.

Chambless, D.L., Baker, M.J., Baucom, D.H. *et al.* (1998). Update on empirically validated therapies II. *Clinical Psychologist*, 51(1), 3–16.

Conason, A.H., Brunstein Klomek, A. and Sher, L. (2006). Recognizing alcohol and drug abuse in patients with eating disorders. *Quarterly Journal of Medicine*, 99, 335–339.

Crisp, A.H., Palmer, R.L. and Kalucy, R.S. (1976). How common is anorexia nervosa? A prevalence study. *British Journal of Psychiatry*, 128, 549–554.

Crisp, A.H., Norton, K., Glowers, S. *et al.* (1991). A controlled study of the effect of therapies aimed at adolescent and family psychopathology in anorexia nervosa. *British Journal of Psychiatry*, 159, 325–333.

DaCosta, M. and Halmi, K.A. (1992). Classifications of anorexia: question of subtypes. *International Journal of Eating Disorders*, 11, 305–311.

Dare, C., Eisler, I., Russell, G. *et al.* (2001). Psychological therapies for adults with anorexia nervosa: randomised controlled trial of outpatient treatments. *British Journal of Psychiatry*, 178, 216–251.

Decaluwe, V. and Braet, C. (2003). Prevalence of binge-eating disorder in obese children and adolescents seeking weight-loss treatment. *International Journal of Obesity*, 27, 404–409.

Dodge, E., Hodes, M., Eisler, I. and Dare, C. (1995). Family therapy for bulimia nervosa in adolescents: an exploratory study. *Journal of Family Therapy*, 17, 59–77.

Epling, W.F. and Pierce, W.D. (1988). Activity-based anorexia: a biobehavioral perspective. *International Journal of Eating Disorders*, 7, 475–485.

Everill, J.T. and Waller, G. (1995). Reported sexual abuse and eating psychopathology: a review of the evidence for a causal link. *International Journal of Eating Disorders*, 17, 127–134.

Fairburn, C.G and Bohn, K (2005). Eating disorder NOS (EDNOS): an example of the troublesome "not otherwise specified" (NOS) category in DSM-IV. *Behavior Research and Therapy*, 43, 691–701.

Fairburn, C.G., Marcus, M.D. and Wilson, G.T. (1993). Cognitive behavioral therapy for binge eating and bulimia nervosa: a comprehensive treatment manual. In: C. Fairburn and G. Wilson (eds), *Binge Eating: Nature, Assessment and Treatment*. New York, NY: Guilford Press, pp. 361–404.

Fairburn, C.G., Welch, S.L., Doll, H.A. *et al.* (1997). Risk factors for bulimia nervosa – a community-based case–control study. *Archives of General Psychiatry*, 54, 500–517.

Fairburn, C.G., Cooper, Z., Doll, H.A. *et al.* (2000). The natural course of bulimia nervosa and binge eating disorder in young women. *Archives of General Psychiatry*, 57, 659–665.

Fichter, M.M. and Quadflieg, N. (2004). Twelve-year course and outcome of bulimia nervosa. *Psychological Medicine*, 34, 1395–1406.

Fingeret, M.C., Warren, C.S., Cepeda-Benito, A. and Gleaves, D.H. (2006). Eating disorder prevention research: a meta-analysis. *Eating Disorders*, 14, 1–23.

Fisher, M., Golden, N.H., Katzman, D.K. *et al.* (1995). Eating disorders in adolescents: a background paper. *Journal of Adolescent Health*, 16, 420–437.

Garner, D.M. and Gerborg, A. (2004). Understanding and diagnosing eating disorders. In: R. H. Coombs (ed.), *Handbook of Addictive Disorders*. Hoboken, NJ: John Wiley & Sons, pp. 275–311.

Gerlinghoff, M., Backmund, H. and Franzen, U. (1998). Evaluation of a day treatment programme for eating disorders. *European Eating Disorders Review*, 6, 96–106.

Gleaves, D.H. and Eberenz, K.P. (1993). The psychopathology of anorexia nervosa: a factor analytic investigation. *Journal of Psychopathology and Behavioral Assessment*, 15, 141–152.

Gleaves, D.H., Lowe, M.R., Green, B.A. *et al.* (2000). Do anorexia and bulimia nervosa occur on a continuum? A taxometric analysis. *Behavior Therapy*, 31, 195–219

Gold, M.S., Frost-Pineda, K. and Jacobs, W.S. (2003). Overeating, binge eating and eating disorders as addictions. *Psychiatric Annals*, 33, 117–122.

Gowers, S., Weetman, J., Shore, A. *et al.* (2000). Impact of hospitalization on the outcome of adolescent anorexia nervosa. *British Journal of Psychiatry*, 176, 138–141.

Green, M., Corr, P. and DeSilva, L. (1999). Impaired color naming of body shape-related words in anorexia nervosa: affective valence or associative priming. *Cognitive, Therapy and Research*, 23, 413–422.

Green, R.S. and Rau, J.H. (1974). Treatment of compulsive eating disturbances with anti-convulsant medication. *American Journal of Psychiatry*, 131, 428–432.

Green, R.S. and Rau, J.H (1977). The use of diphenylhydantoin in compulsive eating disorders: further studies. In: R. Vigersky (ed.), *Anorexia Nervosa*. New York, NY: Raven Press, pp. 377–385

Grilo, C.M., Sanislow, C.A., Shea, M.T. *et al.* (2003). The natural course of bulimia nervosa and eating disorder not otherwise specified is not influenced by personality disorders. *International Journal of Eating Disorders*, 34, 319–330.

Groesz, L.M., Levine, M.P. and Muren, S.K. (2002). The effect of experimental presentation of thin images on body satisfaction: a meta-analytic review. *International Journal of Eating Disorders*, 31, 1–16.

Haworth-Hoeppner, S. (2000). The critical shapes of body image: the role of culture and family in the production of eating disorders. *Journal of Marriage and the Family*, 62, 212–227.

Hay, P. and Fairburn, C. (1998). The validity of the DSM-IV scheme for classifying bulimic eating disorders. *International Journal of Eating Disorders*, 23, 7–15.

Herzog, D.B.(1995). Psychodyamic psychotherapy for anorexia nervosa. In: K. Brownell and C. Fairburn (eds), *Eating Disorders and Obesity: A Comprehensive Handbook*. New York, NY: Guilford Press, pp. 336–353.

Hoek, H.W. and van Hoeken, D. (2003). Review of the prevalence and incidence of eating disorders. *International Journal of Eating Disorders*, 34, 383–396.

Hoek, H.W., van Hoeken, D. and Katzman, M.A. (2003). Epidemiology and cultural aspects of eating disorders: A review. In: M. Maj, K. Halmi, J.J. Lopez-Ibor and N. Sartorius (Eds), *Eating Disorders*. Chichester, Sussex: John Wiley & Sons, pp. 75–104.

Kaye, W.H., Bastisni, A.M. and Moss, H. (1995). Cognitive style of patients with anorexia nervosa and bulimia nervosa *International Journal of Eating Disorders*, 18, 287–290.

Keel, P.K., Heatherton, T.D., Dorer, D.J. *et al.* (2006). Point prevalence of bulimia nervosa in 1982, 1992 and 2002. *Psychological Medicine*, 36, 119–127.

Kent, A. and Waller, G. (2000). Childhood emotional abuse and eating psychopathology. *Clinical Psychology Review*, 20, 887–903.

Killen, J., Taylor, C., Hammer, L. *et al.* (1993). An attempt to modify unhealthy eating attitudes and weight regulation practices of young adolescent girls. *International Journal of Eating Disorders*, 13, 369–384.

Kjelsås, E., Bjornstrom, C. and Götestam, K. G. (2004). Prevalence of eating disorders in female and male adolescents (14–15 years). *Eating Behaviors*, 5, 13–25.

Klump, K.L., McGue, M. and Iacono, W.G. (2000). Age differences in genetic and environment influences on eating attitudes and behaviors in preadolescent and adolescent female twins. *Journal of Abnormal Psychology*, 109, 239–51.

Kotler, L.A. and Walsh, B.T. (2000). Eating disorders in children and adolescents: pharmacological therapies. *European Child and Adolescent Psychiatry*, 19(Suppl. 15), I108–I116.

Kotler, L.A., Devlin, M.J., Davies, M. and Walsh, B.T. (2003). An open trial of Fluoxetine for adolescents with bulimia nervosa. *Journal of Child and Adolescent Psychopharmacology*, 13, 329–335.

Le Grange, D., Lock, J. and Dymeck, M. (2003). Family-based treatment of eating disorders. *American Journal of Psychotherapy*, 57, 237–251.

Lock, J., Le Grange, D., Agras, W.S. and Dare, C. (2001). *Treatment Manual for Anorexia Nervosa: A Family-based Approach*. New York, NY: Guilford Press.

Lunner, K., Werthern, E.H., Thompson, J.K. *et al.* (2000). A cross-sectional examination of weight-related teasing, body image and eating disturbance in Swedish and Australian samples. *International Journal of Eating Disorders*, 28, 430–435.

Marcus, M.D. and Kalarchian, M.A. (2003). Binge eating in children and adolescents. *International Journal of Eating Disorders*, 34, S47–S57.

Marrazzi, M.A. and Luby, E.D. (1986). An auto-addiction opioid model of chronic anorexia nervosa. *International Journal of Eating Disorders*, 5, 191–208.

Marrazzi, M.A., Luby, E.D., Kinzie, J. *et al.* (1997). Endogenous codeine and morphine in anorexia and bulimia nervosa. *Life Sciences*, 60, 1741–1747.

McIntosh, V.V.W., Jordan, J., Carter, F.A. *et al.* (2005). Three psychotherapies for anorexia nervosa: a randomised controlled trial. *American Journal of Psychiatry*, 162, 741–747.

McVey, G.L., Pepler, D., Davis, R. *et al.* (2002). Risk and protective factors associated with disordered eating during early adolescence. *Journal of Early Adolescence*, 22, 75–95.

Michel, D.M. and Willard, S.G. (2004). An overview of family evaluation and therapy for anorexia nervosa, bulimia nervosa and binge eating disorder. In: T. Brewerton (ed.), *Clinical Handbook of Eating Disorders: An Integrated Approach*. New York, NY: Marcel Dekker, Inc.

Mitchell, J.E., Raymond, N. and Specker, S. (1993). A review of the controlled trials of pharmacotherapy and psychotherapy in the treatment of bulimia nervosa. *International Journal of Eating Disorders*, 14, 229–247.

National Institute for Clinical Excellence (2004). *Eating Disorders: Core Interventions in the Treatment and Management of Anorexia Nervosa, Bulimia Nervosa & Related Eating Disorders*. London: National Institute for Clinical Excellence.

Netemeyer, S.B. and Williamson, D.A. (2001). Assessment of eating disturbance in children and adolescents with eating disorders and obesity. In: J.K. Thompson and L. Smolak (eds), *Body Image, Eating Disorders & Obesity in Youth: Assessment, Prevention & Treatment*. Washington, DC: American Psychological Association, pp. 215–233.

O'Herlihy, A., Worral, A., Banerjee, S. *et al.* (2001). *National Inpatient Child and Adolescent Psychiatry Study (NICAPS): Final Report to the Department of Health*. London: Royal College of Psychiatrists' Research Unit.

Paxton, S J. (1993). A prevention program for disturbed eating and body dissatisfaction in adolescent girls: a 1-year follow-up. *Health Education Research*, 8, 43–51.

Polivy, J. and Herman, C.P. (1986). Etiology of binge eating: psychological mechanisms. In: C. Fairburn and G. Wilson (eds), *Binge Eating: Nature, Assessment and Treatment*. New York, NY: Guilford Press, pp. 173–205.

Powers, P.S., Santana, C.A. and Bannon, Y.S. (2002). Olanzapine in the treatment of anorexia nervosa: An open label trial. *International Journal of Eating Disorders*, 32, 146–154.

Pratt, B.M. and Woolfenden, S.R. (2002). Interventions for preventing eating disorders in children and adolescents. *Cochrane Database of Systematic Reviews,* Issue 2, Art No.: CD002891, DOI: 10.1002/14651858. CD002891. Available at http://www.mrw.interscience.wiley.com/cochrane/clsysrev/articles/CD002891/frame.html (retrieved 12 December 2006).

Raffi, A.R., Rondini, M., Grandi, S. and Fava, G. A. (2000). Life events and prodromal symptoms in bulimia nervosa. *Psychological Medicine*, 30, 727–731.

Rodríguez-Villarino, R., González-Lorenzo, M., Fernández-González, Á. and Lameiras-Fernández, M. (2005). Exploring the relationship between shopping addiction and other excessive behaviors: A pilot study. *Adicciones*, 17, 231–240.

Rossiter, E.M and Agras, W.S. (1990). An empirical test of the DSM-III–R definition of binge. *International Journal of Eating Disorders*, 9, 513–518.

Schlundt, D.G. and Johnson, W.G. (1990). *Eating Disorders: Assessment and Treatment*. Needham Heights, MA: Allyn and Bacon.

Schwartz D.M. and Thompson M.G. (1981). Do anorectics get well? Current research and future needs. *American Journal of Psychiatry*, 148, 319–323.

Serpell, L., Treasure, J., Teasdale, J. and Sullivan, V. (1999). Anorexia nervosa: friend or foe? *International Journal of Eating Disorders*, 25, 177–186.

Shoebridge, P. and Gowers, S.G. (2000). Parental height concern and adolescent-onset – a case–control study to investigate direction of causality. *British Journal of Psychiatry*, 176, 132–137.

Simon, J., Schmidt, U. and Pilling, S. (2005). The health service use and cost of eating disorders. *Psychological Medicine*, 35, 1543–1551.

Smolak, L., Levine, M.P. and Gralen, S. (1993). The impact of puberty and dating on eating problems among middle school girls. *Journal of Youth and Adolescence*, 22, 355–368.

Steinhausen, H.C. (2002). The outcome of anorexia nervosa in the 20th century. *American Journal of Psychiatry*, 159, 1284–1293.

Stice, E. (1998). Modeling of eating pathology and social reinforcement of the thin-ideal predict onset of bulimic symptoms. *Behavior Research and Therapy*, 36, 931–944.

Stice, E. (2002). Risk and maintenance factors for eating pathology: a meta-analytic review. *Psychological Bulletin*, 128, 825–848.

Stice, E. and Shaw, H. (2004). Eating disorder prevention programs: a meta-analytic review. *Psychological Bulletin*, 130, 206–227.

Stice, E., Nemeroff, C. and Shaw, H. (1996). A test of the dual pathway model of bulimia nervosa: evidence for the restrained-eating and affect regulation mechanisms. *Journal of Social and Clinical Psychology*, 15, 340–363.

Stice, E., Shaw, H. and Nemeroff, C. (1998). Dual pathway model of bulimia nervosa: Longitudinal support for dietary restraint and affect-regulation mechanisms. *Journal of Social and Clinical Psychology*, 17, 129–140.

Stice, E., Shaw, H., Burton, E. and Wade, E. (2006). Dissonance and healthy weight eating disorder prevention programs: a randomized efficacy trial. *Journal of Consulting and Clinical Psychology*, 74, 263–275.

Stock, S.L., Goldberg, E., Corbett, S. and Katzman, D.K. (2002). Substance use in female adolescents with eating disorders. *Journal of Adolescent Health*, 31, 176–182.

Striegel-Moore, R.H., Silberstein, L. R. and Rodin, J. (1986). Toward an understanding of risk factors for bulimia. *American Psychologist*, 41, 246–263.

Striegel-Moore, R.H. and Kearney-Cooke, C. (1994). Exploring parents' attitudes and behaviors about their child's physical appearance. *International Journal of Eating Disorders*, 15, 337–385.

Striegel-Moore, R.H., Leslie, D., Petrill, S.A. *et al.* (2000). One-year use and cost of inpatient and outpatient services among female and male patients with an eating disorder: evidence from a national database of health insurance claims. *International Journal of Eating Disorders*, 27, 381–389.

Strober, M. and Katz, J.L. (1988). Depression in the eating disorders: a review and analysis of descriptive family and biological findings. In: D.M. Garner and P.E. Garfinkel (eds), *Diagnostic Issues in Anorexia Nervosa and Bulimia Nervosa*. New York, NY: Brunner/Mazel, pp. 80–111.

Strober, M. and Yager, J. (1985). A developmental perspective on the treatment of anorexia nervosa in adolescents. In: D.M. Garner and P.E. Garfinkel (eds), *Handbook of Psychotherapy for Anorexia Nervosa and Bulimia*. New York, NY: Guilford Press, pp. 363–390.

Swarr, A.E. and Richards, M.H. (1996). Longitudinal effects of adolescent girls' pubertal development, perception of pubertal timing and parental relations on eating disorders. *Developmental Psychology*, 32, 636–646.

Tester, M.L. and Gleaves, D.H. (2005). Self-deceptive enhancement and family environment: possible protective factors against internalization of the thin ideal. *Eating Disorders*, 13, 187–199.

Thompson-Brenner, H., Glass, S. and Westen, D. (2003). A multidimensional meta-analysis of psychotherapy for bulimia nervosa. *Clinical Psychology: Science and Practice*, 10, 269–287.

Turnbull, S. Ward, A., Treasure, J. *et al.* (1996). The demand for eating disorder care. An epidemiological study using the general practice research database. *British Journal of Psychiatry*, 169, 705–712.

Vandereycken, W. (1990). The addiction model in eating disorders: some critical remarks and a selected bibliography. *International Journal of Eating Disorders*, 9, 95–101.

Vitousek, K.B. and Hollon, S.D. (1990). The investigation of schematic content and processing in eating disorders. *Cognitive Therapy and Research*, 14, 191–214.

Vogeltanz-Holm, N.D., Wonderlich, S.A., Lewis, B.A. *et al.* (2000). Longitudinal predictors of binge eating, intense dieting and weight concerns in a national sample of women. *Behavior Therapy*, 31, 221–235.

Vohs, K.D., Bardone, A.M., Joiner, T.E. *et al.* (1999). Perfectionism, perceived weight status and self esteem interact to predict bulimic symptoms: a model of bulimic symptom development. *Journal of Abnormal Psychology*, 108, 695–700.

Walsh, B.T. and Garner, D.M. (1997). Diagnostic issues. In: D.M. Garner and P.E. Garfinkel, (eds), *Handbook of Treatment for Eating Disorders*, 2nd edn. New York, NY: Guilford Press, pp. 25–33.

Ward, A., Ramsay, R. and Treasure, J. (2000a). Attachment research in eating disorders. *British Journal of Medical Psychology*, 73, 35–51.

Ward, A., Tiller, J., Treasure, J. and Russell, G. (2000b). Eating disorders: psyche or soma? *International Journal of Eating Disorders*, 27, 279–287.

Warren, C.S., Gleaves, D.H., Cepeda-Benito, A. *et al.* (2005). Ethnicity as a protective factor against internalization of thin ideal and body dissatisfaction. *International Journal of Eating Disorders*, 37, 241–249.

Wertheim, E.H., Paxton, S.J., Schutz, H.K. and Muir, S.J. (1997). Why do adolescent girls watch their weight? An interview study examining sociocultural pressure to be thin. *Journal of Psychosomatic Research*, 42, 345–355.

Whilfley, D.E., Welch, R.R., Stein, R.I. *et al.* (2002). A randomised comparison of group cognitive-behavioral therapy and group interpersonal psychotherapy for treatment of overweight individuals with binge-eating disorder. *Archives of General Psychiatry*, 59, 713–721.

Wiederman, M.W. and Pryor, T. (1991). Substance use and impulsive behaviors among adolescents with eating disorders. *Addictive Behaviors*. 21, 269–271.

Williamson, D.A. (1990). *Assessment of Eating Disorders: Obesity, Anorexia, and Bulimia Nervosa*. New York, NY: Pergamon Press.

Williamson, D.A., Davis, C.J., Goreczny, A.J. and Blouin, D.C. (1989). Body-image disturbances in bulimia nervosa: influences of actual body size. *Journal of Abnormal Psychology*, 98, 97–99.

Williamson, D.A., Gleaves, D.A. and Savin, S.M. (1992). Empirical classification of eating disorder NOS: Support for DSM-IV changes. *Journal of Psychopathology and Behavioral Assessment*, 14, 201–216.

Williamson, D.A., Cubic, B.A. and Gleaves, D.H. (1993). Equivalence of body image disturbance in anorexia and bulimia nervosa. *Journal of Abnormal Psychology*, 102, 177–180.

Williamson, D.A., Thaw, J.M. and Varnado-Sullivan, P.J. (2001). Cost-effectiveness analysis of a hospital-based cognitive-behavioral treatment program for eating disorders. *Behavior Therapy*, 32, 459–477.

Willmuth, M.E., Leitenberg, H., Rosen, J.C. and Cado, S. (1988). A comparison of purging and nonpurging normal weight bulimics. *International Journal of Eating Disorders*, 7, 825–835.

Wilson, G.T. (2000). Eating disorders and addiction. *Drugs and Society*, 15, 87–101.

Wilson, G.T. and Fairburn, C.G. (2002). Treatment for eating disorders. In: P.E. Nathan and J.M. Gorman (eds), *A Guide to Treatments That Work*, 2nd edn. New York, NY: Oxford University Press, pp. 559–592.

Wilson, G.T. and Latner, J.D. (2001). Eating disorders and addiction. In: M. Hetherington (ed.), *Food Cravings and Addiction*. Leatherhead: Leatherhead Publishing, pp. 585–605.

Worthington, E.L., Mazzeo, S.E. and Kliewer, W.L. (2002). Addictive and eating disorders, unforgiveness and forgiveness. *Journal of Psychology and Christianity*, 21, 257–261.

Zipfel, S., Reas, D.L., Thornton, C. *et al.* (2002). Day hospitalization programs for eating disorders: a systematic review of the literature. *International Journal of Eating Disorders*, 31, 105–117.

7

GAMBLING PRACTICES AMONG YOUTH: ETIOLOGY, PREVENTION AND TREATMENT

RINA GUPTA AND JEFFREY L. DEREVENSKY

Even though state-regulated forms of gambling are permitted only to those of legal age (the age varying between jurisdictions and on the type of gambling), children and adolescents are gambling for money in record numbers. If loosely defined as wagering money on the outcome of a game or event, with the hopes of winning larger sums of money, youth gambling participation is ramped. Gambling is not just about going to the casino or racetrack, or playing the lottery; one need not look much further than the home, where card games played for money, and sports wagering, are very commonplace.

Our team at the International Centre for Youth Gambling Problems and High-Risk Behaviors at McGill University in Montreal, Quebec, Canada has been involved since the early 1990s in understanding the complexities involved in youth gambling, treating adolescents and young adults with gambling problems, and preventing youth gambling problems. While youth gambling problems can be viewed as another adolescent risky behavior, it is only recently that is has gained the attention of policy-makers. This chapter is designed to provide an overview of what is currently understood about the correlates, risk factors and protective factors associated with youth gambling and problem gambling, as well as to touch upon prevention and treatment considerations.

Adolescent Addiction: Epidemiology, Assessment and Treatment

GAMBLING PARTICIPATION AMONG YOUTH

There is ample research suggesting that children often start gambling young, usually around 9 or 10 years of age. They frequently report engaging in card-playing with family and friends for money; purchasing and playing lottery products; playing bingo in bingo halls; and wagering on their own activities, including sports and video games (Derevensky and Gupta, 2004). Even before the mass expansion of gambling, Ladouceur and his colleagues conducted a study among 1320 primary school students and found that among their sample 86 percent of children reported some form of gambling for money, and 37 percent admitted to having wagered an object that was very dear to them. They further concluded that a large number of youth were gambling at least once per week, even under the ages of 9 and 10 (Ladouceur *et al.*, 1994a). A smaller sample of elementary students (fourth to sixth grades, age 10–12) in Quebec found similar rates of participation, with 70 percent of respondents reporting having gambled for money, 53 percent doing so at least once per week (Derevensky *et al.*, 1996). While these respondents are not individuals with severe gambling problems, these earlier studies reveal that gambling behavior patterns establish themselves very young, thus confirming retrospective studies where adult pathological gamblers report an early age of onset (Livingston, 1974; Custer, 1982; Productivity Commission, 1999).

More recent investigations have revealed that gambling, or wagering on a myriad number of games, is a relatively common and popular activity among adolescents (Jacobs, 2004). Studies conducted in Canada (Gupta and Derevensky, 1998a; Dickson *et al.*, 2002), the US (Shaffer and Hall, 2001), Australia (Delfabbro and Thrupp, 2003) and New Zealand (Clarke and Rosen, 2000) have consistently identified that between 60 and 80 percent of young people aged 13–17 years gamble at least once per year, and that between 3 and 6 percent display many of the behaviors indicative of adult problem gambling (Gupta and Derevensky, 1998a). These behaviors include an excessive preoccupation with gambling, chasing after losses, lying to peers and parents, and abandonment of important commitments like school work and peer relationships to pursue gambling. It could be argued that adolescents misuse gambling more frequently than adults, since they experience higher rates of problem gambling (Shaffer and Hall, 1996; Stinchfield and Winters, 1997; National Research Council, 1999). The most common locations where gambling takes place include the home, school, and friends' homes. Less frequently, youth report gambling in arcades, corner stores, cruise ships, with some managing to gain access to casinos and bars where electronic machines are frequently located (Gupta and Derevensky, 1998a). Prevalence rates of gambling are often contingent upon the availability and age prerequisites for youth, depending upon their jurisdiction and legal statutes. Of particular concern are the newer forms of electronic gambling, including electronic gambling machines (EGMs, VLTs, slots, Pokies), Internet wagering, mobile gambling, and trends associated with the heavy advertising of gambling (e.g., poker tournaments, Internet websites).

SOCIETAL TRENDS AND INFLUENCES

The activities of today's youth are very much dictated by societal trends and influences. As an example, more youth than ever are spending increased amounts of time in their homes during spare time, either watching television or chatting with friends online via their personal computers. In years past, children were more likely to be playing outside after school or on weekends. Such generational changes can possibly be attributed to a societal trend toward keeping one's children safe (i.e., away from people who could do them harm), increased homework loads assigned by schools, and society's technological advancements with respect to video-gaming, Internet-chatting, increased television programming particularly attractive to youth, and the relatively low cost of home personal DVD and VCR machines. Such societal trends and influences, by changing the way youth use their recreational time, has resulted in public health concerns such as obesity (Stettler *et al.*, 2004; Vandewater *et al.*, 2004) and diabetes rates (Pontiroli, 2004) increasing in young children and adolescents.

Similar arguments can be made in regards to gambling and youth, with increased offer and societal acceptance of gambling resulting in increased public health concerns (Korn and Shaffer, 1999; Derevensky *et al.*, 2004a; Messerlian *et al.*, 2004). Gambling, once considered one of society's sins and vices associated with underground activities, has now taken center stage in many communities, being promoted by governments throughout the world as *gaming* – a change in terminology eliminating the negative connotation that once existed. Once relegated to international centers associated with gambling (such as Las Vegas, Reno, Atlantic City, Monte Carlo), more and more governments have either established their own casinos, electronic gaming machines, lotteries, Internet-gaming, etc., or at the very least have licensed these forms of gambling with heavy regulation and taxation. Growing up in a culture populated with state-sanctioned gambling opportunities and rich in advertisement, it is not surprising that the public has embraced such activities as a socially acceptable form of entertainment.

The very popular and highly publicized game of poker currently represents a social trend that is largely impacting the gambling behaviors of the general public. Celebrity and international poker tournaments, found on many television channels, have placed the game front and center, and have caught the attention and interest of old and young alike. Sports networks are now televising poker tournaments as a *sport*, resulting in yet another cultural shift. The promotion of a gambling activity as a sport carries several concerns, primarily because most people are of the belief that sports are safe and promote health and well-being.

Children and adolescents are not immune to social trends and influences, as well as the negative consequences associated with excessive gambling. While it is still unclear what the social costs are in reality, many now better understand the need to include gambling prevention alongside those of other adolescent addictive and high-risk behaviors (Jessor, 1998; Ghezzi *et al.*, 2000; Dickson *et al.*, 2004). Nevertheless, it still remains that many youth and parents are unaware that what begins as an enjoyable, exciting activity can quickly escalate to impaired control when gambling, with serious social, personal, interpersonal, legal and economic negative consequences. There are so many mixed messages about gambling that many youth, parents and educators are confused and not properly informed. Through our continued work with youth, we have come to understand that many conscientious teens make choices to avoid excessive alcohol and drug use, and elect to gamble instead, believing that they are acting responsibly and in their best interest. Unfortunately, youth who are unaware of the warning signs and potential risks inherent in excessive gambling could unknowingly be placing themselves in harm's way. As a result, the benefits of a *harm-minimization* approach in minimizing gambling problems warrant serious consideration (Dickson *et al.*, 2004) and will be discussed later in this chapter. This approach is nested in the belief that the vast majority of teens are gambling and will continue to do so, that society will continue to readily recognize many forms of gambling as an acceptable form of entertainment, and consequently the best way to help youth is to sensitize them to the risks and raise issues around responsible gambling.

Technology is an ever-evolving phenomenon which inevitably brings with it social change. Today, the majority of people in many jurisdictions around the world have ready, affordable access to computers and to the Internet. Children and teens, even more than adults, are very adept at using and entertaining themselves via Internet access from their homes or Internet cafés, often unsupervised. Griffiths (1999) has long argued that technology will continue to play a meaningful role in the evolution of gambling practices. Griffiths and Parke (2002) explain that patterns of family leisure activities are changing, with the more sophisticated home entertainment systems resulting in a cocooning effect instead of families going out and being active. They argue that these family trends may ultimately affect the choices teens make with regard to the use of their leisure time, with many preferring technologically-based activities. This shift lends itself well to increased gambling involvement, especially when brought into the home via the Internet. In a recent publication, Griffiths *et al.* (2006) address in more detail the impact of technology, highlighting the salient characteristics that could lead to a serious rise in gambling participation by youth. These factors include easy accessibility, anonymity, and convenience amongst others. Gambling has now come to be understood as an activity that individuals engage in for purposes of escape and/or stimulation (Gupta and Derevensky, 1998b), and Griffiths and his colleagues (2006) argue that Internet gambling allow for both. Couple this with adolescents' perceived enjoyment and excitement from gambling, their belief that gambling is a relatively harmless activity, and the potential to win money, and it is no wonder that gambling is enticing.

EFFECTS OF PARENTING ON YOUTH GAMBLING PARTICIPATION

A small-scale study conducted by Magoon and Ingersoll (2006) concluded that parental gambling was associated with levels of gambling amongst adolescents, as well as an increased likelihood of their children being identified as problem gamblers. Higher levels of parent–child attachment were associated with lower levels of adolescent gambling, while strained parental trust and communication was associated with increased problem gambling amongst the teens. Measures of parental monitoring and supervision found similar outcomes in that increased monitoring and supervision resulted in lower levels of adolescent gambling. Their study also suggests that peer influences could be moderated by parental influences. Vachon *et al.* (2004), using a community sample of adolescents, yielded similar conclusions. Their results showed that adolescent gambling frequency was related to both parental frequency of gambling participation and problems. Furthermore, adolescent problem gambling was linked only to fathers' severity of gambling problems. They also examined the impact of parental monitoring and disciplinary practices on the behavior of adolescents. As might be predicted, they concluded that low levels of monitoring and higher levels of discipline inadequacies both adolescents' risk of both getting involved in gambling activities and developing related problems. Other research has consistently pointed to higher rates of problem gambling in adolescents who report excessive parental gambling (Gupta and Derevensky, 1998a; Jacobs, 2000, 2004; Felsher *et al.*, 2003; Langhinrichsen-Rohling *et al.*, 2004).

Parenting style can have an effect on problem gambling even when not modeling the behavior itself. A retrospective study requiring adult pathological gamblers and controls to recall how they were parented found that those reporting lower maternal and paternal care were more likely to be pathological gamblers. In terms of parental bonding patterns based on a combination of care and protection, the pathological gamblers reported low rates of optimal parenting and high rates of neglectful parenting (Grant and Kim, 2002). In another study examining the relationship between parenting styles, family environment and gambling behavior, it was concluded that parenting styles indirectly influenced the gambling behavior of teens via the family environment. More specifically, poor family environments which were characterized by high levels of conflict and low levels of cohesion were found significantly to increase the likelihood of gambling problems among the youth residing in those homes (Ste-Marie, 2006).

RECREATIONAL GAMBLING VS PROBLEM GAMBLING

When addressing the issue of gambling and youth, it is important to make the distinction between problem gambling and general gambling participation (Winters and Anderson, 2000). As is the case with other high-risk activities such as alcohol consumption and drug use, most adolescents experiment with gambling activities while experiencing few or no negative consequences. The majority of young people who gamble do so for enjoyment and excitement, and have no difficulty limiting their participation to social occasions. They gamble only what they can afford to lose, spend a reasonable amount of time doing so, gamble relatively infrequently, and report experiencing considerable fun and entertainment. However, a small but meaningful percentage of teens lose control of their gambling behavior, and as a result of an inability to set or maintain limits or having difficulty stopping, they experience significant gambling-related negative consequences. It is believed that problem gamblers are different from non-problem gamblers in many ways. Nevertheless, it should be noted that not all youth gamblers are problematic. In fact, there is evidence that most youth gamble responsibly, at low levels, with no appreciable problems. However, it is clear that between 4 and 8 percent of adolescents have severe gambling problems, with another 10–15 percent at risk for developing problems (Shaffer and Hall, 1996; National Research Council, 1999).

Youth in detention centers, psychiatric facilities and rehabilitation programs yield pathological gambling rates that are significantly higher than the norm (Winters and Anderson, 2000; Magoon *et al.*, 2005). This is mainly accounted for by the fact that similar risk factors underlie problem gambling as well as other high-risk behaviors, such as substance abuse. Winters and Anderson (2000) highlight that the origins of adolescent problem gambling frequently point to co-morbidity, often established between drug use and pathological gambling. It could thus be argued that multiple high-risk behaviors, in particular those characterized as addictive behaviors, share similar etiological processes. Data from two longitudinal studies, using general population household samples, link gambling to substance use and delinquency, but the association was not found to be strong (Barnes *et al.*, 2005). The lack of a strong association is most likely due to a failure to examine large numbers of problem gamblers.

RISK FACTORS/ETIOLOGY

Risk factors consist of personal attributes, environmental context, or a situational condition that increases the chances of a person engaging in a high-risk behavior. Jessor and colleagues (1995; Jessor, 1988) have identified a host of risk factors that seem to be common to numerous adolescent high-risk behaviors (see Derevensky and Gupta, 2004; Dickson *et al.* 2004; and Dickson-Gillespie *et al.*, 2007 for a comprehensive examination of common high-risk behaviors). Such high-risk behaviors include low self-esteem, depressive mood, being a victim of physical and sexual abuse, poor school performance, a history of delinquency (poor impulse control), being male, having a parental history of addiction, and community and family norms that endorse or facilitate access to gambling venues. More recent research has substantiated this list of risk factors and has identified several additional factors, such as parenting style, a lack of connection to the school community, and the presence of learning problems in earlier educational years (Dickson *et al.*, 2003; Hardoon *et al.*, 2004; Felsher, 2006; Ste-Marie, 2006). Personality traits unique to adolescent problem gamblers have also been identified (Gupta *et al.*, 2006). Utilizing discriminant analysis, Gupta and colleagues found that high levels of disinhibition, boredom susceptibility, cheerfulness and excitability, as well as low levels of conformity and self-discipline, were strongly associated with the function that best predicts the problem gambling severity level. Their findings lend additional support to the premise that certain types of individuals are more susceptible than others to developing a gambling problem.

Jacobs (1987) has long theorized that the severity of gambling in an adolescent is associated with increased stress and inability to cope with negative life events. From this perspective, gambling becomes a maladaptive solution or a coping response to difficult life situations (Gupta and Derevensky, 1998b; Gupta *et al.*, 2004; Hardoon *et al.*, 2004; Bergevin *et al.*, 2006). Co-morbidity may also represent a risk factor. Gambling has been widely correlated with other high-risk behaviors, with adolescent gamblers being more likely to smoke tobacco, drink alcohol and use drugs (Potenza *et al.*, 2000). Adolescents identified as problem or pathological gamblers were more likely to drink alcohol on a weekly basis, to consume drugs or to smoke, compared with those who gambled very little or not at all (Gupta and Derevensky, 1998a; Derevensky and Gupta, 2004).

Experts suggest that risk factors not only play a central role in the initiation and maintenance of gambling behavior, but should also be taken into consideration when targeting interventions, since they consist of complex biological, psychological and sociological factors (DiClemente *et al.*, 2000; Derevensky *et al.*, 2004b, 2004c).

PREVENTION OF UNDERAGE PROBLEM GAMBLING

The issue of gambling prevention programs designed for youth has been gaining considerable attention in recent years. As society and policy-makers become more aware of the risks and negative consequences associated with underage gambling, the movement towards addressing this issue as both a mental and a public health issue has grown, and substantiates the need for effective prevention initiatives (Korn and Shaffer, 1999; Messerlian *et al.*, 2004). Empirically, while little is known about the science of prevention as it pertains to youth gambling, there is a growing body of literature addressing this issue. Prevention experts have often relied heavily upon existing practices common to the prevention of other high-risk and addictive behaviors, as well on the current youth gambling research findings, when developing prevention materials. Based upon theoretical and empirical evidence of common risk and protective factors across adolescent risky behaviors (Battistich *et al.*, 1996; Galambos and Tilton-Weaver, 1998; Jessor, 1998; Loeber *et al.*, 1998; Costello *et al.*, 1999), including problem gambling (Gupta and Derevensky, 1998b; Jacobs, 1998; Dickson *et al.*, 2002, 2004), many have argued the benefit of developing prevention initiatives that target multiple high-risk behaviors (Derevensky *et al.*, 2004b, 2004c). Such comprehensive prevention materials have yet to be developed, but surely represent the future trend in prevention.

Prevention efforts addressing adolescent risky lifestyles have traditionally been aimed towards non-users (primary prevention), screening for potential problems (secondary prevention), and treatment (tertiary prevention) for those who have developed problems (e.g., alcohol use and abuse, substance abuse, smoking). In terms of primary prevention, the goal is avoiding or postponing the initial use of substances or activities such as gambling. Considering the far-reaching consequences that result from a gambling problem in adolescence, the importance of primary prevention administered to youth who have not yet gambled or experienced problems related to their gambling cannot be disputed. Research highlights that age of onset of gambling behavior represents a significant risk factor, with a younger age of initiation being correlated with the development of gambling-related problems (Wynne *et al.*, 1996; Gupta and Derevensky, 1998a; National Research Council, 1999; Jacobs, 2000, 2004; Dickson *et al.*, 2004). Thus, delaying the age of onset of gambling experiences would be fundamental in a successful prevention paradigm for youth in primary school, since many have not yet started engaging in gambling behavior.

The question of whether the traditional approach of promoting non-use amongst adolescents is optimal has been an ongoing topic of discussion (Beck, 1998; Thombs and Briddick, 2000), especially in the field of alcohol use and gambling (Dickson *et al.*, 2004), as it is well understood that the majority of high school students have already engaged in these behaviors at some point in their development. The adoption of a harm-reduction paradigm in the prevention of problem gambling may represent the most logical approach for adolescents who have already initiated gambling behaviors. Even though underage youth are prohibited access to government-regulated forms of gambling and venues, research clearly indicates that early gambling experiences mostly occur with non-regulated forms of gambling amongst peers or family members (e.g., playing cards for money, placing bets on sports events, wagering on games of skill, or parental gambling with their children) (Gupta and Derevensky, 1998a; Jacobs, 2000, 2004). With 70–80 percent of children and adolescents reporting having gambled during the previous year (Gupta and Derevensky, 1998a; National Research Council, 1999; Jacobs, 2000), it could be argued that it would be unrealistic to expect youth to stop gambling completely, especially since it is exceedingly difficult to regulate access to gambling activities organized amongst themselves. And while we remain concerned about the occurrence of serious gambling problems amongst youth, it is also recognized that the majority of youth are able to gamble without developing any significant gambling-related problems, as evidenced in the prevalence rates of underage gamblers who are not meeting the criteria for problem or pathological gambling.

Harm-reduction strategies of all types seek to help individuals without demanding abstinence (Riley *et al.*, 1999; Mangham, 2001). Included in such an approach would be secondary prevention strategies, based upon the assumption that individuals cannot be prevented from engaging in particular risky behaviors (Cohen, 1993; Baer *et al.*, 1998); tertiary prevention strategies (DiClemete, 1999); and a "health movement" perspective (Denning and Little, 2001; Heather *et al.*, 1993; Messerlian *et al.*, 2004). As well, strategies designed as harm-minimization would include the promotion of responsible behavior; teaching and informing youth about the facts and risks associated with excessive gambling; changing erroneous cognitions, misperceptions and beliefs; along with enhancing skills needed to maintain control (setting and adhering to time, frequency and money limits) when gambling. If these skills are encouraged and reinforced through children's formative years, it is plausible that they may become less vulnerable to the risks of a gambling problem once gaining legal access to gambling forums. Given the proliferation and socially accepted practice of gambling, the utility of a harm-reduction approach as a means to prevent problem behavior remains promising. The International Centre for Youth Gambling Problems and High-Risk Behaviors at McGill University (www.youthgambling.com) has developed a number of prevention initiatives based upon a harm-minimization approach, such as *The Amazing Chateau* and *Hooked City* (two interactive CD ROM games for children and adolescents aged 11–18); prevention workshops (PowerPoint) for children aged 11–18; and *Clean Break* (a DVD/VHS docudrama designed for adolescents aged 13–18).

ISSUES PERTAINING TO THE TREATMENT OF ADOLESCENT GAMBLERS

Adolescents with gambling problems in general tend not to present themselves for treatment. There are likely many reasons that they fail to seek treatment, such as a fear of being identified, and the negative stigma often associated with treatment. Adolescents tend to hold self-perceptions of invincibility and invulnerability, and thus rarely recognize their own problems. Also, those who do realize they are in trouble often believe that no one can help them to control their behavior. Inherent in their thinking is the belief in natural recovery and eventual self-control (for a more detailed explanation, see Gupta and Derevensky, 2000, 2004; Derevensky *et al.*, 2003; Derevensky and Gupta, 2004).

Empirically, not very much has been learned about the treatment of young pathological gamblers. We know that a certain percentage of adolescents develop very serious gambling problems, but only a small minority of those individuals present themselves for treatment in facilities where addiction therapists trained to deal with pathological gambling are located. As such, it is very difficult to develop empirical treatment efficacy studies without access to clinical populations, and even more difficult to conduct Empirically Validated Treatment (EVT) designs or Best Practices (Toneatto and Ladouceur, 2003). Minimum criteria for Best Practices include the replicability of findings, randomization of patients to an experimental group, the inclusion of a matched control group, and the use of sufficiently large numbers of participants. Unfortunately, the treatment of adolescent pathological gamblers has not yet evolved to the point that treatment evaluation studies have met such rigorous criteria.

Apart from limited access to adolescent clinical populations, there are several other reasons to explain why more stringent criteria, scientifically validated methodological procedures and experimental analyses concerning the efficacy of treatment programs for youth have not been implemented. Primarily, there exist very few treatment programs prepared to include young gamblers amongst their clientele, and the small number of young people seeking treatment in any given center results in the difficulty of obtaining matched control groups. Matched controls are even more difficult to obtain, considering that young gamblers often present with a significant number and variety of secondary psychological disorders. Another obstacle to treatment program evaluation is that treatment approaches may vary within a center, and may be dependent upon a gambler's specific profile or developmental level, or the therapist's training orientation. Given the lack of empirically-based treatment in the field of pathological gambling (for both adolescents and adults), this issue is relatively new compared with existing treatment models for youth with other addictions and mental health disorders. As such, there remains a continuing and growing interest in identifying effective treatment strategies to help minimize youth gambling problems.

Having acknowledged the limited number of treatment outcome studies, in one empirically-based treatment study Ladouceur and colleagues (1994b) implemented a cognitive-behavioral therapy program, using four adolescent male pathological gamblers. Five components were included within their treatment program – information about gambling, cognitive interventions, problem-solving training, relapse prevention, and social skills training. A mean number of 17 cognitive therapy sessions was provided individually over a period of approximately 3 months. Clinically significant gains were reported, with three of the four adolescents remaining abstinent 3 and 6 months after treatment. Ladouceur and colleagues further concluded that the length of treatment necessary for adolescents with severe gambling problems appeared to be relatively shorter than that required for adults, and that cognitive therapy represents a promising new avenue for treatment. It is important to note that this therapeutic approach is predicated upon the belief that (i) adolescents persist in their gambling behavior in spite of repeated losses primarily as a result of their erroneous beliefs and distorted cognitive perceptions concerning their gambling play, and (ii) winning money is central to their continued efforts. However, the limited sample, while somewhat informative, is not sufficiently representative to depict a complete picture.

Research and clinical accounts with adolescents (Gupta and Derevensky, 2000, 2004) suggest that the clinical portrait of adolescent problematic gamblers is much more complex than merely that of underlying erroneous beliefs and the desire to acquire money. As specified previously, our earlier research demonstrated strong empirical support for Jacobs' General Theory of Addictions for adolescent problem gamblers (Gupta and Derevensky, 1998b). Adolescent problem and pathological gamblers were found to have exhibited abnormal physiological resting states (resulting in a tendency toward risk-taking), greater emotional distress in general (i.e., depression and anxiety), significantly higher levels of dissociation when gambling, and higher rates of comorbidity with other addictive behaviors. The fact that adolescent problem and pathological gamblers differ in their ability successfully to cope with daily events, adversity and situational problems (Gupta *et al.*, 2004; Hardoon *et al.*, 2004; Bergevin *et al.*, 2006) represents a critical component in our treatment approach. Furthermore, contrary to common beliefs and the tenets of the cognitive-behavioral approach, our research and clinical work suggests money is not the predominant reason why adolescents with gambling problems engage in these behaviors (see Gupta and Derevensky, 1998a). Rather, it appears that money is important in that it is merely a means to enable such youth to continue gambling.

Blaszczynski and Silove (1995) further suggest that there is ample empirical support that gambling involves a complex and dynamic interaction between ecological, psycho-physiological, developmental, cognitive and behavioral components. Given this complexity, it would be best to incorporate each of these components into a successful treatment paradigm designed to achieve abstinence and minimize relapse. While Blaszczynski and Silove addressed their concerns with respect to adult problem gamblers, a similar multidimensional approach seems appropriate to successfully address the multitude of problems facing adolescent problem gamblers.

THE McGILL TREATMENT PARADIGM

Over an 8-year period of time, we have developed a treatment approach for adolescents with serious gambling problems (for a comprehensive description, see Gupta and Derevensky, 2000, 2004). We have treated in excess of 60 young problem gamblers, ranging in age from 14 to 21 years. While not a sufficiently large number of clients upon which to draw firm conclusions, this nevertheless has provided us with sufficient diversity of experience. Based upon our clinical observations with these individuals, their reported success in remaining abstinent, and their improvement in their overall psychological well-being, the approach adopted in our clinic has been generally successful in assisting youth to resume a healthy lifestyle.

The criterion by which to evaluate success differs from one treatment facility and approach to the next. In a recent review of the gambling treatment literature, Toneatto and Ladouceur (2003) suggest that several different outcome measures have traditionally been used when assessing treatment effectiveness; these being personal ratings of urges, reduction of gambling involvement, and gambling cessation. Our treatment philosophy is predicated upon the assumption that sustained abstinence is necessary for these youth to recover from their gambling problem, and that their general overall psychological well-being and mental health must be improved (this also includes improvement in their coping skills and adaptive behaviors). It is important to acknowledge that a number of individuals contend that *controlled* gambling for certain adults is a viable alternative to an abstinence approach. During the past 8 years, we have observed a large percentage of youth in treatment who, initially, had controlled gambling as their primary goal. Our clinical work suggests that while controlled gambling (the ability to establish and respect self-imposed limits) can be an interim goal, abstinence is eventually necessary for adolescents with gambling problems.

While our treatment approach is unique, its theoretical basis is predicated upon the principles outlined in Jacobs' General Theory of Addictions and Blaszczynski's Pathways Model (see Nower and Blaszczynski, 2004, for a comprehensive discussion of how the Pathways Model can be adapted to explain youth problem gambling). Both theories presuppose that the interaction of a combination of factors (emotional, psychological and physiological) has an important role in the acquisition and maintenance of a gambling problem. The Pathways Model further elaborates three different subtypes of pathological gamblers – each subtype having a different etiology and different accompanying pathologies. It is postulated and assumed that the different subtypes of pathological gamblers would by necessity require different types of intervention. While there is some overlap between the two models, with both describing the etiology, trajectory and psychology of the addicted gambler, Jacobs' model primarily describes the Pathway 3 gambler articulated by Nower and Blaszczynski. The commonalities lie in the belief that these youth have a combination of emotional and/or psychological distress coupled with a physiological predisposition toward impulsively seeking excitement. This subset of problem gamblers represents our most typical young clients who seek therapy; those tending to gamble impulsively primarily for purposes of escape and as a way of coping with their stress, depression and/or daily problems. Longitudinal data recently published following low-income young boys aged 11–16 years suggests that early indicators of gambling problems include indices of anxiety and impulsivity (Vitaro *et al.*, 2004). Recent research has also replicated earlier findings that adolescent problem gamblers are more likely to be exposed to peer and parent gambling, to be susceptible to peer pressure, to exhibit conduct problems and antisocial behaviors, to engage in substance use, and to have suicide ideation and indicate more suicide attempts (Derevensky and Gupta, 2004; Langhinrichsen-Rohling *et al.*, 2004).

Since adolescents rarely voluntarily seek treatment for gambling problems, a considerable number attend because of parental pressure, mandatory referrals from the judicial system, or are strongly encouraged by significant others (girlfriends, boyfriends, close peers) and comply for fear of losing relationships. As such, many are reticent about participating at first. The youth to whom we have provided treatment tend to share similar profiles. Other than the previously mentioned psychological variables of depression, anxiety, impulsivity and poor coping abilities, it is not uncommon to see youth who have a history of academic difficulties (usually due to a learning disability and/or attention deficit disorder and further compounded by their gambling preoccupation and gambling behavior), have stressed interpersonal relationships with family members and friends, are involved with unhealthy peer groups, and are engaging in delinquent and criminal behaviors to support their gambling. The description of our treatment philosophy and approach is briefly provided to help individuals interested in working with young problem gamblers to acquire a better understanding of the different components necessary when working with these youth. Treating youth with severe gambling problems requires clinical skills, a knowledge of adolescent development, an understanding of the risk factors associated with problem gambling, and a thorough grounding in the empirical work concerning the correlates associated with gambling problems. By no means should this brief description substitute for proper training.

Initial Process

There are three basic processes that are necessary to establishing a successful therapeutic experience:

1. *Establishing mutual trust and respect.* Mutual trust and respect are fundamental to the therapeutic relationship. Total honesty is emphasized and a non-judgmental therapeutic relationship is provided. This results in the adolescent not fearing reactions of disappointment if weekly personal goals are not achieved. However, since treatment is provided without cost, clients are required to respect the therapist's time. This involves calling ahead to cancel and reschedule appointments, punctual attendance of sessions, and a commitment to complete "homework" assignments.

2. *Assessment and setting of individual goals.* Since the emphasis of different therapeutic objectives is tailored to the individual, a more detailed profile of the client is required. This is accomplished through comprehensive clinical interviews (beyond intake assessment), usually taking place over the first three sessions. The initial interview consists of the completion of several instruments primarily designed to screen for gambling severity, impulsivity, conduct problems, depression, antisocial behaviors, and suicide ideation and attempts. Their responses to these measures are followed up through more in-depth diagnostic interviews over the next few sessions, and more details about the consequences associated with their gambling (i.e., academic and/or occupational status, peer and familial relationships, romantic and inter-personal relationships, legal problems, etc.) are obtained. This comprehensive evaluation allows for the therapeutic goals to be established. For example, an adolescent who presents with serious depression will not be approached in the same manner as one who does not evidence depressive symptomatology. If a client presents with a severe depression, this becomes the initial therapeutic objective while the gambling problem becomes a secondary objective. Interestingly, for many youth, once gambling has stopped depressive symptomatology actually increases as youth report that their primary

source of pleasure, excitement and enjoyment has been eliminated. It is therefore important to screen for depressive symptomatology periodically throughout the therapeutic process.

3. *Assessment of readiness to change.* An important factor influencing the therapeutic approach relates to the client's current willingness to make significant changes in his or her life. Our experience suggests that most adolescents experiencing serious gambling-related problems are reluctant to attend and are not convinced that they really want to stop their gambling completely. Rather, most state that they believe in *controlled* gambling, and hold on to this belief for some time in spite of our reluctance and experience. Some individuals seek basic information concerning pathological gambling, but remain open to the idea of making more permanent changes. Others have decided that they really must stop gambling, but are unable to do so without therapeutic assistance and support. Finally, some adolescents have made the decision to stop gambling, and do so prior to their first session but require support in maintaining their abstinence. These three examples depict adolescents in different stages of the process of change.

While there is a multiplicity of approaches taken, depending upon the individual's severity of gambling problems, underlying psychological disorders or problems, age, and risk factors, the overall therapeutic philosophy remains similar, with different weightings of therapeutic goals placed where most needed.

Goals of Therapy

Within our treatment philosophy, the overall framework is to address multiple therapeutic goals simultaneously over time, tailoring the time allocated to each goal to the client. Some require greater emphasis on psychological issues, others on their physiological impulses and others on environmental/social factors, while others require examining their motivations to change. Each client receives individualized therapeutic attention, as an outpatient, in all areas to ensure they are achieving a balanced lifestyle. This approach is consistent with DiClemente and colleagues' (2000) Transtheoretical Model of Intentional Behavior Change for adolescent gambling problems, whereby they call for a multimodal, multi-goaled therapeutic approach.

The McGill Approach adopts the following goals of therapy:

1. *Understanding the motivations for gambling.* Adolescents experiencing serious gambling problems continue gambling in the face of repeated losses and serious negative consequences as result of their need to dissociate and escape from daily stressors. Without exception, youth with gambling problems report that when gambling they enter a "different world," a world without problems and stresses. They report that while gambling, they feel invigorated, excited and alive, they are admired and respected, that time passes quickly, and all their problems are forgotten, be they psychological, financial, social, familial,

academic, work-related or legal. As such, for these individuals gambling becomes the ultimate escape. Once we understand a person's primary and secondary reasons for gambling, we can try to replace the gambling activity for another that may approximate the same benefits.

2. *Analysis of gambling episodes*. Self-awareness is essential to the process of change. By understanding the underlying factors prompting certain behaviors, individuals feel empowered to gain control over their actions and ultimately to make behavioral changes. It is important to achieve an awareness of their gambling triggers, their psychological and behavioral reactions to those triggers, as well as the consequences which ensue from this chain reaction. The following model provides an overview of the framework.

Triggers → Emotional reactions and rationalizations → Behavior → Consequences

Triggers can consist of places, people, times of day, activities, particular situations, and/or emotions. While initially many individuals are unaware of their specific triggers, they can be identified through discussions of prior experiences, as well as by examining written journals (a component within the therapeutic process). Typical triggers include handling of large sums of money, gambling advertisements or landmarks, anxiety or depressive symptomatology, interpersonal difficulties, enticement of peers, stressful situations (e.g., academic failure, exams, a loss of some kind), the need to make money quickly, or quite simply daydreaming of engaging in gambling. Possessing an awareness of his or her triggers provides a person with a better ability to deal with gambling urges.

It is also important to properly understand the times in the individual's day when they do not seem to have the urge to gamble. Identifying the circumstances, time of day, who they are with, their emotional state, activity levels, physical location, etc., is essential. Understanding the circumstances in which the urge to gamble is minimal or absent provides a set of guidelines by which the therapist can help to recreate similar situations at other times in the day.

3. *Establishing a baseline of gambling behavior and encouraging a decrease in gambling*. Once the motivations for gambling are understood and an analysis of gambling patterns completed, efforts are then focused on making changes to the adolescent's gambling behavior. In order to set goals and measure improvements, we find it useful and important initially to establish a baseline of gambling behavior. Adolescents record their gambling behaviors in terms of frequency, duration, time of day, type of gambling activity, amount of money spent, losses and wins (it is interesting to note that adolescent problem gamblers, like their adult counterpart, consistently underestimate their losses).

When establishing goals for a decrease in gambling participation, individuals are guided to establish *reasonable* goals for themselves. Some elect to target multiple factors simultaneously (e.g., frequency, duration and amount wagered), while others may focus on one aspect of their behavior. For these individuals we encourage a decrease in frequency or duration of each gambling episode versus initially focusing on amount wagered. Some meet their goals immediately, at which point we generally support decisions to maintain this decrease for several weeks while setting new goals immediately. Others struggle to meet their goals, at which point goals are generally modified.

4. *Challenging cognitive distortions.* It has been well established that individuals with gambling problems experience multiple cognitive distortions (Langer, 1975; Ladouceur and Walker, 1998). They are prone to having an illusion of control, and perceive that they can exert control over the outcome of gambling events; they underestimate the amount of money lost and over-estimate the amount won; they fail to utilize their understanding of the laws of independence of events; and they firmly believe that if they continue gambling they will likely win back all or most of the money lost ("chasing behavior"). Addressing these cognitive distortions and chasing remains an important treatment goal.

In addition to addressing the erroneous cognitions, it is important to also identify the rationalizations people make to justify their gambling behavior. These rationalizations also represent distortions of reality. An example of a rationalization for gambling is, "If I gamble now, I will be in a good mood and I will be more able to have fun at my friend's party tonight", or "By gambling now, the urge will be out of my system and I'll be more able to focus on studying for my exam". The overarching is to ensure the individual comprehends that the gambling episode will likely result in a bad mood if they are to lose money – and thus a negative mood at the party; or an inability to focus on studying for the exam.

Ultimately, the goal of addressing many of the cognitive distortions is to highlight how their thinking is self-deceptive, to provide pertinent information about randomness, and to encourage a realization that they are incapable of controlling outcomes of random events and games, payout rates, etc.

5. *Establishing the underlying causes of stress and anxiety.* In the light of empirical research and clinical findings, a primary treatment goal is to identify and treat any underlying problems that results in increased stress and/or anxiety. In general, these include one or more of the following problems: personal (e.g., low self-esteem, depression, ADHD, oppositional defiant disorders), familial, peer, academic, loss, vocational and legal. These problems are addressed through traditional therapeutic techniques, and alternative approaches to problem-solving are supported while sublimation, projection, repression and escape are discouraged.

6. *Evaluating and improving coping abilities.* The need to escape their problems usually occurs more frequently among individuals who have poor coping and adaptive skills. Using gambling or other addictive activities to deal with daily stressors, anxiety or depression represents a form of maladaptive coping. Recent research efforts have confirmed these clinical observations, where adolescents who meet the criteria for pathological gambling demonstrated poor coping skills as compared with same-age peers without a gambling problem (Nower *et al.*, 2000; Gupta *et al.*, 2004; Hardoon *et al.*, 2004; Bergevin *et al.*, 2006). A primary therapeutic goal involves building and expanding the

individual's repertoire of coping abilities. As adolescents begin to comprehend the benefits of effective coping abilities and their repertoire of coping responses expands, they are more apt to apply these skills to their daily lives. Examples of healthy coping skills include honest communication with others, seeking social support, and learning to weigh the benefits or downfalls of potential behaviors. Also included in the discussions and role-playing exercises are ways to improve social skills (e.g., learning to communicate with peers, developing healthy friendships, being considerate of others, and developing trust).

7. *Rebuilding healthy interpersonal relationships.* Common consequences of a serious gambling problem involve impaired and severed relationships with friends, peers, family members and employers. Helping the adolescent to rebuild these crucial relationships constitutes an important therapeutic goal. Often friends and family members have become alienated through lies and manipulative behaviors resulting from the individual's gambling problem, leaving unresolved negative feelings. Once a youth has been identified as being a liar or a thief, it becomes difficult to earn back the trust of others and to resume healthy relationships – something the adolescent has difficulty accepting once his or her gambling has stopped. It is important to explain to family members and friends that these deceptive actions are part of the constellation of problematic behaviors exhibited by individuals having difficulty controlling their gambling. Consequently, once the actual gambling is under control, family member and friends can anticipate being treated with more respect. Family members, peers, and significant others become extremely important support personnel to help ensure abstinence, and can take an active role in relapse prevention. We contend that youth with gambling problems will be happier and are more likely to abstain from gambling if they feel they belong to a peer group and are supported by family and friends. As a result, the occasional inclusion of family members and friends in therapy sessions can prove to be very beneficial.

8. *Restructuring free time.* Adolescents struggling to overcome a gambling problem experience more positive outcomes when not faced with large amounts of unstructured time. Some adolescents in treatment are still in school and/or have a job, and as such their free time consists mainly of evenings and weekends. Others have dropped out of school and may have a part-time job while others are not working. For these youth, structuring their time becomes paramount as they initially find it exceedingly difficult to resist urges to gamble when they are bored. With the use of a daily agenda, we help them to articulate ways of spending time with friends, family, school- or work-related activities. Other activities can involve participating in organized sports activities, engaging in a hobby, and performing volunteer work. A successful week is measured not only by meeting their goals in regard to their gambling participation, but also by how they use their free time. This approach tends to keep the young gamblers from being discouraged, and motivates them to keep trying to attain a balanced lifestyle.

9. *Fostering effective money-management skills.* These skills are typically lacking in adolescents who have a gambling problem. Therapeutic goals involve

educating them as to the value of money (as they tend to lose perspective after gambling large sums), building money management skills, and helping them to develop effective and reasonable debt-repayment plans.

10. *Relapse prevention*. Despite a lack of strong empirical evidence, our clinical work suggests that abstinence from gambling is necessary in order to prevent a relapse of pathological gambling behaviors. It should be noted that small, occasional relapses throughout the treatment process are to be expected. However, once gambling has ceased for an extended period of time (i.e., 4–6 months), an effective relapse prevention program should help these individuals to remain free of gambling. Relapse prevention includes continued access to their primary therapist, the existence of a good social support network, engagement in either school or work, the practice of a healthy lifestyle, and avoidance of powerful triggers. Gamblers representative of Nower and Blaszczynski's (2004) Pathways 2 and 3 are more apt to need additional support after the termination of therapy.

OTHER CONSIDERATIONS

While we have not elaborated upon how to treat youth with multiple addictions, it is clear that gamblers with concomitant substance abuse problems pose a greater challenge for treatment (Ladd and Petry, 2003). Youth with clinical levels of depression, high levels of impulsivity and anxiety disorders are often referred to psychiatry to simultaneously engage in pharmacological treatment while undergoing therapy. The use of serotonin re-uptake inhibitors tend to be effective in helping these youth manage their depression and anxiety, and preliminary research suggests that they may be useful in lowering the levels of impulsivity which often underlie pathological gambling behavior (Grant *et al.*, 2003, 2004).

FINAL REMARKS

While the incidence of severe gambling problems amongst youth remains relatively small, the devastating short- and long-term consequences for affected individuals, their families and friends are significant. New forms of gambling have changed the landscape considerably. There is beginning to be evidence that more youth are engaging in online gambling, and that a high percentage of these youth are experiencing gambling-related problems (Derevensky *et al.*, 2006). While some governments (in particular the US government) are seeking to restrict Internet gambling, many others throughout the world are licensing, regulating or operating sites. Simultaneously, many other land-based forms of gambling are appearing daily, with significant increases in sports wagering, and lotteries, electronic gaming machines and casinos springing up in most countries.

Gambling has become a primary form of entertainment, and one of the fastest-growing industries throughout the world. The widespread acceptance of and greater opportunities for accessing multiple venues are going to be a significant challenge. While these venues are primarily being developed for adults, the rate of gambling for young adults is amongst the highest for all age groups. Not withstanding the operators' perspective and diligence to ensure that underage gambling is prohibited, underage youth have managed to be engaged in all forms of personal and state-sponsored and regulated gambling. In North America, some of the more highly rated television shows and movies have significant gambling themes. The adventuresome *James Bond* is one persona that youth admire.

Today's youth treat the winners of the World Championship Poker series as cult heroes who are known and admired. More and more international stars are sponsoring or have major stakes in Internet companies. The appeal, thrill of winning and lure of gambling are becoming increasingly attractive. The fact that few adolescents fear getting caught gambling and are often encouraged to play poker in their homes by their parents (gambling and poker is viewed as less problematic than most other addictive behaviors) without acknowledging any of the potential warning signs for excessive gambling is particularly problematic.

The fact that the prevalence rate for youth with severe gambling problems remains higher than that for adults is of significant concern. Societal trends continue to indicate that gambling is becoming more mainstream, and youth are being influenced and exposed through traditional media such as television, mobile phones and the Internet. The complete etiology of problem gambling among youth is unclear, but we do know that parenting style, acceptability, exposure, access to gambling venues, personality traits, impulsivity and emotional disposition all interact together to place certain individuals at increased risk at a very young age. It is important, now more than ever, that youth adopt healthy attitudes towards gambling, such that they recognize it is not a way to make money, nor is it a healthy way to escape from life stressors. As one teen told us, "Gambling is an equal opportunity destroyer. I wouldn't wish my gambling problems on my worst enemy as it is way too harsh a punishment". The implementation of prevention programs, as well as providing therapeutic support for those experiencing problems, remains essential.

While somewhat similar in many ways to other adolescent high-risk behaviors, gambling problems among youth have gone relatively unnoticed. Often referred to as the hidden addiction, all individuals working with adolescents are well-advised to understand and address this issue.

REFERENCES

Baer, J., MacLean, M. and Marlatt, G. (1998). Linking etiology and treatment for adolescent substance abuse: toward a better match. In: R. Jessor (ed.), *New Perspectives on Adolescent Risk Behavior*. Cambridge, Cambridgeshire: Cambridge University Press, pp. 182–220.

Barnes, G.M., Welte, J.W., Hoffman, J.H. and Dintcheff, B.A. (2005). Shared predictors of youthful gambling, substance use and delinquency. *Psychology of Addictive Behaviors*, 19, 165–174.

Battistich, V., Schaps, E., Watson, M. and Solomon, D. (1996). Prevention effects of the Child Development Project: Early findings from an ongoing multisite demonstration trial. *Journal of Adolescent Research*, 11, 12–35.

Beck, J. (1998). 100 Years of "Just say no" versus "Just say know". Reevaluating drug education goals for the coming century. *Evaluation Review*, 22, 15–45.

Bergevin, T., Gupta, R., Derevensky, J and Kaufman, F. (2006). Adolescent gambling: understanding the role of stress and coping. *Journal of Gambling Studies*, 22, 195–208.

Blaszczynski, A.P. and Silove, D. (1995). Cognitive and behavioral therapies for pathological gambling. *Journal of Gambling Studies*, 11, 195–220.

Clarke, D. and Rossen, F. (2000). Adolescent gambling and problem gambling: a New Zealand study. *New Zealand Journal of Psychology*, 29, 10–16.

Cohen, J. (1993). Achieving a reduction in drug-related harm through education. In: N. Heather, A. Wodak, E. Nadelmann and P. O'Hare (eds), *Psychoactive Drugs and Harm Reduction: From Faith to Science*. London: Whurr Publishers Ltd, pp. 65–76.

Costello, E.J., Erkanli, A., Federman, E. and Angold, A. (1999). Development of psychiatric comorbidity with substance abuse in adolescents: effects of timing and sex. *Journal of Clinical Child Psychology*, 28, 298–311.

Custer, R.L. (1982). An overview of compulsive gambling. In: P. Carone, S. Yoles, S. Keiffer and L. Krinsky (eds), *Addictive Disorders Update*. New York, NY: Human Sciences Press, pp. 107–124.

Delfabbro, P. and Thrupp, L. (2003). The social determinants of youth gambling in South Australian adolescents. *Journal of Adolescence*, 26, 313–330.

Denning, P. and Little, J. (2001). Harm reduction in mental health: the emerging work of harm reduction psychotherapy. *Harm Reduction Communication*, 11, 7–10.

Derevensky, J. and Gupta, R. (2004). Adolescents with gambling problems: a synopsis of our current knowledge. *e-Gambling: The Electronic Journal of Gambling Issues*, 10, 119–140.

Derevensky, J. L., Gupta, R. and Della-Cioppa, G. (1996). A developmental perspective of gambling behavior in children and adolescents. *Journal of Gambling Studies*, 12, 49–66.

Derevensky, J.L., Gupta, R. and Winters, K. (2003) Prevalence rates of youth gambling problems: are the current rates inflated? *Journal of Gambling Studies*, 19, 405–425.

Derevensky, J., Gupta, R. and Magoon, M. (2004a). Adolescent problem gambling: legislative and policy decisions. *Gambling Law Review*, 8, 107–117.

Derevensky, J., Gupta, R. and Dickson, L. (2004b). Adolescent gambling problems: prevention and treatment implications. In: J.E. Grant and M.N. Potenza (eds), *Understanding and Treating Pathological Gambling*. Washington, DC: APPI Press, pp. 159–168.

Derevensky, J., Gupta, R., Dickson, L. and Deguire, A.-E. (2004c). Prevention efforts toward reducing gambling problems. In: J. Derevensky and R. Gupta (eds), *Gambling Problems in Youth: Theoretical and Applied Perspectives*. New York, NY: Kluwer Academic/Plenum Publishers, pp. 211–230.

Derevensky, J., Gupta, R. and McBride, J. (2006). "Internet gambling among youth: a cause for concern." Paper presented at the Global Remote and E-Gambling Research Institute Conference, Amsterdam, Netherlands, August.

Dickson, L., Derevensky, J.L. and Gupta, R. (2002). The prevention of youth gambling problems: a conceptual model. *Journal of Gambling Studies*, 18, 161–184.

Dickson, L., Derevensky, J.L. and Gupta, R. (2003). *Youth Gambling Problems: The Identification of Risk and Protective Factors*. Report prepared for the Ontario Problem Gambling Research Centre, Guelph, Ontario, Canada.

Dickson, L., Derevensky, J.L. and Gupta, R. (2004). Harm reduction for the prevention of youth gambling problems: lessons learned from adolescent high-risk prevention programs. *Journal of Adolescent Research*, 19, 233–263.

Dickson-Gillespie, L., Derevensky, J. and Gupta, R. (2007). Youth gambling problems: an examination of risk and protective factors. *International Gambling Studies* (in press).

DiClemente, C.C. (1999). Prevention and harm reduction for chemical dependency: a process perspective. *Clinical Psychology Review*, 19, 173–186.

DiClemente, C.C., Story, M. and Murray, K. (2000). On a roll: the process of initiation and cessation of problem gambling among adolescents. *Journal of Gambling Studies*, 16, 289–313.

Felsher, J.R. (2006). "Etiological factors related to gambling problems: the impact of childhood maltreatment and subsequent psychological stressors." Unpublished doctoral dissertation, McGill University, Montreal.

Felsher, J.R., Derevensky, J.L. and Gupta, R. (2003). Parental influences and social modelling of youth lottery participation. *Journal of Community and Applied Social Psychology*, 13, 361–377.

Galambos, N.L. and Tilton-Weaver, L.C. (1998). Multiple risk behavior in adolescents and young adults. *Health Review*, 10, 9–20.

Ghezzi, P.M., Lyons, C.A. and Dixon, M.R. (2000). Gambling in socioeconomic perspective. In: W.K. Bickel and R.E. Vuchinich (eds), *Reframing Health Behavior Change with Behavioral Economics*. New York, NY: Lawrence Erlbaum Associates, pp. 313–338.

Grant, J.E. and Kim, W.S. (2002). Parental bonding in pathological gambling disorder. *Psychiatric Quarterly*, 73, 239–247.

Grant, J.E., Kim, S.W. and Potenza, M. N. (2003). Advances in pharmacotherapy of pathological gambling disorder. *Journal of Gambling Studies*, 19, 85–109.

Grant, J.E., Chambers, A.D. and Potenza, M.N. (2004). Adolescent problem gambling: neurodevelopment and pharmacological treatment. In: J. Derevensky and R. Gupta (eds), *Gambling Problems in Youth: Theoretical and Applied Perspectives*. New York, NY: Kluwer Academic/Plenum Publishers, pp. 81–98.

Griffiths, M. (1999). Gambling technologies: prospects for problem gambling. *Journal of Gambling Studies*, 15, 265–283.

Griffiths, M. and Parke, J. (2002). The social impact of internet gambling. *Social Science Computer Review*, 20, 312–320.

Griffiths, M., Parke, A., Wood, R. and Parke, J. (2006). Internet gambling: an overview of psychological impacts. *UNLV Gaming Research and Review Journal*, 10, 27–39.

Gupta, R. and Derevensky, J. (1998a). Adolescent gambling behavior: a prevalence study and examination of the correlates associated with excessive gambling. *Journal of Gambling Studies*, 14, 319–345.

Gupta, R. and Derevensky, J. (1998b). An empirical examination of Jacobs' General Theory of Addictions: do adolescent gamblers fit the theory? *Journal of Gambling Studies*, 14, 17–49.

Gupta, R. and Derevensky, J.L. (2000). Adolescents with gambling problems: from research to treatment. *Journal of Gambling Studies*, 16, 315–342.

Gupta, R. and Derevensky, J. (2004). A treatment approach for adolescents with gambling problems. In: J. Derevensky and R. Gupta (eds), *Gambling Problems in Youth: Theoretical and Applied Perspectives*. New York, NY: Kluwer Academic/Plenum Publishers, pp. 165–188.

Gupta, R., Derevensky, J. and Marget, N. (2004). Coping strategies employed by adolescents with gambling problems. *Child and Adolescent Mental Health*, 9(3), 115–120.

Gupta, R., Derevensky, J. and Ellenbogen, S. (2006). Personality characteristics and risk-taking tendencies among adolescent gamblers. *Canadian Journal of Behavioral Science*, 38, 201–213.

Hardoon, K., Gupta, R. and Derevensky, J. (2004). Psychosocial variables associated with adolescent gambling: a model for problem gambling. *Psychology of Addictive Behaviors*, 18(2), 170–179.

Heather, N., Wodak, A., Nadelmann, E. and O'Hare, P. (1993). *Psychoactive Drugs and Harm Reduction: From Faith to Science*. London: Whurr Publishers Ltd.

Jacobs, D.F. (1987). A general theory of addictions: application to treatment and rehabilitation planning for pathological gamblers. In: T. Galski (ed.), *The Handbook of Pathological Gambling*. Springfield, IL: Charles C. Thomas, pp. 169–194.

Jacobs, D.F. (2000). Juvenile gambling in North America: an analysis of long term trends and future prospects. *Journal of Gambling Studies*, 16, 119–152.

Jacobs, D.F. (2004). Youth gambling in North America: long-term trends and future prospects. In: J. Derevensky and R. Gupta (eds), *Gambling Problems in Youth: Theoretical and Applied Perspectives*. New York, NY: Kluwer Academic/Plenum Publishers, pp. 1–26.

Jessor, R. (1998) (ed.). *New Perspectives on Adolescent Risk Behavior*. Cambridge, Cambridgeshire: Cambridge University Press.

Jessor, R., van den Bos, J., Vanderryn, J. *et al.* (1995). Protective factors in adolescent problem behavior: moderator effects and developmental change. *Developmental Psychology*, 31, 923–933.

Korn, D. and Shaffer, H. (1999). Gambling and the health of the public: adopting a public health perspective. *Journal of Gambling Studies*, 15, 289–365.

Ladd, G.T. and Petry, N.M. (2003). A comparison of pathological gamblers with and without substance abuse treatment histories. *Experimental and Clinical Psychopharmacology*, 11, 202–209.

Ladouceur, R. and Walker, M. (1998). Cognitive approach to understanding and treating pathological gambling. In: A.S. Bellack and M. Hersen (eds), *Comprehensive Clinical Psychology*, New York, NY: Pergamon, 588–601.

Ladouceur, R., Dubé, D. and Bujold, A. (1994a). Gambling among primary school students. *Journal of Gambling Studies*, 10, 363–370.

Ladouceur, R., Boisvert, J-M. and Dumont, J. (1994b). Cognitive-behavioral treatment for adolescent pathological gamblers. *Behavior Modification*,.18, 230–242.

Langer, E.J. (1975). The illusion of control. *Journal of Personality and Social Psychology*, 32, 311–321.

Langhinrichsen-Rohling, J., Rohde, P., Seeley, J. and Rohling, M. (2004). Individual, family and peer correlates of adolescent gambling. *Journal of Gambling Studies*. 20, 23–46.

Livingston, J. (1974). Compulsive gamblers: observations on action and abstinence. New York, NY: Harper and Row.

Loeber, R., Farrington, D., Stouthamer-Loeber, M. and van Kammen, W. (1998). Multiple risk factors for multi-problem boys: co-occurrence of delinquency, substance use, attention deficit, conduct problems, physical aggression, covert behavior, depressed mood and shy/withdrawn behavior. In: R. Jessor (ed.), *New Perspectives on Adolescent Risk Behavior*. Cambridge, Cambridgeshire: Cambridge University Press, pp. 90–149.

Magoon, M. and Ingersoll, G. (2006). Parental modeling, attachment and supervision as moderators of adolescent gambling. *Journal of Gambling Studies*, 22, 1–22.

Magoon, M., Gupta, R. and Derevensky, J. (2005). Juvenile delinquency and adolescent gambling: implications for the juvenile justice system. *Criminal Justice and Behavior*, 32, 690–713.

Mangham, C. (2001). Harm reduction or reducing harm? *Canadian Medical Association Journal*, 164, 173.

Messerlian, C., Derevensky, J. and Gupta, R. (2004). A public health perspective for youth gambling: a prevention and harm minimization framework. *International Gambling Studies*, 4, 147–160.

National Research Council (1999). *Pathological Gambling: A Critical Review*. Washington, DC: National Academy Press.

Nower, L. and Blaszczynski, A. (2004). The pathways model as harm minimization for youth gamblers in educational settings. *Child and Adolescent Social Work Journal*, 21(1), 25–45.

Nower, L.M., Gupta, R. and Derevensky, J. (2000). "Youth gamblers and substance abusers: a comparison of stress-coping styles and risk taking behavior of two addicted adolescent populations." Paper presented at the 11th International Conference on Gambling and Risk-Taking, Las Vegas, June.

Pontiroli, A.E. (2004). Type 2 diabetes mellitus is becoming the most common type of diabetes in school children. *Acta Diabetologica*. 41(3), 85–90.

Potenza, M.N., Steinberg, M.A., McLaughlin, S.D. *et al.* (2000). Illegal behaviors in problem gambling: analysis of data from a gambling helpline. *Journal of the American Academy of Psychiatry and the Law*. 28(4), 389–403.

Productivity Commission (1999). *Australia's Gambling Industries*, Report No. 10. Canberra: AusInfo (available at http://www.pc.gov.au/).

Riley, D., Sawka, E., Conley, P. *et al.* (1999). Harm reduction: Concepts and practice – a policy discussion paper. *Substance Use and Misuse*, 34, 9–24.

Shaffer, H.J. and Hall, M.N. (1996). Estimating the prevalence of adolescent gambling disorders: a quantitative synthesis and guide toward standard gambling nomenclature. *Journal of Gambling Studies*, 12, 193–214.

Shaffer, H.J. and Hall, M.N. (2001). Updating and refining prevalence estimates of disordered gambling behavior in the United States and Canada. *Canadian Journal of Public Health*, 92, 168–172.

Ste-Marie, C. (2006). "Parenting styles and family environment: influences on youth problem gambling." Unpublished doctoral dissertation, McGill University, Montreal.

Stettler N., Signer T.M. and Suter, P.M. (2004). Electronic games and environmental factors associated with childhood obesity in Switzerland. *Obesity Research*, 12, 896–903.

Stinchfield, R. and Winters, K.C. (1997). Measuring change in adolescent drug misuse with the Personal Experience Inventory (PEI). *Substance Use and Misuse*, 32(1), 63–76.

Toneatto, T. and Ladouceur, R. (2003). Treatment of pathological gambling: a critical review of the literature. *Psychology of Addictive Behaviors*, 17, 284–292.

Thombs, D. and Briddick, W. (2000). Readiness to change among at-risk Greek student drinkers. *Journal of College Student Development*, 41, 313–322.

Vachon, J., Vitaro, F., Wanner, B. and Tremblay, R.E. (2004). Adolescent gambling: relationships with parent gambling and parenting practices. *Psychology of Addictive Behaviors*, 18(4), 398–401.

Vandewater, E.A., Shim, M.S. and Caplovitz, A.G. (2004). Linking obesity and activity level with children's television and video game use. *Journal of Adolescence*, 27(1), 71–85.

Vitaro, F., Wanner, B., Ladouceur, R. *et al.* (2004). Trajectories of gambling during adolescence. *Journal of Gambling Studies*, 20(1), 47–69.

Winters, K.C. and Anderson, N. (2000). Gambling involvement and drug use among adolescents. *Journal of Gambling Studies*, 16(2–3), 175–198.

Wynne, H.J., Smith, G.J. and Jacobs, D.F. (1996). *Adolescent Gambling and Problem Gambling in Alberta*. Alberta: Alberta Alcohol and Drug Abuse Commission.

8

INTERNET AND VIDEO-GAME ADDICTION

MARK GRIFFITHS

The popularity of video-game and Internet use as a leisure phenomenon has led to them becoming an ever-increasing part of many people's lives. Coupled with this, there is a growing number of reports in the media about excessive use of both the Internet and video-games. Although the concept of an addiction to the Internet or video-games appears to have its supporters in the media, there is much skepticism amongst the academic community – not least among those working in the field of addiction research. It is not hard to understand such attitudes. For many, the concept of Internet or video-game addiction seems far-fetched, particularly if their concepts and definitions of addiction involve the taking of drugs. Despite the predominance of drug-based definitions of addiction, there is now a growing movement which views a number of behaviors as potentially addictive, including many behaviors which do not involve the ingestion of a psychoactive drug (e.g., gambling, computer game playing, exercise, sex, Internet use) (Griffiths, 2005a). Such diversity has led to new all-encompassing definitions of what constitutes addictive behavior.

DEFINITION

This author has consistently argued that excessive gambling is no different from (say) alcoholism or heroin addiction in terms of the core components of addiction (Griffiths, 2007). If it can be shown that a behavior such as excessive gambling can be a *bona fide* addiction, then there is a precedent that any behavior which can provide continuous rewards in the absence of a psychoactive substance can be potentially addictive (i.e., a behavioral as opposed to a chemical addiction). Such a precedent "opens the floodgates" for other excessive behaviors to be theoretically considered as potential addictions (such as Internet and video-game use) (Griffiths, 2005a).

It has been alleged for many years that social pathologies exist among excessive Internet users and video-game players. For instance, Soper and Miller (1983) claimed "video-game addiction" was like any other behavioral addiction, and consisted of a compulsive behavioral involvement, a lack of interest in other activities, association mainly with other addicts, and physical and mental symptoms when attempting to stop the behavior (e.g., the "shakes"). Young (1998) argued a similar case for excessive Internet users. Such addictions have been termed "technological addictions" (Griffiths, 1995a, 1996a), and have been operationally defined as non-chemical (behavioral) addictions that involve excessive human–machine interaction. They can either be passive (e.g., television), or active (e.g., video-games), and usually contain inducing and reinforcing features which may contribute to the promotion of addictive tendencies (Griffiths, 1995a). Technological addictions can thus be viewed as a subset of behavioral addictions (Marks, 1990), and feature core components of addiction first outlined by Brown (1993) and modified by Griffiths (1996b, 2005a) – i.e., salience, mood modification, tolerance, withdrawal, conflict and relapse.

Research into the area of video-game and Internet addiction needs to be underpinned by three fundamental questions:

1. What is addiction?
2. Does Internet or video-game addiction actually exist?
3. If Internet and video-game addiction exists, what are people actually addicted to?

The first question continues to be much debated, both amongst psychologists within the field of addiction research and among those working in other disciplines. For many years, this author has operationally defined addictive behavior as any behavior that features all the core components of addiction. It is this author's contention that any behavior (e.g., video-game playing, Internet use) that fulfils these six criteria is therefore operationally defined as an addiction. In the case of Internet or video-game addiction, criteria would be:

1. *Salience*. This occurs when Internet use or video-game play becomes the most important activity in a person's life, dominating their thinking (preoccupations and cognitive distortions), feelings (cravings) and behavior (deterioration of socialized behavior). For instance, even if not actually on the Internet or playing on a video-game, the individual will be thinking about the next time that he or she will be.

2. *Mood modification*. This refers to the subjective experiences that people report as a consequence of engaging in Internet use or video-game play, and can

be seen as a coping strategy (i.e., they experience an arousing "buzz" or a "high" or, paradoxically, a tranquilizing feel of "escape" or "numbing").

3. *Tolerance*. This is the process whereby increasing amounts of Internet use or video-game play are required to achieve the former mood-modifying effects. This basically means that people gradually build up the amount of the time they spend engaged in Internet use or video-gaming.

4. *Withdrawal symptoms*. These are the unpleasant feeling states and/or physical effects that occur when Internet use or video-game play is discontinued or suddenly reduced (e.g., the shakes, moodiness, irritability).

5. *Conflict*. This refers to the conflicts between the Internet user or video-game player and those around them (interpersonal conflict), conflicts with other activities (job, schoolwork, social life, hobbies and interests) or from within the individual themselves (intrapsychic conflict and/or subjective feelings of loss of control) which are concerned with spending too much time engaged in Internet use or video-game play.

6. *Relapse*. This is the tendency for repeated reversions to earlier patterns of Internet use or video-game play, and for even the most extreme patterns typical of the height of excessive Internet use or video-game play to be quickly restored after periods of abstinence or control.

Having operationally defined addiction, it is this author's belief that, in answer to the second question, Internet and video-game addictions do indeed exist, but that they affect only a very small minority of users and players (including adolescents). There appear to be many people who use the Internet or play video-games excessively but are not addicted as measured by these (or any other) criteria. The third question is perhaps the most interesting and the most important when it comes to researching this field. What are people actually addicted to when they use the Internet or play video-games excessively? Is it the interactive medium of playing? Is it aspects of its specific style (i.e., an anonymous and disinhibiting activity)? Is it the specific types of games (aggressive games, strategy games, etc.)? This has led to much debate amongst those working in this field. Research being carried out into Internet addiction may lead to insights regarding video-game addiction, and *vice versa*. For instance, Young (1999) has claimed that Internet addiction is a broad term covering a wide variety of behaviors and impulse control problems. This is categorized by five specific subtypes:

1. Cybersexual addiction: compulsive use of adult websites for cybersex and cyberporn.
2. Cyber-relationship addiction: over-involvement in online relationships
3. Net compulsions: obsessive online gambling, shopping or day-trading
4. Information overload: compulsive web surfing or database searches
5. Computer addiction: obsessive computer game playing (e.g., *Doom*, *Myst*, *Solitaire*, etc.).

In reply to Young, this author has argued that many of these excessive Internet users are not "Internet addicts" but just use the Internet excessively as a medium to fuel other addictions (Griffiths, 1999, 2000a). Put very simply, gambling addicts or a video-game addicts who engage in their chosen behavior online are not addicted to the Internet; the Internet is just the place where they engage in the behavior. However, in contrast to this, there are case-study reports of individuals (including adolescents) who appear to be addicted to the Internet itself (e.g., Griffiths, 1996a, 1998, 2000b; Young, 1998). These are usually people (and very often adolescents in their late teenage years) who use Internet chat rooms or play fantasy role-playing games – activities that they would not engage in except on the Internet itself. These individuals to some extent are engaged in text-based virtual realities, and take on other social personas and social identities as a way of making them feel good about themselves. In such cases, the Internet may provide an alternative reality to users and allow them feelings of immersion and anonymity that may lead to an altered state of consciousness. This in itself may be highly psychologically and/or physiologically rewarding. Obviously, for those playing online computer games (theoretically a combination of both Internet use and video-game play) these speculations may provide insights into the potentially addictive nature of video-games for those playing in this medium.

VIDEO-GAME ADDICTION: A BRIEF OVERVIEW

Research has shown that males are the most excessive users of video-games (Kaplan, 1983; Griffiths, 1991, 1993, 1997a), and this mirrors many other youth addictions (Griffiths, 1995b). Reasons why males play video-games significantly more than females have been generally lacking, but explanations may include the following:

- The content of the game – most video-games have traditionally contained masculine images (Braun *et al.*, 1986), although this is changing with the introduction of strong female lead characters like Lara Croft. Furthermore, video-games are designed by males for males (Gutman, 1982), although some "female" forms of game hardware and software have been introduced (e.g., *Ms Pac-man*, Nintendo's *Game Girl*). However, these are often seen as patronizing by female gamers.
- Socialization – women are not encouraged to express aggression in public, and feel uncomfortable with games of combat or war (Surrey, 1982). It could be that the male domination of video-games is due more to its social rules and socialization factors (e.g., arcade atmosphere and subculture) than to the games themselves.
- Sex differences – males, on average, have better visual and spatial skills (for example, hand–eye co-ordination), particularly depth perception (Maccoby and Jacklin, 1974), which are essential to good game playing (Keisler *et al.*, 1983). Therefore, the average male player is more likely to score higher than the average female player and thus to persist in playing.

It is also apparent that there are gender differences between the types of games played. For example, Griffiths and Hunt (1995) reported that males preferred "beat 'em ups" and "puzzlers" and females preferred "platform" games. Another study by Griffiths (1997b) reported that males play more "beat 'em ups" and sport simulations, and that females play more "puzzlers" and "platformers". Although there are some slight differences in these findings, they do seem to suggest that males prefer the more aggressive type of games. In fact, Griffiths (1997b) went on to report that 42 percent of boys' favorite games were violent, as opposed to only 9 percent of the girls'. This was echoed by Parsons (1995), who reported that females prefer less aggressive games than males, while males prefer violence.

Insights into the potentially addictive nature of video-games have come from research into slot-machine gaming. For instance, both video-game machines and slot machines may be considered under the generic label of "amusement machines" (Griffiths, 1991). The main difference between video-game machines and slot machines are that video-games are (usually) played to accumulate as many points as possible, whereas slot machines are played (i.e., gambled upon) to accumulate money. It has been suggested that playing a video-game could be considered to be a non-financial form of gambling (Griffiths, 1991). Both types of machine (in the case of arcade games) require insertion of a coin to play, although the playing time on a slot machine is usually much less than on a video-game machine. This is because on video-games the outcome is almost solely due to skill, whereas on slot machines the outcome is more likely to be a product of chance. However, the general playing philosophy of both slot-machine players and (arcade) video-game players is to stay on the machine for as long as possible, using the least amount of money (Griffiths, 1990a, 1990b) – playing *with* money rather than *for* it.

Besides the generic labeling, their geographical juxtaposition and the philosophy for playing, it could be argued that, on both psychological and behavioral levels, slot-machine gambling and video-game playing share many similarities (e.g., similar demographic differences such as age and gender breakdown, similar reinforcement schedules, similar potential for "near miss" opportunities, similar structural characteristics involving the use of light and sound effects, similarities in skill perception, similarities in the effects of excessive play, etc.) (Griffiths, 2005b). The most probable reason the two forms have rarely been seen as conceptually similar is because video-game playing does not involve the winning of money (or something of financial value), and therefore cannot be classed as a form of gambling. However, the next generation of slot machines is starting to use video-game graphics and technology (Griffiths, 2006). While many of these relate to traditional gambling games (e.g., roulette, poker, blackjack, etc.), there are plans for developing video gambling games in which people would win money based on their game scores. This obviously gives an idea of the direction in which slot machines and the gaming industry are heading.

Furthermore, there is a growing number of researchers who suggest that arcade video-games share some common ground with slot (gambling) machines, including the potential for dependency (see, for example, Griffiths, 1991, 1993, 1997a, 2005b; Brown and Robertson, 1992; Fisher, 1994; Gupta and Derevensky, 1997; Wood *et al.*, 2004). As Fisher and Griffiths (1995) pointed out, arcade video-games and slot machines share some important structural characteristics, these being:

- The requirement for response to stimuli which are predictable and governed by the software loop
- The requirement for total concentration and hand–eye coordination
- A rapid span of play, negotiable to some extent by the skill of the player (more marked in video-games)
- The provision of aural and visual rewards for a winning move (e.g., flashing lights, electronic jingles)
- The provision of an incremental reward for a winning move (points or cash), which reinforces "correct" behavior
- Digitally displayed scores of "correct" behavior (in the form of points or cash accumulated)
- The opportunity for peer-group attention and approval through competition.

As with excessive slot-machine playing, excessive video-game playing partly comes about by the partial reinforcement effect (PRE) (Wanner, 1982). This is a critical psychological ingredient of video-game addiction whereby the reinforcement is intermittent – i.e., people keep responding in the absence of reinforcement, hoping that another reward is just around the corner. Knowledge about the PRE gives the video-game designer an edge in designing appealing games. Magnitude of reinforcement is also important. Large rewards lead to a fast response and greater resistance to extinction – in short, to more "addiction". Instant reinforcement is also satisfying. Video-games rely on multiple reinforcements (i.e., the "kitchen sink" approach) in that different features might be differently rewarding to different people. Success on video-games comes from a variety of sources, and the reinforcement might be intrinsic (e.g., improving your highest score, beating your friend's high score, getting your name on the "hall of fame", mastering the machine) or extrinsic (e.g., peer admiration).

To date, there has been very little research directly investigating video-game addiction; furthermore, almost all of it has concentrated on adolescents only. Shotton (1989) carried out a study specifically on "computer addiction", using a sample of 127 people (half being children, half adult; 96% male) who had been self-reportedly "hooked" on home video-games for at least 5 years. Of these, 75 were measured against two control groups, and it was reported that the computer-dependent individuals were highly intelligent, motivated and achieving people, but were often misunderstood. After a 5-year follow-up, Shotton found that the younger cohort had done well educationally, gone on to university and then into high-ranking jobs. However, Shotton's research was carried out with people who were familiar with the older generation of video-games that were popular in the earlier part of the 1980s. Video-games from the 1990s onwards may in some way be more psychologically rewarding than the games of a decade ago in that they require more complex skills and improved dexterity, and feature socially relevant topics and better graphics. Anecdotal accounts of greater psychological rewards could mean that the newer games are more "addiction inducing", although such an assertion needs empirical backing.

A questionnaire study undertaken by Griffiths and Hunt (1995, 1998) with almost 400 adolescents (12–16 years of age) attempted to establish the level of "dependence" using a scale adapted from the DSM-III-R criteria for pathological gambling (American Psychiatric Association, 1987). Eight questions relating to the DSM-III-R criteria were adapted for computer game playing, and examined a number of addiction components, including:

- Salience ("Do you frequently play most days?")
- Tolerance ("Do you frequently play for longer periods of time?")
- Mood modification ("Do you play for excitement or a 'buzz'?")
- Chasing ("Do you play to beat your personal high score?")
- Relapse ("Do you make repeated efforts to stop or decrease playing?")
- Withdrawal ("Do you become restless if you cannot play?")
- Conflict ("Do you play instead of attending to school related activities?", "Do you sacrifice social activities to play?")

A cut-off point of four was assumed to indicate a participant was playing at dependent (i.e., addictive) levels at the time of the study. Scores on the adapted DSM-III-R scale indicated that 62 players (19.9%) were dependent on computer games (i.e., scored four or more on the scale). Furthermore, 7 percent of the sample claimed they played for over 30 hours a week. The dependence score correlated with gender – significantly more males than females were dependent – and with how often individuals played computer games, the mean session length playing time, and the longest single-session playing time. Further analysis indicated that those who were dependent were significantly more likely to have started playing computer games to impress friends, because there was nothing else to do, for a challenge, and to meet friends. Dependent players were also significantly more likely to report aggressive feelings as a direct result of their computer game playing. However, there are several problems with the findings of this study.

Although the criteria for the scale were all based on the different components of dependence common to other addictive behaviors (salience, euphoria, tolerance, withdrawal, conflict, etc.), it could be that these are less relevant for excessive computer game playing. There was also an assumption made that computer game playing was similar to gambling in terms of the consequences of excessive behavior. Alternative explanations could be that excessive computer game playing cannot be conceptualized as an addiction at all, or that the scale is more a measure of preoccupation rather than dependence. A part replication study found very similar results (Griffiths, 1997b). It is also worth noting that 7 percent of the sample in the study by Griffiths and Hunt (1995, 1998) claimed to play computer games for over 30 hours a week. Similar findings have also been reported in other studies (see, for example, Fisher, 1994; Parsons, 1995; Phillips *et al.*, 1995; Griffiths, 1997b; Tejeiro-Delguero and Moran, 2002). However, it is worth noting that Charlton's (2002) factor analytic study of computer addiction showed a blurring of distinction between non-pathological high engagement and addiction. Therefore, it could alternatively be the case that there are very excessive gamers who show few negative consequences in their life.

There is no doubt that, for a minority of adolescents, video-games can take up considerable time. Whether these studies suggest video-games are truly addictive is perhaps not the most salient issue here. The question to ask is, what does the longitudinal effect of any activity (not just video-game playing) that takes up 30 hours of leisure time a week have on the educational and social development of children and adolescents? At present we do not know the answer. However, it could be argued any child who engages in any activity excessively (whether defined as an addiction or not) every day over a number of years from a young age will have his or her social and/or educational development negatively affected in some way.

There is also the question raised earlier: if video-games are addictive, then what is the addictive process? One potential way of answering this question is to produce possible theoretical accounts of video-game addiction and test the hypotheses empirically. McIlwraith (1990) proposed four theoretical models of television addiction in the popular and psychological literature that would seem good models to test the boundaries of video-game addiction. Substituting "video-game" for "television" in McIlwraith's account would leave the four explanations as thus:

1. That video-game addiction is a function of the video-game's effects on imagination and fantasy life – i.e., people who play video-games to excess have a poor imagination
2. That video-game addiction is a function of the video-game's effects on arousal level – i.e., people who play video-games to excess either do so for its arousing or tranquillizing effects
3. That video-game addiction is a manifestation of oral, dependent or addictive personality – i.e., people who play video-games to excess do so due to their inner personality as opposed to the external source of the addiction
4. That video-game addiction is a distinct pattern of uses and gratifications associated with the video-game medium – i.e., people who play video-games to excess enjoy the physical act of playing, or play only when they are bored, etc.

Few of these explanations for home video-game playing have been empirically studied, although some empirical evidence by Griffiths and Dancaster (1995) and evidence regarding arcade video-game addiction (Fisher, 1994) appears to support the second theoretical orientation – i.e., that video-game addiction is a function of the video-game's effects on arousal level. Research by Koepp *et al.* (1998) demonstrated dopaminergic neurotransmission during the playing of a video-game. This may have implications for understanding the underlying addictive process in the playing of such games. If it is accepted that video-game playing can be addictive, then it is appropriate to look for the neural foundation of such behavior. Over the last decade, the role of the mesotelencephalic (nucleus accumbens) dopaminergic system that is constructed as a circuit between the midbrain and the forebrain (within the medial forebrain bundle) has been widely accepted as the neural substrate of reinforcement (Julien, 1995).

In addition to neurochemical research, there are further reports of behavioral signs of video-game dependency among adolescents. Dependency signs reported include stealing money to play arcade games or to buy new games cartridges (Klein, 1984; Keepers, 1990; Griffiths and Hunt, 1995, 1998), truanting from school to play (Keepers, 1990; Griffiths and Hunt, 1998), not doing homework/getting bad marks at school (Phillips *et al.*, 1995; Griffiths and Hunt, 1998), sacrificing social activities to play (Egli and Meyers, 1984; Griffiths and Hunt, 1998), irritability and annoyance if unable to play (Rutkowska and Carlton, 1994; Griffiths and Hunt, 1998), and playing longer than intended/time loss (Egli and Meyers, 1984; Griffiths and Hunt, 1998; Wood and Griffiths, 2007; Wood *et al.*, 2007). There is no doubt that, for a minority of people (particularly adolescents), video-games can take up considerable time, and to all intents and purposes they are "addicted" to them. However, the prevalence of such an addiction is still a matter of great controversy, as is the mechanism by which people may become addicted. This is one area where research appears to be much needed. The need to establish the incidence and prevalence of clinically significant problems associated with video-game addiction is of paramount importance. There is no doubt that clearer operational definitions are required if this is to be achieved.

It has been argued that the only way of determining whether non-chemical (i.e., behavioral) addictions (such as video-game addiction) are addictive in a non-metaphorical sense is to compare them against clinical criteria for other established drug-ingested addictions. However, most people researching in the field have failed to do this, which has perpetuated the skepticism shown in many quarters of the addiction-research community. The main problems with the addiction criteria suggested by most researchers in the field is that the measures used (i) have no measure of severity, (ii) have no temporal dimension, (iii) have a tendency to over-estimate the prevalence of problems, and (iv) take no account of the context of video-game use. There are also concerns about the sampling methods employed. As a consequence, none the surveys to date conclusively show that video-game addiction exists or is problematic to anyone but a small minority. At best, they indicate that video-game addiction may be prevalent in a significant minority of individuals (usually adolescents), but that more research using validated survey instruments and other techniques (e.g., in-depth qualitative interviews) are required. Case studies of excessive video-game players may provide better evidence of whether video-game addiction exists by the fact that the data collected are much more detailed. Even if just one case study could be located, it would indicate that video-game addiction actually does exist – even if it were unrepresentative. There are case-study accounts in the literature which appear to show that excessive video-game players display many signs of addiction (see, for example, Keepers, 1992) including those that play online (Griffiths, 2000b; Griffiths *et al.*, 2003, 2004a, 2004b). These case studies tend to show that the video-games are used to counteract other deficiencies and underlying problems in a person's life (e.g., relationships, lack of friends, dissatisfaction with physical appearance, disability, coping, etc.). Again, further work of a more in-depth qualitative nature is needed to confirm the existence of video-game addiction.

There has been speculation that online gaming may be more problematic and/or addictive than offline (stand alone) games (Griffiths *et al.*, 2004a). For instance, Grüsser and colleagues (2007) investigated the addictive potential of online video-gaming. A self-selected sample comprising 7069 gamers, mostly male (94%), with an average age of 21 years, answered two online questionnaires. One in nine of them (840 gamers) fulfilled at least three diagnostic criteria of addiction concerning their gaming behavior. Addictive signs were modeled on key symptoms of the dependence syndrome outlined by the World Health Organization, and included craving, tolerance, withdrawal symptoms, loss of control, neglect of other activities, and other negative consequences. Those gamers who displayed at least three addictive signs were then compared with the remaining gamers. The "addicted" gamers predictably played for significantly longer daily periods of time. They were also significantly more likely to report withdrawal symptoms and craving. Although these gamers show some signs of addiction normally found in other more traditional addictions, the results did not conclusively show that the gamers are genuinely addicted. Many gamers play excessively and display few negative consequences. However, the 24-hours-a-day never-ending online games may provide a potentially addictive medium for those with a predisposition to excessive game playing.

Other indirect evidence of addictive and excessive play comes from the many health consequences that have been reported in the literature. The risk of epileptic seizures while playing video-games in photosensitive individuals (usually adolescents) with epilepsy is well established (see, for example, Maeda *et al.*, 1990; Graf *et al.*, 1994; Harding and Jeavons, 1994; Quirk *et al.*, 1995; Millett *et al.*, 1997). Graf *et al.* (1994) reported that seizures are most likely to occur during rapid scene changes, and with high intensity repetitive and flickering patterns. However, for many individuals, seizures during play will represent a chance occurrence without a causal link. Furthermore, there appears to be little direct link to excessive and/or addictive play, as occasional players appear to be just as susceptible.

In addition to photosensitive epilepsy, the medical profession has, for over 25 years, voiced a number of concerns about excessive video-game playing. Back in the early 1980s, rheumatologists described cases of "*Pac-man's* Elbow" and "*Space Invaders'* Revenge", in which players suffered skin, joint and muscle problems from repeated button-hitting and joystick-pushing on the game machines (Loftus and Loftus, 1983). Early research by Loftus and Loftus indicated that two-thirds of (arcade) video-game players examined complained of blisters, calluses, sore tendons, and numbness of fingers, hands and elbows, directly as a result of their playing. There have been a whole host of case studies in the medical literature reporting some of the adverse effects of playing video-games (see Griffiths, 2003a, 2005c). These have included auditory hallucinations (Spence, 1993), enuresis (Schink, 1991), encoprisis (Corkery, 1990), wrist pain (McCowan, 1981), neck pain (Miller, 1991), elbow pain (Miller, 1991), tenosynovitis – also called "nintendinitis" – (Reinstein, 1983; Brasington, 1990; Casanova and Casanova, 1991; Siegal, 1991), hand–arm vibration syndrome (Cleary *et al.*, 2002), repetitive strain injuries (Mirman and Bonian, 1992), and peripheral neuropathy (Friedland and St John, 1984). Admittedly, some of these adverse effects are quite rare, and "treatment" simply involved non-playing of the games in question. In fact, in the cases involving enuresis and encoprisis, the children were so engaged in the games that they did not want to go to the lavatory. In these particular cases, they were simply taught how to use the game's "pause" button!

Other negative aspects of video-game playing that have been reported include the belief that it is socially isolating, causes social anxiety and prevents children from developing social skills (see, for example, Zimbardo, 1982; Lo *et al.*, 2005). For instance, Selnow (1984) reported that some video-game players use the machine as "electronic friends". However, this does not necessarily mean that players play the machines instead of forming human friendships and interacting with their peer groups. Further to this, Colwell *et al.* (1995) reported that heavy video-game players see friends more often outside school (and have a need for friends) more than non-heavy players. Rutkowska and Carlton (1994) reported there was no difference in "sociability" between high- and low-frequency players, and reported that games foster friendship. This finding was echoed by Phillips and colleagues (1995), who found no difference in social interactions between players and non-players.

It has also been suggested that video-game playing may prevent children and adolescents from participating in more educational or sporting pursuits (Egli and Meyers, 1984; Professional Association of Teachers, 1994). In this context, it is worth noting that childhood obesity has also been linked with video-games. For instance, Shimai and colleagues (1993) found that obesity was correlated with long periods of video-game playing in Japanese children. This finding has also been found in young French children (Deheger *et al.*, 1997) and US children (Vandewater *et al.*, 2004). In the UK, Johnson and Hackett (1997) reported that there was an inverse relationship between physical activity and playing video-games in schoolgirls.

TREATMENT

To date there have been very few accounts of treating video-game addiction, although there are many overviews providing advice to parents (see, for example, Griffiths, 2002, 2003b). Kuczmierczyk and colleagues (1987) reported the case of an 18-year-old college student who had been playing video-games for 3–4 hours a day at an average cost of $5 a day over a 5-month period. They assumed that compulsive video-game playing was conceptually similar to pathological gambling, and used a cognitive-behavioral modification approach in their treatment. Using a combination of self-monitoring, GSR biofeedback assisted relaxation training, *in vivo* exposure and response prevention, a 90 percent reduction of playing was observed and continued at 6- and 12-month follow-up. In addition, the patient reported a more satisfying interpersonal life, had developed an interest in the martial arts, and was significantly less anxious and withdrawn.

The only other reported case of treating a video-game addict was that of Keepers (1990). A 12-year-old boy was brought in by his mother for psychiatric help because he had been playing video-games for 4–5 hours a day at an average cost of $30–50 a day over a 6-month period. The amount was far beyond the boy's means, and he had been stealing and truanting from school in order to play. Keepers reported that the boy was physically abused by his father (as was the mother), and was placed in a residential treatment centre and given family therapy. During therapy, the boy remained reluctant to discuss his home situation or his parents. In an effort to uncover some of his feelings, the boy was asked to design his own video-game. Using video-games as a vehicle for communication, the boy was gradually able to talk about his fear of his father and his feelings of helplessness. Family therapy was again undertaken, with the eventual outcome of parental separation and return of the boy to his mother. At 6-month follow-up, no recurrence of the boy's difficulty was noted. Keepers also considered his patient's behavior to be reminiscent of pathological gambling.

What is clear from the case studies displaying the more negative consequences of playing is that they all involved people who were excessive users of video-games. From prevalence studies in this area, there is little evidence of serious acute adverse effects on health from moderate play. Adverse effects are likely to be relatively minor and temporary, resolving spontaneously with decreased frequency of play, or to affect only a small subgroup of players. Excessive players are the most at risk of developing health problems, although more research appears to be much needed. The need to establish the incidence and prevalence of clinically significant problems associated with video-game play is of paramount importance. There is also no doubt that clearer operational definitions are required if this is to be achieved. Taking all factors and variables into account, and considering the prevalence of play, the evidence of serious adverse effects on health is rare. An overview of the available literature appears to indicate that adverse effects are likely to affect only a very small subgroup of players, and that frequent players are the most at risk of developing health problems. Those that it does affect will experience subtle, relatively minor and temporary effects that resolve spontaneously with decreased frequency of play.

INTERNET ADDICTION: A BRIEF OVERVIEW

Unlike the research on video-game play, the vast majority of research on excessive Internet use has concentrated on undergraduate students and other adult populations. The extent to which excessive Internet use is a problem in adolescence thus remains somewhat speculative. As noted above, this author has argued (Griffiths, 2000a) that many excessive Internet users are not "Internet addicts", but just use the Internet excessively as a medium to fuel other addictions. Therefore, there is a need to distinguish between addictions *to* the Internet and addictions *on* the Internet. We will return to this later in the chapter. As we shall see, there have been increasing numbers of academic papers about excessive use of the Internet. These can roughly be divided into five categories:

1. Survey studies that compare excessive Internet users with non-excessive users
2. Survey studies that have examined groups that are vulnerable to excessive Internet use, most notably students
3. Studies that examine the psychometric properties of excessive Internet use
4. Case studies of excessive Internet users and treatment case studies
5. Correlational studies examining the relationship of excessive Internet use with other behaviors (e.g., psychiatric problems, depression, self-esteem, etc.).

Therefore, each of the areas outlined above will be briefly reviewed in turn, although it must be reiterated that very few of these studies have specifically examined adolescent Internet addiction.

COMPARISON SURVEY STUDIES OF INTERNET ADDICTION AND EXCESSIVE INTERNET USE

The earliest empirical research study to be carried out looking into excessive Internet use was by Young (1996a). The study addressed the question of whether or not the Internet can be addictive, and the extent of problems associated with its misuse. The DSM-IV criteria for pathological gambling were modified to develop an eight-item questionnaire, as pathological gambling was viewed to be the closest in nature to pathological Internet use. Participants who answered "yes" to five or more of the eight criteria were classified as being addicted to the Internet (i.e., "dependents"). A self-selected sample of 496 people responded to the questionnaire, with the vast majority ($n = 396$) being classed as dependents. The majority of respondents were female (60%), and none of the sample were adolescents.

It was found that dependents spent more time online (38.5 hours a week) compared with non-dependents (4.9 hours a week), and mostly used the more interactive functions of the Internet, such as chat rooms and forums. Dependents also reported that their Internet use caused moderate to severe problems in their family, social and professional lives. Young concluded that (i) the more interactive the Internet function, the more addictive it is, and (ii) while normal users reported few negative effects of Internet use, dependents reported significant impairment in many areas of their lives, including health, occupational, social and financial.

However, there were many limitations to the study, including the (relatively) small self-selected sample. Furthermore, the dependents and non-dependents had not been matched in any manner. Moreover, Young advertised for "avid Internet users" to take part in her study, which would have biased her results. There was also an assumption that excessive Internet use was akin to pathological gambling, and that the criteria used to operationalize excessive Internet use were reliable and valid. Despite the methodological shortcomings of Young's study, it could be argued that she kick-started a new area of academic enquiry.

Egger and Rauterberg (1996) also conducted an online study by asking similar questions to those asked by Young, although their categorization of addiction was based purely on whether the respondents themselves felt they were addicted. Using an online survey, they gathered 450 participants, 84 percent of whom were males. Again, there were no adolescents in the sample, and the researchers reached similar conclusions to Young. Respondents who self-reported as "addicts" reported negative consequences of Internet use, complaints from friends and family over the amount of time spent online, feelings of anticipation when going online, and feeling guilty about their Internet use. As with Young's study, it suffered from similar methodological limitations. Furthermore, most of the participants were males from Switzerland.

Brenner (1997) devised an instrument called the Internet-Related Addictive Behavior Inventory (IRABI), consisting of 32 dichotomous (true/false) items. These items were designed to assess experiences comparable to those related to Substance Abuse in the DSM-IV. Of the 563 adult respondents, the majority were male (73%), and they used the Internet for (a mean average) of 19 hours a week. All 32 items seemed to measure some unique variance, as they were all found to be moderately correlated with the total score. Older users tended to experience fewer problems compared with younger users despite spending the same amount of time online (which may have implications for adolescents). No gender differences were reported. The data appeared to suggest that a number of users experienced more problems in role performance because of their Internet usage. Brenner concluded that the skewed distribution was consistent with the existence of a deviant subgroup of people who experiences more severe problems due to Internet use. He also claimed there was evidence of tolerance, withdrawal and craving. The major limitation to the study was that it was not clear whether items in the IRABI really tapped into behaviors that indicated genuine signs of addiction (Griffiths, 1998).

In a much bigger study – the Virtual Addiction Survey (VAS) – Greenfield (1999) conducted an online survey with 17 251 (mostly adult) respondents. The sample was mainly Caucasian (82%) and male (71%), with a mean age of 33 years. The VAS included demographic items (e.g., age, location, educational background, etc.), descriptive information items (e.g., frequency and duration of use, specific Internet usage, etc.) and clinical items (e.g., disinhibition, loss of time, behavior online). It also included 10 modified items from DSM-IV criteria for pathological gambling. Approximately 6 percent of respondents met the criteria for addicted Internet usage patterns. Tentative *post hoc* analysis proposed several variables that made the Internet attractive:

- Intense intimacy (41% of total sample, 75% of dependents)
- Disinhibition (43% of total sample, 80% of dependents)
- Loss of boundaries (39% of total sample, 83% of dependents)
- Timelessness (most of the sample replied "sometimes", most of the dependents replied "almost always")
- Out of control (8% of total sample, 46% of dependents).

One of the additional areas examined was whether Internet addiction shared the same characteristics as other forms of addiction, including substance-based addictions. Early analysis revealed numerous symptoms, which Greenfield viewed as being consistent with the concept of tolerance and withdrawal in dependents, including preoccupation with going online (58%), numerous unsuccessful attempts to cut back (68%), and feeling restless when attempting to cut back (79%). Despite the large sample size, only a very preliminary analysis was conducted. Therefore, results should be interpreted with caution. Furthermore, it is hard to make generalizations to adolescents, as there were very few people under the age of 20 years in the study.

SURVEY STUDIES OF INTERNET ADDICTION IN VULNERABLE GROUPS

A number of other studies have highlighted the danger that excessive Internet use may pose to students as a population group. This population is deemed to be vulnerable and at risk, given the accessibility of the Internet and the flexibility of their schedules (Moore, 1995). For instance, Scherer (1997) studied 531 students at the University of Texas at Austin. Of these, 381 students used the Internet at least once per week and were further investigated. Based on the criteria paralleling chemical dependencies, 49 students (13%) were classified as "Internet dependent" (71% male; 29% female). Dependent users averaged 11 hours/week online as opposed to the average of 8 hours for non-dependents. Dependents were three times more likely to use interactive synchronous applications. The major weakness of this study appears to be that dependents only averaged 11 hours a week online (i.e., just over an hour a day). This could hardly be called excessive or addictive (Griffiths, 1998).

Morahan-Martin and Schumacher (2000) conducted a similar online study. Pathological Internet Use (PIU) was measured by a 13-item questionnaire assessing problems due to Internet use (e.g., academic, work, relationship problems, tolerance symptoms, and mood-altering use of the Internet). Those who answered yes to four or more of the items were defined as pathological Internet users. They recruited 277 undergraduate Internet users, of whom 8 percent were classed as pathological users. Pathological Internet users were more likely to be male and to use technologically sophisticated sites. On average, they spent 8.5 hours a week online. It was also found that pathological users used the Internet to meet new people, for emotional support and to play interactive games, and were more socially disinhibited. Again, an average of 8.5 hours a week online does not appear excessive, although the authors argued that it was indicative of problems surfacing in relatively short periods of being online. Furthermore, the items used to measure dependency were similar to Brenner's IRABI items. Therefore, the results claimed to be indicative of Internet addiction without substantiating its existence (Griffiths, 1998).

Anderson (1999) collected data from a mixture of colleges in the US and Europe, yielding 1302 respondents (with an almost 50–50 gender split). On average, his participants used the Internet 100 minutes a day, and roughly 6 percent of the participants were considered to be high users (above 400 minutes a day). The DSM-IV substance-dependence criteria were used to classify participants into dependents and non-dependents. Those endorsing more than three of the seven criteria were classified as being dependent. Anderson reported a slightly higher percentage of dependent student users (9.8%), most of whom were those majoring in hard sciences. Of the 106 dependents, 93 were males. They averaged 229 minutes a day compared with non-dependents who averaged 73 minutes a day. The participants in the high-user category reported more negative consequences compared with the low-user participants.

Kubey and colleagues (2001) surveyed 576 students in Rutgers University. Their survey included 43 multiple-choice items on Internet usage, study habits, academic performance and personality. Internet dependency was measured with a five-point Likert-scale item, asking participants how much they agreed or disagreed with the following statement: "I think I might have become a little psychologically dependent on the Internet". Participants were categorized as being Internet dependent if they chose "agree" or "strongly agree" as the answer to the statement. Of the 572 valid responses, 381 (66%) were females; the age ranged between 18 and 45 years old, with a mean age of 20.25 years. Fifty-three participants (9.3%) were classified as Internet dependent, and males were more prevalent in this group. Age was not found to be a factor, but first-year students (mean age not reported) were found to make up 37.7 percent of the dependent group. Dependents were four times more likely than non-dependents to report academic impairment due to their Internet use, and they were significantly "more lonely" than other students. In terms of their Internet usage, dependents who were also academically impaired were found to be nine times as likely to use synchronous functions of the Internet (MUDs and IRC/chat programs). The authors proposed that these types of applications are an important outlet for lonely people (especially students who have just moved away to college), as they can keep in touch with family and friends, and find someone to chat with at anytime. No other medium can offer such an opportunity. The results suggest that the younger the user is, the more problems he or she may have as a result of Internet use – which again may have implications for adolescent Internet usage.

Niemz and colleagues (2005) surveyed 371 British students. In a questionnaire which included the pathological Internet use (PIU) scale (Morahan-Martin and Schumacher, 2000), the General Health Questionnaire (GHQ-12), a self-esteem scale and two measures of disinhibition. Results showed that 18.3 percent of the sample were considered to be pathological Internet users whose excessive use of the Internet was causing academic, social and interpersonal problems. Other results showed that pathological Internet users had lower self-esteem and were more socially disinhibited. However, there was no significant difference in GHQ scores. There are methodological concerns, though, as the study used the PIU Scale and relied on a self-selected sample.

Other studies, such as those by Kennedy-Souza (1998), Chou (2001), Tsai and Lin (2003), Chin-Chung and Sunny (2003), Nalwa and Anand (2003). Kaltiala-Heino *et al.* (2004) and Wan and Chiou (2006), which surveyed very small numbers of students and adolescents have simply been too small and/or methodologically limited to make any real conclusions. From the studies so far discussed (in this section and the preceding one, on comparison studies), it is clear that most of these "prevalence type" studies share common weaknesses. Most use convenient, self-selected participants who volunteer to respond to the survey. It is therefore difficult to plan any kind of comparable groups. Most studies did not use any type of validated addiction criteria (such as withdrawal symptoms, salience, tolerance, relapse, etc.), and those that did assumed that excessive Internet use was akin to other behavioral addictions like gambling, and/or used very low cut-off scores which would increase the percentage of those defined as addicted. As Griffiths (2000a) observed, the instruments (like those in video-game play) used have no measure of severity, no temporal dimension, they have a tendency to over-estimate the incidence of the problems, and they do not consider the context of Internet use (for example, it is possible for some people to be engaged in very excessive use because it is part of their job or they are in an online relationship with someone geographically distant).

It is perhaps worth noting that in addition to direct studies of Internet addiction, there have been a number of longitudinal studies examining the relationship between general Internet use (including heavy use) and various aspects of psychosocial well-being (Kraut *et al.*, 1998, 2002; Wästlund *et al.*, 2001; Jackson *et al.*, 2003). However, none of these studies show consistent findings, and none specifically investigated Internet addiction or attempted to measure it. Furthermore, none of them have examined the relationships among adolescent Internet users.

PSYCHOMETRIC STUDIES OF INTERNET ADDICTION

As can be seen from early studies, a number of differing diagnostic criteria have been used in "Internet addiction" studies. One of the most commonly used criteria was that used by Young (1996a) and subsequently by others. The diagnostic questionnaire consisted of eight items modified from the DSM-IV criteria for pathological gambling (see Table 8.1). She maintained the cut-off score of five, according to the number of criteria used to diagnose pathological gambling, although the latter had two additional criteria. Even with the more rigorous cut-off score, it was found that almost 80 percent of the respondents in her study were classified as dependents.

Beard and Wolfe (2001) attempted to modify Young's criteria, based on concerns about the objectivity and the reliance on self-report. Some criteria can easily be reported or denied by a participant, whose judgment might be impaired, thus influencing the accuracy of the diagnosis. Secondly, some of the items were deemed to be too vague, and some terminologies needed to be clarified (for example, what exactly is meant by "preoccupation"?). Thirdly, they questioned whether or not the criteria for pathological gambling are the most accurate to use as a basis for identifying Internet addiction. Beard and Wolfe therefore proposed modified criteria (see Table 8.2). It was recommended that all of the former five criteria be required for a diagnosis, since they could be met without any impairment in the person's daily functioning. Furthermore, at least one of the latter three criteria should be required for diagnosis, as these criteria impact the person's ability to cope and function.

Another attempt at formulating a set of diagnostic criteria for Internet addiction was made by Pratarelli and colleagues (1999). Factor analysis was employed in this research to examine possible constructs underlying computer/Internet addiction. There were 341 completed surveys with 163 male and 178 female participants (mean age of 22.8 years) recruited from Oklahoma State University.

TABLE 8.1 Young's (1996) Diagnostic Criteria for Internet Addiction

1. Do you feel preoccupied with the Internet (think about previous online activity or anticipation of next online session)?
2. Do you feel the need to use the Internet with increasing amounts of time in order to achieve satisfaction?
3. Have you repeatedly made unsuccessful efforts to control, cut back, or stop Internet use?
4. Do you feel restless, moody, depressed, or irritable when attempting to cut down or stop Internet use?
5. Do you stay online longer than originally intended?
6. Have you jeopardized or risked the loss of a significant relationship, job, educational or career opportunity because of the Internet?
7. Have you lied to family members, therapist, or others to conceal the extent of involvement with the Internet?
8. Do you use the Internet as a way of escaping from problems or of relieving a dysphoric mood (e.g., feelings of helplessness, guilt, anxiety, depression)?

TABLE 8.2 Criteria for Identifying Internet Addiction (Beard and Wolfe, 2001)

All the following 1–5 must be present
1. Is preoccupied with the Internet (think about previous online activity or anticipate next online session)
2. Needs to use the Internet with increased amounts of time in order to achieve satisfaction
3. Has made unsuccessful efforts to control, cut back or stop Internet use
4. Is restless, moody, depressed, or irritable when attempting to cut down or stop Internet use
5. Has stayed online longer than originally intended

and at least one of the following:
1. Has jeopardized or risked the loss of a significant relationship, job, educational or career opportunity because of the Internet
2. Has lied to family members, therapist, or others to conceal the extent of involvement with the Internet
3. Uses the Internet as a way of escaping from problems or of relieving a dysphoric mood (e.g., feelings of helplessness, guilt, anxiety, depression)

A questionnaire consisting of 93 items was constructed, 19 of which were categorical demographic and Internet-use questions, and 74 dichotomous items. Four factors were extracted from the 93 items; two principal and two minor.

- Factor 1 focused on problematic computer-related behaviors in heavy users of the Internet. This factor was characterized by reports of loneliness, social isolation, missing appointments, and other general negative consequences of their Internet use.
- Factor 2 focused on the use and usefulness of computer technology in general, and of the Internet in particular.
- Factor 3 focused on two different constructs that concerned the use of the Internet for sexual gratification and shyness/introversion.
- Factor 4 focused on the lack of problems related to Internet use, coupled with mild aversion/disinterest in the technology.

The data collected in this study supported the idea that a mixture of obsessive-like characteristics are present in some individuals in terms of their Internet use, and that they prefer online interactions rather than face-to-face. Although this study used a more statistically tested instrument in measuring Internet addiction, some of the factors extracted (e.g., Factors 2 and 4) did not seem to indicate components of addiction in general. Furthermore, the sample consisted mainly of young adults. Generalization to adolescents or older groups was not confirmed.

More recently, Shapira and colleagues (2003) proposed a revised classification and diagnostic criteria for problematic Internet use. Furthermore, Black and colleagues (1999) pointed out that Internet Addiction Disorder (IAD) seemed to have high comorbidity with other psychiatric disorders. Because of this, the criteria need to be unique in order to evaluate the validity of Internet abuse as a distinct disorder. Shapira and colleagues discussed the concept of Glasser's (1976) work on "positive addiction". However, the concept has been questioned, as the criteria for positive addiction do not resemble many of the components of more established addictions – such as tolerance and withdrawal (Griffiths, 1996b). Moreover, in terms of Internet dependency, negative consequences have been reported along with the amount of time spent online.

Internet dependency has most commonly been conceptualized as a behavioral addiction which operates on a modified principle of classic addiction models, but the validity and clinical usefulness of such claims have again been questioned (Holden, 2001). Other studies have also supported the concept that problematic Internet use might be associated with features of DSM-IV impulse control disorder (Shapira *et al.*, 2000; Treuer *et al.*, 2001), at least in adult populations.

However, other researchers have questioned the existence of PIU and IAD itself. Mitchell (2000) does not believe it deserves a separate diagnosis, as it is still unclear whether it develops of its own accord or is triggered by an underlying comorbid psychiatric illness. It has become virtually impossible to make the distinction as to which develops first, especially considering how integrated the Internet has become in people's lives. It is therefore difficult to establish a clear developmental pattern, especially as there is very little research specifically on excessive adolescent usage. In addition, behavioral patterns of individuals with problematic Internet use are varied and hard to identify. The only general agreement seems to be that it can be associated with material and psychological consequences. Shapira *et al.* (2003) suggested that future research should delineate problems – for example, some individuals may have problems during a manic episode only, some because of the demographics of choosing the Internet as a medium to shop or to gamble. Once these factors are extricated, the individuals who are left can be assessed regarding addiction and impulsivity purely in terms of their Internet use.

Based on the current (yet limited) empirical evidence, Shapira *et al.* (2003) proposed that problematic Internet use be conceptualized as an impulse control disorder. They admitted that although the category is already a heterogeneous one, over time, specific syndromes have been indicated as clinically useful. Therefore, in the style of DSM IV-TR's impulse-control disorder criteria, and in addition to the proposed impulse-control disorder of compulsive buying, Shapira and colleagues proposed broad diagnostic criteria for problematic Internet use (see Table 8.3).

TABLE 8.3 Diagnostic Criteria for Problematic Internet Use (Shapira *et al.*, 2003)

A. Maladaptive preoccupation with Internet use, as indicated by at least one of the following:
   - Preoccupations with use of the Internet that are experienced as irresistible
   - Excessive use of the Internet for periods of time longer than planned

B. The use of the Internet or the preoccupation with its use causes clinically significant distress or impairment in social, occupational, or other important areas of functioning

C. The excessive Internet use does not occur exclusively during periods of hypomania or mania and is not better accounted by other Axis I disorders

Rotunda and colleagues (2003) used an instrument they simply called the Internet Use Survey. It contained three formal components that explored (i) demographic data and Internet usage, (ii) the negative consequences and experience associated with Internet use, and (iii) personal history and psychological characteristics of participants. Components (ii) and (iii) included several items from DSM-IV criteria for pathological gambling, substance use dependence, and a particular personality disorder (e.g., schizoid). Their sample consisted of 393 students, 53.6 percent females ($n = 210$) and 46.4 percent males ($n = 182$). The age range was between 18 and 81 years, with a mean of 27.6 years. The average use was 3.3 hours a day, with 1 hour for personal use (the other time on the Internet being spent for work-related purposes). The most common usage was e-mail, surfing the web for information and news, and chat rooms. The negative consequences included 18 percent of participants reporting preoccupation with the Internet, 25 percent sometimes feeling excited or euphoric when online, 34 percent admitting to going online to escape other problems to some degree, and 22.6 percent reporting socializing online more than in person. Staying online longer than planned and losing track of time were also found to be common reports.

Factor analysis revealed four main factors. The first was labeled "absorption" (i.e., over-involvement with the Internet, time management failure), the second "negative consequences" (i.e., distress or problematic behavior such as preferring to be online rather than spending time with the family), the third "sleep" (i.e., sleep-pattern disruption, such as scheduling sleep around online time), and the fourth "deception" (i.e., lying to others online about identity, or how long is spent online). Internet-related impairment was conceptualized based on user absorption and negative consequences instead of frequency of use. The authors concluded by stating that in order to assume frequent Internet use is excessive, pathological or addictive is potentially misleading, as it ignores contextual and dispositional factors associated with this behavior. Again, the data were collected from adult users rather than adolescents.

INTERNET ADDICTION, COMORBIDITY AND RELATIONSHIP WITH OTHER BEHAVIORS

Previous studies have found that problematic Internet use in adults co-occurs with other psychiatric disorders (Black *et al.*, 1999, Shapira *et al.*, 2000). Griffiths (2000a) has postulated that in the majority of the cases the Internet seems to act as a medium for other excessive behaviors, and the Internet is largely being used only to carry out these behaviors – in other words, the Internet is acting as a medium and not a causal factor (Shaffer *et al.*, 2000). Some of the factors found to be associated with IAD are personality traits, self-esteem and other psychiatric disorders.

Young and Rodgers (1998) examined the personality traits of individuals who were considered dependent on the Internet using the Sixteen Personality Factor

Inventory (16 PF). Dependent users were found to rank highly in terms of self-reliance (i.e., they did not feel the sense of alienation others feel when sitting alone, possibly because of the interactive functions of the Internet), emotional sensitivity and reactivity (i.e., they are drawn to mental stimulation through endless databases and information available online), vigilance, low self-disclosure, and non-conformist characteristics (i.e., they might be drawn to the anonymity of the Internet). The findings of this study seem to suggest that specific personality traits may predispose individuals to develop PIU. Similar findings were obtained by Xuanhui and Gonggu (2001), examining the relationship between Internet addiction and the 16 PF. Whether such findings can be generalized to adolescents remains to be seen.

Armstrong and colleagues (2000) investigated the extent to which sensation seeking and low self-esteem predicted heavier Internet use, using the Internet Related Problem Scale (IRPS). The IRPS is a 20-item scale covering factors such as tolerance, craving and negative impacts of Internet use. Results indicated that self-esteem is a better predictor of "Internet addiction", compared with impulsivity. Individuals with low self-esteem seem to spend more time online, and had higher scores on the IRPS. Although this study yielded some interesting results, it should be interpreted with caution due to the small number of participants ($n = 50$). Moreover, Armstrong and colleagues maintained that the 20 items indicated 9 different symptoms without any statistical evidence. It would be interesting to investigate whether the items really did measure the symptoms they claimed to. Other studies have looked at the relationship between Internet addiction and self-esteem (see, for example, Widyanto and McMurran, 2004), but again the very low sample sizes make it hard to generalize findings.

Lavin and colleagues (1999) also tested sensation seeking and Internet dependence in college students ($n = 342$). Of the total participants, 43 were defined as dependents and 299 as non-dependents. Dependents had a lower score on the Sensation Seeking Scale, which contradicted their hypothesis. The authors explained by stating that dependents tended to be sociable in their Internet usage but not to the point of sensation seeking, as it differed from the traditional concept. The traditional form of sensation seeking involves more physical activities, such as sky-diving and other thrill-inducing activities, while Internet users are less physical in their sensation seeking. It is possible that the scale used to measure sensation seeking touched more on the physical sensations rather than the non-physical sensations.

Petrie and Gunn (1998) examined the link between Internet addiction, sex, age, depression and introversion. One key question was whether participants defined themselves as Internet addicts or not. Of the 445 participants (roughly equal gender split), nearly half (46%) stated that they were addicted to the Internet. This group was the Self-Defined Addicts (SDAs) group. No gender or age differences were found between SDAs and non-SDAs. The 16 questions that had the highest factor analytical loadings were used to construct an Internet Use and Attitudes Scale (IUAS). Respondents' scores on this scale ranged from

5 to 61, with high scores indicating high use of and positive attitudes towards the Internet. SDAs scored significantly higher than non-SDAs, with SDAs having a mean IUAS score of 35.6 and non-SDAs a mean IUAS score of 20.9. SDAs were also found to have higher levels of depression, and they were more likely to be introverted. The main problem with the study was the fact that addiction was self-defined and not assessed formally.

Shapira and colleagues (2000) employed a face-to-face standardized psychiatric evaluation to identify behavioral characteristics, family psychiatric history, and comorbidity of adult individuals with problematic Internet use. The study sample consisted of 20 participants (11 men and 9 women) with an average age of 36 years. Problems associated with Internet use were: significant social impairment (in 19 of the participants), marked personal distress over their behaviors (in 12 of the participants), vocational impairment (in 8 of the participants), financial impairment (in 8 participants), and legal problems (in 2 participants). It was found that every participant's problematic Internet use met DSM-IV criteria for an Impulse Control Disorder Not Otherwise Specified, while only three participants' Internet use met DSM-IV criteria for Obsessive-Compulsive Disorder. All participants met criteria for at least one lifetime DSM Axis I diagnosis. The limitations to the study include the small sample size, self-reported interviews, the possible existence of experimenter's bias, the lack of a control group, and the possibility of overestimating certain psychiatric disorders – especially bipolar disorders.

More recently, Mathy and Cooper (2003) measured the duration and frequency of Internet use across five domains, namely past mental health treatments, current mental health treatments, suicidal intent, and past and current behavioral difficulties. It was found that the frequency of Internet use was related to past mental health treatments and suicidal intent. Participants who acknowledged them spent significantly greater number of hours a week online. Duration of Internet use was related to past and current behavioral difficulties. Participants who admitted to past and current behavioral problems with alcohol, drugs, gambling, food or sex also reported being relatively new Internet users.

Black and colleagues (1999) attempted to examine the demographic and clinical features and psychiatric comorbidity in adult individuals reporting compulsive computer use ($n = 21$). They reported spending between 7 and 60 hours a week on non-essential computer use (mean, 27 hours a week). Nearly 50 percent of the participants met the criteria for a current disorder, with the most common being substance use (38%), mood (33%), anxiety (19%) and psychotic disorders (14%). Nearly 25 percent of the sample had current depressive disorder (depression or dysthymia). Results showed that eight participants (38%) had at least one disorder, with the most common being compulsive buying (19%), gambling (10%), pyromania (10%) and compulsive sexual behavior (10%). Three of the participants reported physical abuse and two reported sexual abuse during childhood. Other results showed that 11 participants met the criteria for at least one personality disorder, with the most frequent being borderline (24%), narcissistic (19%)

and antisocial (19%) disorders. Perhaps it was due to the sensitive nature of this particular study that there were a very small number of participants. However, caution is advised when interpreting the results. Other studies have postulated relationships between Internet addiction, shyness (Chak and Leung, 2004), depression (Morgan and Cotton, 2003) and attention deficit hyperactivity disorder (Yoo *et al.*, 2004). Furthermore, none of these studies examined adolescent populations.

INTERNET ADDICTION CASE STUDIES

This author has stressed the importance of case studies in the study of Internet addiction (Griffiths, 2000a, 2000b), and his operational definition of addictive behavior is any behavior (including Internet use) that includes the six core components of addiction outlined earlier – namely salience, mood modification, tolerance, withdrawal symptoms, conflict and relapse. Using these criteria, this author has consistently asserted that Internet addiction exists in only a very small percentage of users, and most of the individuals who use the Internet excessively just use it as a medium through which they can engage in a chosen behavior (Griffiths, 2000a, 2000b). Most studies to date have failed to show that Internet addiction exists outside a small minority of users. It is suggested, therefore, that case studies might help in indicating whether or not Internet addiction exists, even if these are unrepresentative.

The current author outlined five case studies of excessive users that were gathered over the space of 6 months (Griffiths, 2002b). Of the five case studies discussed, only two were "addicted" according to the components criteria. In short, these two case studies ("Gary" and "Jamie", both adolescent males) demonstrated that the Internet was the most important thing in their lives, that they neglected everything else in their lives to engage in the behavior, and that it compromised most areas of their lives. They also built up tolerance over time, suffered withdrawal symptoms if they were unable to engage in using the Internet, and showed signs of relapse after giving up the behavior for short periods.

In the other cases of very excessive Internet use, this author claimed that the participants had used the Internet as a way to cope with and counteract other inadequacies (such as lack of social support in real life, low self-esteem, physical disability, etc.). It was also observed that all of the participants seemed to be using the Internet mainly for social contact, and the author postulated that it was because the Internet could be an alternative, text-based reality where users are able to immerse themselves by taking on another social persona and identity to make them feel better about themselves, which in itself would be highly rewarding psychologically (Griffiths, 2000b).

Young (1996b) highlighted the case of a 43-year-old homemaker who appeared to be addicted to the Internet. This particular case was chosen because it was contrary to the stereotype of a young, computer-savvy male online user as an Internet addict. The woman was not technologically oriented, had reported a contented home life, and had no prior psychiatric problems or addictions. Due to the menu-driven and user-friendly nature of the web browser provided by her service provider, she could navigate the Internet easily despite referring to herself as being "computer-phobic and illiterate". She initially spent a few hours a week in various chat-rooms, but within 3 months she reported the need to increase her online time to up to 60 hours a week. She would plan to go online for 2 hours, but often stayed there longer than she intended, reaching up to 14 hours a session. She started withdrawing from her offline social involvements, stopped performing household chores in order to spend more time online, and reported feeling depressed, anxious and irritable when she was not online.

She denied that the behavior was abnormal, as she did not see it as a problem. Regardless of her husband's protests about the financial cost and her daughter's complaints that she was ignoring them, she refused to seek treatment and had no desire to reduce her online time. Within a year of getting her computer, she was estranged from her two daughters and was separated from her husband. An interview took place 6 months later, and she admitted that the loss of her family resulted in her successfully cutting down her online time without any therapeutic intervention. However, Young stated that she could not eliminate her online use completely, nor re-establish relationship with her family, without intervention. It was also suggested that this case indicated that certain risk factors, such as the type of function used and the level of excitement experienced while being online, may be associated with the development of addictive Internet use.

Black and colleagues (1999) also outlined two case studies. The first was of a 47-year-old man who reported spending 12–18 hours a day online. He owned three personal computers and was in debt from purchasing the associated paraphernalia. He admitted to developing several romantic relationships online, despite being married with three children. He had been arrested several times for computer hacking, he spent little time with his family, and he reported feeling powerless over his usage. The second case was of a 42-year-old divorced man who admitted to wanting to be online all day. He admitted to spending 30 hours a week online, mostly in chat rooms to make new friends and meet potential partners. He had dated several women he met online, and had made no attempt to cut back despite his parents' complaints over his "addiction". While these cases may be excessive, and there were negative consequences in the first case, the users do not seem to be addicted but rather to use the Internet excessively for functional purposes (for example, to engage in online relationships).

More interestingly, Leon and Rotunda (2000) reported two contrasting case studies of individuals who used the Internet for 8 hours or more a day. Both were college students, and neither was seeking treatment. The first was the case of Neil, a 27-year-old white male who was described as being outgoing and sociable by his college friends. He discovered an online computer game called *Red Alert* during his third year of college. The game began to replace his social activities, and he changed his sleeping patterns so he could play online with the other "good players". He also reported dropping all but two of his classes and spending up to 50 hours a week online. Friends reported that his personality changed. He became short-tempered and overly sensitive, especially when it came to the time he spent online. Eventually he stopped all his social activities and skipped classes, his grades deteriorated, he slept all day and played all night. He did not go out to buy food, as he used his grocery money to buy a faster modem. The connection speed was extremely important to him, and he would become upset and angry if the game server went offline. Due to his excessive online time, he was also close to being evicted from his apartment and he constantly lied about the extent of his involvement with the Internet. All this happened within a year of Neil discovering the online game.

The second case was Wu Quon, a 25-year-old male foreign exchange student from Asia who had very few friends in North America. He stated that it was due to cultural differences, and the lack of other Asian students in college. He bought a personal computer and used the Internet to make contact with people globally, read news about his home country, and listen to radio broadcasts from Asia. He also used Internet-Relay Chat (IRC) to keep in touch with friends and family in China. He stated that the Internet occupied his life outside of study and college time, spending 8 hours a day online. He said that being able to contact his family and friends daily relieved his depression and homesickness. He claimed that he was not addicted to the Internet; it had simply become an important part of his life and routine. He admitted feeling uncomfortable when he was offline, but said that it was due to feeling disconnected and out of touch with what was happening at home. Overall, he rated his experience on the Internet as being positive.

Leon and Rotunda (2000) concluded that only Neil seemed to be dependent on the Internet, as his personal and occupational life was problematic due to the time he spent online. Moreover, it was argued that Neil met the criteria for Schizoid Personality Disorder and Circadian Rhythm Disorder. Both of these were the result of his Internet use. In contrast, Wu Quon's Internet use could be seen as a remedy for his homesickness. His online time seemed to make him a happy and functional individual, although it could also be seen as a mechanism that caused him further isolation. In summary, Leon and Rotunda contended that to assume that frequent Internet use is excessive, pathological or addictive was simplistic and ignored the contextual and dispositional factors associated with the behavior. This author (Griffiths, 2000a) would argue that Neil was a computer game addict and not an Internet addict, as the Internet was clearly being used to fuel his gaming behavior. However, gaming is increasingly moving online and the immersive nature of the Internet may facilitate excessive play, leading to increased addiction in some players.

TREATMENT

Another indirect indicator that Internet addiction may exist, from a case-study perspective, comes from the few reports of its treatment. Most of these have used a cognitive-behavioral approach therapy to treat IAD, although these accounts usually contain some commonsense elements (see, for example, Orzack and Orzack, 1999; Young, 1999; Hall and Parsons, 2001; Yu and Zhao, 2004). None of these treatment accounts show that the people treated were definitely addicts, although all those under treatment certainly felt they had a problem with their excessive Internet use. Young and colleagues (1999) also conducted a survey among therapists who had treated clients suffering from cyber-related disorders. The sample consisted of 23 female and 12 male therapists, with an average of 14 years of clinical practice experience. They reported an average caseload of 9 clients that they would classify as being Internet addicts treated within the past year, with a range of 2–50 patients. The patients were more likely to complain about direct compulsive Internet use (CIU), along with its negative consequences and prior addictions, rather than psychiatric illness. Almost all the therapists (95%) felt that the problem of CIU was more widespread than the number of cases indicated.

WHY DOES EXCESSIVE INTERNET USE OCCUR?

Most of the research that has been discussed appears to lack theoretical basis, as surprisingly few researchers have attempted to propose a theory of the cause of Internet addiction despite the number of studies conducted in the field. Davis (2001) proposed a model of the etiology of pathological Internet use (PIU) using the cognitive-behavioral approach. The main assumption of the model was that PIU resulted from problematic cognitions coupled with behaviors that intensify or maintain maladaptive response. It emphasized the individual's thoughts/cognitions as the main source of abnormal behavior. Davis stipulated that the cognitive symptoms of PIU might often precede and cause the emotional and behavioral symptoms, rather than *vice versa*. Similar to the basic assumptions of cognitive theories of depression, it focused on maladaptive cognitions associated with PIU.

Davis described Abramson and colleagues' (1989) concepts of *necessary*, *sufficient* and *contributory* causes. A necessary cause is an etiological factor that must be present or must have occurred in order for symptoms to appear. A sufficient cause is an etiological factor whose presence/occurrence guarantees the occurrence of symptoms, while a contributory cause is an etiological factor that increases the likelihood of the occurrence of symptoms, but is neither necessary nor sufficient. Abramson also distinguished between *proximal* and *distal* causes. In an etiology chain that results in a set of symptoms, some causes lie toward the end of the chain (proximal) and others towards the beginning (distal). In the case of PIU, Davis claimed that the distal cause was underlying psychopathology (e.g., depression, social anxiety, other dependence, etc.), while the proximal cause was maladaptive cognitions (i.e., negative evaluation of oneself and the world in general). The main goal of the paper was to introduce maladaptive cognitions as proximal sufficient cause of the set of symptoms for PIU.

Distal contributory causes of PIU were discussed. It was explained using a diathesis–stress framework, whereby an abnormal behavior was caused by a predisposition/vulnerability (diathesis) and a life event (stress). In the cognitive-behavioral model of PIU, existing underlying psychopathology was viewed as the diathesis, as many studies had shown the relationship between psychological disorders such as depression, social anxiety and substance dependence (Kraut *et al.*, 1998). The model suggested that psychopathology was a distal necessary cause of PIU – i.e., psychopathology must be present or must have occurred in order for PIU symptoms to occur. However, in itself, the underlying psychopathology would not result in PIU symptoms, but was a necessary element in its etiology.

The model assumed that although a basic psychopathology might predispose an individual to PIU, the set of associated symptoms was specific to PIU and therefore should be investigated and treated independently. The stressor in this model was the introduction of the Internet, or the discovery of a specific function of the Internet. Although it might be difficult to trace back an individual's encounter with the Internet, a more testable event would be the experience of a function found online – for example, the first time the person used an online auction, found pornographic material online, etc.

Exposure to such functions was viewed as a distal necessary cause of PIU symptoms. In itself, this encounter did not result in the occurrence of symptoms of PIU. However, as a contributory factor, the event could be a catalyst for the developmental process of PIU. A key factor here was the reinforcement received from an event (i.e., operant conditioning, whereby positive response reinforced continuity of activity). The model proposed that stimuli such as the sound of a modem connecting or the sensation of typing could result in a conditioned response. Thus, these types of secondary reinforcers could act as situational cues that contribute to the development of PIU and the maintenance of symptoms.

Central to the cognitive-behavioral model was the presence of maladaptive cognitions that were viewed to be proximal sufficient cause of PIU. Maladaptive cognitions were broken down into two subtypes; perceptions about one's self, and perceptions about the world. Thoughts about self are guided by ruminative cognitive style. Individuals who tend to ruminate would experience a higher degree in severity and duration of PIU, as studies have supported that rumination is likely to intensify or maintain problems, partly by interfering with instrumental behavior (i.e., taking action) and problem-solving. Other cognitive distortions include self-doubt, low self-efficacy and negative self-appraisal. These cognitions dictate the way in which individuals behave, and some cognitions would cause specific or generalized PIU. Specific PIU referred to the over-use and abuse of a specific Internet function. It was assumed to be the result of a pre-existing psychopathology that became associated with an online activity (for example, compulsive gamblers might realize that they could gamble online and ultimately showed symptoms of specific PIU as the association between need and immediate reinforcement became stronger). However, it should be noted that not every compulsive gambler showed symptoms of PIU.

On the other hand, generalized PIU involved spending excessive amounts of time online with no direct purpose, or just wasting time. The social context of the individual, especially the lack of social support he or she received and/or social isolation, was one key factor that played a role in the causality of general PIU. Individuals with general PIU were viewed as being more problematic, as their behavior would not even exist in the absence of the Internet.

Based on Davis' model, Caplan (2003) further proposed that problematic psychosocial predispositions causes excessive and compulsive computer-mediated (CM) social interaction in individuals, which in turn increases their problems. The theory proposed by Caplan, examined empirically, had three main propositions:

1. Compared with others, individuals with psychosocial problems (e.g., depression and loneliness) hold more negative perceptions of their social competence
2. Such individuals prefer CM interactions to face-to-face ones, as the former is perceived to be less threatening and they perceive themselves to be more efficient in an online setting
3. This preference in turn leads to excessive and compulsive use of CM interactions, which then worsens their problems and creates new ones at school, work and home.

In Caplan's (2003) study, the participants consisted of 386 undergraduates (279 females and 116 males), with the age ranging from 18 to 57 years (mean age, 20 years). This study used Caplan's (2002) Generalized Problematic Internet Use Scale (GPIUS), a self-report assessing the prevalence of cognitive and behavioral symptoms of pathological Internet use along with the degree to which negative consequences affected the individual. The GPIUS had seven subscales – mood alteration, perceived social benefits, perceived social control, withdrawal, compulsivity, excessive Internet use, and negative outcomes. Also included in this study were validated depression and loneliness scales.

It was found that depression and loneliness were significant predictors of preference for online social interaction, accounting for 19 percent of the variance. In turn, participants' preference for online social interaction was found to be a significant predictor of their scores on pathological Internet use and negative outcomes. The data also suggested that excessive use was one of the weakest predictors of negative outcomes, whereas preference for online interaction, compulsive use, and withdrawal were among the strongest. Overall, loneliness and depression were not found to have large, independent effects on negative outcomes. The result of this study appeared to support the proposition that preference for online socialization was a key contributor to the development of problematic Internet use.

Caplan noted two unexpected results in the data. First, loneliness played a more significant role in the development of problematic Internet use compared with depression. He attempted to explain this finding by stating that loneliness was theoretically the more salient predictor, as negative perception of social competence and communication skills is more pronounced in lonely individuals. On the other hand, a wide variety of circumstances that might not be related to a person's social life could result in depression (e.g., traumatic experiences). Secondly, using the Internet to alter mood was found to be lacking in influence on negative outcomes. For instance, it was proposed by Caplan that there are various different circumstances in which individuals use the Internet to alter their mood, and different usages would cause different mood alterations – for example, online game playing might be exciting and fun, while reading the news might be relaxing. Therefore, in itself, using the Internet to alter mood might not necessarily lead to the negative consequences associated with preference for online social interaction, excessive and compulsive use, and experiencing psychological withdrawal.

The limitations to this study include the need for future empirical evidence pertaining to the causality of specific CM communication characteristics that could lead to the preference for online social interaction. Also, the data were collected from a primarily sample that did not display very high degrees of problematic Internet use (median for preference was 1.28 on a scale ranging from 1 to 5; most participants did not prefer online over face-to-face social interactions). Finally, the study did not take into account the role that an individual's actual social skill and communication preference played in the development of problematic Internet use, despite the theory's emphasis on perceived social competence.

SUMMARY

This chapter has demonstrated that research into video-game and Internet addiction is a relatively little studied phenomenon, although there is more research regarding adolescent video-game addiction than there is on adolescent Internet addiction. Obviously, more research is needed before the debate on whether video-game and Internet addictions are distinct clinical entities is decided. From the sparse research, it is evident that playing video-games and Internet use appear to be at least potentially addictive. With respect to video-games, there is also a need for a general taxonomy of such games, as it could be the case that particular types of games are more addictive than others. Another major problem is that video-games can be played in lots of different ways, including on handheld consoles, personal computers, home video-game consoles, arcade machines, the Internet, and other portable devices (e.g., mobile phones, i-Pods). It may be the case that some of these media for playing games (such as in an arcade or on the Internet) may be more addictive because of other factors salient to that medium (for example, disinhibition on the Internet). Therefore, future research needs to distinguish between excessive play in different media.

There is also the question of developmental effects – that is, do video-games have the same effect regardless of age? It could well be the case that video-games have a more pronounced addictive effect in young children, but less of an effect (if any) once they have reached their adult years. There is also the social context of playing – that is, does playing in groups or individually, with or against each other, affect the potential addictiveness of games in any way? These points all need further empirical investigation.

It does appear that excessive video-game playing can have potentially damaging effects upon a minority of individuals who display compulsive and addictive behavior, and who will do anything possible to "feed their addiction". Such individuals need monitoring. Using these individuals in research would help to identify the roots and causes of addictive playing and the impact of such behavior on family and school life. It would be clinically useful to illustrate problem cases, even following them longitudinally and recording developmental features of the adolescent video-game addict. This would help to determine the variables that are salient in the acquisition, development and maintenance of video-game addiction. It may be that video-game addiction is age-related, like other more obviously "deviant" adolescent behaviors (e.g., glue sniffing), since there is little evidence to date of video-game addiction in adults – at least in offline games.

There is no doubt that video-game play usage among the general population will continue to increase over the next few years, and that if social pathologies (including video-game addiction) do exist then this is certainly an area for development that should be of interest and concern to all those involved in the addiction research field. Real-life problems need applied solutions and alternatives, and until there is an established body of literature on the psychological, sociological and physiological effects of video-game playing and video-game addiction, directions for education, prevention, intervention and treatment will remain limited in scope.

With respect to excessive Internet use, the labels Internet Addiction, Internet Addiction Disorder, Pathological Internet Use, Problematic Internet Use, Excessive Internet Use and Compulsive Internet Use have all been used to describe more or less the same concept – i.e., that an individual is so involved in their online use as to neglect other areas of his or her life. However, it would seem premature at this stage to use one label for the concept, as most of the studies conducted in the field so far have presented varying degrees of differences and conflicting results.

There is clearly a need to distinguish between addictions *to* the Internet and addictions *on* the Internet. Gambling addicts who chooses to engage in online gambling, as well as a computer game addicts who play online, are not Internet addicts; the Internet is just the place where they conduct their chosen (addictive) behavior. These people display addictions *on* the Internet. However, there is also the observation that some behaviors engaged on the Internet (e.g., cybersex, cyberstalking, etc.) may be behaviors that the person would only carry out on the

Internet because the medium is anonymous, non-face-to-face, and disinhibiting (Griffiths, 2000c, 2001).

In contrast, it is also acknowledged that there are some case studies that seem to report an addiction to the Internet itself (see, for example, Young, 1996b; Griffiths, 2000b). Most of these individuals use functions of the Internet that are not available in any other medium, such as chat rooms or various role-playing games. These are people addicted *to* the Internet. However, despite these differences there seem to be some common findings, most notably reports of the negative consequences of excessive Internet use (neglect of work and social life, relationship breakdowns, loss of control, etc.) which are comparable to those experienced with other, more established addictions. In conclusion, it would appear that if Internet addiction does indeed exist, it affects only a relatively small percentage of the online population and there is very little evidence that it is problematic among adolescents. However, exactly what it is on the Internet that they are addicted to still remains unclear.

REFERENCES

Abramson, L., Metalsky, G.I. and Alloy, L.B. (1989). Hopelessness depression: a theory-based subtype of depression. *Psychological Review*, 96, 358–372.

American Psychiatric Association (1987). *Diagnostic and Statistical Manual for Mental Disorders*, 3rd edn. Washington, DC: American Psychiatric Association.

Anderson, K.J. (1999). "Internet use among college students: should we be concerned?" Paper presented at the Annual Meeting of the American Psychological Association, Boston.

Armstrong, L., Phillips, J.G. and Saling, L.L. (2000). Potential determinants of heavier Internet usage. *International Journal of Human Computer Studies*, 53, 537–50

Beard, K. and Wolfe, E. (2001). Modification in the proposed diagnostic criteria for Internet addiction. *Cyberpsychology and Behavior*, 4, 377–383.

Black, D., Belsare, G. and Schlosser, S. (1999). Clinical features, psychiatric comorbidity and health-related quality of life in persons reporting compulsive computer use behavior. *Journal of Clinical Psychiatry*, 60, 839–843.

Brasington, R. (1990). Nintendinitis. *New England Journal of Medicine*, 322, 1473–1474.

Braun, C.M.J., Goupil, G., Giroux, J. and Chagnon, Y. (1986). Adolescents and microcomputers: sex differences, proxemics, task and stimulus variables. *Journal of Psychology*, 120, 529–542.

Brenner, V. (1997). Psychology of Computer Use: XLVII. Parameters of Internet use, abuse and addiction: the first 90 days of the Internet Usage Survey. *Psychological Reports*, 80, 879–882.

Brown, R.I.F. (1993). Some contributions of the study of gambling to the study of other addictions. In: W.R. Eadington and J.A. Cornelius (eds), *Gambling Behavior and Problem Gamblin*. Reno, NV: University of Nevada Press, pp. 241–272.

Brown, R.I.F. and Robertson, S. (1993). Home computer and video-game addictions in relation to adolescent gambling: conceptual and developmental aspects. In: W.R. Eadington and J.A. Cornelius (eds), *Gambling Behavior and Problem Gambling*. Reno, NV: University of Nevada Press, pp. 451–471.

Caplan, S.E. (2002). Problematic Internet use and psychosocial well-being: development of a theory-based cognitive-behavioral measurement instrument. *Computers in Human Behavior*, 18, 553–575.

Caplan, S.E. (2003). Preference for online social interaction: a theory of problematic Internet use and psychosocial well-being. *Communication Research*, 30, 625–648.

Casanova, J. and Casanova, J. (1991). Nintendinitis. *Journal of Hand Surgery*, 16, 181.

Chak, K. and Leung, L. (2004). Shyness and locus of control as predictors of Internet addiction and Internet use. *CyberPsychology and Behavior*, 7, 559–570.

Charlton, J.P. (2002). A factor analytic investigation of computer "addiction" and engagement. *British Journal of Psychology*, 93, 329–344.

Chin-Chung, T. and Sunny, L. (2003). Internet addiction of adolescents in Taiwan: an interview study. *CyberPsychology and Behavior*, 6, 649–652.

Chou, C. (2001). Internet heavy use and addiction among Taiwanese college students: an online interactive study. *CyberPsychology and Behavior*, 4, 573–585.

Cleary, A.G., Mckendrick, H. and Sills, J.A. (2002). Hand–arm vibration syndrome may be associated with prolonged use of vibrating computer games. *British Medical Journal*, 324, 301.

Colwell, J., Grady, C. and Rhaiti, S. (1995). Computer games, self-esteem and gratification of needs in adolescents. *Journal of Community and Applied Social Psychology*, 5, 195–206.

Corkery, J.C. (1990). Nintendo power. *American Journal of Diseases in Children*, 144, 959.

Davis, R. (2001). A cognitive-behavioral model of Pathological Internet Use. *Computers in Human Behavior*, 17, 187–195.

Deheger, M., Rolland-Cachera, M.F. and Fontvielle, A.M. (1997). Physical activity and body composition in 10-year-old French children: linkages with nutritional intake? *International Journal of Obesity*, 21, 372–379.

Egger, O. and Rauterberg, M. (1996). Internet behavior and addiction. Available at http://www.idemployee.id.tue.nl/g.w.m.rauterberg/ibq/res.htm (accessed 14 October 2005) from the Swiss Federal Institute of Technology, Zurich.

Egli, E.A. and Meyers, L.S. (1984). The role of video-game playing in adolescent life: is there a reason to be concerned? *Bulletin of the Psychonomic Society*, 22, 309–312.

Fisher, S. E. (1994). Identifying video-game addiction in children and adolescents. *Addictive Behaviors*, 19, 5, 545–553.

Friedland, R.P. and St. John, J.N. (1984). Video-game palsy: distal ulnar neuropathy in a video-game enthusiast. *New England Journal of Medicine*, 311, 58–59.

Glasser (1976). *Positive Addictions*. New York, NY: Harper & Row.

Graf, W.D., Chatrian, G.E., Glass, S.T. and Knauss, T.A. (1994). Video-game related seizures: a report on 10 patients and a review of the literature. *Pediatrics*, 3, 551–556.

Greenfield, D.N. (1999). Psychological characteristics of compulsive Internet use: a preliminary analysis. *CyberPsychology and Behavior*, 2, 403–412.

Griffiths, M.D. (1990a). The acquisition, development and maintenance of fruit machine gambling in adolescence. *Journal of Gambling Studies*, 6, 193–204.

Griffiths, M.D. (1990b). The cognitive psychology of gambling. *Journal of Gambling Studies*, 6, 31–42.

Griffiths, M.D. (1991). Amusement machine playing in childhood and adolescence: a comparative analysis of video-games and fruit machines. *Journal of Adolescence*, 14, 53–73.

Griffiths, M.D. (1993). Are computer games bad for children? *The Psychologist: Bulletin of the British Psychological Society*, 6, 401–407.

Griffiths, M.D. (1995a). Technological addictions. *Clinical Psychology Forum*, 76, 14–19.

Griffiths, M.D. (1995b). *Adolescent Gambling*. London: Routledge.

Griffiths, M.D. (1996a). Internet "addiction": an issue for clinical psychology? *Clinical Psychology Forum*, 97, 32–36.

Griffiths, M.D. (1996b). Behavioral addictions: an issue for everybody? *Journal of Workplace Learning*, 8(3), 19–25.

Griffiths, M.D. (1997a). Video-games and children's behavior. In: T. Charlton and K. David (eds), *Elusive Links: Television, Video-games, Cinema and Children's Behavior*. Gloucester, Gloucestershire: GCED/Park Publishers, pp. 66–93.

Griffiths, M.D. (1997b). Computer game playing in early adolescence. *Youth and Society*, 29, 223–237.

Griffiths, M.D. (1998). Internet addiction: does it really exist? In: J. Gackenbach (ed.), *Psychology and the Internet: Intrapersonal, Interpersonal and Transpersonal Applications*. New York, NY: Academic Press, pp. 61–75.

Griffiths, M.D. (1999). Internet addiction: Internet fuels other addictions. *Student British Medical Journal*, 7, 428–429.

Griffiths, M.D. (2000a). Internet addiction – time to be taken seriously? *Addiction Research*, 8, 413–418.

Griffiths, M.D. (2000b). Does Internet and computer "addiction" exist? Some case study evidence. *Cyberpsychology and Behavior*, 3, 211–18.

Griffiths, M.D. (2000c). Excessive Internet use: implications for sexual behavior. *CyberPsychology and Behavior*, 3, 537–552.

Griffiths, M.D. (2001). Sex on the Internet: observations and implications for sex addiction. *Journal of Sex Research*, 38, 333–342.

Griffiths, M.D. (2002). *Gambling and Gaming Addictions in Adolescence*. Leicester, Leicestershire: British Psychological Society/Blackwells.

Griffiths, M.D. (2003a). The therapeutic use of video-games in childhood and adolescence. *Clinical Child Psychology and Psychiatry*, 8, 547–554.

Griffiths, M.D. (2003b). Video-games: advice for teachers and parents. *Education and Health*, 21, 48–49.

Griffiths, M.D. (2005a). A "components" model of addiction within a biopsychosocial framework. *Journal of Substance Use*, 10, 191–197.

Griffiths, M.D. (2005b). The relationship between gambling and video-game playing: a response to Johansson and Gotestam. *Psychological Reports*, 96, 644–646.

Griffiths, M.D. (2005c). Video-games and health. *British Medical Journal*, 331, 122–123.

Griffiths, M.D. (2006). Impact of gambling technologies in a multi-media world. *Casino and Gaming International*, 2, 15–18.

Griffiths, M.D. (2007). *Gambling Addiction and its Treatment within the NHS*. London: British Medical Association.

Griffiths, M.D. and Dancaster, I. (1995). The effect of Type A personality on physiological arousal while playing computer games. *Addictive Behaviors*, 20, 543–548.

Griffiths, M.D. and Hunt, N. (1995). Computer game playing in adolescence: prevalence and demographic indicators. *Journal of Community and Applied Social Psychology*, 5, 189–194.

Griffiths, M.D. and Hunt, N. (1998). Dependence on computer games by adolescents. *Psychological Reports*, 82, 475–480.

Griffiths, M.D., Davies, M.N.O. and Chappell, D. (2003). Breaking the stereotype: the case of online gaming. *CyberPsychology and Behavior*, 6, 81–91.

Griffiths, M.D., Davies, M.N.O. and Chappell, D. (2004a). Online computer gaming: a comparison of adolescent and adult gamers. *Journal of Adolescence*, 27, 87–96.

Griffiths, M.D., Davies, M.N.O. and Chappell, D. (2004b). Demographic factors and playing variables in online computer gaming. *CyberPsychology and Behavior*, 7, 479–487.

Grüsser, S.M., Thalemann, R. and Griffiths, M.D. (2007). Excessive computer game playing: evidence for addiction and aggression? *Cyberpsychology and Behavior*, 10, 290–292.

Gupta, R. and Derevensky, J.L. (1997). The relationship between gambling and video-game playing behavior in children and adolescents. *Journal of Gambling Studies*, 12, 375–394.

Gutman, D. (1982). Video-games wars. *Video-game Player*, Fall, whole issue.

Hall, A.S. and Parsons, J. (2001). Internet addiction: college student case study using best practices in cognitive behavior therapy. *Journal of Mental Health Counselling*, 23, 312–327.

Harding, G.F.A. and Jeavons, P.M. (1994). *Photosensitive Epilepsy*. London: Mac Keith Press.

Holden, C. (2001). "Behavioral" addictions: do they exist? *Science*, 294, 5544.

Jackson, L.A., von Eye, A., Biocca, F.A. *et al.* (2003). Personality, cognitive style, demographic characteristics and Internet use – findings from the HomeNetToo project. *Swiss Journal of Psychology*, 62, 79–90.

Johnson, B. and Hackett, A.F. (1997). Eating habits of 11- to 14-year-old schoolchildren living in less affluent areas of Liverpool, UK. *Journal of Human Nutrition and Dietetics*, 10, 135–144.

Julien, R.M. (1995). *A Primer of Drug Action: A Concise, Nontechnical Guide to the Actions, Uses and Side Effects of Psychoactive Drugs*. Oxford, Oxfordshire: Freeman.

Kaltiala-Heino, R., Lintonen, T. and Rimpela, A. (2004). Internet addiction? Potentially problematic use of the Internet in a population of 12- to 18-year-old adolescents. *Addiction Research and Theory*, 12, 89–96.

Kaplan, S.J. (1983). The image of amusement arcades and differences in male and female video-game playing. *Journal of Popular Culture*, 16, 93–98.

Keepers, G.A. (1990). Pathologicical preoccupation with video-games. *Journal of the American Academy of Child and Adolescent Psychiatry*, 29, 49–50.

Keisler, S., Sproull, L. and Eccles, J.S. (1983). Second class citizens. *Psychology Today*, 17(3), 41–48.

Kennedy-Souza, B. (1998). Internet addiction disorder. *Interpersonal Computing and Technology: An Electronic Journal for the 21st Century*, 6(1–2). Available at http://www.emoderators.com/ipct-j/1998/n1-2/kennedy-souza.html (accessed 10 December 2003).

Klein, M.H. (1984). The bite of Pac-man. *Journal of Psychohistory*, 11, 395–401.

Koepp, M.J., Gunn, R.N., Lawrence, A.D. *et al.* (1998). Evidence for striatal dopamine release during a video-game. *Nature*, 393, 266–268.

Kuczmierczyk, A.R., Walley, P.B. and Calhoun, K.S. (1987). Relaxation training, in vivo exposure and response-prevention in the treatment of compulsive video-game playing. *Scandinavian Journal of Behavior Therapy*, 16, 185–190.

Kraut, R., Patterson, M., Lundmark, V. *et al.* (1998). Internet paradox: a social technology that reduces social involvement and psychological well being? *American Psychologist*, 53, 1017–1031.

Kraut, R., Kiesler, S., Boneva, B. *et al.* (2002). Internet paradox revisited. *Journal of Social Issues*, 58, 49–74.

Kubey, R.W., Lavin, M.J. and Barrows, J.R. (2001). Internet use and collegiate academic performance decrements: early findings. *Journal of Communication*, 51, 366–382.

Lavin, M., Marvin, K., McLarney, A. *et al.* (1999). Sensation seeking and collegiate vulnerability to Internet dependence. *Cyberpsychology and Behavior*, 2, 425–430.

Leon, D. and Rotunda, R. (2000). Contrasting case studies of frequent Internet use: is it pathological or adaptive? *Journal of College Student Psychotherapy*, 14, 9–17.

Lo, S., Wang, C. and Fang, W. (2005). Physical interpersonal relationships and social anxiety among online game players. *CyberPsychology and Behavior*, 8(1), 15–20.

Loftus, G.A. and Loftus, E.F. (1983). *Mind at Play: The Psychology of Video-games*. New York, NY: Basic Books.

Maccoby, E.E. and Jacklin, C.N. (1974). *The Psychology of Sex Differences*. Stanford, CA: Stanford University Press.

Maeda, Y., Kurokawa, T., Sakamoto, K. *et al.* (1990). Electroclinical study of video-game epilepsy. *Developmental Medicine and Child Neurology*, 32, 493–500.

Marks, I. (1990). Non-chemical (behavioural) addictions. *British Journal of Addiction*, 85, 1389–1394.

Mathy, R. and Cooper, A. (2003). The duration and frequency of Internet use in a nonclinical sample: suicidality, behavioural problems and treatment histories. *Psychotherapy: Theory, Research, Practice, Training*, 40, 125–135.

McCowan, T.C. (1981). Space Invaders' wrist. *New England Journal of Medicine*, 304, 1368.

McIlwraith, R. (1990, August). "Theories of television addiction." Paper presented at the Annual Meeting of the American Psychological Association, Boston.

Miller, D.L.G. (1991). Nintendo neck. *Canadian Medical Association Journal*, 145, 1202.

Millett, C.J., Fish, D.R. and Thompson, P.J. (1997). A survey of epilepsy-patient perceptions of video-game material/electronic screens and other factors as seizure precipitants. *Seizure*, 6, 457–459.

Mirman, M.J. and Bonian, V.G. (1992). "Mouse elbow": a new repetitive stress injury. *Journal of the American Osteopath Association*, 92, 701.

Mitchell, P. (2000). Internet addiction: genuine diagnosis or not? Lancet, 355, 632.

Moore, D. (1995). *The Emperor's Virtual Clothes: The Naked Truth about the Internet Culture.* Chapel Hill, NC: Alogonquin.

Morahan-Martin, J. and Schumacher, P. (2000). Incidents and correlates of pathological Internet use among college students. *Computers in Human Behavior*, 16, 13–29.

Morgan, C. and Cotton, S.R., (2003). The relationship between Internet activities and depressive symptoms in a sample of college freshman. *CyberPsychology and Behavior*, 6, 133–143.

Nalwa, K. and Anand, A.P. (2003). Internet addiction in students: a cause of concern. *CyberPsychology and Behavior*, 6, 653–656.

Niemz, K., Griffiths, M.D. and Banyard, P. (2005). Prevalence of pathological Internet use among university students and correlations with self-esteem, GHQ and disinhibition, *CyberPsychology and Behavior*, 8, 562–570.

Orzack, H. and Orzack, D. (1999). Treatment of computer addicts with complex comorbid psychiatric disorders. *Cyberpsychology and Behavior*, 2, 465–473.

Parsons, K. (1995). "Educational places or terminal cases: young people and the attraction of computer games." Paper presented at the British Sociological Association Annual Conference, University of Leicester.

Petrie, H. and Gunn, D. (1998). "Internet 'addiction': the effects of sex, age, depression and introversion." Paper presented at the British Psychological Society London Conference, London.

Phillips, C.A., Rolls, S., Rouse, A. and Griffiths, M. (1995). Home video-game playing in schoolchildren: a study of incidence and patterns of play. *Journal of Adolescence*, 18, 687–691.

Phillips, W.R. (1991). Video-game therapy. *New England Journal of Medicine*, 325, 1056–1057.

Pratarelli, M., Browne, B. and Johnson, K. (1999). The bits and bytes of computer/Internet addiction: a factor analytic approach. *Behavior Research Methods, Instruments and Computers*, 31, 305–314.

Professional Association of Teachers (1994). *The Street of the Pied Piper: A Survey of Teachers' Perceptions of the Effects on Children of the New Entertainment Technologies.* Derby: Professional Association of Teachers.

Quirk, J.A., Fish, D.R., Smith, S.J.M. *et al.* (1995). First seizures associated with playing electronic screen games: a community based study in Great Britain. *Annals of Neurology*, 37, 110–124.

Reinstein, L. (1983). De Quervain's stenosing tenosynovitis in a video-games player. *Archives of Physical and Medical Rehabilitation*, 64, 434–435.

Rotunda, R.J., Kass, S.J., Sutton, M.A. and Leon, D.T. (2003). Internet use and misuse: preliminary findings from a new assessment instrument. *Behavior Modification*, 27, 484–504.

Rutkowska, J.C. and Carlton, T. (1994). "Computer games in 12- to 13-year-olds' activities and social networks." Paper presented at the British Psychological Society Annual Conference, University of Sussex.

Scherer, K. (1997). College life on-line: healthy and unhealthy Internet use. *Journal of College Student Development*, 38, 655–665.

Schink, J.C. (1991). Nintendo enuresis. *American Journal of Diseases in Children*, 145, 1094.

Selnow, G.W. (1984). Playing video-games: the electronic friend. *Journal of Communication*, 34, 148–156.

Shaffer, H., Hall, M. and Vander Bilt, J. (2000). "Computer addiction": a critical consideration. *American Journal of Orthopsychiatry*, 70, 162–168.

Shapira, N., Goldsmith, T., Keck, P. Jr *et al.* (2000). Psychiatric features of individuals with problematic Internet use. *Journal of Affective Disorders*, 57, 267–272.

Shapira, N., Lessig, M., Goldsmith, T. *et al.* (2003). Problematic Internet use: proposed classification and diagnostic criteria. *Depression and Anxiety*, 17, 207–216.

Shimai, S., Yamada, F., Masuda, K. and Tada, M. (1993). TV game play and obesity in Japanese school children. *Perceptual and Motor Skills*, 76, 1121–1122.

Shotton, M. (1989). *Computer Addiction? A Study of Computer Dependency*. London: Taylor & Francis.

Siegal, I.M. (1991). Nintendonitis. *Orthopedics*, 14, 745.

Soper, W.B. and Miller, M.J. (1983). Junk time junkies: an emerging addiction among students. *School Counsellor*, 31, 40–43.

Spence, S.A. (1993). Nintendo hallucinations: a new phenomenological entity. *Irish Journal of Psychological Medicine*, 10, 98–99.

Surrey, D. (1982). "It's like good training for life". *Natural History*, 91, 71–83.

Tejeiro-Dalguero, R.A.T. and Moran, R.M.B. (2002). Measuring problem video-game playing in adolescents. *Addiction*, 97, 1601–1606.

Treuer, T., Fabian, Z. and Furedi, J. (2001). Internet addiction associated with features of impulse control disorder: is it a real psychiatric disorder? *Journal of Affective Disorders*, 66, 283.

Tsai, C-C. and Lin, S.S.J. (2003). Internet addiction of adolescents in Taiwan: an interview study. *CyberPsychology and Behavior*, 6, 649–652.

Vandewater, E.A., Shim, M. and Caplovitz, A.G. (2004). Linking obesity and activity level with children's television and video-game use. *Journal of Adolescence*, 27, 71–85.

Wan, C. and Chiou, B. Why are adolescents addicted to online gaming? An interview study in Taiwan. *CyberPsychology and Behavior* 9, 762–766.

Wanner, E. (1982). The electronic bogeyman. *Psychology Today*, 16(10), 8–11.

Wästlund, E., Norlander, T. and Archer, T. (2001). Internet blues revisited: replication and extension for an Internet paradox study. *Cyberpsychology and Behavior*, 4, 385–391.

Widyanto, L. and McMurran, M. (2004). The psychometric properties of the Internet addiction test. *CyberPsychology and Behavior*, 7, 443–450.

Wood, R.T.A. and Griffiths, M.D. (2007). Time loss whilst playing video-games: is there a relationship to addictive behaviors? *International Journal of Mental Health and Addiction*, 5, 141–149.

Wood, R.T.A., Griffiths, M.D., Chappell, D. and Davies, M.N.O. (2004). The structural characteristics of video-games: a psycho-structural analysis. *CyberPsychology and Behavior*, 7, 1–10.

Wood, R.T.A., Griffiths, M.D. and Parke, A. (2007). Experiences of time loss among video-game players: an empirical study. *CyberPsychology and Behavior*, 10, 45–56.

Xuanhui, L. and Gonggu, Y. (2001). Internet addiction disorder, online behavior and personality. *Chinese Mental Health Journal*, 15, 281–283.

Yoo, H.J., Cho, S.C., Ha, J. *et al.* (2004). Attention deficit hyperactivity symptoms and Internet addiction. *Psychiatry and Clinical Neurosciences*, 58, 487–494.

Young, K. (1996a). Internet addiction: the emergence of a new clinical disorder. *CyberPsychology and Behavior*, 3, 237–44.

Young, K. (1996b). Psychology of computer use: XL. Addictive use of the Internet: a case that breaks the stereotype. *Psychological Reports*, 79, 899–902.

Young, K. (1998). *Caught in the Net: How to Recognize the Signs of Internet Addiction and a Winning Strategy for Recovery*. New York, NY: Wiley.

Young K. (1999). Internet addiction: evaluation and treatment. *Student British Medical Journal*, 7, 351–352.

Young, K. and Rodgers, R. (1998). "Internet addiction: personality traits associated with its development." Paper presented at the 69th Annual meeting of the Eastern Psychological Association.

Young, K. Pistner, M., O'Mara, J. and Buchanan, J. (1999). Cyber disorders: the mental health concern for the new millennium. *Cyberpsychology and Behavior*, 2, 475–479.

Yu, Z. F. and Zhao, Z. (2004). A report on treating Internet addiction disorder with cognitive behavior therapy. *International Journal of Psychology*, 39, 407.

Zimbardo, P. (1982). Understanding psychological man: a state of the science report. *Psychology Today*, 16, 15.

9

TEEN SEXUAL ADDICTION

STEVE SUSSMAN

Very little thought or research has been directed to the topic of teen sexual addiction. This *status quo* is due to differences in opinion regarding the concept of sexual addiction as it applies to teens. This chapter provides a pioneer examination of this concept. Its definitions, definitional problems, epidemiology, course/consequences, predictors (risk and protective factors), prevention and treatment are described. It is concluded that there probably does exist a phenomenon of sexual addiction that applies across the life course (including the teenage years), and which deserves much more study alongside other types of addictive behaviors.

DEFINITION

Schaef (1987) proposed a typology to attempt to differentially classify various addictive behaviors. According to him, substance addictions involve all mood-altering products, including drugs (e.g., caffeine, nicotine, alcohol, cocaine, heroin, etc.) and food-related disorders (e.g., anorexia, bulimia, overeating, etc.). Substance addictions involve direct manipulation of pleasure through use of products that are taken into the body. Process addictions (Schaef, 1987) consist of a series of actions that expose an individual to "mood-altering events" from which that person achieves pleasure and on which he or she becomes dependent (e.g., gambling, workaholism, excessive exercise and sex, excessive spending, excessive television watching, and so on). Compulsive sexual behavior is a process addiction, according to Schaef (see Schneider and Irons, 2001, for additional discussion).

Process addictions involve a more indirect manipulation of pleasure through situational and physical activity manipulations, which may then alter neurotransmitter function, particularly mesolimbic dopaminergic turnover (Mani *et al.*, 2000; Bradley and Meisel, 2001; Sussman and Ames, 2001). Through repetitive sexual behavior, an individual may attempt to achieve a desired psychological state, similar to that desired by a substance addiction. In some cases, out-of-control sexual behavior may operate like prototypical compulsive behavior – that is, to remove a negative state as opposed to achieve a positive state – though many argue it primarily operates as a pleasure-producing behavior (Carnes, 1996; Schneider and Irons, 2001). The words "compulsive" and "addictive" will be used interchangeably throughout the rest of this chapter.

The range of human sexual activity is quite variable, and it is difficult to differentiate normal from abnormal sexual behavior in form and frequency. Sexual addiction is not so much mere form or frequency of sexual behavior. Sexual addiction is a pattern of sexual behavior that is initially pleasurable but becomes unfulfilling and self-destructive, and that a person is unable to stop. That is, sexual addiction refers to a loss of control over an individual's sexual behavior that causes negative consequences in his or her life. According to The Society for the Advancement of Sexual Health (SASH), there are three general questions that may be asked regarding the likelihood of having a sexual addiction (http://www.sash.net/general/addict_faqs.aspx):

> The three basic questions you can ask yourself are:
>
> 1. Do I feel like I've lost the ability to control my sexual behavior (e.g., crossed lines I didn't think I would cross, set limits that I have failed to meet, made promises to stop a behavior and then continued it)?
> 2. Do I experience consequences because of my sexual behavior (e.g., miss work or call in late because of acting out, risk my relationships, loss of spirituality, legal consequences)?
> 3. Do I constantly think about sexual activity even when I don't want to (e.g., spend hours cruising for sexual experiences, dream about sexual behavior regularly, spend time preparing for sexual behaviors, dwell on sexual experiences long after they are over)?
>
> (Adapted from Schneider, 1994; see also Schneider and Irons, 2001)

There appear to be three social manifestations of compulsive sexual behavior assessed on the various self-report measures utilized by The Society for the Advancement of Sexual Health (SASH) and the five main twelve-step sexual-addiction organizations (discussed towards the end of the chapter; see questionnaires at: www.sash.net, www.saa-recovery.org, www.slaafws.org, www.sa.org; www.sca-recovery.org, e-mail: sexualrecovery.org). These social manifestations are: (i) solitary acts (excessive masturbation, possibly excluding other forms of sex); (ii) unilateral acts (one acting on a passive other, such as repetitive flirting, or sexual comments, body touching, ogling, abusive sex); or (iii) mutual participatory acts involving two or more people.

In addition, these assessments indicate that there are many behavioral forms that a sexual addiction may take. Forms of compulsive sex may include: (i) regularly reading romance novels or sexually explicit magazines, sexual daydreams or searching for sexual images in daily life scenes (e.g., ogling, popular magazines); (ii) exchanging money or gifts for sex; or (iii) engagement in sexual "perversions" (statistically unusual behavior). There is a long list of potential perversions, which include the following:

- Sado-masochistic behavior (e.g., bondage and discipline)
- Fixation (paraphilia) on certain body parts (e.g., feet, breasts), objects used to stimulate sexual organs (e.g., vibrators, penis rings), objects used in role plays (e.g., baby in diapers, nylons, playing doctor), animals (e.g., dogs, horses) or certain locations (e.g., public bathrooms, elevators)
- Excretory-sexual integrations (e.g., golden showers, scat)
- Sex with persons of different age groups (e.g., older people, minors)
- High-tech or cyber sex (chat rooms, considering chat-room sex as not cheating on another person, Internet pornography, CD-ROM pornography, fantasy online /telephone acts that would be illegal if real)
- Involvement in "swing parties", orgies or anonymous sex (agreed upon or not agreed upon affairs with one or multiple persons, with one or both genders, or with transgender persons)
- Sex while using particular drugs (e.g., cocaine, poppers/inhalants).

The functions that sexually addictive behaviors serve include the following:

- A means of spending time (like a hobby)
- Validation of oneself as a virile person (e.g., keeping a list of "conquests", feeling like a competent person as a lover)
- To relax or feel elated ("high", "really alive")
- To escape from other life problems (a distraction, entertainment)
- To feel "whole" or "fixed" by another
- To feel that life has meaning (e.g., as if it were a spiritual experience)
- Confusing sex with love, totally compartmentalizing sex apart from love, or otherwise eliminating negative or positive feelings that could be sensed as initially overwhelming through replacing them with sexual obsessions.

Loss of control over sexual behavior is assessed through reports of any of several types of events. Individuals may have sought help from someone else due to their uncontrolled sexual thoughts or behavior, or may have broken promises to themselves or lied to others about their sexual behavior. They may have found that the frequency, variety, or intensity of their sexual activities has increased over time, or gone through periods of sexual binges such as having multiple partners followed by periods of celibacy. They may have tried consciously to control the frequency or situations under which they engage in sex, or have tried to stop or control the frequency of a form of sexual behavior and failed. They may feel that their urges for sex are out of control. They may feel unable to refuse another's sexual advance, and may also be grossly insensitive to the plight of another in their pursuit for sexual release.

Negative consequences (unmanageability) of compulsive sex, other than loss of control, may include a number of outcomes. There are several types of negative self-evaluations *or* feelings that individuals may assert or experience due to their sexual behavior: (i) feeling abnormal or sick; (ii) feeling degraded, guilty, shamed by the behavior; (iii) feeling regret, depression or discomfort over the behavior; (iv) feeling numb, hollow or empty after sexually acting out; and (v) feeling desperate about their chances of having a solid and healthy relationship. There are several associated aspects of this sense of desperation, including that the individual may feel dependent on providers of sex yet want to get away from the sex partner as soon as possible after the act, and may have sex with people they generally would not be friends with in locations they generally would not want to be at. They may notice a lack of true intimacy in relationships and feel lonely. They may resort to fantasies in thought or behavior while having sex with a significant other (which may distance one partner from the other emotionally) and experience difficulty concentrating about other topics.

Individuals may have lost school, family or work time due to time spent searching for and engaging in sexual experiences. They may have created problems for their family, including hurt feelings/worry, isolation from the family, or being secretive about their life, or they may have exerted a financial drain on themselves or others. They may have been arrested for a sex-related offence (e.g., voyeurism, exhibitionism, prostitution, sex with minors, indecent phone calls), worry about or be suffering from a sex-related disease (STDs, HIV, AIDS), or have experienced an unwanted or unexpected pregnancy, a worsening of their reputation, or victimization (e.g., by being drawn to dangerous people).

The DSM-IV-TR (APA, 2000) provides diagnoses for Sexual and Gender Identity Disorders, which are subdivided into Sexual Dysfunctions, Paraphilias, Gender Identity Disorders, and Sexual Disorder Not Otherwise Specified. The term "sexual addiction" is not found in the DSM-IV; however, the Sexual Disorder Not Otherwise Specified section includes a sexual addiction-type example and permits most such classifications therein (Irons and Schneider, 1996). It is also possible that a diagnosis of Paraphilia or of an Impulse Control Disorder Not Otherwise Specified might be used, as well as other qualifying categories, depending on patient symptomatology (Irons and Schneider, 1996). There are working groups that are attempting to establish sexual addiction as a separate formal category in the DSM-V (Robert E. Longo, personal communication). To repeat, classical symptoms, as with other addictions, include obsession, loss of control, continuation despite adverse consequences, escalation of behaviors, and high relapse rates after treatment (Sussman and Ames, 2001).

DIFFICULTY IN DEFINING SEXUAL ADDICTION IN TEENAGERS

These same social manifestations, behavioral forms, functions, loss of control and negative consequences related to sexual addiction may occur among teens. However, there also are several differences between identification of sexual addiction among teens versus adults. Adolescent sexual addiction may differ from adult sexual addiction in at least five ways. First, occasional sexual behavior may or may not be considered abnormal in adults, whereas it may be considered abnormal in youth because of the potential of such behavior to interfere with emotional development and adjustment (Sussman, 2005). For example, it may be considered imprudent to engage in such behavior prior to achieving a fully developed brain in which cortical inhibitory processes are fully functional (Sussman, 2005).

Sussman (2005) examined 29 studies found in a search of the literature (on adolescent sexual behavior and cigarette smoking) that examined varying perspectives of risky sexual behavior among teens. Two general perspectives were found. Some researchers defined risky sexual behavior among teens as being participation in any mutual acts, while other researchers defined risky sexual behavior among teens as being dangerous behaviors (e.g., not using condoms, multiple partners). Sussman found that in a set of 19 US studies located, 9 used an early sexual behavior perspective whereas 10 used the hazardous sexual behavior perspective. Of ten other studies conducted outside of the US (four in the Americas, two in Northern Europe and four in the Far East or Africa), seven used the early sexual behavior perspective and three used the hazardous sexual behavior perspective. Thus, researchers appear roughly evenly split between the two perspectives regarding what constitutes unhealthy sexual behavior among teens, at least in those 29 studies. Of course, if any sexual behavior is considered abnormal, then it would seem to more-or-less preclude the need for consideration of a term for teen sexual addiction, which involves repeated acts.

Conversely, teens may be considered to be highly sexually charged as a group. As such, they might be relatively likely to engage in frequent sexual acts due to rapidly changing hormonal levels occurring in this stage of development. If so, then some people may consider uncontrolled, repeated acts as being typical of a teenage status and not addictive (Robert E. Longo, personal communication). In summary, any mutual sexual behavior, hazardous sexual behavior, or perhaps only hazardous (but not frequent) sexual behavior might be considered to reflect sexual addiction among teens. There is quite a wide range to consider. Given the definitions offered at the beginning of this chapter, perhaps hazardous sexual behavior, or sexual behavior that reflects a subjective lack of control and consequential negative affect, may be reasonable criteria to define a sexual addiction among most teens.

Second, high-risk situations may differ between adolescents and adults. In particular, adolescents may be relatively likely to sexually act out while not being responsible for the care-taking of others. Thus, they may bring worry to their parents or friends but not someone that is dependent on them (not including teen parentage). Furthermore, it is possible that the types of risky, compulsive sexual behavior may differ for teens. While adults may engage in a variety of acts, it may be speculated that teens are relatively likely to engage in acts specifically involving the Internet (see, for example, Boies *et al.*, 2004; Peter and Valkenberg, 2006; Weiss and Schneider, 2006). In addition, a relatively greater percentage of their sexual behavior is likely to be solitary acts.

Third, teens may experience relatively higher rates of dual diagnosis – that is, comorbidity of sexual acting out, substance use disorders and other mental health disorders (Brannigan *et al.*, 2004). For example, well over half of the youth in treatment for substance use disorders have other psychopathology in addition to substance use problems (e.g., depressive and anxiety disorders, social phobia, PTSD, conduct disorders or oppositional defiant disorder, sexual acting out; see Abrantes *et al.*, 2004; Tomlinson *et al.*, 2004; Malow *et al.*, 2006a). Fourth, teens may be relatively less likely to seek treatment, and relapse more quickly than adults do after treatment (O'Leary *et al.*, 2002; Cornelius *et al.*, 2003). Finally, adolescents may have a higher likelihood of suffering social consequences specific to adolescence (e.g., problems at school, statutory difficulties, truncated development; see Newcomb and Bentler, 1988; Blum, 1995).

Contacting the Experts

In July and August of 2006, the current author contacted 12 leading experts in the field of sexual addiction: Patrick Carnes, PhD (Executive Director of Gentle Path Program at Pine Grove Recovery Center in Hattiesburg, Mississippi, and Associate Editor of the journal *Sexual Addiction and Compulsivity*), M. Deborah Corley, PhD (Director of Research and Family Services at Sante Center for Healing in Argyle, Texas), David L. Delmonico, PhD (Associate Professor at Duquesne University School of Education in Pittsburgh, Pennsylvania, and Editor of the journal *Sexual Addiction and Compulsivity*), Ralph H. Earle, PhD, ABPP (President of New Hope Educational Foundation and Director of Psychological Counseling Services in Scottsdale, Arizona, and on the editorial board of the journal *Sexual Addiction and Compulsivity*), Elizabeth Griffin, MA (Chief Operating Officer of the American Foundation for Addiction Research in Minneapolis, Minnesota, and on the editorial board of the journal *Sexual Addiction and Compulsivity*), Seth Kalichman, PhD (Professor of Social Psychology at the University of Connecticut in Storrs), Robert E. Longo, MRC, LPC (Clinical Director of Youth Residential Services, Old Vineyard Youth Services, Universal Health Services, Inc., Winston-Salem, North Carolina), Robert Malow, PhD (Professor and Director of AIDS Prevention Program, Department of Public Health, Florida International University in Miami), Marilyn Murray, MA (President of Health Restoration International in Scottsdale, Arizona), David Price, LMHC, MS, CAS, BS (Professional Counselor, Information Consultant, SPSES, Assistant Clinical Director of Deveroux Foundation, Rutland, Massachusettts), Jennifer P. Schneider, MD, PhD (Internist at Arizona Community Physicians, and Associate Editor of the journal *Sexual Addiction and*

Compulsivity), and Rob Weiss, LCSW, CAS (Clinical Director of the Sexual Recovery Institute in Los Angeles, California). None of them knew of empirical studies on teen sexual addiction *per se*, and Seth Kalichman and Robert Longo queried whether or not teens can develop such an addiction, given that this is a time of rapid development and exploration. Pat Carnes stated that over the years he had met many sex addicts who knew by their adolescence that there was something different about their approach to sexual behavior. Further, he mentioned that up to the present time no one has engaged in systematic retrospective assessments of adult addicts on their adolescence. He also cautioned that addiction and adolescence look alike – "So your focus could be differential diagnosis which would be useful for many" (Pat Carnes, personal communication).

Likewise, M. Deborah Corley commented that:

> since teens can become addicted to food, gambling, exercise and substances, it only makes logical sense that they can become addicted to sex as well. My experience with a couple thousand sex addicts (excluding cybersex addicts – that onset is often quicker and can be long-time addiction continued or just stumbling into the abyss online) is that most report their acting out behavior started in preadolescence or adolescence (a few started masturbation earlier as way to self-soothe or self-injure and it is related to trauma repetition/compulsion). The gateway drug for nearly 100 percent of male sex addicts is pornography of some sort. Although some female sex addicts report starting to act out in adolescence, we just don't see enough female sex addicts for me to respond with confidence about adolescence experiences. Unfortunately, many behaviors that we hear about from addicts are also what we often hear from males in general as "normal" behavior in adolescent years – only the behavior does not balance itself out when raging hormones relax a bit and other distractions come along – and as the brain matures and values and impulse control is developed.

She continues:

> Normal adolescent sexual behavior does not seem to have the huge shame that comes along with addict behavior. I think in making a diagnosis, one has to be careful not to look at frequency but more about what impact the sexual behaviors are having on the adolescent.
>
> (M. Deborah Corley, personal communication).

The area of teen sexual addition appears to be an omission, or a very difficult concept to qualify. Differential diagnosis appears to involve assessment of the effect of the sexual behavior on the teen. Negative consequences reflecting a result of sexual "acting out" (e.g., engaging in repetitive masturbation as a means to regulate affect, acquiring an STD as the result of having unprotected sex with several partners) appears to be a key element of differential diagnosis among teens. This statement, of course, precludes consideration that some adults may view any sexual engagement by teens as being abnormal. More systematic research is needed to increase our understanding of the specifics of adolescent sexual addiction.

In November of 2006, I met with Robert Weiss, LCSW, CAS, Executive Director, and Omar Minwalla, PsyD, Clinical Director, of the Sexual Recovery Institute (SRI) in Los Angeles. The SRI has seen over 1000 male sex addicts since opening its doors in 1995. The two directors suggested some unique features that teens with developing sex addictions might display, based on retrospective reports they recalled from their clients. These features include:

1. Masturbation to self-soothe (e.g., after an argument with parents, when feeling anxiety), perhaps feeling drained or depressed after ejaculating, perhaps masturbating to the point of injury
2. A tendency to try to get emotional needs met through sexual fantasy or behavior
3. Pursuit of sexual pleasure beginning to become a priority
4. Many life situations becoming interpreted in sexual terms, life becoming sexualized
5. Potential withdrawal from others and institutions into a more sexually-focused world (e.g., a teen may seek out adult females, may get STDs).

Thus, the underlying aspects of teen sexual addiction, according to them, appear to be dysfunctional relations of sexual activity with affect, imparting many stimuli with sexual connotations, and focusing on sex as a main reinforcer (source of direction).

EPIDEMIOLOGY, COMORBIDITY AND USE OF MENTAL HEALTH SERVICES

EPIDEMIOLOGY

It has been estimated that sexual addiction affects 3–6 percent of the US population (Carnes, 1991), and is relatively highly prevalent among emerging adults (Seegers, 2003). Among teens, however, it is difficult to make an estimate of prevalence, since any teen sexual behavior is seen by some people as being a problem (Sussman, 2005) whereas excessive thoughts about sex may be considered part of normal adolescent development by others (Robert E. Longo, personal communication; Seth Kalichman, personal communication). It is known that approximately 50 percent of high school students (across the ninth through twelfth grades) in the US have reported having ever had sexual intercourse (54% in 1991 to 47% in 2005; CDC, 2006) and between 14 percent (2005) and 19 percent (1991) have reported having four or more sexual partners in their lifetime (Valois *et al.*, 1999; CDC, 2006). The percentages reporting ever having had sexual intercourse by grade were as follows: 34 percent in ninth grade, 43 percent in tenth grade, 51 percent in eleventh grade, and 63 percent in twelfth grade (6% reported having had sexual intercourse before 13 years of age). Furthermore, between 34 percent (2005) and 38 percent (1991) reported being currently sexually active, while only 46 percent (1991) to 63 percent (2005) of currently sexually active youth reported having used a condom at last sexual intercourse, 18 percent (2005) to 21 percent (1991) reported having used the birth control pill for the same situation, and 22 percent (1991) to 23 percent (2005) reported alcohol or drug use before last sexual intercourse (CDC, 2006). In 2005, African-American youth were much more likely to have reported four of more lifetime sexual partners (28%) than were Hispanic (16%) and White (11%) youth.

Very similar data are reported in Canada. In 1998, 9997 ninth-, tenth- and twelfth-grade public school students in five western Canadian provinces reported whether or not they had had sexual intercourse (vaginal or anal) in the past 12 months. Overall, 38.6 percent of the sample reported having had sexual intercourse in the last year (37.5% of males and 39.7% of females); 24 percent of ninth-graders, 37 percent of tenth-graders and 55.3 percent of twelfth-graders. Among those that had had sex, 65.5 percent reported the occurrence of unplanned sex, 40.9 percent reported multiple sexual partners, and 49.9 percent reported inconsistent condom use (Poulin and Graham, 2001). Regarding reasons for inconsistent condom use, 60 percent reported not having a condom, 28 percent reported that condom use interferes with sex, and 25 percent reported being under the influence of a substance. Between 10 and 15 percent of the sample reported the price of condoms, or partner refusal to use of condom, or embarrassment about buying a condom as being a reason for inconsistent condom use.

Arguably, these teens' dangerous sexual behavior will continue into adulthood, since the best predictor of future behavior tends to be past behavior (Sussman and Ames, 2001). It seems wise to assert that engagement in risky sex among teens is consistent with the intent of a category of teen sexual addiction. Certainly, having sex with multiple partners, or while using drugs or without protection is suggestive of losing control over sexual activities.

COMORBIDITY

The relationship between risky teen sexual behavior and other risky behaviors is not merely an expression of health-compromising behaviors (e.g., malnutrition or lack of exercise; Turbin *et al.*, 2000). It clusters more strongly with other deviant behaviors (e.g., substance use) than with health-compromising behaviors such as maintaining a poor diet (Donovan and Jessor, 1985; Warren *et al.*, 1997; Bardone *et al.*, 1998; Robinson *et al.*, 1999; Schwartz *et al.*, 1999; Turbin *et al.*, 2000; Wolf and Freedman, 2000; Busen *et al.*, 2001; Poulin and Graham, 2001; Schneider and Irons, 2001). For example, crack cocaine addiction among young females (aged 18–29 years) has been found to be associated with a much larger number of lifetime male sex partners than in non-addict females of the same age, perhaps reflecting an addictive ritual across the two behaviors as well as an economic exchange (Schneider *et al.*, 2005). Use of alcohol and other drugs delineates up to a 50 percent increase in likelihood that a teen will engage in sexual behavior (Malow *et al.*, 2006a, 2006b, 2006c).

It is plausible that sexual acting out is at relatively high prevalence among teens that have all ready suffered serious drug problems (Gorski and Miller, 1986; Schrier *et al.*, 1997; Schneider and Irons, 2001). For example, adolescents who visit STD clinics are twice as likely to be cigarette smokers as teens who visit general community health centers (MacKenzie *et al.*, 1998). Persons in recovery from drug addictions may engage in substitute behaviors that serve similar pleasurable functions as did their drug of choice, including compulsive sexual behavior (Gorski and Miller, 1986; Murphy and Hoffman, 1993; Schneider and Irons, 2001; Sussman and Ames, 2001; Sussman *et al.*, 2005).

Sexual abuse as a child also may facilitate compulsive sexual behavior, unprotected sexual acts as an adult, and alcohol abuse (Carnes, 1991; NIMH Multisite HIV Prevention Trial Group, 2001; Schneider and Irons, 2001; Schneider *et al.*, 2005). Related, a pattern of physically or emotionally abusive relationships may facilitate sexual acting out. Adult sex addicts have been found to report being depressed, low in self-esteem and feeling alone (Carnes, 1991). To try to determine whether risky sexual behavior and other psychiatric problems are linked, researchers in New Zealand followed a group of 992 people from the time they were 3 years old until age 21. They found that when the group reached adolescence, young people with symptoms of depression, schizophrenia, antisocial disorders or substance abuse problems were most likely to engage in risky sexual behaviors, such as early intercourse, multiple partners, and having sex without condoms, and they were also more likely to acquire sexually transmitted diseases. Likewise, in another study, youth in the US that tended not to use condoms during sex included those reporting feeling sad or hopeless or who had considered suicide (Anderson *et al.*, 2006).

USE OF MENTAL HEALTH SERVICES

There are very few mental health services available for teens suffering from sexual addiction at this time. It may be assumed that teens with sexual addiction-related problems are seen in treatment for other problems such as for STDs, but there is no research to support this assumption at present. No direct treatment-providers for teen sexual addiction related to, or independent of, other problems were found on 12 searches on Google accessed from May 1, 2006 through July 31, 2006.

COURSE AND OUTCOME

The first major study of sexual addiction was published by Patrick Carnes (Carnes, 1991). It was based on questionnaires filled out by 752 adult males and 180 adult females diagnosed as sex addicts, most of them admitted for treatment in the inpatient Sexual Dependency Unit of a hospital in Minnesota. Others included in the survey had participated for at least 3 years in one of the 12-step programs for recovery from sexual addition. Of the sex addicts in this survey,

63 percent were heterosexual, 18 percent homosexual and 11 percent bisexual, and 8 percent were unsure of their sexual preference.

The sexual addicts who responded to Carnes' questionnaire typically were unable to form close friendships. Their feelings of shame and unworthiness made them unable to accept real intimacy. They were certain they would be rejected if others knew what they were "really" like, so they found myriad obsessive ways to turn away a potential friend or loving partner. Despite a large number of superficial sexual contacts, they suffered from loneliness, and many developed a sense of leading two lives – one sexual, the other centered on their occupation or other "normal" activity.

In Carnes' survey, 97 percent responded that their sexual activity led to loss of self-esteem. Other emotional costs reported were strong feelings of guilt or shame (96%); strong feelings of isolation and loneliness (94%); feelings of extreme hopelessness or despair (91%); acting against personal values and beliefs (90%); feeling like two people (88%); emotional exhaustion (83%); strong fears about own future (82%); and emotional instability (78%). Carnes found that 42 percent of sex addicts in his sample also had a problem with either alcohol or drug dependency, and 38 percent had eating disorders.

In addition, 64 percent reported that they continued their sexual behavior despite risk of disease or infection, and 38 percent of the men and 45 percent of the women had contracted venereal diseases. Of the women, 70 percent routinely risked unwanted pregnancy by not using birth control, and 42 percent reported having unwanted pregnancies. Many patients had pursued their sexual activities to the point of exhaustion (59%) or even physical injury requiring medical treatment (38%). Many (58%) had pursued activities for which they felt they could be arrested, and 19 percent actually were arrested. Sleep disorders were reported by 65 percent; they usually resulted from stress or shame connected with the sexual activity. Of the survey respondents, 56 percent experienced severe financial difficulty because of their sexual activity. Loss of job productivity was reported by 80 percent, and 11 percent were actually demoted as a result (Carnes, 1991).

Recent work has been completed utilizing a sexual compulsivity scale and examining its associations with various consequences. For example, among primarily African-American adults being seen for treatment of STDs and HIV, individuals with scores above the eightieth percentile on a sexual compulsivity scale (translating to over one standard deviation above the mean) had more sex partners, engaged in higher rates of sexual risk behaviors with casual or one-time sex partners, and were nearly four times as likely to have been recently diagnosed with multiple STIs than were individuals who scored below the eightieth percentile (Kalichman and Cain, 2004). Results have been equivocal among younger, college-age subjects. In one study, significant relationships were found among sexual compulsivity, frequencies of sexual behaviors and numbers of sexual partners (Dodge *et al.*, 2005), but an opposite result was found by Gullette and Lyons (2005).

Course and outcomes data are lacking among teens. It is the case that masturbation without ejaculation often begins to be practiced long before the onset of adolescence. Secondary sexual characteristics, including rapid increases in levels of sex-related hormones, operate during the teen years, and heighten sexual awareness and sensitivity. It is likely that some type of sexual experimentation will occur, culminating in orgasm. Among the Fourteen Characteristics of Sexual Compulsives Anonymous, the first characteristic asserts that as teens, adult sexual compulsives used fantasy and masturbation to avoid feelings, and carried this behavior into adulthood with these or other types of compulsive sex (www.sca-recovery.org). Perhaps an early sign of sexual addiction is excessive masturbation among teens, perhaps related to sexual fantasies experienced in imagery, visual stimuli or reading material. The masturbation engaged in is likely perceived as pleasurable, assisting the young teen in falling asleep, switching thoughts away from daily worries, or as a type of fantasy play.

As discussed previously in this chapter, the appropriateness of sexual behavior among teens is subject to divergent views. Many investigators define any sexual relations as unhealthy or dangerous among teens (see, for example, Stuart-Smith, 1996; Hallfors *et al.*, 2004). Thus, there is empirical work presented in this chapter that defines “risky” sexual behavior among teens as having any sex – also referred to as “early sex”. Early sex can refer more specifically to such behaviors as petting or sexual intercourse (see Sussman, 2005). Since over 50 percent of teens have engaged in sexual intercourse by the time they graduate high school, such conventions are met with great resistance among teens. It is not likely that sexual behavior, *per se*, could be considered statistically abnormal, except as practiced by very young teens.

A few investigators (see, for example, Springarn and DuRant, 1996; Everett *et al.*, 2000; Lam *et al.*, 2001; Poulin and Graham, 2001) recognize sexual behavior among teens as reflecting historically normative behavior (Lerman, 2000), and define “risky” sexual behavior among teens (particularly among older or high-risk teens) as including such hazardous activities as having multiple sexual partners, not using condoms consistently, or using alcohol during sex (see Sussman, 2005). This behavior, which was mentioned earlier in this chapter as being consistent with an addictive behavior perspective, is associated with a variety of negative consequences. In particular, in large samples of HIV+ persons, 15 percent of the sample may fall within a 15- to 29-year-old age range (Aidala *et al.*, 2005). Currently, it is estimated that at least 50 percent of all HIV cases are acquired prior to age 25 (UNICEF, 2002; Marston and King, 2006). In addition, several comorbid conditions may stem from or be made worse by (unpleasant) repeated risky sexual experiences among teens, including drug abuse, experience of physical violence and dating violence, post-traumatic stress disorder, difficulty socially bonding with others, and depression, as well as unwanted pregnancy (up to 100 cases per 1000), STDS (accounting for 3 million new cases each year) and HIV/AIDS (Valois *et al.*, 1999; Carter-Jessop *et al.*, 2000; Ybarra and Mitchell, 2005).

Perhaps the most frightening aspect about the course and outcome of teenage sexual addiction is that it likely sets up a life-long struggle in which an individual's focus of activity, reward system, affect and behavior are intertwined with themes of sexual pleasure. Because of what may develop as a teen, adult sex addicts may suffer the culmination of years of addiction, including loss of family, job and self-respect.

RISK AND PROTECTIVE FACTORS

Variables that are positively or inversely predictive of risky teen sexual behavior consist of those that reside within the individual (e.g., neurotransmission; disinhibition tendency-related variables, such as sensation seeking; cognitive processing; and affect) and those that reside outside of the individual (e.g., role-modeling, peer group effects, and large social environmental effects such as the mass media). These "risk" and "protective" factors are discussed next.

NEUROTRANSMISSION

Dopamine release may stimulate sexual behavior (Wersinger and Rissman, 2000), and sexual behavior may alter mesolimbic dopaminergic transmission. Dopamine is the neurotransmitter thought to underlie novelty-related pleasure and facilitate dependence on a drug or behavior (Sussman and Ames, 2001). In other words, the effect of substances and behaviors on dopamine release is not independent of their potential roles as addictions, as dopamine is the primary neurotransmitter implicated in the addictions (Sussman and Ames, 2001). Further, when pleasure centers in the human brain are stimulated, chemicals called endorphins are released into the bloodstream. Endorphins are believed to be associated with the mood changes that follow sexual release. Any chemical that causes mood changes can be addictive, with repeated exposure altering brain chemistry to the point that more of the chemical is "required" in order to feel "normal" (see also Sussman and Unger, 2004).

DISINHIBITION TENDENCY

Sexual behavior among teens also may be a function of behavioral disinhibition – that is, this behavior may reflect impulsive, sensation-seeking behavioral preferences (Ary *et al.*, 1999; Robbins and Bryan, 2004; Noar *et al.*, 2006). The relationship between drug use and (risky) teen sexual behavior could be conceptualized as a result of the disinhibition effects of drugs consumed and subsequent diminished decision-making and judgment (see, for example, Leigh and Schafer, 1993; Valois *et al.*, 1999; Peugh and Belenko, 2001; Malow *et al.*,

2006), which could include sexual behavior. In addition, among teens, cognitive immaturity, reflected by incomplete myelination of the frontal lobe of the brain and incomplete connections between the limbic system and the neocortex until later in adolescence, may lead to impulsive, immediately pleasurable activities that are removed from more foresight or planning (Stuart-Smith, 1996). This status of neuro-cognitive development may be considered in the context of the development of secondary sexual characteristics. Those youth who are more physically mature and report greater sexual feelings are relatively likely to initiate sexual intercourse in young adolescence (i.e., 1-year after a self-report provided in seventh or eighth grades; L'Engle *et al.*, 2006a).

COGNITIVE PROCESSING

There has been research suggesting that teens perceive themselves to be relatively invulnerable to consequences of their behavior (Malow *et al.*, 2006a). Therefore, they may engage in repeated and risky sexual acts, expecting no negative consequences. Furthermore, memory associations of sexual behavior with cues and initially pleasurable outcomes may set in motion continuing sexual behavior that can later get out of control (e.g., lack of condom use among adults in the community; Stacy *et al.*, 2000).

One recent qualitative review (Marston and King, 2006) suggested several cognitive themes that appeared to direct teens' sexual behavior. These include judging potential partners as "clean" or "unclean", thinking that use of condoms indicates mistrust, and having perceived social expectations that may limit communication about sexual behavior (e.g., women may be expected never directly to indicate an interest in sex). These findings were interpreted by the authors as reflecting social influence processes, but were measured as perceptions of social processes – hence involving cognitive interpretations. In another study that found limited support for a national demonstration project on knowledge but not beliefs or intentions to use condoms (Healthy Respect, in Scotland), unchanging beliefs included that using a condom would be embarrassing and would reduce sexual enjoyment (Tucker *et al.*, 2006). Perceived personal immunity, implicit cognition and sex-related beliefs may be useful in the prediction of later sexual addiction. Unfortunately, most relevant studies have been completed with adults in clinical or community settings. Little work has been completed on teens, and much more research is needed.

FAMILY ROLE-MODELING

Teens may engage in risky sexual behavior due to observing any type of problem behavior among their family. For example, Wilder and Watt (2002) reported from the National Longitudinal Study of Adolescent Health (in which data were collected in the home from both teens and parents) that teens whose parents engaged in risky behaviors (smoking, drinking, and seat-belt nonuse) were relatively likely to smoke cigarettes, be sexually active and report having had sex before 15 years of age. Teens may (i) directly model parents' behavior, (ii) explore new behaviors as the result of parents' tolerance of deviant behavior, (iii) take risks as a reaction to a high level of family conflict, or (iv) learn symbolic relations from parents as "adults" (e.g., engaging in sex is what adults do; Ary *et al.*, 1999; Blum *et al.*, 2000; Paul *et al.*, 2000; Sussman and Ames, 2001; Wilder and Watt, 2002).

Another study found greater sexual experience among 14- to 17-year-olds that lived with a single parent (Silver and Bauman, 2006), perhaps suggestive of lack of parental monitoring or family conflict. In a longitudinal study of 5000 Scottish teenagers, low parental monitoring has been found to predict early sexual activity for both genders, whereas perceived comfort talking with parents about sex failed to be related to sexual activity (Wight *et al.*, 2006). In most studies, greater parental monitoring, less parental permissiveness, perceived parental warmth and support, conservative parental attitudes about sex, and frequent parent–teen communication about sex-related topics have been associated with more responsible teen sexual behavior and less sexual experience (Donenberg and Pao, 2005). Still, at least one study of teens' self-reports has suggested minimal parental influence on teen sexual behavior (Beal *et al.*, 2001), and one other study has suggested that parental permissiveness and peer influence are only linked to risky sex among teens that reported using drugs and alcohol (Donenberg *et al.*, 2006). Additional research is needed.

PEER GROUP EFFECTS

Several studies indicate that peer-modeling or direct peer social influence may lead to engagement in sexual behavior (Kinsman *et al.*, 1998; Ary *et al.*, 1999; Beal *et al.*, 2001; Wilder and Watt, 2002). Certainly, the perception that a person's peers are sexually active is predictive of that person's own sexual behavior 1 year later (L'Engle *et al.*, 2006a). Association or identification with deviant peers is relatively likely to lead a teen to adopt the values of the group and participate in common group behaviors that may include early entry into adult roles such as work, poor academic performance, and sexual behavior (Ary *et al.*, 1999; Wilder and Watt, 2002; Silver and Bauman, 2006).

The processes involved in peer dating relationships are also related to risky sexual behavior. In general, knowing a partner as a friend (versus being an acquaintance) prior to involvement in a romantic relationship is protective against engaging in sexual intercourse among teens (Kaestle and Halpern, 2005). However, exposure to violence in dating relationships is related to engagement in sex with a greater number of sexual partners (Valois *et al.*, 1999), perhaps suggesting that exposure to abusive peer relationships may facilitate teen sexual frequency and perhaps lead to sexual addiction.

LARGE SOCIAL-ENVIRONMENTAL EFFECTS

Sexual portrayals in the mass media may influence teens' sexual behavior. One comprehensive review suggested that the mass media depicts sexual behavior as glamorous and risk-free, and may influence teen behavior through social modeling effects (Brown and Witherspoon, 2002). Also, as suggested by Sussman (2005), many older and recent media products (e.g., movies such as *Animal House* or *Saved*) tend to portray youth that participate in sexual and other risky behaviors as more honest, independent and courageous than other youths (who are hypocrites, anyway, according to this conceptualization). Rock-and-roll music as well depicts many sexual-related scenes and romantic feelings, and degrading (i.e., objectifying) sexual lyrics have been found to predict later petting behaviors among teens (Martino *et al.*, 2006). Adolescents are bombarded with many such media portrayals within the context of "controlling" adults that might tell them to postpone sexual experimentation.

There is no universally expressed attitude toward teen sexual behavior. Thus, exposure to internet pornography or to music with sexually explicit lyrics among teens is a major introduction to sexual material that may lead to modeling effects, as well as providing an outlet of expression for sensation-seeking youth, and eventually addictive sexual behavior (Ybarra and Mitchell, 2005; Martino *et al.*, 2006). In fact, one study found evidence that 13 percent of the variance in young adolescents' intentions to have sexual intercourse in the near future is due to type of media exposure (L'Engle *et al.*, 2006b).

SUMMARY AND PROTECTIVE FACTORS

Both intrapersonal factors (e.g., neurotransmission and behavioral disinhibition) and extrapersonal factors (e.g., role-modeling) may explain the occurrence of compulsive sexual behavior among teens. These myriad of factors may operate together to determine a variety of co-occurring lifestyle-related behaviors. These behaviors often are referred to as "problem behaviors" because they place youth at risk for negative consequences, and transgress social norms of appropriate teen behavior (Turbin *et al.*, 2000; Sussman and Ames, 2001).

Protective factors are those characteristics that reduce the chances of risky sexual behavior and promote positive development. Certainly, a baseline sense of balance in neurotransmission, relatively low sensation-seeking orientation, use of deliberate processes such as decision-making, belief that abstinence is a means to plan better for the future, having a strong future orientation, and role-modeling of conservative others is the "flip-side" of the aforementioned risk factors. In addition, cooperativeness, social competence, attachment to parents, family supervision, having conventional friends, high achievement in school, neighborhood cohesiveness and lack of direct exposure to promotion of sexual activity are among factors that have been found to be protective against behaviors such as risky sexual behavior (Sussman and Ames, 2001). With knowledge of such risk and protective factors, it has been possible to begin the design of prevention and cessation programs.

PREVENTION AND TREATMENT

PREVENTION

Teens are exposed to more conflicting information about sex than ever before. Some schools offer counseling on birth control and sexual disease prevention; others preach absolute abstinence. A recent emphasis on abstinence-only education has shown some effects on creating conservative shifts in attitudes in some studies (Carter-Jessop *et al.*, 2000). However, in general this approach has had little impact on behavior (Rose, 2005).

There is no consistent set of prevention strategies consensually agreed on. Specifically, among teens, types of prevention programming to decrease risky sexual behavior have included (i) school-group based or other small group, (ii) one-on-one counseling, (iii) case management, (iv) family-based, and (v) community-level programming (e.g., media, health services, outreach and group support), with most research being addressed (successfully) to small-group programming (Malow *et al.*, 2006a). Key strategies that overlap across several different levels of programming but provide a significant preventive impact may include instruction in STI knowledge, goal-setting, alteration of perceived peer group norms, cognitive-behavioral skills instruction (e.g., refusal assertion, how to use condoms, conversational skills), personalization of consequences information, motivational enhancement, family education and counseling, media awareness and education, and use of community outreach services (Fisher *et al.*, 2002; Auerbach *et al.*, 2006; Malow *et al.*, 2006a). Creating links to social, health and instrumental support, which can then create "human capital" and increase social competence, is thought to be another "key" to successful HIV prevention among teens – particularly at-risk groups (Malow *et al.*, 2006c). In addition, instruction that emphasizes ethnic and gender pride may be better able to impart sex prevention information among minority females (Wingood *et al.*, 2006). Evidence-based prevention interventions have shown generalizability effects in developing countries (see, for example, Karnell *et al.*, 2006; Kirby *et al.*, 2006).

Programs that consensually (no or few data-based evaluations) have been thought to be effective HIV prevention programs by experts likewise include the delineation of specific objectives for specific populations, have multiple components delivered through multiple modalities, involve behavioral theories, and closely monitor its activities (Eke *et al.*, 2006). Most sex-education programming, however, has produced only short-term effects (up to 3 months; Coyle *et al.*, 2006; Malow *et al.*, 2006a), although this programming hasn't been found to do any harm, such as encouraging sexual activity (Sabia, 2006).

There are a few recently evaluated promising prevention programs on the horizon. For example, Life Skills Training, a 30-session school-based drug abuse prevention program, was examined for long-term generalization effects to HIV-risk behavior (Griffin *et al.*, 2006). The program instructed personal and social competence (e.g., developing personal relationships, conversation skills), and skills to resist drug use. Data were collected in 1985 among 12-year-olds in seventh grade and at a long-term follow-up in 1998 (average age of 24). HIV-risk behavior was measured as an index score composed of items including number of sex partners, having sex while intoxicated, and extent of condom use. An approximate 5 percent absolute reduction on each of the HIV risk behaviors was found 13 years later, comparing the program condition with the control condition in this randomized design, apparently mostly mediated by reduction in drug use.

Family-based programs have been promoted extensively by organizations such as the National Association of Social Workers (Malow *et al.*, 2006a) and the Sex Information and Education Council of the United States (SIECUS; www.familiescaretalking.org/teen/teen0000.html; siecus@siecus.org). Debra Haffner, President and CEO of SIECUS), advises:

> Don't wait for your teens to ask you about sex – they may not. We don't wait to talk to our kids about other important matters of health and safety. Why should the subject of sex be any different?

If parents monitor their children, and provide them with accurate information, they may help to set values for responsible sexual decision-making.

Some parents feel that if they bring up the subject of birth control, they may be encouraging their child to have sexual intercourse. However, offering information isn't the same as offering the tools themselves. According to SIECUS (the Sex Information and Education Council of the United States), "with open communication, young people are more likely to turn to their parents in times of trouble. Without it, they will not." (See also Burgess *et al.*, 2005.) Outcome and self-efficacy expectations may mediate the likelihood that parents will communicate with their children about sex (e.g., father–son; DiLorio *et al.*, 2006), and thus might need instruction.

Of course, parents can take some health-protection preventive measures, particularly regarding online exposure to porn. The computer with Internet access can be placed in the house in an area where it can be easily monitored, the web history on the child's Internet can be checked, home web pages (e.g., My Space) can be monitored and blocking software can be installed. In addition, parents can talk with their teen about the importance of hiding their identity on-line (Weiss and Schneider, 2006).

There are many books, pamphlets and videos available for parents and teens, including a comprehensive and very readable report from the National Commission on Adolescent Sexual Health entitled "Facing Facts". Possibly, tailoring these mass media materials for sensation-seeking youth may exert a stronger preventive effect on sexual attitudes and behavior (Noar *et al.*, 2006). Also, very recently a study examined the effectiveness of a computer-delivered, individually tailored HIV/AIDS risk-reduction intervention in a randomized trial with 157 college students (Kiene and Barta, 2006). Two brief computer-delivered sessions that used elements of Motivational Interviewing were implemented (HIV intervention versus a nutrition education tutorial control group). Subjects in the HIV intervention group reported a greater frequency of keeping condoms available, and greater condom use, at 4-week follow-up. Much research needs to be completed, but this does appear to be a promising modality.

While seldom investigated, state governmental policies, such as taxes on beer and restrictions on the location of cigarette-vending machines, and placement of family-planning clinics, influence adolescents' behavior (i.e., have been shown to exhibit significant deterrent effects; Bishai *et al.*, 2005). Thus, possibly policy-determined, large environmental manipulations may provide a preventive effect on risky sexual behavior among teens.

There is a collection of evidence-based, primarily school-based efforts that have been created for teen pregnancy and HIV/AIDS prevention, and it is possible that this programming can be adapted for specific populations (Eke *et al.*, 2006; Solomon *et al.*, 2006). This may be accomplished by knowing the core elements of the program and the population it is being adapted to, and then fitting the two together. Also, arguably, perhaps the fact that sexual addictions are correlated with other addictive or problem behaviors among teens (e.g., substance misuse, violence) indicates that prevention programming might target multiple behaviors and thereby provide a more palatable format for also including information on sexual addiction (Guilamo-Ramos *et al.*, 2005). Much more prevention research is needed, and it may need to address specifically repetitive, out-of-control dimensions of addictive sexual behavior.

TREATMENT

There have been four primary substance abuse treatment models used with adolescents (Hovarth, 1999; Sussman *et al.*, 2006):

1. The Minnesota Model, which is based on the 12 steps of Alcoholics Anonymous (AA)
2. The therapeutic community (TC) model, in which all treatees are also treaters
3. Family therapy (or other group therapy)
4. Cognitive-behavioral therapy.

Possibly, these models (or elements of these models) could be used for treatment of teen sexual addiction – that is, if teens and adults permit this diagnosis to be publicly stated as a reality which needs treatment. As of now, there is little available in terms of treatment of teen sexual addiction (in December 10, 2006, a Google search under "teen sexual addiction", "teen sex addiction", "adolescent sexual addition" or "adolescent sex addiction" revealed only six web pages, mostly 12-step or religion-based programming).

Recognition that self-destructive sexual behavior can be an addiction has spawned the rapid growth of five nationwide self-help organizations in the US for persons trying to recover from this problem. All are 12-step recovery programs patterned after Alcoholics Anonymous, and a vast majority of members are adults. These five fellowships that provide 12-step support to sexual addicts include: Sexaholics Anonymous (www.sa.org), Sex Addicts Anonymous (www.saa-recovery.org), Sex and Love Addicts Anonymous (www.slaafws.org), Sexual Recovery Anonymous (e-mail: sexualrecovery.org) and Sexual Compulsives Anonymous (www.sca-recovery.org).

A little over 10 years ago, a membership survey of Sex and Love Addicts Anonymous found that 58 percent of its members were male, 92 percent Caucasian, 44 percent in professional jobs, 24 percent with a postgraduate degree and 31 percent with a college degree. The sexual orientation of its members was 63 percent heterosexual, 11 percent bisexual and 26 percent gay or lesbian. (Documentation provided by Sex and Love Addicts Anonymous to R.J. Heuer, Defense Personnel Security Research Center, 13 January 1992.). These data apparently have stayed fairly consistent to the present day (Rob Weiss, personal communication). It is normal for recovery groups like this to have a disproportionate number of highly educated members, but that is only because well-educated persons are more likely to seek out self-help programs. There is no evidence that well-educated persons are more likely than others to suffer from sexual addiction.

At present, it is not clear that teens would be attracted to 12-step programming for sexual addiction. Only approximately 9 percent of the members of AA are 21–30 years old, and only 2 percent are under 21 years old (Alcoholics Anonymous, 2001). Admitting to a sense of powerlessness, a key principle of 12-step programs, may conflict with teens' search for autonomy, as well as the difficulty in perceiving themselves as having to remain "sober" (perceiving themselves as having "hit bottom"; Rivers *et al.*, 2001) – both potential barriers preventing 12-step program participation. Also, treatment among teens needs to grapple with the tendency to engage in a relatively great deal of limit-testing (Kaminer, 2001). However, attendance at 12-step meetings among teens (teens with teens) has been found to predict better outcomes. These outcomes are mediated by motivation but not coping (Kelly *et al.*, 2000).

One potential approach to dealing with sexual behavior among older teens and emerging adults is to introduce harm-reduction approaches, such as use of microbicides among females or male circumcision, to protect against spread of disease while engaging in addictive sexual behavior (e.g., Short, 2006). Still, such approaches do not reduce the sense of shame or dependence people may feel regarding this behavior. It is possible to attempt to normalize aspects of sexual behavior, but there are limits, including subjective self- or other harm.

Some state-of-the-art treatment approaches to sexual addiction are discussed by Weiss and Schneider (2006). It may be speculated that these techniques might be successfully used with teens. They suggest use of an "accountability partner" – someone to help the sex addict prepare to change (like a 12-step "sponsor"). In addition, the addict is requested to engage in a variety of cognitive-behavioral type tasks, including use of stimulus control strategies (e.g., throwing out all pornography, and actively planning and avoiding risky situations), organism strategies (self-affirmations), response control strategies (development of a "sexual boundary plan" such as not keeping secrets from significant others about sexual behavior, limiting sexual behavior to one significant other, going to support groups and focusing on physical health), and reinforcement strategies (e.g., enjoyment of new activities, family involvement, work, and having one's emotional needs better taken care of).

SUMMARY

The roots of out-of-control sexual behavior may be quite varied. It may be caused by an underlying personality disorder, an "addiction" or a physical disorder. Disorders of exaggerated sexuality, nymphomania in the female and satyriasis in the male, believed to be caused by pituitary gland dysfunction or irritation of the brain cortex by a tumor, arteriosclerosis or epilepsy, are quite rare (Barth and Kinder, 1987). It is very likely, however, that sex addiction as a disorder extends across the lifespan, beginning in adolescence as secondary sexual characteristics mature, conditional on presence of biological and personality factors (e.g., insufficient mesolimbic dopaminergic turnover reflective of risk-taking characteristics) and subjective affective discomfort, embedded within social environmental contexts that expose teens to sexually explicit stimuli and related social learning of the reinforcing value of these stimuli. With successful outcomes of initial experiences with sex for gratification, and repetition of such experiences, the teen may bypass other more prosocial or potentially productive means of coping with their *status quo*.

As the years accumulate, a myriad of stimuli are associated or endowed with sexual connotations, and numerous negative consequences ensue. At this point in adulthood, often after 10–30 years of sexual acting out, individuals might seek out treatment (or be forced into treatment) that may involve lifelong attendance at 12-step meetings or therapy, and possibly drug therapy (e.g., use of SSRIs) (Schneider and Irons, 2001). By recognizing that sexual addiction may begin in the teenage years, through assessment, information campaigns, and prevention and treatment education, corrective channeling of teenage sexual energy may be accomplished. This is a real challenge for the future, and will not occur until much debate and awareness of the problem rises above the public horizon.

ACKNOWLEDGMENTS

This research was supported by grants from the National Institute on Drug Abuse Nos. (DA16094, DA016090, DA020138).

REFERENCES

Abrantes, A.M., Brown, S.A. and Tomlinson, K.L. (2004). Psychiatric comorbidity among inpatient substance abusing adolescents. *Journal of Child and Adolescent Substance Abuse*, 13, 83–101.

Aidala, A., Cross, J.E., Stall, R. *et al.* (2005). Housing status and HIV risk behaviors: implications for prevention and policy. *AIDS and Behavior*, 9, 251–265.

Alcoholics Anonymous (2001). *Alcoholics Anonymous 2001 Membership Survey*. New York, NY: AA World Services.

American Psychiatric Association (2000). *Diagnostic and Statistical Manual of Mental Disorders*, 4th edn, revised. Washington, DC: APA.

Anderson, J.E., Santelli, J.S. and Morrow, B. (2006). Trends in adolescent contraceptive use, unprotected and poorly protected sex, 1991–2003. *Journal of Adolescent Health*, 38, 734–739.

Ary, D.V., Duncan T.E., Biglan, A. *et al.* (1999). Development of adolescent problem behavior. *Journal of Abnormal Child Psychology*, 27, 141–150.

Auerbach, J.D., Hayes, R.J. and Kandathil, S.M. (2006). Overview of effective and promising interventions to prevent HIV infection. *World Health Organization Technical Report Services*, 938, 43–78.

Bardone, A.M., Moffitt, T.E., Caspi, A. *et al.* (1998). Adult physical health outcomes of adolescent girls with conduct disorder, depression and anxiety. *Journal of the American Academy of Child and Adolescent Psychiatry*, 37, 594–601.

Barth, R.J. and Kinder, B.N. (1987). The mislabeling of sexual impulsivity. *Journal of Sex and Marital Therapy*, 1, 15–23.

Beal, A.C., Ausiello, J. and Perrin, J.M. (2001). Social influences on health-risk behaviors among minority middle school students. *Journal of Adolescent Health*, 28, 474–480.

Bishai, D.M., Mercer, D. and Tapales, A. (2005). Can government policies help adolescents avoid risky behavior? *Preventive Medicine*, 40, 197–202.

Blum, R.W. (1995). Transition to adult health care: setting the stage. *Journal of Adolescent Health*, 17, 3–5.

Blum, R.W., Beuhring, T., Shew, M.L. *et al.* (2000). The effects of race/ethnicity, income and family structure on adolescent risk behaviors. *American Journal of Public Health*, 90, 1879–1884.

Boies, S.C., Knudson, G. and Young, J. (2004). The Internet, sex and youths: implications for sexual development. *Sexual Addiction and Compulsivity*, 11, 343–363.

Bradley, K.C. and Meisel, R.L. (2001). Sexual behavior induction of c-Fos in the nucleus accumbens and amphetamine-stimulated locomotor activity are sensitized by previous sexual experience in female Syrian hamsters. *Journal of Neuroscience*, 21, 2123–2130.

Brannigan, R., Schackman, B.R., Falco, M. and Millman, R.B. (2004). The quality of highly regarded adolescent substance abuse treatment programs: results of an in-depth national survey. *Archives of Pediatrics and Adolescent Medicine*, 158, 904–909.

Brown, J.D. and Witherspoon, E.M. (2002). The mass media and American adolescents' health. *Journal of Adolescent Health*, 31, 153–170.

Burgess, V., Dziegielewski, S.F. and Green, C.E. (2005). Improving comfort about sex communication between parents and their adolescents: practice-based research within a teen sexuality group. *Brief Treatment and Crisis Intervention*, 5, 379–390.

Busen, N.H., Modeland, V. and Kouzekanani, K. (2001). Adolescent cigarette smoking and health risk behavior. *Journal of Pediatric Nursing*, 16, 187–193.

Carnes, P. (1991). *Don't Call It Love: Recovery from Sexual Addiction.* New York, NY: Bantam Books, pp. 22–23, 30–34.

Carnes, P.J. (1996). Addiction or compulsion: politics or illness? *Sexual Addiction and Compulsivity*, 3, 127–150.

Carter-Jessop, L., Franklin, L.N., Heath, J.W. Jr *et al.* (2000). Abstinence education for urban youth. *Journal of Community Health*, 25, 293–305.

Centers for Disease Control and Prevention (CDC) (2006) Surveillance Summaries, *Morbidity and Mortality Weekly Report*, 55, SS–5, 112 pages (Youth Risk Behavior Surveillance, 2005).

Cornelius, J.R., Maisto, S.A., Pollock, N.K. *et al.* (2003). Rapid relapse generally follows treatment for substance use disorders among adolescents. *Addictive Behaviors*, 28, 381–386.

Coyle, K.K., Kirby, D.B., Robin, L.E. *et al.* (2006). All4You!: a randomized trial of an HIV, other STDs and pregnancy prevention intervention for alternative school students. *AIDS Education and Prevention*, 18, 187–203.

DiLorio, C., McCarty, F. and Denzmore, P. (2006). An exploration of social cognitive theory mediators of father–son communication about sex. *Journal of Pediatric Psychology*, 31, 917–927.

Dodge, B., Reece, M., Cole, S.L. and Sandfort, T.G. (2005). Sexual compulsivity among heterosexual college students. *Journal of Infectious Diseases*, 191, S127–S138.

Donenberg, G. and Pao, M. (2005). Youths and HIV/AIDS: psychiatry's role in a changing epidemic. *Journal of the American Academy of Child and Adolescent Psychiatry*, 44, 728–747.

Donenberg, G.R., Emerson, E., Bryant, F.B. and King, S. (2006). Does substance use moderate the effects of parents and peers on risky sexual behavior? *AIDS Care*, 18, 194–200.

Donovan, J.E. and Jessor, R. (1985). Structure of problem behavior in adolescence and young adulthood. *Journal of Consulting and Clinical Psychology*, 53, 890–904.

Eke, A.N., Mezoff, J.S., Duncan, T. and Sogolow, E.D. (2006). Reputationally strong HIV prevention programs: lessons from the front line. *AIDS Education and Prevention*, 18, 163–175.

Everett, S.A., Malarcher, A.M., Sharp, D.J. *et al.* (2000). Relationship between cigarette, smokeless tobacco and cigar use and other health risk behaviors among US high school students. *Journal of School Health*, 70, 234–240.

Fisher, J.D., Fisher, W.A., Bryan, A.D. and Misovich, S.J. (2002). Information-motivation-behavioral skills model-based HIV risk behavior change intervention for inner-city high school youth. *Health Psychology*, 21, 177–186.

Gorski, T.T. and Miller, M. (1986). *Staying Sober. A Guide for Relapse Prevention.* Independence, MO: Independence Press.

Griffin, K.W., Botvin, G.J. and Nichols, T.R. (2006). Effects of a school-based drug abuse prevention program for adolescents on HIV risk behavior in young adulthood. *Prevention Science*, 7, 103–112.

Guilamo-Ramos, V., Litardo, H.A. and Jaccard, J. (2005). Prevention programs for reducing adolescent problem behaviors: implications of the co-occurrence of problem behaviors in adolescence. *Journal of Adolescent Health*, 36, 82–86.

Gullette, D.L. and Lyons, M.A. (2005). Sexual sensation seeking compulsivity and HIV risk behaviors in college students. *Journal of Community Health Nursing*, 22, 47–60.

Hallfors, D.D., Waller, M., Ford, C.A. *et al.* (2004). Adolescent depression and suicide risk: association with sex drug behavior. *American Journal of Preventive Medicine*, 27, 223–231.

Hovarth, A.T. (1999). *Sex, Drugs, Gambling and Chocolate: A Workbook for Overcoming Addictions.* San Luis Obispo, CA: Impact.

Irons, R. and Schneider, J.P. (1996). Differential diagnosis of addictive sexual disorders using the DSM-IV. *Sexual Addiction and Compulsivity*, 3, 7–21.

Kaestle, C.E. and Halpern, C.T. (2005). Sexual activity among adolescents in romantic relationships with friends, acquaintances, or strangers. *Archives of Pediatric and Adolescent Medicine*, 159, 849–853.

Kalichman, S.C. and Cain, D. (2004). The relationship between indicators of sexual compulsivity and high risk sexual practices among men and women receiving services from a sexually transmitted infection clinic. *Journal of Sex Research*, 41, 235–241.

Kaminer, Y. (2001). Alcohol and drug abuse: adolescent substance abuse treatment: where do we go from here? *Psychiatric Services*, 52, 147–149.

Karnell, A.P., Cupp, P.K., Zimmerman, R.S. *et al.* (2006). Efficacy of an American alcohol and HIV prevention curriculum adapted for use in South Africa: results of a pilot study in five township schools. *AIDS Education and Prevention*, 18, 295–310.

Kelly, J.F., Myers, M.G. and Brown, S.A. (2000). A multivariate process model of adolescent 12-step attendance and substance use outcome following inpatient treatment. *Psychology of Addictive Behaviors*, 14, 376–389.

Kiene, S.M. and Barta, W.D. (2006). A brief individualized computer-delivered sexual risk reduction intervention increases HIV/AIDS preventive behavior. *Journal of Adolescent Health*, 39, 404–410.

Kinsman, S.B., Romer, D., Furstenberg, F.F. and Schwartz, D.F. (1998). Early sexual initiation: the role of peer norms. *Pediatrics*, 102, 1185–1192.

Kirby, D., Obasi, A. and Laris, B.A. (2006). The effectiveness of sex education and HIV education interventions in schools in developing countries. *World Health Organization Technical Report Services*, 938, 103–150.

Lam, T.H., Stewart, S.M. and Ho, L.M. (2001). Smoking and high-risk sexual behavior among young adults in Hong Kong. *Journal of Behavioral Medicine*, 24, 503–518.

Leigh, B.C. and Schafer, J.C. (1993). Heavy drinking occasions and the occurrence of sexual activity. *Psychology of Addictive Behaviors*, 7, 197–200.

L'Engle, K.L., Jackson, C. and Brown, J.D. (2006a). Early adolescents' cognitive susceptibility to initiating sexual intercourse. *Perspectives on Sexual and Reproductive Health*, 38, 97–105.

L'Engle, K.L., Brown, J.D. and Kenneavy, K. (2006b). The mass media are an important context for adolescents' sexual behavior. *Journal of Adolescent Health*, 38, 186–192.

Lerman, E. (2000). *Safer Sex: The New Morality*. Buena Park, CA: Morning Glory.

MacKenzie, T.D., Steiner, J.F., Davidson, A.J. *et al.* (1998). Tobacco use and other risk behaviors among adolescents in an STD clinic. *Preventive Medicine*, 27, 792–797.

Malow, R.M., Rosenberg, R. and Devieux, J. (2006a). Human immunodeficiency virus and adolescent substance abuse. In: H.A. Liddle and C.L. Rowe (eds), *Adolescent Substance Abuse: Research and Clinical Advances*. New York, NY: Cambridge University Press, pp. 284–309.

Malow, R.M., Devieux, J.G., Rosenberg, R. *et al.* (2006b). Alcohol use severity and HIV sexual risk among juvenile offenders. *Substance Use and Misuse*, 41, 1769–1788.

Malow, R.M., Rosenberg, R., Donenberg, G. and Devieux, J. (2006c). Interventions and patterns of risk in adolescent HIV/AIDS prevention. *American Journal of Infectious Diseases*, 2, 80–89.

Mani, S.K., Mitchell, A. and O'Malley, B.W. (2000). Progesterone receptor and dopamine receptors are required in delta-9-tetrahydrocannabinol modulation of sexual receptivity in female rats. *Proceedings of the National Academy of Sciences*, 98, 1249–1254.

Marston, C. and King, E. (2006). Factors that shape young people's sexual behavior: a systematic review. *Lancet*, 368, 1581–1586.

Martino, S.C., Collins, R.L., Elliott, M.N. *et al.* (2006). Exposure to degrading versus nondegrading music lyrics and sexual behavior among youth. *Pediatrics*, 118, 430–441.

Murphy, S.A. and Hoffman, A.L. (1993). An empirical description of phases of maintenance following treatment for alcohol dependence. *Journal of Substance Abuse*, 5, 131–143.

Newcomb, M.D. and Bentler, P.M. (1988). Impact of adolescent drug use and social support on problems of young adults: a longitudinal study. *Journal of Abnormal Psychology*, 97, 64–75.

NIMH Multisite HIV Prevention Trial Group (2001). A test of factors mediating the relationship between unwanted sexual activity during childhood and risky sexual practices among women enrolled in the NIMH Multisite HIV Prevention Trial. *Women's Health*, 33, 163–180.

Noar, S.M., Zimmerman, R.S., Palmgreen, P. *et al.* (2006). Integrating personality and psychosocial theoretical approaches to understanding safer sexual behavior: implications for message design. *Health Communication*, 19, 165–174.

O'Leary, T.A., Brown, S.A., Colby, S.M. *et al.* (2002). Treating adolescents together or individually? Issues in adolescent substance abuse interventions. *Alcoholism: Clinical and Experimental Research*, 26, 890–899.

Paul, C., Fitzjohn, J., Herbison, P. and Dickson, N. (2000). The determinants of sexual intercourse before age 16. *Journal of Adolescent Health*, 27, 136–147.

Peter, J. and Valkenburg, P.M. (2006). Adolescents' exposure to sexually explicit material on the internet. *Communication Research*, 33, 178–204.

Peugh, J. and Belenko, S. (2001). Alcohol, drugs and sexual function: a review. *Journal of Psychoactive Drugs*, 33, 223–232.

Poulin, C. and Graham, L. (2001). The association between substance use, unplanned sexual intercourse and other sexual behaviours among adolescent students. *Addiction*, 96, 607–621.

Rivers, S.M., Greenbaum, R.L. and Goldberg, E. (2001). Hospital-based adolescent substance abuse treatment: comorbidity, outcomes and gender. *Journal of Nervous and Mental Disease*, 189, 229–237.

Robbins, R.N. and Bryan, A. (2004). Relationships between future orientation, impulsive sensation seeking and risk behaviors among adjudicated adolescents. *Journal of Adolescent Research*, 19, 428–445.

Robinson, K.L., Telljohann, S.K. and Price, J.H. (1999). Predictors of sixth graders engaging in sexual intercourse. *Journal of School Health*, 69, 369–375.

Rose, S. (2005). Going too far? Sex, sin and social policy. *Social Forces*, 84, 1207–1233.

Sabia, J.J. (2006). Does sex education affect adolescent sexual behaviors and health? *Journal of Policy Analysis and Management*, 25, 783–802.

Schaef, A. W. (1987). *When Society Becomes An Addict.* New York, NY: Harper Collins.

Schneider, J. P. (1994). Sex addiction: controversy within mainstream addiction medicine, diagnosis based on the DSM-III-R and physician case histories. *Sexual Addiction and Compulsivity*, 1, 19–44.

Schneider, J.P. and Irons, R.R. (2001). Assessment and treatment of addictive sexual disorders: relevance for chemical dependency relapse. *Substance Use and Misuse*, 36, 1795–1820.

Schneider, J.P., Sealy, J. and Montgomery, J. (2005). Ritualization and reinforcement keys to understanding mixed addiction involving sex and drugs. *Sexual Addiction and Compulsity*, 12, 121–148.

Schrier, L.A., Emans, S.J., Woods, E.R. and DuRant, R.H. (1997). The association of sexual risk behaviors and problem drug behaviors in high school students. *Journal of Adolescent Health*, 20, 377–383.

Schwartz, R.H., Milteer, R., Sheridan, M.J. and Horner, C.P. (1999). Beach week: a high school graduation rite of passage for sun, sand, suds and sex. *Archives of Pediatrics and Adolescent Medicine*, 153, 180–183.

Seegers, J.A. (2003). The prevalence of sexual addiction symptoms on the college campus. *Sexual Addiction and Compulsivity*, 10, 247–258.

Short, R.V. (2006). New ways of preventing HIV infection: thinking simply, simply thinking. *Philosphical Transactions of the Royal Society B*, 361, 811–820.

Silver, E.J. and Bauman, L.J. (2006) The Association of Sexual Experience with Attitudes, Beliefs and Risk Behaviors of Inner-City Adolescents. *Journal of Research on Adolescence*, 16, 29–45.

Solomon, J., Card, J.J. and Malow, R.M. (2006). Adapting efficacious interventions: advancing translational research in HIV prevention. *Evaluation and the Health Professions*, 29, 162–194.

Springarn, R.W. and DuRant, R.H. (1996). Male adolescents involved in pregnancy: associated health risk and problem behaviors. *Pediatrics*, 98, 262–268.

Stacy, A.W., Newcomb, M.D. and Ames, S.L. (2000). Implicit cognition and HIV risk behavior. *Journal of Behavior Medicine*, 23, 475–499.

Stuart-Smith, S. (1996). Teenage sex: cognitive immaturity increases the risks. *British Medical Journal*, 312, 390–391.

Sussman, S. (2005). The relations of cigarette smoking with risky sexual behavior among teens. *Sexual Addiction and Compulsivity*, 12, 181–199.

Sussman, S. and Ames, S.L. (2001). *The Social Psychology of Drug Abuse*. Buckingham, Buckinghamshire: Open University Press.

Sussman, S. and Unger, J.B. (2004). A "drug abuse" theoretical integration: a trans-disciplinary speculation. *Substance Use and Misuse*, 39, 2055–2069.

Sussman, S., Patten, C.A. and Order-Connors, B. (2005). Tobacco use. In: R. Coombs (ed.), *Addiction Counseling Review*. Mahwah, NJ: Lawrence Erlbaum, pp. 203–224.

Sussman, S., Skara, S. and Ames, S.L. (2006). Substance abuse among adolescents. In: T.G. Plante (ed.), *Mental Disorders of the New Millennium*, Vol. 2, *Public and Social Problems*. Westport, CT: Praeger, pp. 127–169.

Tomlinson, K.L., Brown, S.A. and Abrantes, A.M. (2004). Psychiatric comorbidity and substance use treatment outcomes of adolescents. *Psychology of Addictive Behaviors*, 18, 160–169.

Tucker, J.S., Fitzmaurice, A.E., Imanura, M. *et al.* (2006). The effect of the national demonstration project Healthy Respect on teenage sexual health behavior. *Developmental Neuropsychology*, 30, 633–657.

Turbin, M.S., Jessor, R. and Costa, F.M. (2000). Adolescent cigarette smoking: health-related behavior or normative transgression? *Prevention Science*, 1, 115–124.

UNICEF (2002). Young people and HIV/AIDS:opportunity in crisis. Geneva: UNICEF (www.unicef.org/publications/index_4447.html).

Valois, R.F., Oeltmann, J.E., Waller, J. and Hussey, J.R. (1999). Relationship between number of sexual intercourse partners and selected health behaviors among public high school adolescents. *Journal of Adolescent Health*, 25, 328–353.

Warren, C.W., Kann, L., Small, M.L. *et al.* (1997). Age of initiating selected health-risk behaviors among high school students in the United States. *Journal of Adolescent Health*, 21, 225–231.

Weiss, R. and Schneider, J. (2006). *Untangling the Web: Sex, Porn and Fantasy Obsession in the Internet Age*. New York, NY: Alyson Books.

Wersinger, S.R. and Rissman, E.F. (2000). Dopamine activates masculine sexual behavior independent of the estrogen receptor alpha. *Journal of Neuroscience*, 20, 4248–4254.

Wight, D., Williamson, L. and Henderson, M. (2006). Parental influences on young people's sexual behavior: a longitudinal analysis. *Journal of Adolescence*, 29, 473–494.

Wilder, W.I. and Watt, T.T. (2002). Risky parental behavior and adolescent sexual activity at first coitus. *The Milbank Quarterly: A Journal of Public Health and Health Care Policy*, 80, 481–524.

Wingood, G.M., DiClemente, R.J., Harrington, K.F. *et al.* (2006). Efficacy of an HIV prevention program among female adolescents experiencing gender-based violence. *American Journal of Public Health*, 96, 1085–1090.

Wolf, R. and Freedman, D. (2000). Cigarette smoking, sexually transmitted diseases and HIV/AIDS. *International Journal of Dermatology*, 39, 1–9.

Ybarra, M.L. and Mitchell, K.J. (2005). Exposure to Internet pornography among children and adolescents: a National survey. *CyberPsychology and Behavior*, 8, 473–486.

PART

III

EPILOGUE

10

Comorbidity of Addictive Problems: Assessment and Treatment Implications

Cecilia A. Essau

The term "comorbidity" has recently become fashionable among mental health professionals to indicate the presence of more than one disorder in a person in a specific period of time (Wittchen and Essau, 1993). Comorbidity can be examined using the "lifetime" or "current" approaches. The lifetime approach is advantageous because it makes it possible to determine the occurrence and clustering of disorders over the individual's lifespan, while the current approach determines the presence of multiple disorders at the time of the investigation. Both the patterns of comorbidity and the temporal sequencing of comorbid disorders can be very different in different individuals. For example, in some individuals anxiety disorders may occur before substance use disorders (SUD), whereas in others SUD and anxiety may occur at the same time, or SUD may occur before anxiety disorders.

Although the concept of comorbidity has been described as far back as the Hippocratic time, heightened interest in comorbidity is associated with the shifts towards the "neo-Kraepelinian" paradigm during the 1970s, and with the advent of the third edition of the *Diagnostic and Statistical Manual of Mental Disorders* (DSM-III, American Psychiatric Association, 1980). The DSM-III and its subsequent versions provide: (i) explicit and operationalized diagnoses; (ii) the reduction of diagnostic hierarchies; (iii) a stronger emphasis on lifetime phenomena; and (iv) an increase in the number of specific diagnostic categories, in contrast to the broad and loosely defined generic classes such as "neurosis" (Wittchen and Essau, 1993). The changes inherent in these principles have had an impact on clinical and research strategies and findings. That is, due to the higher number of specific diagnoses, the use of the lifetime perspective and the lack of diagnostic hierarchies, many adolescents who would previously have received only one diagnosis receive multiple diagnoses. These changes in the DSM system have been criticized because they have led to an artificial increase the prevalence of comorbidity rates, and to making distinctions that may not be clinically useful (Frances *et al.*, 1990). On the other hand, no judgment regarding their clinical usefulness could be made without making such distinctions.

In the following section, specific comorbid patterns will be presented. Because most of the existing studies have found comorbidity between alcohol/drug use disorders and anxiety, depressive, and disruptive behavioral disorders, we will focus on these specific comorbid patterns.

COMORBID PATTERNS

One of the most consistent findings in adolescent psychopathology is the high comorbidity rates, with the degree of comorbidity being even more common than in adults. As reported by Anderson and colleagues (1987), about 60 percent of children and adolescents with a diagnosable condition have two or more additional disorders. Furthermore, after reviewing six community studies, Angold and Costello (1992) concluded that the presence of one disorder in adolescents increased the probability of having another disorder by at least 20 times.

Similar to other adolescent psychopathology, addictive problems such as substance use disorders (SUD) (e.g., alcohol, drug, nicotine abuse/dependence) and gambling addiction co-occur frequently with other psychiatric disorders (Bukstein *et al.*, 1989; Fergusson *et al.*, 1993; Lewinsohn *et al.*, 1993), although the precise rate of comorbidity varies widely across studies due to differences on the operationalization of SUD, the age and gender, the timeframe assessed (lifetime, current) and the settings from which the samples were recruited. In the Bremen Adolescent Study (Essau *et al.*, 1998), for example, about half (47.2%) of the adolescents who met the diagnosis of any SUD were diagnosed with only these disorders; 37.1 percent had one additional and 12.7 percent had at least two other psychiatric disorders. In the Oregon Adolescent Depression Project (OADP), over 80 percent of the adolescents with an alcohol use disorder (AUD) had another psychiatric disorder: about 20 percent of the adolescents had comorbid internalizing disorders, 35 percent had externalizing disorders, and the remaining 45 percent suffered from both internalizing and externalizing disorders (Rohde *et al.*, 1996).

SUBSTANCE USE DISORDERS

SUD include substance dependence and substance abuse. The former refers to a physiological and/or psychological dependence on a substance, while the latter has a less severe symptom presentation than substance dependence. A person with a substance abuse may continue using the substance despite problems in various life domains. Recent years have seen an increased number of studies investigating the prevalence of SUD and their comorbidity with other psychiatric disorders (see Chapter 4 in this volume). Comorbidity has been found to occur not only between SUD and other psychiatric disorders, but also within the SUD. In Essau and colleagues' study (1998), about one-third of those with one type of SUD had at least other types of abuse/dependence, with AUD being the most common comorbid disorder. In the EDSP (Perkonigg *et al.*, 1997), 80 percent of the young adults with cannabis use disorder were exclusively abusing or dependent on this substance. About 18 percent also used amphetamines, 11.7 percent cocaine and 4.1 percent hallucinogens. Among those with hallucinogen or amphetamine use disorders, not one single case was identified as having only this disorder. About 88 percent of those with amphetamine use disorders also had a cannabis use disorder, while 76 percent had hallucinogen and 20 percent had opioid use disorders. The finding of the high comorbidity between SUD and other disorders (especially illicit drug use, delinquent-type behavior and tobacco use) was interpreted as being consistent with problem-behavior theory as proposed by Jessor and Jessor (1977). According to their theory, this problem behavior is a single syndrome which is associated with the underlying construct of unconventionality.

ANXIETY DISORDERS

Anxiety disorders are among the most common disorders in the general population, affecting up to 20 percent of adolescents (Essau *et al.*, 2000). Adolescents meeting the criteria of anxiety disorders have been described as generally withdrawn, fearful of situations or objects, afraid of being in a social situation, and inhibited (APA, 1994). Anxiety disorders that commonly occur in adolescents include separation anxiety disorder (i.e., excessive fears about separation from a care-giver), social phobia (i.e., an irrational fear of being judged in social situations), specific phobias (i.e., a fear of specific objects or situations), generalized anxiety disorder (i.e., excessive and uncontrollable worry about life events), obsessive-compulsive disorder (i.e., intrusive illogical thoughts and repetitive behaviors often related to the obsessions), panic disorder (i.e., discrete fear attacks that are associated with cognitive and physical symptoms), post-traumatic stress disorder (i.e., a severe trauma that is characterized by re-experiencing an event, hyperarousal and avoidance symptoms), and agoraphobia (i.e., fear of being in places that are difficult to escape).

High comorbidity rates between SUD and anxiety disorders have been reported in both clinical samples and the general population. For example, in a study by Clark and Jacob (1992), 50 percent of the adolescent with AUD had at least one lifetime anxiety disorder. The temporal sequence of anxiety and AUD is variable, depending on the type of anxiety disorder; social phobia and agoraphobia usually precede alcohol abuse, while panic disorder and generalized anxiety disorder tend to follow the onset of alcohol abuse (Kushner *et al.*, 2000).

At least three models have been put forward to explain the comorbidity between social anxiety and SUD, including (1) the tension reduction theory (i.e., alcohol use to relieve tension in social situation; Conger, 1956); (2) the Stress Response Dampening Model (i.e., using alcohol to reduce reactivity to stressful situation; Khantzian, 1997); and (3) the Self-Medication Hypothesis (i.e., the psychotropic effects of alcohol on an individual's anxiety symptoms could lead to the development of alcohol dependence). However, studies that attempt to test these models have reported inconsistent findings (see Chapter 4 in this volume).

DEPRESSIVE DISORDERS

Depressive disorders are characterized by the presence of depressed mood along with a set of additional symptoms, persisting over time, and causing disruption and impairment of function. Two depressive disorders commonly reported in adolescents are major depressive disorder and dysthymic disorder (APA, 1994); major depressive disorder denotes a severe and acute form of depressive disorder, while dysthymic disorder is a chronic but less severe form of depressive disorder.

Depression appears to have a strong association with SUD, more so in females than in males (see, for example, Brook *et al.*, 1996; Cornelius *et al.*, 2004). According to numerous previous studies, the comorbidity rates of SUD and depression range from 11 to 32 percent; however, the comorbidity rates tend to vary across classes of drug (Armstrong and Costello, 2002). Specifically, the highest comorbidity rate was found between depression and tranquilizer use, followed by non-prescription drugs, inhalants, alcohol, and tobacco.

The role of depression on SUD and *vice versa* has been examined in several studies. In a study by Milberger and colleagues (1997), alcohol consumption and cigarette smoking were found to trigger depression. In Kandel and colleagues' study (1997), weekly use of alcohol, daily cigarette smoking, and drug use independently increased the depressive rates to about 19 percent. In a recent study by Chinet and colleagues (2006), depression and substance use varied overtime, and were closely but synchronically related. Specifically, a decrease in the severity of substance use paralleled a decrease in depression. With regard to smoking, the presence of depression greatly reduces the ability of smokers to quit (see, for example, Glassman *et al.*, 1990), which, according to the nicotine withdrawal escape model (e.g., Parrott, 1999), suggest that smokers achieve a reduction in negative affect through relief of nicotine withdrawal symptoms.

DISRUPTIVE BEHAVIORAL DISORDERS

Disruptive behavioral disorders include three separate disorders: conduct disorder, oppositional defiant disorder, and Attention-Deficit/Hyperactivity Disorder (ADHD). Conduct disorder is a persistent behavior pattern in which the basic rights of others or age-appropriate societal norms are repeatedly violated (APA, 1994). Oppositional defiant disorder is a recurring pattern of defiant, disobedient, negativistic and hostile behavior toward authority figures. ADHD is a persistent pattern of inattention and/or hyperactivity-impulsivity which is more severe and frequent than is commonly seen in persons of similar age and developmental level.

Studies of adolescents with SUD in clinical settings have also reported the common presence of disruptive behaviors, with rates ranging from 40 to 70 percent (Bukstein, 2000). ADHD has been reported to occur in 20–30 percent of adolescents with SUD (Kaminer, 1992; Horner and Scheibe, 1997); however, this association tends to be moderated by conduct disorder (Pihl and Peterson, 1991; Disney *et al.*, 1999). Conduct disorder also increased the risk of drug use in adolescence (see, for example, Slutske *et al.*, 1998) and doubled the probability of future AUD (Rohde *et al.*, 2001). The nature of comorbidity between SUD and conduct disorder is still unclear; however, several explanations have been discussed (Conner 2002). First, an early-onset conduct disorder may increase the risk of developing SUD in adolescence and adulthood. As reported by Myers and colleagues (1998), the onset of conduct disorder by age 10 years among referred adolescents predicted the development of SUD during adolescence. Brook and colleagues (1996) similarly found early onset of aggressive behavior/conduct disorder symptoms (i.e., at age 5–10 years) to be predictive of SUD during adolescence and adulthood. Second, SUD may increase the risk of displaying aggressive behavior through the physiological and behavioral effects of the substance being used – for example, to overcome the negative experiences of substance withdrawal symptoms, addicted person may be motivated towards antisocial behavior in order to obtain more of the substance. Third, SUD may be part of a large spectrum of psychopathology. As shown by several authors, individuals with SUD and those with aggressive behavior or conduct disorder-related behavior have been reported to show executive cognitive function deficits (Kreutzer *et al.*, 1995; Giancola *et al.*, 1998).

TEMPORAL SEQUENCE OF DISORDERS

Most studies that have examined the temporal sequence of comorbid disorders have focused on SUD and other psychiatric disorders. In adult studies, most patients with comorbid disorders reported the onset of the psychiatric disorders prior to that of substances (see, for example, Ross *et al.*, 1988; Kessler *et al.*, 1996), which is not surprising, because many psychiatric disorders emerge in childhood or early adolescence, before the period of highest risk for developing SUD. As reported in the Dunedin Study, psychiatric disorders at age 18 which preceded the occurrence of SUD at age 21 included history of conduct disorder (43%), depressive disorder (38%), anxiety disorder (29%) and ADHD (11%).

In the OADP (Rohde *et al.*, 1996), 58.1 percent of adolescents with alcohol use disorder who had a history of major depression, reported the occurrence of depression before that of alcohol. In about 87.5 percent and 80 percent of the adolescents, anxiety and disruptive behavioral disorders, respectively, preceded that AUD (Rohde *et al.*, 1996). Similar findings have been reported by Hovens *et al.* (1994), in that 53 percent of the adolescents with dysthymia and AUD reported dysthymia preceding AUD. Among adolescents with conduct disorder and AUD, conduct disorder not only frequently predates but also predicts alcohol use or an AUD (Clark *et al.*, 1998; Lynskey and Fergusson, 1995). It has been argued that adolescents with conduct disorder tend to "act out" and frequently seek new experiences, and may consequently begin drinking at an early age and have an increased risk of developing alcohol problem (Lewis and Bucholz, 1991). Another explanation for the relationship between conduct disorder and AUD could be that each disorder shares common risk factors. According to this explanation, the development of both antisocial behaviors and early alcohol use results from common risk factors, such as poor parental support and supervision, deviant peer group association, and low academic achievement (Donovan and Jessor 1985).

POSSIBLE EXPLANATIONS FOR COMORBIDITY

Despite the high comorbidity rates between addictive problems and other psychiatric disorders, the meaning of comorbidity for psychopathology and classification issues remains unclear. There has been much debate as to whether comorbidity is "real" or an artefact. Artefactual explanations include methodological and assessment bias.

Methodological biases include a treatment or sampling bias in which adolescents with two or more disorders have a greater chance of being hospitalized or treated. As such, the clinic samples generally comprise individuals with comorbid disorders. This phenomenon arises because the chance of being referred to mental health services is higher for adolescents with a comorbid disorder than for those with only one disorder. Comorbidity found in clinical setting could reflect severe psychopathology and psychosocial impairment; thus, adolescents with comorbid disorders are more likely to be referred than those with non-comorbid disorders.

Assessment bias may include the lack of discrete diagnostic definitions in which a large degree of symptoms overlap exists between two diagnostic categories, or the application of diagnostic hierarchies which may mask an association between disorders (Widiger and Ford-Black, 1994). As argued by Maj (2005), comorbidity may occur as a by-product of some specific features of our current classification systems; he claimed "If demarcations are made where they do not exist in nature, the probability that several diagnosis have to be made in an individual case will obviously increase" (Maj, 2005: 182). He further argued that artificially splitting a clinical problem into pieces not only prevents a holistic approach to the individual, but also encourage unwarranted polypharmacy.

However, there are also some indicators to support the presence of "true" comorbidity. Rutter, for example, has argued that the core of every disorder is a struggle for adaptation, but the way in which the phenotype is expressed depends on environmental conditions and person – environment interactions. According to Merikangas (1989), the co-occurrence of disorders could be etiologic in that one disorder causes the second disorder (i.e., causal association). As argued by Schuckit (2006), the frequent use of substance could either unmask a latent predisposition toward having a psychiatric disorder, or cause changes in the brain which in turn lead to long-term depression. Comorbidity may also develop if the second disorder (e.g., AUD) develops as a result of the patient's effort to reduce problems with the first disorder (e.g., depression). That is, the frequent use of a substance to alleviate depressive feelings could lead to the development of SUD. Others (such as Felitti *et al.*, 1998) have argued that high comorbidity among disorders could be attributed to common environmental risk factors for psychiatric disorders (e.g., stress, poverty, early trauma), which involve different pathways.

THE IMPACT OF COMORBIDITY

Comorbidity of addictive problems and psychiatric disorders is of significance to health services, healthcare providers, adolescents and their family members, because of both its frequency and its negative impact. Psychiatric disorders are generally chronic and severe, are less likely to benefit from treatments, and are often associated with impairment in various life domains, including social, occupational, family, economic and/or health functions (Lewinsohn *et al.*, 1995). In addition to impairment in these life domains, addictive problems are associated with increased vulnerability to legal, community, family and self-support risks. The presence of comorbid disorders makes it difficult to differentiate impairment as a result of addictive problems from impairment due to other psychiatric disorders.

In a recent study by Rowe and colleagues (2004), adolescents with substance abuse and comorbid disorders ("Mixed" group) showed higher levels of overall symptoms and internalizing symptoms than the other groups at intake to treatment. These adolescents also came from families with more significant alcohol, drug and legal problems, poorer family relationships, and higher levels of conflict and mental health problems, than families of adolescents with substance abuse only (the Exclusive Substance Abusers group; Rowe *et al.*, 2004). Adolescents who abuse substances and have comorbid disorders have been found to have earlier onset and greater frequency of substance, and more chronic use compared with those without comorbid disorders (Rohde *et al.*, 1996; Horner and Scheibe, 1997; Miller-Johnson *et al.*, 1998). Furthermore, depression seems to predict escalation in adolescent drug use (Henry *et al.*, 1993) and correlates positively with the severity of drug use (Riggs *et al.*, 1995). Studies have also shown substance abuse and dependence to be independent and interactive risk factors for suicidal ideation, attempts and completed suicides (Brent, 1995).

Furthermore, the prevalence of comorbid disorder in adolescents increased the likelihood of receiving mental health treatment for their disorder. However, despite using more mental health services, comorbid drug abusers showed poorer treatment outcomes in standard community treatment programs, and also in empirically supported interventions (Rowe *et al.*, 2004). For example, in Rowe and colleagues' study (2004), adolescents in the "Exclusive Substance Abusers" group reported an increase in the amount of substance use during treatment, but responded more positively during the follow-up period. In contrast, adolescents in the "Mixed" group showed slight reductions in substance use from intake to discharge; however, their gains seemed to level off between discharge and 6 months, then returned to intake levels by the 12-month follow-up assessment. It was argued that, among adolescents with comorbid psychopathology, a lack of significant improvement in their emotional and behavioral symptoms may have led to the leveling off of drug use treatment gains in the longer term.

Studies have also shown that comorbid substance abuse is not only a more challenging clinical phenomenon to treat (Grella *et al.*, 2001; Rohde *et al.*, 2001), but also about twice as costly to treat as to treat substance abuse or mental health problems in isolation (King *et al.*, 2000). Why adolescents with comorbid disorders are more difficult to treat than those with only addictive problems is unclear. According to one study, factors that complicated treatment of adolescents with substance abuse and conduct disorder included greater severity of family, school and legal problems (Grella *et al.*, 2001).

Comorbidity has also been reported to have a role in premature termination of treatment, although findings have been inconsistent across studies. In the study by Kaminer *et al.* (1992) comorbidity was related to premature termination of treatment, where as in several other studies comorbidity did not significantly predict attendance (Rowe *et al.*, 2004).

Comorbidity has both advantages and disadvantages. Specifically, comorbidity avoids treatment errors which result from misattribution of symptoms associated with one disorder and missing the comorbid disorders (Drake and Wallach, 2007). However, comorbidity could lead to an expansion of polypharmacy and underutilization of psychological interventions for the prevention, treatment and rehabilitation of addictive problems and comorbid psychiatric disorders (Drake and Wallach, 2007). Others argued that focusing on comorbid disorders could lead to an overemphasis of treatment on specific addictive problems and disorders, without taking important life domains (e.g., social and family relationship) into consideration (Mueser and Drake, 2007). Furthermore, because treatment tends to be domain-specific, effective treatment for a particular addictive problem cannot be expected to lead to improvement in other life domains. However, there are no studies that investigate which particular interventions are more effective for adolescents with specific comorbid problems.

ASSESSMENT IMPLICATIONS OF COMORBIDITY

Assessment represents a fundamental step in understanding addictive problems and other psychiatric disorders. The general goals of assessment include diagnosis and prognosis, treatment planning, and treatment monitoring and evaluation. In clinical practice, assessment precedes treatment but is also an ongoing, fluid and dynamic process. The success of the intervention often depends on the information obtained during the initial assessment process and the dynamic interplay between ongoing assessments throughout treatment.

The high comorbidity rates among the addictive problems suggest that when assessing adolescents with addictive problems, a wide range of other disorders should be assessed routinely – especially because certain addictive problems (e.g., substance) can mask symptoms or are used to "medicate" psychiatric illness. Because unstructured clinical interviews often result in inaccurate diagnostic formulations, standardized diagnostic interview schedules (e.g., the Diagnostic Interview for Children and Adolescents (Herjanic and Campbell, 1977) and the Diagnostic Interview Schedule for Children (Costello *et al.*, 1987)) are needed to provide accurate profiles. The major advantage of using diagnostic interview schedules is their comprehensive coverage of psychiatric disorders and their ability to help reduce variability through clear specification, definition and instruction regarding the items involved.

In many settings, evaluation of psychiatric symptoms occurs only at intake, however, because comorbid psychiatric disorders may emerge and develop at a different pace and level of severity during the treatment period, the presence of a wide variety of psychiatric symptoms should be monitored. This means that assessment should be made on an ongoing basis or at specific intervals to capture the emergence of any new disorders and any clinical changes in the primary diagnosis. This in turn may help to understand sequencing of disorders and to tailor treatment to addictive problems and their interaction with other disorders (Piotrowski, 2007). Whitmore and Riggs (2006) recently suggested using the "lifetime timeline" approach to organize the assessment information (Table 10.1). This approach enables the collection of information, from birth to present, which can be mapped onto important developmental and family history. The use of the timeline approach provides a clear conceptualization of events that influence the adolescent's clinical presentation, and integrates this information longitudinally.

In assessing addictive problems, adolescents should be asked about the patterns of their addictive problems (frequency, severity), the consequences of use, past treatment history (types of treatment, intensity of treatment, and length of treatment), any family history of mental illness and addictive problems, their perceptions regarding their addictive problems, and motivation to quit their addiction. It is also important to know the way in which symptoms of both addictive problems and psychiatric disorders are expressed and experienced, because there is no stereotypical trajectory across age groups and gender – for example, girls with alcohol abuse may not show the same symptoms of

TABLE 10.1 Integrating Treatment for Substance Abuse and Comorbid Disorders

Stage	Components
Starting treatment	Establish rapport
	Functional analysis of addictive problems
	Establish goals for treatment
	Encourage parent's involvement in the treatment process
Use of pharmacotherapy	Weigh the risk of drug-medication interactions against the risk of the untreated comorbid disorders
	Choose specific medications for comorbid disorders
	Initiation of pharmacotherapy to treat comorbid disorders such as anxiety and depression
	Patient psychoeducation, especially on the safety and effectiveness of medication
Evaluating improvement	Examine the efficacy of the medication
	Re-evaluate the appropriate of the medication
	Re-evaluate the diagnosis
Dealing with relapse	Increase the intensity and frequency of treatment to restabilize illness and to prevent further decline in functioning

Adapted from Whitmore and Riggs (2006).

alcohol misuse as boys (e.g., reckless/drunk driving, or fights/arguments with others). Contextual/environmental factors (e.g., difficult family relationships, the lack of adequate parental supervision, and deviant peer affiliations) should also be assessed, given their role in the development and maintenance of addictive problems and in treatment planning (Clark *et al.* 1998).

Addictive problems with comorbid disorders will naturally take more time to administer. Owing to both the complexity and the time-consuming nature of administration and interpretation, the cost of assessing comorbid disorders will be higher than when assessing addictive problems only (Piotrowski, 2007).

TREATMENT IMPLICATIONS OF COMORBIDITY

Adolescents with comorbid disorder put a tremendous social and financial strain on the public healthcare system because disorders tend to interact in a circular manner, thus exacerbating subsequent problems. As reported by several authors, adolescents with comorbid disorders tend to be younger and to experience higher levels of substance use, report severe psychosocial impairment, legal problems, suicidal behavior and sexual or physical abuse, and to report the presence of parental drug use and psychopathology (King *et al.*, 2000; Kelly *et al.*, 2004). These findings are a clear indication that adolescents' addictive problems are linked to diverse areas of life and youth culture. For this reason, treatment needs to be multifaceted by focusing not only on the addictive problems, but also on the comorbid disorders and a range of interrelated problems.

The presence of comorbid disorders raises questions about which disorder should be treated first or considered the most serious, whether each disorder should be treated separately, whether a single treatment can be used for all disorders, and whether outcomes should be evaluated for only the target disorder or for all problems. Answers to these questions may help in designing effective treatment for addictive problems with comorbid disorders. Generally, once a thorough assessment has been made the next step is to decide which disorder (i.e., primary diagnosis) should be the main focus of treatment. Primary diagnosis has been defined differently, being based either on the chronology of onset (i.e., the disorder which occurred first), or its etiology (i.e., the disorder which caused the occurrence of another disorder), or its cause of impairment (i.e., the disorder which causes the most impairment) (Brown and Barlow, 1992).

Comorbid disorders also present a challenge to the clinician, as they can could cloud the treatment's focus and lead the clinician to drift in his or her treatment goal. According to Curry and colleagues (2003), comorbidity necessitates the choice of three systematic approaches: sequential treatment (i.e., treating the primary disorder first and the comorbid disorder second); common process treatment (i.e., targeting common process of both disorders); or modular treatment (i.e., an integrative approach to both disorders which involves addressing the process that are specific to each). For the treatment of patients with SUD and comorbid psychiatric disorders, the widely used American Society of Addiction Medicine Patient Placement Criteria currently focus on SUD to evaluate the appropriate treatment for patients (Minkoff *et al.*, 2003).

In addition to Curry's suggestion (2003), some authors have suggested that effective interventions for adolescent substance abusers with comorbid psychiatric disorders need to have an integrative conceptualization and systematic approach to addressing these multiple problems (Riggs and Whitmore, 1999; Rounds-Bryant *et al.*, 1999). As reported by Liddle and colleagues (2001), family-based approaches which target change in the multiple systems that are involved in the development and maintenance of both drug use and psychiatric problems are among the most effective treatments for adolescent substance abusers with comorbid conduct disorder. Bukstein (1995) similarly argued that treatment strategies which include family interventions, contingency management programs and social skills training have been reported to be successful in treating adolescents with comorbid AUDs and conduct disorder.

The importance of using a specific treatment for comorbid disorders among adolescents with SUD has been much debated. Furthermore, the use of pharmacotherapy for the treatment of comorbid depression and AUD, for example, is still in its embryonic stage (Cornelius *et al.*, 2004). In the clinical setting, the use of antidepressant medication for adolescents with AUD and comorbid depression is quite common, and showed an increased from 18 percent to 55 percent from 1991 to 2000. Empirical studies on the effectiveness of pharmacological treatment when used in adolescents with SUD and comorbid disorders are, though, lacking. The high cost of a comprehensive program may have limited its application. However, as argued by some authors, the cost of neglecting the most problematic adolescents could be greater than the cost of the most extensive intervention (cott *et al.*, 2001; Clark, 2004).

The cost of treating comorbid disorder also tends to be higher because of the need for more services and integrated care. For example, Kessler and colleagues (1994) reported that six of ten individuals with multiple comorbid disorders received treatment. Findings such as this stress the importance of improving our intervention programs so that those with comorbid disorders can be treated effectively. Treatment of addictive problems with comorbid disorders also requires knowledge regarding how treatment for one disorder may interact with treatment of other disorders.

TRAINING IMPLICATIONS OF COMORBIDITY

Comorbidity not only has assessment and treatment implications; it also has training implication. Because of the frequency and complexity of comorbidity in addictive problems, clinical training should address comorbidity directly at pre- and post-doctoral levels and beyond. At pre- and post-doctoral levels, there is a need to provide training regarding the general concept of comorbidity, and the assessment and treatment of comorbid disorders. In addition, at the post-doctoral level, research training and clinical practice need to continue to address comorbidity and its variations. Furthermore, continuing education materials need to be developed in order to facilitate clinicians' knowledge and find methods to inform research and training practice in specific areas of application (Piotrowski, 2007). Moreover, educating clinicians about symptoms of substance addiction greatly improves both their recognition of the problem and the treatment of other problems which previously have been neglected (Mueser *et al.*, 2005).

SUMMARY

Addictive problems co-occur frequently, both among themselves and with other psychiatric disorders. Despite the high comorbidity rates, the meaning of comorbidity for classification and etiological mechanism remains unclear. What our review clearly shows is the negative impact of comorbidity on the course and outcome of addictive problems, and the challenge it produces in assessing and treating adolescents with addictive problems and comorbid disorders.

To design more effective interventions for adolescents with comorbid addictive problems and psychiatric problems is an enormous challenge, and should therefore be the highest priority for clinicians and researchers alike. There is a need for greater attention to and more comprehensive assessment of psychiatric comorbidity in working with adolescents with addictive problems and their families. Such assessments should lead to more appropriate treatment planning and intervention. It is also the first step towards moving away from a unidimensional disease model in which one size fits all. Progress in treating adolescents with addictive problems will remain limited until comorbid disorders are adequately assessed and targeted in treatment. Additionally, there are numerous areas which need further development in the assessment and treatment of adolescents with addictive problems and comorbid disorders, including the following:

- Examination of the etiological relationship between addictive problems and comorbid psychiatric disorders, and of the common and shared aspects of pathophysiology, using family and genetic studies, neuroimaging studies and biological studies (Nunes and Rounsaville, 2006)
- Identification of the characteristics (e.g., diagnostic status and developmental stage) of adolescents with comorbid disorders
- Determination of the course and outcome of addictive problems, with or without comorbid disorders
- Development and evaluation of pharmacological and psychological interventions for adolescents with comorbid disorders – both the appropriate combination and sequencing of pharmacological and psychological interventions need to be explored
- Development of evaluation measures for treatment outcome for different patterns of comorbid disorders.

REFERENCES

American Psychiatric Association (1980). *Diagnostic and Statistical Manual of Mental Disorders*, 3rd edn. Washington, DC: APA.

American Psychiatric Association (1994). *Diagnostic and Statistical Manual of Mental Disorders*, 4th edn. Washington, DC: APA.

Anderson, J.C., Williams, S., McGee, R. and Silva, P.A. (1987). DSM-III disorders in preadolescent children. Prevalence in a large sample from the general population. *Archives of General Psychiatry*, 44, 69–76.

Angold, A. and Costello, E.J. (1992). Comorbidity in children and adolescents with depression. *Child and Adolescent Psychiatric Clinics of North America*, 1, 31–51.

Armstrong, T.D. and Costello, E.J. (2002). Community studies on adolescent substance use, abuse, or dependence and psychiatric comorbidity. *Journal of Consulting and Clinical Psychology*, 70, 1224–1239.

Brent, D.A. (1995). Risk factors for adolescent suicide and suicidal behaviour. *Suicide Life Threat Behavior,* 25, 52–63.

Brook, J.S., Whiteman, M., Finch, S.J. and Cohen, P. (1996). Young adult drug use and delinquency: childhood antecedent and intervening processes. *Journal of the American Academy of Child and Adolescent Psychiatry*, 34, 1076–1084.

Brown, T.A. and Barlow, D.H. (1992). Comorbidity among anxiety disorders: implications for treatment and DSM-IV. *Journal of Consulting and Clinical Psychology*, 60, 835–844.

Bukstein, O.G. (1995). *Adolescent Substance Abuse: Assessment, Prevention* and *Treatment.* New York, NY: John Wiley.

Bukstein, O.G. (2000). Disruptive behavior disorders and substance use disorders in adolescents. *Journal of Psychoactive Drugs*, 32, 67–79.

Bukstein, O.G., Brent, D.A. and Kamier, Y. (1989). Comorbidity of substance abuse and other psychiatric disorders in adolescents. *American Journal of Psychiatry*, 146, 1131–1141.

Chinet, L., Plancherel, B., Bolognini, M. *et al.* (2006). Substance use and depression. Comparative course in adolescents. *European Child and Adolescent Psychiatry*,15, 149–155.

Clark, D.B. and Jacobs, R.G. (1992). Anxiety disorders and alcoholism in adolescents. A preliminary report. *Alcoholism: Clinical and Experimental Research*, 16, 371.

Clark, D.B. (2004). The natural history of adolescent alcohol use disorders. *Addiction*, 99, 5–22.

Clark, D.B., Neighbors, B.D., Lesnick, L.A. *et al.* (1998). Family functioning and adolescent alcohol use disorders. *Journal of Family Psychology*, 12, 81–92.

Conger, J. (1956). Reinforcement theory and the dynamics of alcoholism. *Quarterly Journal of Studies on Alcohol*, 17, 296–305.

Conner, D.F. (2002). *Aggression and Antisocial Behaviour in Children and Adolescents: Research and Treatment.* New York, NY: Guilford Press.

Cornelius, J.R., Maisto, S.A., Martin, C.S. *et al.* (2004). Major depression associated with earlier alcohol relapse in treated teens with AUD. *Addictive Behaviors*, 29, 1035–1038.

Costello, A.J., Edelbrock, C., Dulcan, M.K. *et al.* (1987). *The Diagnostic Interview Schedule for Children (DISC).* Pittsburgh, PA. University of Pittsburgh.

Curry, J.F., Wells, K.C., Lochman, J.E. *et al.* (2003). Cognitive-behavioral intervention for depressed, substance-abusing adolescents: development and pilot testing. *Journal of the American Academy of Child and Adolescent Psychiatry*, 42, 656–665.

Disney, E.R., Elkins, I.J., McGue, M. and Iacono, W.G. (1999). Effects of ADHD, conduct disorder and gender on substance use and abuse in adolescence. *American Journal of Psychiatry*, 156, 1515–1521.

Donovan, J.E. and Jessor, R. (1985). Structure of problem behavior in adolescence and young adulthood. *Journal of Consulting and Clinical Psychology*, 53, 890–904.

Drake, R.E. and Wallach, M.A. (2007). Is comorbidity a psychological science? *Clinical Psychology: Science and Practice*, 14, 20–22.

Essau, C.A., Karpinski, N.A., Petermann, F. and Conradt, J. (1998). Häufigkeit und Komorbidität von Störungen durch Substanzkonsum. *Zeitschrift Kindheit und Entwicklung*, 7, 199–207.

Essau, C.A., Conradt, J. and Petermann, F. (2000). Frequency, comorbidity, and pyschosocial impairment of anxiety disorders in adolescents. *Journal of Anxiety Disorders*, 14, 263–279.

Felitti, V.J., Anda, R.F., Nordenberg, D. *et al.* (1998). Relationship of childhood abuse and household dysfunction to many of the leading causes of death in adults: the Adverse Childhood Event (ACE) study. *American Journal of Preventive Medicine*, 14, 245–258.

Fergusson, D.M., Horwood, L.J. and Lynskey, M.T. (1993). Prevalence and comorbidity of DSM-III-R diagnoses in a birth cohort of 15-year-olds. *Journal of the American Academy of Child and Adolescent Psychiatry*, 32, 1127–1134.

Frances, A., Widiger, T. and Fyer, M.R. (1990). The influence of classification methods on comorbidity. In: J.D. Maser and C.R. Cloinger (eds), *Comorbidity of Mood and Anxiety Disorders.* Washington, DC: American Psychiatric Press, pp. 41–59.

Giancola, P.R., Mezzich, A.C. and Tarter, R.E. (1998). Executive functioning, temperament and antisocial behavior in conduct-disordered adolescent females. *Journal of Abnormal Psychology*, 107, 629–641.

Glassman, A.H., Helzer, J.E., Covey, L.S. *et al.* (1990). Smoking, smoking cessation and major depression. *Journal of the American Medical Association*, 264, 1546–1549.

Grella, C.E., Hser, Y., Joshi, V. and Rounds-Bryant, J. (2001). Drug treatment outcomes for adolescents with comorbid mental and substance use disorders. *Journal of Nervous and Mental Disorders*, 189, 384–392.

Henry, B., Moffitt, T.E., Robins, L.N. *et al.* (1993). Early family predictors of child and adolescent antisocial behaviour. Who are the mothers of delinquents? *Criminal Behavior and Mental Health*, 3, 97–118.

Herjanic, B. and Campbell, W. (1977). Differentiating psychiatrically disturbed children on the basis of a structured interview. *Journal of Abnormal Child Psychology*, 5, 127–134.

Horner, B.R. and Scheibe, K.E. (1997). Prevalence and implications of Attention-Deficit Hyperactivity Disorder among adolescents in treatment for substance abuse. *Journal of the American Academy of Child and Adolescent Psychiatry*, 36, 30–36.

Hovens, J.G.F.M., Cantwell, D.P. and Kiriakos, R. (1994). Psychiatric comorbidity in hospitalized adolescent substance abusers. *Journal of the American Academy of Child and Adolescent Psychiatry*, 33, 476–483.

Jessor, R. and Jessor, S.L. (1977). *Problem Behavior and Psychosocial Development: A Longitudinal Study of Youth*. New York, NY: Academic Press.

Kaminer, Y. (1992). Desipramine facilitation of cocaine abstinence in an adolescent. *Journal of the American Academy of Child and Adolescence Psychiatry*, 31/2, 312–317.

Kandel, D.B., Johnson, J.G., Bird, H.R. *et al.* (1997). Psychiatric disorders associated with substance use among children and adolescents. Findings from the Methods for the Epidemiology of Child and Adolescent Mental Disorders (MECA) Study. *Journal of Abnormal Child Psychology*, 25, 121–132.

Kelly, T.M., Cornelius, J.R. and Clark, D.B. (2004). Psychiatric disorders and attempted suicide among adolescents with substance use disorders. *Drug and Alcohol Dependence*, 73, 87–97.

Kessler, R.C., McGonagle, K.A., Zhao, S. *et al.* (1994). Lifetime and 12-month prevalence of DSM-III-R psychiatric disorders in the United States: Results from the National Comorbidity Survey. *Archives of General Psychiatry*, 51, 8–19.

Kessler, R.C., Nelson, C.B., McGonagle, K.A. *et al.* (1996). The epidemiology of co-occurring addictive and mental disorders in the National Comorbidity Survey: implications for prevention and service utilization. *American Journal of Orthopsychiatry*, 66, 17–31.

Khantzian, E. (1997). The self-medication hypothesis of substance use disorders: a reconsideration and recent applications. *Harvard Review of Psychiatry*, 4, 231–244.

King, R.D., Gaines, L.S., Lambert, E.W. *et al.* (2000). The co-occurrence of psychiatric and substance use diagnosis in adolescents in different service systems: frequency, recognition, cost and outcome. *Journal of Behavioral Health Services & Research*, 27, 417–430.

Kreutzer, J.S., Marwitz, J.H. and Witol, A.D. (1995). Interrelationships between crime, substance abuse and aggressive behaviours among persons with traumatic brain injury. *Brain Injury*, 9, 757–768.

Kushner, M.G., Abram, K. and Borchardt, C. (2000). The relationship between anxiety disorders and alcohol use disorders: a review of the major perspectives and findings. *Clinical Psychiatric Review*, 20, 149–171.

Lewinsohn, P.M., Hops, H., Roberts, R.E. *et al.* (1993). Adolescent psychopathology: I. Prevalence and incidence of depression and other DSM-III-R disorders in high school students. *Journal of Abnormal Psychology*, 102, 133–144.

Lewinsohn, P. M., Rohde, P. and Seeley, J. R. (1995). Adolescent psychopathology: III. The clinical consequences of comorbidity. *Journal of the American Academy of Child and Adolescent Psychiatry*, 34, 510–519.

Lewis, C.E. and Bucholz, K.K. (1991). Alcoholism, antisocial behavior and family history. *Addiction*, 86, 177–194.

Liddle, H.A., Dakof, G.A., Parker, K. *et al.* (2001). Multidimensional family therapy for adolescent drug abuse: results of a randomized clinical trial. *American Journal of Drug and Alcohol Abuse*, 27, 651–688.

Lynskey, M.T. and Fergusson, D.M. (1995). Childhood conduct problems, attention deficit behaviosr and adolescent alcohol, tobacco and illicit drug use. *Journal of Abnormal Child Psychology*, 23, 281–302.

Maj, M. (2005). "Psychiatric comorbidity": an artefact of current diagnostic systems? *British Journal of Psychiatry*, 186, 182–184.

Merikangas, K.R. (1989). Comorbidity for anxiety and depression: review of family and genetic studies. In: J.D. Maser and C.R. Cloninger (eds), *Comorbidity of Mood and Anxiety Disorders*. Washington, DC: American Psychiatric Press, pp. 331–348.

Meuser, K.T. and Drake, R.E. (2007). Comorbidity: what have we learned and where are we going? *Clinical Psychology: Science and Practice*, 14, 64–69.

Milberger, S., Biederman, J., Faraone, S.V. *et al.* (1997). Further evidence of an association between attention-deficit/hyperactivity disorder and cigarette smoking. Findings from a high-risk sample of siblings. *American Journal of Addiction*, 6, 205–217.

Miller-Johnson, S., Lochman, J.E., Coie, J.D. *et al.* (1998). Comorbidity of conduct and depressive problems at sixth grade: substance use outcomes across adolescence. *Journal of Abnormal Child Psychology*, 26, 221–232.

Minkoff, K., Zweben, J., Rosenthal, R. and Ries, R. (2003). Development of service intensity criteria and program categories for individuals with co-occurring disorders. *Journal of Addictive Disorder*, 22, 113–29.

Mueser, K.T., Drake, R.E., Sigmon, S.C. and Brunette, M.F. (2005). Psychosocial interventions for adults with severe mental illnesses and co-occurring substance use disorders: a review of specific interventions. *Journal of Dual Diagnosis*, 1, 57–82.

Myers, M.G., Stewart, D.G. and Brown, S.A. (1998). Progression from conduct disorder to antisocial personality disorder following treatment for adolescent substance abuse. *American Journal of Psychiatry*, 155, 479–485.

Nunes, E.V. and Rounsaville, B.J. (2006). Comorbidity of substance use with depression and other mental disorders: from *Diagnostic and Statistical Manual of Mental Disorders*, fourth edition (DSM-IV) to DSM-V. *Addiction*, 101, 89–96.

Parrott, A.C. (1999). Does cigarette smoking cause stress? *American Psychologist*, 54, 817–820.

Perkonigg, A., Lieb, R. and Wittchen, H.-U. (1997). Prevalence of use, abuse and dependence of illicit drugs among adolescents and young adults in a community sample. *European Addiction Research*, 134, 1–15.

Pihl, R. and Peterson, J. (1991). Attention deficit hyperactivity disorder, childhood conduct disorder and alcoholism. *Alcohol Health and Research World*, 15, 25–31.

Piotrowski, N.A. (2007). Comorbidity and psychological science: does one size fit all? *Clinical Psychology: Science and Practice*, 14, 6–19.

Riggs, P.D. and Whitmore, E.A. (1999). Substance use disorders and disruptive behaviour disorders. In: R.L. Hendren (ed.), *Review of Psychiatry*, Vol. 18, *Disruptive Behaviour Disorders in Children and Adolescents*. Washington, DC: American Psychiatric Press, pp. 33–174.

Riggs, P.D., Baker, S., Mikulich, S.K. *et al.* (1995). Depression in substance-dependent delinquents. *Journal of the American Academy of Child and Adolescent Psychiatry*, 34, 764–771.

Rohde, P., Lewinsohn, P.M. and Seeley, J.R. (1996). Psychiatric comorbidity with problematic alcohol use in high school adolescents. *Journal of the American Academy of Child and Adolescent Psychiatry*, 35, 101–109.

Rohde, P., Lewinsohn, P.M., Kahler, C.W. *et al.* (2001). Natural course of alcohol use disorders from adolescence to young adulthood. *Journal of the American Academy of Child and Adolescent Psychiatry*, 40, 83–90.

Ross, H.E., Glaser, F.B. and Germanson, T. (1988). The prevalence of psychiatric disorders in patients with alcohol and other drug problems. *Archives of General Psychiatry*, 45, 1023–1031.

Rounds-Bryant, J.L. and Staab, J. (2002). Patient characteristics and treatment outcomes for African American, Hispanic and White adolescents in DATOS-A. *Journal of Adolescent Research*, 16, 624–641.

Rowe, C.L., Liddle, H.A., Greenbaum, P.E. and Henderson, C.E. (2004). Impact of psychiatric comorbidity on treatment of adolescent drug abusers. *Journal of Substance Abuse Treatment*, 26, 129–140.

Rutter, M. (1994). Comorbidity: meanings and mechanisms. *Clinical Psychology: Science and Practice*, 1, 100–103.

Schuckit, M.A. (2006). Comorbidity between substance use disorders and psychiatric conditions. *Addiction*, 101, 76–88.

Scott, S., Knapp, M., Henderson, J. and Maughan, B. (2001). Financial cost of social exclusion: follow-up study of antisocial children into adulthood. *British Medical Journal*, 323, 1–5.

Slutske, W.S., Heath, A.C., Dinwiddie, S.H. *et al.* (1998). Common genetic risk factors for conduct disorder and alcohol dependence. *Journal of Abnormal Psychology*, 107, 363–374.

Whitmore, E.A. and Riggs, P.D. (2006). Developmentally informed diagnostic and treatment considerations in comorbid conditions. In: H.A. Liddle and C.L. Rowe (eds), *Adolescent Substance Abuse: Intervention and Management*. Cambridge, Cambridgeshire: Cambridge University Press, pp. 264–283.

Widiger, T.A. and Ford-Black, M.M. (1994). Diagnoses and disorders. *Clinical Psychology: Science and Practice*, 1, 84–87.

Wittchen, H.-U. and Essau, C.A. (1993). Epidemiology of anxiety disorders. In: P.J. Wilner (eds), *Psychiatry*. Philadelphia, PA: J.B. Lippincott Company, pp. 1–25.

11

Social and Political Implications

Paul McArdle

This chapter attempts to examine, from a clinician's perspective, the influence of political factors on international and UK policy concerning youth substance use and misuse. It argues that, to a significant degree, governments are influenced by the concepts, guidance and data provided by supranational bodies such as the United Nations, European Community or World Bank and their subsidiary organizations such as the United Nations Office on Drugs and Crime (UNODC), and the European Commission or European Monitoring Centre for Drugs and Drug Addiction (EMCDDA). However, these bodies address issues that, in the first place, have become politically salient to national governments. Consequently, supranational bodies express the consensus emerging from dialogue between national governments. Perhaps especially because of its link with crime, substance misuse has become a major focus of their attention.

The emerging documentation ultimately articulates frameworks that potentially equip politicians to generate policy "solutions" in international and national jurisdictions. It is useful to be aware of this influential hinterland in attempting to understand or indeed challenge national policy and the actions of national politicians and civil servants.

WORLD BODIES

Even in its title, UNODC reflects the conflation of "drugs and crime" in the mind of international politicians. This organization is concerned that in recent decades international trends in youth drug abuse "have started to converge" on levels previously attained only within high-use regions such as the US or Northern Europe (e.g., EMCDDA Annual Report, 2006). Even prior to this, the recently retired UN General Secretary, Kofi Annan (UN General Assembly, 1998), had remarked that "the proliferation of drugs over the past 30 years is an example of the previously unimaginable becoming reality very quickly. A tragic reality." Currently, according to UNODC, rates of not only "drug-related problems... of crime and violence" but also "susceptibility to HIV/AIDS and hepatitis, demand for treatment and emergency room visits and a breakdown in social behavior" are also being driven upwards across the world. (www.unodc.org/unodc/en/drug_demand_reduction.html). Indeed, according to UNODC the illicit trade in substances is a global business of such scale and value, dwarfing the GDP of the majority of states, that "it erodes the rule of law {and} may potentially destabilize states... the dark side of globalization allows multinational criminal syndicates to broaden their range of operations from drug and arms trafficking to money laundering and trafficking in human beings" (www.unodc.org/unodc/en/crime_prevention.html). Although some may see in this an implausibly apocalyptic view of illicit drugs, who is to say it could not be also prophetic, UNODC implies, should this malign phenomenon continue to grow?

In its *Declaration on the Guiding Principles of Demand Reduction* (United Nations General Assembly, 1998), the UN set out guiding principles for confronting this drug use and abuse. These state that:

> There shall be a balanced approach between demand reduction and supply reduction, each reinforcing the other, in an integrated approach to solving the drug problem.

and

> Demand reduction policies shall: (i) aim at preventing the use of drugs and at reducing the adverse consequences of drug abuse; (ii) provide for and encourage active and coordinated participation of individuals at the community level, both generally and in situations of particular risk, by virtue, for example, of their geographic location, economic conditions or relatively large addict populations; (iii) be sensitive to both culture and gender; (iv) contribute towards developing and sustaining supportive environments.

The UN (1998) has argued for prevention by "facilitating healthy, productive and fulfilling alternatives to" drug abuse. The Declaration proposed reducing supply by measures against illicit crops and manufacture, money laundering (said to comprise 2–5% of the world's GDP), law enforcement and judicial cooperation. Indeed, the current Western military campaign in Afghanistan is partly justified by referring to destruction of the opium crop (Reid, 2006).

The UN indicates that demand reduction (UN, 1998) should include reversing the disintegration of communities that has contributed to drug abuse becoming endemic. Although it offers no explicit guidance about how to engage in "rebuilding and empowering communities", other more "micro" demand-reduction strategies seek to "prevent the onset of drug use, help drug users break the habit and provide treatment through rehabilitation and social reintegration." (www.unodc.org/unodc/en/drug_demand_reduction.html). It argues too for not only prevention but also counseling, treatment, rehabilitation, relapse prevention, aftercare and social reintegration. It advocates widespread "multisectoral collaborations" of interested parties, including "healthcare professionals", with "special attention being paid to youth", for whom programs should be "effective, relevant and accessible".

The World Bank uses the language of economics, expressing its concern that "these early decisions {to use psychoactive substances} can have far reaching consequences depleting the economy of productive human capital and adding to public health costs." In its view, it remains "the willingness of young parents to invest in their children {which} is the single most important factor determining the outcome for future generations". This is at a time that the UK think tank, the Institute for Public Policy Research (IPPR), has written of the "less engaged parents" of the UK (Margo *et al.*, 2006). The World Bank (Figure 11.1) advocates investing in the human capital of youth by "policies that dispense the information and incentives that enable them to make good decisions". Since "... not having second chances can lead to a free fall in outcomes", like the UN it, crucially, argues for the capacity to put "put young people back on the path to build

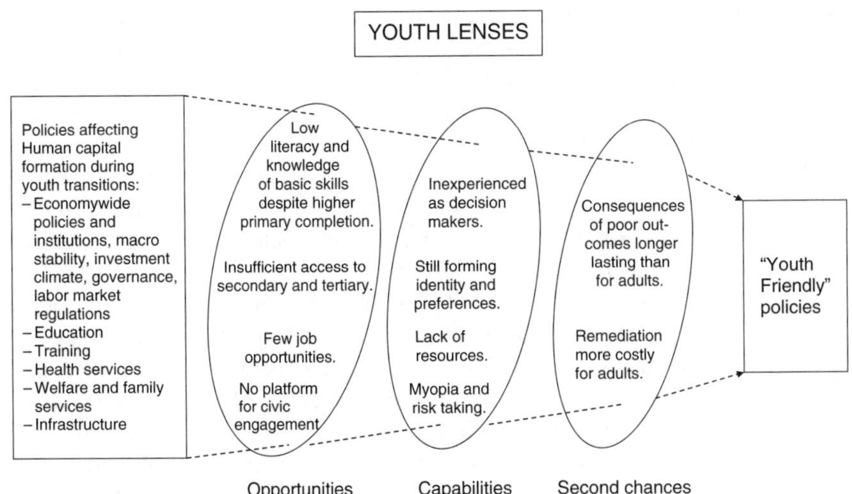

FIGURE 11.1 Transitions seen through three lenses focus policies and magnify impact.

their human capital for the future". However, citing the example of very low levels of primary school attainment in certain developing countries despite high levels of school attendance, it cautions that interventions should be of adequate quality and that measurement of quality is crucial. (Interestingly, on a matter important for clinicians, UNODC advocates a conservative approach to consent. It notes that prosecutions of traffickers are lost through what it terms a "false" understanding of consent, often in this case to prostitution by trafficked women. It argues that "children under 18 cannot give valid consent", and states that if there is evidence of any of improper means (e.g., coercion, fraud, deception), then any alleged consent to subsequent exploitation is irrelevant. Although not explicitly focused on drug use, this is a more conservative view of consent than applies in the UK, and could perhaps facilitate active intervention in situations of drug abuse and prostitution that all services meet from time to time. See www.unodc.org/unodc/en/trafficking_victim_consents.html.

In a UNODC paper, McClellan (2003) argues that whether it is "a sin, a crime, a bad habit, an illness, society has a right to expect that an effective public policy will reduce drug related crime, unemployment, family dysfunction and disproportionate use of medical care" (UNODC, 2003: 32), ultimately countering the "social decay" (p. i) that accompanies widespread substance abuse. UNODC also argues for the superiority of treatment over no treatment or, indeed, criminal justice alternatives. One of his key points concerns the need to treat addiction like a chronic disease, addressing the multiple risks for relapse, "medical, psychiatric symptoms and social instability", in part by retaining severely affected individuals in treatment for extended periods. Treatments should be "well integrated into society to permit ready access for monitoring purposes and to forestall relapse" (UNODC, 2003: iii). However, treatment of addiction differs from the management of chronic relapsing conventional disease in that its aim is not simply to make the patient feel better but to also reduce the consequences for society of the individual's social dysfunction – a crucial point in "selling" drug treatment to politicians. It also differs because many abusers are not in contact with services, requiring an emphasis on early detection, often through healthcare settings and outreach.

Although McClellan does not quote evidence in any detail, these views would reflect those of many practitioners. Indeed, in formulating its advice UNODC draws on "basic research, evaluation reports and field experience". Interestingly, this runs counter to the so-called "evidence based" philosophy of the UK National Institute for Clinical Excellence (NICE), which explicitly discounts field experience, or the National Institute on Drug Abuse (www.nida/nih.gov), which ignores it – a possibly wider emerging conflict between field workers and evidence based-practice (see, for example, Links, 2006; McArdle, 2007).

UNODC argues that "detoxification should be seen in the context of broader social and treatment interventions", requiring "a basic medical and social support infrastructure {and} a multidisciplinary team composed of medical, social and counseling providers" in order to enable "involvement of the family, mobilization of the community" and progress to "rehabilitation {in part through} marketable skills training {toward} eventual social reintegration". It advises, "integration of treatment and rehabilitation services within existing health services or systems should take place wherever possible without creating a separate drug system." Although not explicitly focused on youth, these principles can be adapted to their needs, particularly by focusing more on working with families, education and training.

EUROPE

A World Health Organization ministerial conference (WHO, 2001) noted that Europe is the continent with the highest alcohol consumption. It listed a range of ambitious targets, including (i) "to reduce substantially the number of young people who start using alcohol", and (ii) "to increase access to health and counseling" for young people adversely affected by alcohol. Its European Alcohol Action Plan (EAAP) focuses on alcohol use and alcohol-related harm, such as drunkenness, binge drinking and alcohol-related social problems, that are common among European adolescents and young people. As the Australian Alcohol Strategy (Commonwealth of Australia, 2006) comments, "too many . . . now partake in drunken cultures rather than drinking cultures".

Table 11.1 indicates the position of alcohol among the leading 12 selected risk factors as a global cause of disease burden.

TABLE 11.1 Alcohol in the Leading 12 Selected Risk Factors as Global Causes of Disease Burden

	Developed countries	
Developing countries	High mortality	Low mortality
Underweight	*Alcohol*	*Tobacco*
Unsafe sex	Blood pressure	Blood pressure
Unsafe water	*Tobacco*	*Alcohol*
Indoor smoke	Underweight	Cholesterol
Zinc deficiency	Body mass index	Body mass index
Iron deficiency	Cholesterol	Low fruit/vegetable intake
Vitamin A deficiency	Low fruit/vegetable intake	Physical inactivity
Blood pressure	Indoor smoke	*Illicit drugs*
Tobacco	Iron deficiency	Unsafe sex
Cholesterol	Unsafe water	Iron deficiency
Alcohol	Unsafe sex	Lead exposure
Low fruit/vegetable intake	Lead exposure	Childhood sexual abuse

Source: Adapted from *Alcohol in the Global Burden of Disease*, 2000 (% total DALYS) (WHO, 2002).

AUSTRALIA

AUSTRALIAN ALCOHOL STRATEGY 2006

Like UNODC, WHO also argues for "the development of structured and controlled programmes to minimize risk". It identifies primary healthcare facilities and general hospitals as key potential settings for identifying and treating individuals with alcohol-related problems in many countries. However, there is both a therapeutic nihilism (McClelland, 2003) and a "skill deficit" in the capability of professionals in those settings to assess and treat children who present with alcohol- (or other drug-) related harm.

In a commentary on the EAAP, Gual and Colom (2001) suggested that the overall drop in alcohol consumption in Southern European countries was due to the replacement of wine- by beer-drinking – part of a process of Europe-wide "homogenization". This and other practices, such as alcopop-drinking, reflect the power of marketing against which the influence of scientists, the WHO or indeed the EU is "limited". Indeed, they note that one of the striking differences from the previous EAAP was the disappearance of references to population-based interventions such as taxation, implying that this was itself a reflection of the power of the drinks and hospitality industry. The Australian strategy illustrates frankly the dilemma facing governments: alcohol is responsible for harm estimated at costing approximately A$7 billion, but this is outweighed by the combination of alcohol-related taxes of A$5.5 and alcohol-related employment and exports worth over A$18 billion to the wider Australian economy. No government would want seriously to disturb this state of affairs. This has wider implications for proponents of legalization of psychoactive substances in general; the harm would have to be on a colossal scale to "outbid" the state's interest in high levels of taxable and employment-generating consumption by populations. The state has an incentive to drive down illegal use, but, in collaboration with the drinks and hospitality industry, to drive up legal use; the wellbeing of the exchequer outbids that of the people – sound finances, but risking, perhaps, moral bankruptcy.

Nevertheless, following the UN lead, the current European Union (EU) drug strategy (http://www.emcdda.eu.int/) proposes that the programs of action should simultaneously focus on demand and supply reduction, the former essentially a task of law enforcement. Following a public health model, the demand reduction should incorporate prevention, early intervention and treatment, including "social reintegration programmes". Following the spirit of UNODC, it hopes for "adequate consultation with . . . scientific centres {and} professionals". In particular, it also aims at

> the development and improvement of an effective and integrated comprehensive knowledge-based demand reduction system including prevention, early intervention, treatment, harm reduction, rehabilitation and social reintegration measures within the EU Member States

and

> improving access to targeted and diversified treatment programmes, including integrated psychosocial and pharmacological care.

The standard of effectiveness of treatment programs should be continuously evaluated. Treatment of health problems resulting from the use of psychoactive substances should become an integral part of health policies.

UNITED STATES OF AMERICA

In the US, the Substance Abuse and Mental Health Services Administration (SAMHSA) acts as a coordinating and grant-giving federal organization with an overall budget of $3.3bn. Youth-related expenditure is divided between directly funding prevention and acting to coordinate state treatment services. It aims at "improving the quality and availability of prevention, treatment, and rehabilitation services in order to reduce illness, death, disability, and cost to society resulting from substance abuse and mental illnesses". Its website does not appear explicitly to address youth substance abuse. However, it does refer to the Youth Violence report by the US Surgeon General (http://mentalhealth.samhsa.gov/youth violence/surgeongeneral/SG_Site/chapter5/sec1.asp). Much more so than World or European policies, this endorses evidence-based interventions. This document asserts the crucial importance of certificated training for professionals in evidence-based interventions lest "operational entropy" set in whereby program directors sacrifice quality for volume. However, this vision could imply what in the US will amount to a virtual army of para-professionals certificated in the various "patented" evidence-based interventions. Like recent NICE draft advice (NICE 2006), it could be interpreted to advocate a system of intervention separate from healthcare or education, running counter to the UNODC argument for integration.

UK POLICY

The UK Health Act 1999 introduced the possibility of health- and social-care pooled funds to commission services for a particular "client group". This approach appears to have developed from concern that infirm elderly patients were remaining in hospital beds because of lack of access to social-care facilities. The pooled-fund approach was established to provide "integrated provision". This "partnership" approach has spread within the public sector and has begun to influence the shape of services. However, it has its problems.

For instance, the Audit Commission ("an independent public body responsible for ensuring that public money is spent . . . efficiently") reported in 2004 on local "partnerships" formed around misuse and other youth-related difficulty. It noted that because constituent organizations (e.g., health, social and police services) have different priorities, partnerships contain tensions that may leave substance misuse services in a marginalized position. Some have found a way around this; but within health- and social-care partnerships substance misuse may not achieve a high priority. The risk was recently illustrated in respect of another "Cinderella" area, sexually transmitted disease, whereby health administrators raided funds dedicated for treatment of STDs but that were insufficiently ring-fenced (*Guardian*, 2007). The establishment of the National Treatment Agency, the board of which is heavily dominated by the Home Office, is an attempt to guard against health services raiding the substance misuse budget.

In similar vein to its international counterparts, and reflecting the consensual language international bodies, the report draws attention to the importance of "whole person" assessment and "wrap around" services including attention to "accommodation, employment . . . transport . . . and relationships", comprehensive assessment, "care planning" necessary to complete "recovery journeys". While oriented to adult predicaments, these clearly have counterparts in relation to childhood and youth. Focusing on the common problem of drop-out from treatment it recommends "improving fairly basic administration and customer care {to address} delayed letters, staff who miss appointments {and} dilapidated premises".

The Audit Commission also notes the sometimes "fraught" relations between those who commission services, and the health providers involved in treatment. While accepting that commissioning has problems, it implies that tighter performance expectations will draw health services into line. There is no suggestion in this that administrators (who man the committees that run the partnerships) should ever listen to professionals. Finally, it is striking that the advisory group which authored the Audit Commission document did not contain a single academic or senior (or indeed any) clinician, of any medical background. It is possible to consider that not only are drug users marginalized but, at least in some jurisdictions, the stigma extends to those who are professionally associated with them. The notion that professionals are part of the problem perhaps is part of a wider political view of professionals as potentially self-interested and "conservative" (Stevens, 2003) and perhaps too from admiration of the more spontaneous qualities of the voluntary or third sector (Conservative Party, 2006).

The UK Conservative Party's *Interim Report on the State of the Nation* (2006) sees the voluntary sector as providing "remarkable value" and proposes a higher level of individual donations to "non-cuddly areas such as drug abuse". For instance, "with proper training, a few hours relationship counselling can help keep a vulnerable family together {preventing} . . . long term social exclusion". Practitioners of any sector might be somewhat skeptical about this judgment. At face value, these ideas do not appear to be capable either of countering the skills deficits or of mounting the sustained and complex interventions, evidence-based or not, noted above. It does not suggest any preparedness to invest, commensurate with need, in prevention or treatment.

The National Treatment Agency was established in 2001 as an arms-length agency of government to take charge of drug treatment in England and Wales. Treatment is one of the four arms of the current UK government drug policy: "to enable people with drug problems to overcome them and to live healthy, crime-free lives". It currently receives most of its funding from the Department of Health (*c.* £10 m) and from the Home Office (*c.* £2 m) – a modest sum in total. Its concern for engagement and retention in treatment is emphasized by the NTA draft care planning criteria (NTA, 2007). These include, "Services to have systems in place to minimize client 'did not attend' (DNA) and dropout rates, and to support clients being retained in treatment" and highlighting the importance of comprehensive assessment and care pathways that include the facilitation of interagency referral, all reflecting themes raised by the AC. Its most important roles are to advocate standards of intervention, ensure services are in place, maximize numbers attending services, and guard drug budgets against encroachment. However, the then Prime Minister Tony Blair made it clear that its fundamental purpose is to play a part in reducing crime (http://www.pm.gov.uk/output/Page1717.asp).

From the perspective of healthcare, National Service Frameworks (NSFs) are described as "long term strategies for improving specific areas of care (that) set measurable goals within set time frames". The UK Children's NSF intends that "all children and young people achieve optimum health and well being and are supported in achieving their potential". The NSF asserts that "children and young people and families {should} receive high quality services . . . coordinated around their individual and family needs and take account of their views". A second standard urges that "young people have access to age-appropriate services . . . responsive to their specific needs as they grow into adulthood". It does note the importance of training related to substance misuse. In keeping with government and international policy, it sees multi-agency "partnerships" as the vehicle to deliver "services to young people with mental . . . disorders who are misusing drugs and alcohol". It too refers to the so-called "Child and Young Persons Local Strategic Partnerships" to commission local services, but does not explicitly mention the lowered priority for substance abuse in that system noted by the Audit Commission. The principles outlined in the NSF are perhaps useful levers when negotiating about the shape of services and correctives against over-focus on one aspect of a user's presentation. Nevertheless, there is a lack of serious thought in the NSF about substance misuse as a major cause of morbidity and mortality among young people. This reflects the true driver of substance use policy. It is possible to believe that without the impetus from those concerned about crime, services for substance users would receive a very low priority indeed.

The UK government strategy toward drug use has been criticized by the non-establishment left (e.g., http://www.narconews.com) and, more recently, from a more establishment source (http://www.rsadrugscommission.org/). The Royal Society of Arts (2007) argues that drugs policy has been conceived in an atmosphere of moral outrage ("the demonization of drugs") rather than of cool deliberation. (It also denies that cannabis is dependence-forming, but later cites the ACMD view that it may be dependence forming (p. 76). The RSA acknowledges that "For some heavy cannabis users problems with memory and attention may last for weeks after they have stopped using the drug", but later (p. 79) state that there is no "conclusive proof that the use of cannabis during adolescence affects social or cognitive development".) It argues that colossal efforts of enforcement have resulted in no real increase in cost or decrease in availability of illicit substances, and indeed describes a paradox whereby to reduce the size of illegally transported substances there is a drive to increase their potency. Of considerable interest, the RSA quotes Prime Minister's Strategy Unit documents that argue against reducing supply (if that were possible, which the RSA judges it not to be) as that would have the effect of driving up crime in an effort to afford continued use. It would be more effective to reduce "demand by 'gripping high harm users' in coerced treatment". This consideration, the RSA says, led to Drug Treatment and Testing Orders in the Crime and Disorder Act 1998. According to the Strategy Unit document, drug related offences contribute approximately 56 percent of the total number of criminal acts committed in the UK and approve of the 'prolific and priority offenders' scheme, whereby the 5000 most prolific offenders responsible for 10% of all crime are targeted with an intensive rehabilitation package.

In contrast, the Strategy Unit document appears to criticize the historical "psychiatrisation of the problem" but does not acknowledge the skills deficits in the healthcare system in particular, nor explain how the acknowledged high level of comorbidity is to be addressed. The Strategy Unit is uneasy about the current " strange strategic alliance between law enforcement and... treatment... reconceptualized... {to reduce} criminal behavior" (p. 113) which is explicitly led by criminal justice. As noted above, without this "strange alliance", there might be no drug treatment at all.

Nevertheless, in keeping with the UN, UNODC, the AC and the NTA, the Strategy Unit document defines treatment in terms of "wraparound care" addressing "health conditions", addiction itself, accommodation, money, child care, re-entering society, and "multi-disciplinary and multi-sectoral" intervention, and see drug addiction as a "chronic relapsing condition". Also, the report criticizes the "total lack of services" present in many areas. "Treatment that is poorly provided (i.e., not multidisciplinary and not multi-sectoral) may have little effect". They cite survey data indicating the public's support for treatment, "an effectively resourced treatment service", and argue for better access to residential treatment and that mental health services need to make the assessment and treatment of drug use a routine... and central... element".

In considering new legislation, they endorse the Blakemore–Nutt hierarchy of harms (Figure 11.2).

The report also estimates that the number that have used Class A drugs is more than ten times that of problematic drug users (pp. 66) – "in other words... the number of people who are not harming themselves or others... exceeds by a wide margin the number of people whose drug use causes harm" (pp. 68). UNODC might argue with the RSA's implicit user-focused definition of harm

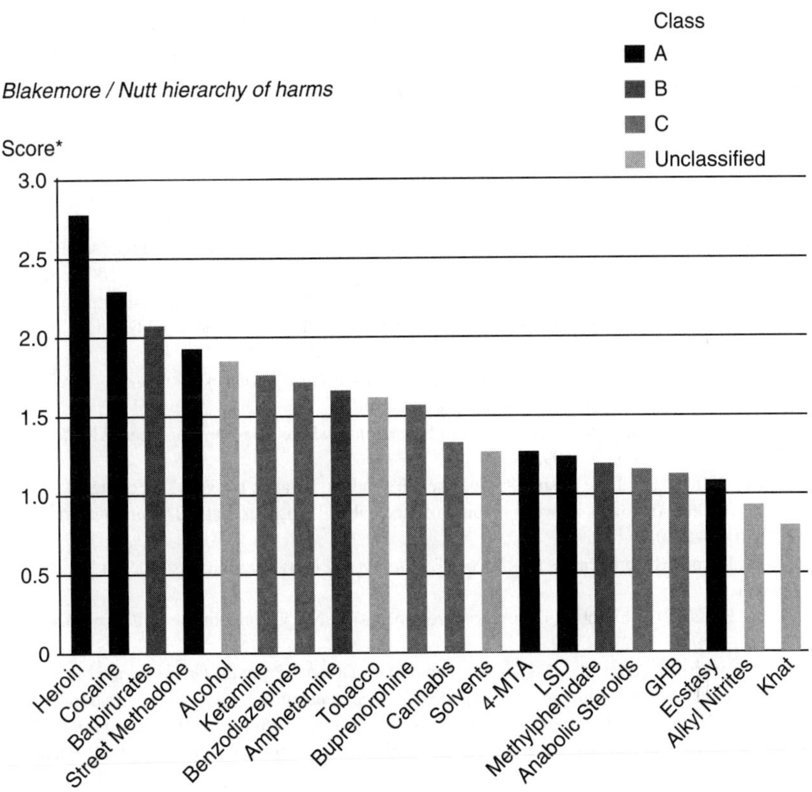

FIGURE 11.2 Blakemore–Nutt hierarchy of harms.

and that users are helping to fund international crime with serious consequences for vulnerable individuals elsewhere.

SUMMARY

It is clear from the international documentation in particular that there is an argument for the "demonization of drugs". On the other hand, if drugs were legalized then governments could not be trusted not to collude surreptitiously in their promotion. It is also clear that without the link with crime, there would be much less concern about drug abuse. It hardly gets a mention in the UK NSF for children.

Indeed, it is hard to evade the view that the RSA notion of "strange alliances" is not to be deprecated, but that they are at the heart of successful enterprise in relation to drug abuse. Field workers need to embrace strange alliances, with policy formers, statutory and non-statutory sectors, multiple agencies, with politicians, the "evidence", with families and with drug users themselves. Indeed, the last task may be the simplest.

REFERENCES

Audit Commission (2004). http://www.audit-commission.gov.uk/Products/NATIONAL-REPORT/BCD29C60-2C98-11d9-A85E-0010B5E78136/Drug percent20misuse percent202004.pdf

Commonwealth of Australia (2006). National Alcohol Strategy. The Australian alcohol document is available at http://www.alcohol.gov.au/internet/alcohol/publishing.nsf/content/B83AD1F91AA632ADCA25718E0081FIC3/$File/nas.06.09.pdf

EMCDDA (2006) *Annual Report: The State of the Drugs Problem in Europe* (available at http://ar2006.emcdda.europa.eu/en/home-en.html?).

Gual, A. and Colom, J. (2001) From Paris to Stockholm, where does the European Alcohol Action Plan lead? *Addiction*, 96, 1093–1096.

Guardian (2007) NHS Trusts using "sexual health funds to balance books". 15 February.

Links, M. (2006). Analogies between reading of medical and religious texts. *British Medical Journal*, 333, 1068–1070.

Margo, J., Dixon, M. and Pearce, M. (2006). *Freedom's Orphans*. London: Institute for Public Policy Research.

McArdle, P. (2007). Childhood depression: comments on NICE Guidelines. *Child and Adolescent Mental Health*, 12(2), 66–69.

National Treatment Agency (2007). *Care Planning: a Good Practice Guide* (available at http://www.nta.nhs.uk/areas/clinical_guidance/docs/nta_care_planning_briefing_consultation0207.doc).

NICE (2006). *Community-based Interventions to Reduce Substance Misuse Among Vulnerable and Disadvantaged Young People*. Available at http://www.nice.org.uk/nicemedia/pdf/PHI004guidance.pdf

Reid J. (2006) *House of Commons Hansard Debates* for 14 Nov 2005 (pt 2). London: House of Commons.

Royal Society of Arts (2007). Drugs-Facing Facts: the Report of the RSA Commission on illegal Drugs, Communities and Public Policy. http://www.rsadrugscommission.org/

Stevens S. (2003). Reform strategies for the English NHS. *Health Affairs*, 23, 37–44.

Substance Abuse and Mental Health Services Administration (2005). Background paper (available at http://rcsp.samhsa.gov/_pubs/background_paper.pdf).

United Nations General Assembly (1998). *Declaration on the Guiding Principles of Drug Demand Reductions*, A/S-20/II. Vienna: United Nations.

UNODC (2003). "Investing in drug abuse treatment: A discussion paper for policy makers." New York, NY: UN.

WHO (2001). *Drinking Among Young Europeans* (available at www.eurocare.org/pdf/who/2001-alcoholyp.pdf).

WHO (2002). *Alcohol in the Global Burden of Disease*. Geneva: WHO.

World Bank. http://siteresources.worldbank.org/WBI/Resources/wbi37196.pdf

http://unesdoc.unesco.org/images/0012/001281/128131eb.pdf

Index